Paper Boy

READ ALL ABOUT IT!

HOWIE CARR

Howie Carr

Frandel, LLC

To all my readers, listeners, and viewers.

Thank you!

Table of Contents

ACKNOWLEDGMENTS

Assembling a book like this requires the diligent efforts of many people, and I would like to thank some of those most involved in producing *Paper Boy*.

First of all, my wife Kathy, also known as the mailroom manager. And my staff at the radio network who were involved in one facet of another of the effort – my producers Taylor Cormier and Jarred Diglio, as well as digital editor Emma Foley.

Thanks also to Maureen O'Leary, who came up with the subtitle: "Read All About It!"

Thanks as well to the Boston *Herald*, for generously allowing me to use their iconic Paper Boy logo, as well as the photo of me sitting behind Billy Bulger at the Congressional hearing in 2003 (page 209). The *Herald* also provided the photos of Dapper O'Neil in his office (page 127) and with his fellow city councilors Freddie Langone and Joe Tierney (page 54).

Baker & Taylor Publisher Services did another outstanding job in getting this book into your hands in a timely fashion. Thanks especially to Jennifer Welsch.

PROLOGUE

Ever since I was a kid, all I ever wanted to do was work for a newspaper. I dabbled in other trades, but eventually I always drifted back to newspapers.

It's all over now, of course. Newspapers are as dead as doornails, except for maybe the *New York Post* and the *Wall Street Journal*—and who knows what will happen even to them once Rupert Murdoch finally cashes in his chips.

Oh sure, some newspapers are still printed, sort of, but there's seldom anything worth reading in any of them. They're on life support.

A handful of hedge funds are trying to wring a few final drops of blood out of these shriveled relics before they finally expire, unnoticed and unloved. What newspapers do survive employ ever fewer people. Most sad newsroom hangers-on are either just trying to last a few more years, if they're close to retirement, or merely for a few more paychecks before their newspapers' legal notices are stripped out next and gobbled up by the Internet, in the fashion of first the classifieds and then the display ads.

There aren't any rising young stars in newsrooms anymore. For that matter, there are hardly any newsrooms anymore.

It's true that most newspapers never did a great job of kicking the ass of the ruling class, but they thought about it, or at least claimed they did.

The old saying (at least in the newsrooms and the journalism schools) was that newspapers afflicted the comfortable and comforted the afflicted. Not that newspapers have any mission now other than to limp onward into the next quarter with as few layoffs as possible. But almost all have come to the same conclusion, that the best way to survive is to turn the old saying on its head.

Afflict the afflicted and comfort the comfortable.

Afflicting the comfortable is pretty much verboten these days, or would be, if anyone was left in the city rooms to ponder such an abstract concept. Most newspapers are no longer part of the ruling class. They're too irrelevant and broke—which is part of being irrelevant. And most "journalists" who are hanging on in those picked-over, skeletal remains of what were once proud newspapers have no interest in rocking the boat.

For one thing, there's no longer any practical way for a reporter to rise out of the tank towns anymore. Especially if you're not a member of one of the protected classes. On the off chance that somebody with an IQ greater than that of a soft-boiled egg stumbles into the newspaper business now, he'll soon be off to a more rewarding career, say, managing a Thom McAn shoe store—except that they're out of business too, come to think of it, just like your local newspaper for all practical purposes.

The point is, although I've titled this book *Paper Boy,* as you get deeper into it, you will be reading less and less about newspapers, and more about other media, some of which are almost as *in extremis* as print media.

I can't claim to have lived in the golden age of newspapers—that would be the early part of the 20th century. But until 15 or 20 years ago, if you were a certain type of person—reasonably bright, from a working-class background—a city room could be a wonderful place to make a living, especially in a big city with a large mass-transit system, meaning that you had thousands and thousands of readers every morning on subways and buses.

Believe it or not, as impossible as it seems now, everybody read newspapers.

If you worked for a newspaper—even the also-ran in town—it was such a thrill, picking up the paper, preferably a tabloid, and reading your stuff in the first edition. Some nights I'd find myself standing at the bar at J.J. Foley's in the South End. I'd be sneaking peeks to see if what I'd just written an hour or two earlier would get a rise out of anyone perusing "the edition"—the bartender, perhaps, or the pressman who'd just walked the papers down, or maybe a plain-clothes cop or two getting off his swing shift at District 4.

Or in the mornings, I'd catch the Orange Line at Sullivan Square in Charlestown and scan the other riders on the train to see who was reading the *Herald,* watching them thumb through the pages, until they reached the page my story was on.

If they smiled, or nodded to themselves, I knew I'd produced a winner. If they just scanned the headline and quickly turned the page, I knew I'd struck out (or maybe I'd blame the copy desk for writing a bad headline, or slashing my deathless prose into unrecognizability).

Newspapers seemed like such an exciting way to make a living. You got a free front-row seat to everything interesting that the world had to offer, and on top of that you were paid. In some respects, it was like being a cop—you didn't even have to dress that well, because you had the clout of a powerful institution behind you.

A good, tough reporter didn't have to be a salesman, a Willy Loman riding on a smile and a shoeshine. He was more like Sgt. Joe Friday of *Dragnet*—just the facts, ma'am.

You met all the most interesting people—the boldface celebs, A to D list, whether they were in sports, entertainment, politics, organized crime, or some combination thereof. You might not make a lot of money, but at least you would always be able to keep up your end of the conversation, in whatever social settings you might find yourself.

This was what I'd always wanted to do, ever since I was a 15-year-old kid in the Press Club at Deerfield Academy. It was such a thrill to call the prep desk of the *Boston Herald* collect on fall Saturday afternoons in the sixties to dictate the results of the Choate or Andover football game. Then, on Sunday mornings, I'd rush out to check the sports page to see how much they'd rewritten my red-hot copy. (Totally, every time.)

I've always been a newspaperman, although the kind of newspapers that I worked on no longer exist in any recognizable form.

You pick up any paper you haven't read for a while, and you'll immediately realize that there's next to nothing in any of them anymore—very little local news, few obituaries and even fewer classified ads.

Local pro sports are often covered by editorial assistants or cub reporters if the teams are home, and almost always by the wire services if they're on the road. Or an intern watches the game on television and writes off that. What little editorial product remains often isn't news. What it is, 98 percent of the time, is Democrat party agitprop.

As John Hinderaker observed at Powerlineblog.com, "One of the requirements to be a reporter these days is a total lack of curiosity about anything that reflects poorly on the establishment in general, and the Democratic Party in particular."

Granted, this is a traditional complaint in any industry—that they're not making reporters-cops-linebackers-hijackers (fill in the blank) like they used to back in the glory days, which is to say, the youth of whoever's singing the blues.

As parlous as newspapers had become even before COVID-19 arrived from China, they became even worse once the Panic was ginned up. The media swallowed the Fauci bullshit hook, line, and sinker. Nobody was going to work, so street sales collapsed. Even if the papers could convince their ever-dwindling numbers of elderly print junkies to buy online "subscriptions," all the readers got from their newspapers was an endless stream of Panic Porn around the clock.

Every day, the papers—and all other media—would lead with what amounted to nothing more than government press releases, and from the sketchiest, least credible sort of sources at that—"public health agencies," such as the federal Centers for Disease Control and Massachusetts' scandal-scarred Department of Public Health.

These corrupt bureaucracies' pernicious nonsense—often in direct contradiction of the previous day's pronouncements with their continually "adjusted" statistics depending on the latest political whims and needs of the Democrat party—was printed without even the slightest hint of skepticism.

I kept thinking to myself, this is the kind of dim-witted flackery that in my youth as a city editor I would have assigned to an editorial assistant—and one of the slower ones, at that. After it had been typed up, I would have thrown it on the obit page, if I hadn't just plain spiked it. And yet every day, these handouts, as we used to call them, were now being splashed across the top of the front page—complete with bylines.

And the same nonsense from the same "experts" would likewise be leading the evening TV news. And the national news . . .

The sky is falling! The sky is falling!

And they wonder why their circulations, and ratings, are cratering. I have seen the future, and it is CNN+.

All the media I have worked in are shadows of their former selves. Who watches local TV news anymore, or any kind of network programming, for that matter? Weather, traffic, sports—there are apps for everything.

Magazines are deader than the *Evening Transcript*. Even radio is heading for the ropes—it's still sort of functional, thank goodness. But it's less and less about "broadcasting," and more and more about streaming, or podcasts, or setting up a camera and doing a video version of a radio show on YouTube or Rumble.

Paper Boy

I know what I sound like—an old fart. What's happened is not a conspiracy per se, it's mostly just that technology has changed everything—Schumpeter's theory of the creative destruction of capitalism proven once again.

But other dynamics are at work as well in the demise of newspapers, indeed all mass media, as they were known for so long. The big problem is that the "mass media" isn't—mass, that is. They have lost the masses. That's not a bad thing for me personally, as I've been fortunate enough to develop and sustain niche audiences across assorted platforms.

But what's happened is not a positive development for society at large—look at the Fake News Media, CNNMSNBCABCCBSNBC, as well as the far-left newspapers that now read more like religious tracts for the Democratic Party.

But I digress. This will be mostly a professional memoir, about my long career, such as it is. In *A Fan's Notes,* Frederick Exley referred to "that long malaise, my life." I've had my ups and downs, but to borrow a line from Sinatra about regrets, I've had a few, but then again, too few to mention. That's not right either, though. I'll be mentioning more than a few regrets, but I'll try not to dwell on them.

I will not be including much about my personal family life here. The title is *Paper Boy*, not *Family Man.*

Sometimes I've read reviews of memoirs or autobiographies that make a point of noting how many old scores the author settled. Usually, it's considered a mark of character if you pull your punches. We'll have none of that here, as Jerry Angiulo used to say when talking about whether he would go to prison to protect his son.

Besides, what do I care about reviews? They appear—or used to appear—in newspapers, and as we've already discussed, nobody reads 'em anymore. I doubt this tome will generate much response among the chattering classes, whose chattering is heard by fewer and fewer people every day.

Why am I writing this now? Well, to quote Auberon Waugh, one of several newspapermen I will be mentioning in this book, "A professional writer has only so many shots in his locker, and autobiography is one of them."

I've done well in the organized-crime genre, but that's a vein that's pretty much tapped out at this point. Same with the Kennedy family—Patches Kennedy has sobered up, Joe Kennedy III didn't make it to the Senate, and the family's last fatal drug overdose in Hyannis Port was of a young woman who went to the same prep school I did.

Right now, *Kennedy Babylon* is not looking like a trilogy, even with Bobby Kennedy Jr. running for president.

As for my meager output of hard-boiled detective fiction, I wish I could have succeeded as a "paperback writer." Churning out the 21st-century versions of 25-cent Gold Medal paperbacks like some modern-day Jim Thompson or John D. MacDonald—that was something I long aspired to, like so many American paper boys of the last century.

Forget Raymond Chandler or Dashiell Hammett, I'd have gladly settled for becoming, say, the next Brett Halliday, or someone you've probably never even heard of such as William Fuller or Roger Torrey or Frank Kane.

But it was not to be. Maybe someday my series detective Jack Reilly will return, but probably not.

Fiction is different from newspapers. As Cyril Connolly once wrote, "Literature is the art of writing something that will be read twice; journalism what will be grasped at once, and they require separate techniques."

I guess you've figured out which technique I'm better at.

One of the most successful newspapermen of all time was Walter Winchell, a Hearst man like myself. At the end of his career, after he lost his column, Winchell said he was working on his autobiography, and he was going to name his enemies from A to Z, and if he didn't reach the end of the alphabet, he'd have died an unhappy man.

I won't go that far, but why bother with this kind of project if you can't point a few fingers here and there.

As H. L. Mencken wrote in 1941 in his memoir, *Newspaper Days,* "This book is mainly true."

In other words, I make no claims that everything in this book is absolutely 100 percent factually accurate. I'm sure there are errors. After all, as Waugh put it, all lives ultimately reduce "to a scrapbook of false or partial recollections, deliberate evasions and suppressions?"

In recounting some parts of my career, I am bound by the usual assortment of confidentiality agreements, sealed decrees, gentlemen's understandings, and so on. But I'll try to come as clean as possible. To quote the line I've used so often from Hunter S. Thompson's attorney in *Fear and Loathing in Las Vegas:*

"You can trust me, I'm not like the others."

1
PALM BEACH PUBLIC

As for some basic biographical facts, I've been married twice. I have five children, all daughters, and eight grandchildren. Like Henry Wadsworth Longfellow, I was born on Congress Street in Portland, Maine, "the beautiful town/That is seated by the sea." Like Longfellow, I played in Deering Oaks as a boy, and as an adult moved to Cambridge, Massachusetts. He wrote about Hiawatha, and I've written about Lieawatha—the fake Indian, Sen. Elizabeth Warren.

That's about it for the similarities between me and Longfellow.

Genetically, my DNA test results show that I'm 53 percent Irish, 47 percent English. My father was the seventh son of a seventh son, raised on Oxford Street, which I suppose is considered the back side of the now semi-trendy Munjoy Hill neighborhood of Portland.

My mother was from Monroe, North Carolina. She went to high school with the late Sen. Jesse Helms, who once told me she was a lot smarter back then than he was. I'm pretty sure he was telling me the truth.

After high school, she was learning a trade—typing, shorthand, filing, etc.—at the secretarial school at Women's College, what would later become UNC Greensboro. She was almost through the one-year course when the richest man in town, the founder of what was eventually called Burlington Industries, J. Spencer Love, called the school and asked them to send over their smartest girl.

Soon my mother, at the age of 18, was living in Palm Beach, in one of The Breakers' big rental cottages (now rebuilt as $23 million townhouse condos) just

1

Baptism in Portland, 1952, with Cousin Patti and Aunt Mabel Carr.

north of the main hotel. Every night, she'd ride her bicycle up to The Breakers to put Mr. Love's business correspondence in the overnight mail. The Breakers' reservations manager, 36-year-old Del Carr, noticed the brunette teenager and one thing led to another.

They were married in January 1943.

He was in the Army Air Corps until Mr. Love decided he needed him for assorted chores, including the occasional deliveries of envelopes full of cash to Democratic politicians. So Love got Sen. Bob Reynolds from North Carolina to arrange for his wartime discharge—a very rare occurrence during World War II. My parents lived in Washington, D.C., Greensboro, North Carolina and Palm Beach. I was born in Portland in 1952. My brother Jonathan came along a year later.

I grew up on the East Coast, here, there, and everywhere. My father worked, off and on, for The Breakers, which was then a seasonal hotel, heading north to work summers in different resorts, sometimes in New Hampshire. My mother worked, off and on, for her old boss at Burlington Industries until he dropped dead on his tennis court on South Ocean Boulevard in 1962.

Christmas in Palm Beach, 1958, with family.

My brother and I would spend the winters in Palm Beach, living with our parents, and the summers in Portland, with my aunt Mabel. Summers, my father spent in New Hampshire and my mother worked in her boss's New York offices, or sometimes down in the corporate headquarters in Greensboro.

Until I was 13 I bounced around back and forth between Portland, Palm Beach, and Greensboro.

Wherever we were, there was a common theme—not very much money. Nobody on either side of the family could ever seem to turn a buck. It wasn't poverty, per se, nothing particularly dysfunctional, no broken homes, alcoholism, the usual hard-knocks stuff. It was just . . . no dough.

If I ate doughnuts in Portland, they were day-olds, from the Cushman Bakery on Elm Street. Once I had a broken leg in Portland, and the doctors at Maine Medical Center wanted to take another X-ray, and it cost $25. I thought my father, down from the Mountain View House in Whitefield New Hampshire, was going to keel over when he saw the bill.

My parents owned a cottage on Little Diamond Island in Casco Bay, now a very upscale place, but they had to sell it. Among other things, the cost of the

3

lawn mowing—three dollars a week—was crushing them. There were no rich relations on either side to fall back on. My aunt Mabel was like a second mother to me. My mother made sure that whatever money she paid to Mabel, she'd report the income to Social Security, because Mabel's teacher's pension from the City of Portland was going to be next to nothing.

In Palm Beach, we lived in a cottage on Mr. Love's estate on South Ocean Boulevard. The Love kids went to what was then called Palm Beach Private School and my brother and I attended the school on the other end of Seaview Avenue—Palm Beach Public. It was my first, but not my last, exposure to an *Upstairs, Downstairs* sort of life.

Still, I got to hang out in a lot of the fancy places frequented by the carriage trade. I occasionally ate at Ta-Boo on Worth Avenue—some of my classmates at Palm Beach Public had their birthday parties there. I took dance lessons at the Bath & Tennis Club—my parents scrimped and saved to pay Mrs. de Rham to teach me about what the *New York Times* called "ballroom dancing, poise and good manners." My parents thought if I could only learn the social graces I might be able to . . . pass.

It would become a recurring theme in my life. I would always be there, with the swells, but somehow I just couldn't quite pass.

So near, and yet so far.

The lobby at The Breakers was in my father's time a renowned public gathering place, a social destination in Palm Beach. It's still one of the better places to people-watch on the island. But in the old days, it was the ultimate location to hang out in. Even people who weren't allowed to stay at the hotel, for social rather than economic reasons—among them former Boston mayors James Michael Curley and John "Honey Fitz" Fitzgerald—loitered in the lobby, hobnobbing with the swells.

The headmaster of Deerfield Academy, in western Massachusetts, was a little man named Frank L. Boyden. He'd been headmaster since his graduation from Amherst College in 1902, a few years behind Calvin Coolidge.

He'd been planning to go to law school after a few years, but he stayed to build one of the nation's greatest prep schools. The problem was, he had neither the time nor the inclination to build the kind of endowment that the other great schools in New England developed.

Since then, Deerfield has upped its game. One of the Koch brothers, David, graduated in 1959, and until his death, he was a "life" trustee, as well as he should have been. Later, whenever I'd read about the evil "Koch brothers,"

I would always consider the billions he gave to worthy causes, not just to Deerfield, but to New York hospitals and every other damn thing. Demonizing the Kochs—just more fake news.

During his 66-year tenure that ended in 1968, Boyden had to develop different sources of revenue to keep the school going. And he discovered that if he journeyed to Palm Beach every spring break, usually with one of his younger masters, who would drive him, he could just hang out in the lobby of The Breakers all day and chat up . . . whomever.

Mr. Boyden got to know my father, who became a scout of sorts for him, because no one knew more about the guests and visitors in The Breakers' lobby than Del Carr. He instinctively understood who were the best ones to put the touch on. And so my father got to listen as the Quid, as Mr. Boyden was known to his all-male student body, made his pitch for the school to any likely philanthropic prospects in the lobby.

My father, by then pushing 60 and weary of the resort-hotel circuit, asked Mr. Boyden if there were any jobs open at Deerfield. Of course, he had no college degree, nor did my mother, but they were willing to do anything. They wanted me and my brother to have a better chance than they had had to get ahead, to . . . pass.

My father told me and my brother to come up to The Breakers (where we often hung out anyway, usually around either the staff dining room or at the old golf club on Coconut Row). He introduced us to the Quid, who was a very unprepossessing man. He always seemed to be wearing the same wrinkled double-breasted blue suit.

Around the campus, I was soon to learn, he drove a golf cart, although he still maintained a stable with a couple of horses for the buggy he'd used to get around in for most of his years as headmaster. The buggy usually only came out on special occasions, such as homecoming in the fall, or Spring Day in May, when large numbers of the alumni were back on Albany Road, feeling nostalgic.

Every year when he left Florida, Mr. Boyden told Del he'd keep him in mind if any jobs opened up at the school. One day in 1965, he called and said that the manager of the school store had decided to retire and would Del be interested in the job? It wouldn't pay much, but it included an apartment, and food, and, oh yes, as residents of the town of Deerfield, the boys could enroll as students for free.

I started Deerfield in the fall of 1965. I was 13, one of the youngest boys in the school, a year ahead of my natural class. Mr. Boyden told my father he

With my father as a freshman at Deerfield, 1965.

usually kept the Florida boys back a year, but that I seemed bright enough to handle the workload. I struggled with algebra, but otherwise I had no problems academically. Even at age 86, the Quid had a pretty good instinct for what his boys were capable of.

I lived at home my first year, but I ate my meals in the main school dining room. I wasn't quite a day student, as they were defined at Deerfield. They ate their lunch separately, went home at night, and had to take a fifth year before they could graduate. Although I ate with the boarders, I didn't live in a dorm either. I was a hybrid student, but a lot of the boarders called me a "dago." That puzzled me, because I didn't have any Italian blood.

Deerfield was always one of the more egalitarian of the elite prep schools—everyone had to wait tables, or work in the kitchen, regardless of their social or economic standing. Snobbery was not a big thing, thank goodness. Still, I would find out a lot more at Deerfield about the class structure of American society than I'd ever learned as a kid in Palm Beach.

Deerfield had a motto: "Be Worthy of Your Heritage." I've never figured out what that was supposed to mean.

2
JIMMY OLSEN

The first newspaper I can remember reading was the *Press Herald* in Portland in 1959. I was getting into baseball and the box scores on the sports page fascinated me. I was amazed how Early Wynn could be 39 years old and still winning ball games for the White Sox.

My uncle Ray had followed my father, his younger brother, into resort hotels, and he was a room clerk at The Breakers every winter. He'd come back to Portland every fall after his own summer job at one of the big resorts in Spring Lake, New Jersey, ended.

Every morning when he was home, Ray would stroll down Brighton Avenue to the local newsstand, where he'd pick up the tabloids available in Portland. If he got up early enough he would bring home the *Daily News*, which quickly became my favorite newspaper. I would sit at the kitchen table staring at the grainy photos of the dead bodies of stab victims in barrooms in the Bronx.

Sometimes, though, if he'd slept late, the *Daily News* would be sold out and he'd come home with a copy of the Boston tabloid, the *Record American*. That was always a disappointment. Instead of gangland hit photos, they'd have staged photos of corpulent grandees posing at various dinners at places like Anthony's Pier 4, then the biggest restaurant in the country.

I wondered what was wrong with the *Record*, why it wasn't nearly as much fun to read as the *Daily News*. In about 15 years, I would find out for myself.

When I got to Deerfield, I quickly realized I wasn't going to have an easy time getting into an elite college. I wasn't that outstanding at anything. But I did have a certain way with words. I was a facile writer, maybe because I was always reading, especially newspapers.

At Deerfield, the school store that my father ran was responsible for delivering the out-of-town newspapers that almost all the boarding students got every morning. We'd put them in the boarders' mailboxes as soon as they were delivered. The most popular newspaper among the student body was the *New York Herald Tribune*, the dying liberal Republican daily that was owned first by the Reids and then by the Whitneys, both of whom were Deerfield families.

Those connections meant that the *Herald Tribune* only cost a nickel, compared to a dime for the *New York Times*, which was why it was the top seller. I felt like an adult, getting my own copy of the *Trib* every morning. It seemed rather dry—I don't remember ever reading either Jimmy Breslin or Tom Wolfe back then. But since I often stuffed the mailboxes with the papers in the morning, I usually got a chance to peruse my favorite tabloid—the *Daily News*.

There were still plenty of dead bodies sprawled across the double truck, and as I got older I also began to enjoy both Dick Young's wiseguy sports column, *Young Ideas,* as well as the punchy, no-holds-barred editorials—written by a now-forgotten legend named Reuben Maury.

In his own 1982 obituary, Maury was quoted explaining his philosophy of writing for a tabloid:

"Just say what you think, or what the paper thinks, in plain English. But by God don't try to write down to anybody—because they spot it right away."

As for the Boston papers in the sixties—they bored the hell out of me. The *Boston Herald*, then the Yankee paper, had as you might expect the greatest circulation among the local dailies at Deerfield. The *Boston Globe*—"the maid's newspaper," as *The New Republic* would later describe what it was in those days—had far fewer readers.

Only a handful of the 500 or so boarding students subscribed to Hearst's tabloid *Record American*. It puzzled me that anybody would ever read the *Record* instead of the *Daily News* if they had a choice, no matter where they were from.

Even at the age of 13, I knew that I wasn't what is now called a "legacy." For college, I would need a scholarship, as Mr. Boyden's son John pointedly reminded me one evening when he caught me cutting the Sunday Night Sing and heading back to my parents' house to watch *The FBI* on Channel 40 out of Springfield.

I liked basketball, and one of my first coaches nicknamed me "Cooz," after Bob Cousy. It was a nickname that stuck, even though I was strictly a scrub, in all sports. That too was unfortunate for my college prospects, because to get into a good school, a student—a "boy"—needed extracurricular activities, and sports were the gold standard.

If sports were out, what could I do? What was I good at? I kept coming back to writing, and at the top of the possibilities was the school newspaper, the *Deerfield Scroll*. The faculty adviser was Bryce Lambert, a confirmed bachelor—you know where I'm going with this now, right? Yes, after his death, Lambert would be named as an abuser, but not of me. Somehow I was never molested, either by a Catholic priest or by one of these confirmed-bachelor Yankee prep-school masters, even though I was around both varieties, more of the latter than the former.

Lambert was from Maine, and that gave me a slight edge over the non-Mainers. In English class, for extra credit, he'd ask a question about Maine slang, for example, Down East, what does "spider" mean in the kitchen? (It's a frying pan; I was the only one in the class who got it right.)

I made the *Scroll* "editorial board" and started working my way up. The paper came out twice a month. Competition was keen for the top slots—those were supposed to be guaranteed tickets to the Ivy League—so I calculated the odds and decided that I'd be better off sticking to sports writing.

I became sports editor. I had a column called *Sports Carr*. It was fun, and I was quite pleased my senior year when the local newspaper, what was then the *Greenfield Recorder-Gazette*, lifted one of my columns and reprinted it, word for word. I cut it out of the paper and had my mother make a few copies. (She was the new headmaster's secretary by then.)

Another of my extracurriculars was something I've made a joke of over the years on my radio show. I was on the bridge team, and we were the New England champions my senior year. The adviser was a guy named Peter Hindle, another guy who was, you guessed it, later outed as a homosexual predator. "Hindu," as he was then known (later he became "the Czar"), had an office around the locker rooms. He always did his paperwork late in the afternoon, when all the boys were taking their showers. Everybody noticed, but nobody talked about his peculiar routine.

I never had him as a math teacher, but I was with Hindu every Sunday night, playing duplicate bridge in the Science Building. He collected matchbooks, and wherever I went, I grabbed some for him. It was the sixties and it was a simpler time.

Going into my senior year, when it came to Ivy League prospects, I was on the bubble, so to speak. I was in the top third of my class (meaning, the bottom of the top third). I had decent SATs (1300 out of 1600). The fact that I still remember these numbers after all these years shows just how important they were to me.

I applied to Harvard, but I knew I had zero chance. The admissions officer, a future Deerfield headmaster, had been a master at Deerfield before he returned to Cambridge, and he'd never thought much of me—he was appalled when I mentioned at dinner one night that I liked to watch *Batman* when I went home, as all the boarding students were "grinding it out" at the evening study hall.

Harvard gave out grades back then to candidates. A meant you were getting in, B maybe but don't count on it, C meant forget about it. I got a C.

I did get into Brown, which was then second-tier Ivy. Now, it's Beautiful People to the max. The problem was, it cost $3,200 a year, and they didn't give me a dime of scholarship money. My father had gone on Social Security the previous fall at age 63 when Frank Boyden had finally retired after 66 years as headmaster.

My mother was making maybe $4,500 a year. They did still get a free house just off campus, and they could eat at the school, but still . . . $3,200 for a college? They still owned a house in Greensboro, without a mortgage, which they rented out.

They offered to get a mortgage on it to raise the money for me to go to Brown, but that didn't seem like a good idea. Suppose I didn't get a scholarship my sophomore year either—then I, or my parents, would have had to go even further into the hole.

And if I knew my parents were sacrificing for me, how much could I enjoy myself in Providence? And believe me, after four years at an all-boys school, in the sixties no less, I was ready for a little R&R.

My "safety" school was the University of North Carolina at Chapel Hill. I used the house that my parents owned in Greensboro as my in-state residence. There was never any question about UNC; I was in. As an in-state student, even if I really wasn't one, UNC cost practically nothing—a few hundred dollars a year.

In June, I got a final postcard from Brown, sent to my parents' P.O. Box 243 in Deerfield. It told me that if I wanted to reserve my slot in the Class of 1973, I should send $50.

Again, so close, and yet so far.

In Greensboro, my father knew a guy who owned a motel. He'd sold off the front of the land the motel was on to the local YMCA, but he still operated a few rooms in the back. His motel's address was 1045 West Market Street, the same as the YMCA's.

That became my mailing address as an in-state student, the YMCA in Greensboro. I wonder if I could get away with that today. Later, when I had a car, I registered it in Massachusetts. I had a Massachusetts driver's license as well. Nobody ever checked.

One thing about UNC—they had a newspaper, *The Daily Tar Heel.* I did a little research and discovered that the sports editor was another Massachusetts guy, from Newton. When I got to Chapel Hill in September 1969, I went to the paper's offices, in the Student Union, and presented myself to my fellow Bay Stater. I gave him a copy of my column in the Greenfield paper.

He glanced at it, nodded, and gave me my first assignment: freshman football.

That was the start of my career in daily journalism. I was living in Ehringhaus, the football dorm on the South Campus. It was an interesting place to room—during rush, sorority pledges would be dispatched to run the elevators, and fend off the jocks.

Saturday nights in the fall were always exciting, especially if there was a home game. There were still cigarette vending machines in the basement, and when the jocks got drunk, sometimes they'd drag the machines into the elevator, take them up to the top floor, and then hurl them off the balconies onto the ground.

Then they'd steal all the cigarettes. Sometimes, there'd be enough left for us non-jocks in the dorm—if we were willing to settle for the less popular brands, like Raleighs and Belairs.

After my freshman year, I couldn't get out of the dorm fast enough—I moved into a cheap, rented house trailer north of town. But the Ehringhaus experience came in handy later because I still knew a few of the players.

By my junior year, I was more interested in the news side of the DTH—especially writing columns—op-eds, they were sometimes called. They weren't sports, that was the main thing. I found that I liked writing columns, and the recognition I got from them. But my "job," for $1.25 an issue, was still sports.

Labor Day 1971 was brutally hot, but the football team was getting ready for the season. The coach, Bill Dooley, was a typical SEC redneck coach of the era, who had decided to migrate to the less-cutthroat Atlantic Coast Conference. He'd been hired in 1967, to reinvigorate a moribund program. As part of the reinvention, he'd had to run off, as they say, a bunch of the previous loser coach's dilettante recruits.

The "reeducation" program was still being talked about at Ehringhaus when I was a freshman two years later. The coaches had pitted the scrubs against each other in no-holds-barred wrestling, once between twins, or so the story went. Then they'd make them run laps at Kenan Stadium, and when the players pulled up short as they reached the concrete walls, the coaches would yell at them, "I didn't tell you to stop, did I?"

That's the way football was back then, even at the high school level to some degree. I remember one of the jocks telling me about one game in his high school. His team was getting crushed. At halftime, in the locker room, the coach started weeping and yelling at them, "All the real men are in Vietnam!"

On this sweltering Labor Day afternoon in 1971, a Carolina offensive line-man from Staten Island named Billy Arnold collapsed in the 100-degree heat. The coaches left him lying there, in the hot sun. No one made a move to help him. When practice ended, the coaches sent the rest of the team to the showers, but left Arnold lying there, unconscious, on the practice field.

Finally, after the managers threw the tackling dummies into the back of the team pickup truck, a couple of them picked up Arnold and tossed him into the truck on top of the dummies, and finally drove him to N.C. Memo-rial Hospital.

His temperature spiked to 108 degrees. I don't know if he'd had a stroke or what, but his brain was fried. They got some rich Chapel Hill alumnus to use his private plane to fly Billy Arnold's parents down from New York, but by then their son was dead.

Coach Dooley had a lot of explaining to do.

I started working on the story with an older DTH writer who would go on to law school and eventually become a state judge. A couple of former players whom I'd known casually at Ehringhaus were likewise trying to figure out what had in fact happened, because the Dooley regime was not exactly forthcoming.

Finally, with the DTH advancing the story a little bit every day, the ex-players formed a group seeking justice (or something) for Billy Arnold. They'd leak to us whatever they discovered, and we'd run with it, and include a quote or two from them and the standard "no comment" from the athletic department.

It became a big story. The *New York Times* even sent a sports reporter down to write something. He told us that we were doing a great job on the story.

Paper Boy

The daily drip-drip-drip of revelations was driving Coach Dooley crazy. One afternoon, as the little group of ex-jocks was having a press conference upstairs in a room at the Student Union, the door swung open and in walked Coach and dozens of his players, in practice gear. Dooley began snarling at the former players, then turned to his team and asked them if any of them agreed with the protest. Of course, they didn't. Not if they knew what was good for them.

And that turned out to be the end of the Billy Arnold story. Try finding something about it on the Internet today. It's vanished, almost totally. It was never spoken of again in Chapel Hill, except in 1973, when the Tar Heels went from an 11–1 record to 4–7. Everybody blamed it on bad recruiting two years earlier—"you know, Billy Arnold."

As far as sports writing was concerned, after Billy Arnold it wasn't nearly as much fun hanging out in locker rooms after the games anymore.

Don't get me wrong, I still enjoyed sitting in the press box at Kenan Stadium, and having food brought to me by coeds in hot pants. But finally, after the game, I always was supposed to write something. And that was dreary beyond belief, especially anything about the minor sports. As Dan Jenkins once said, "The only thing more boring than track is field."

I decided to slide over to the news side.

This was the age of the New Journalism, as Tom Wolfe would put it in 1973. By then I was already into it, bigtime. Forget sports, I wanted to write "long-form" journalism.

I can still remember reading *Radical Chic* for the first time. It was written, of course, by Wolfe, for *New York* magazine. It wasn't just the writing, which was exquisite, it was the reporting. I'd already discovered Jimmy Breslin, another *Herald Tribune* alum, from his collected columns. He was more of a street guy, very talented, but he and Wolfe came out of different schools, so to speak.

Wolfe was something else. So erudite, so droll. I was blown away. I read *Radical Chic* again and again. I still read it now, in book form, with its companion piece, *Mau-Mauing the Flak Catchers,* which is almost as brilliant.

I started studying general-interest magazines more carefully. It was always a big day when one of them—*Esquire,* say, or *Harper's*—arrived at my trailer in Chapel Hill. One night I picked up the new issue of *Esquire* and started reading Ed McClanahan's piece, *Famous People I Have Known,* as soon as I got inside.

By the time I finished it was dark, and quite cold. I realized the pilot light in the heater had gone out and the trailer was frigid. But I hadn't even noticed

13

because I'd been so engrossed in the story. All the above writers had one thing in common: they were very, very funny. And the funniest of them all was Hunter S. Thompson. At the 1973 Super Bowl, he perfectly summed up in a single sentence why I had become so jaded about sports writing.

"The precision jack-hammer attack of the Miami Dolphins stomped the balls off the Washington Redskins today by stomping and hammering with one precise jack-thrust after another up the middle, mixed with pinpoint precision passes into the flat and numerous hammer-jack stomps around both ends. . . ."

I first encountered Hunter S. Thompson in *Rolling Stone*, in 1971 when he took up an entire issue with what became the book *Fear and Loathing in Las Vegas*. Whether it was fact or fiction, the only thing about the piece that mattered to me was that it was so damn entertaining.

As Thompson described the nuts and bolts of his "gonzo" journalism: "Total coverage, final wisdom, free lunch."

Words to live by, indeed.

I was also reading newspapers, of course. My parents had always sent me a lot of clippings from Boston, and soon I was getting columns from someone named George Frazier. My father recalled him from the *Boston Herald* in the early 1960s, but the *Globe* was my first exposure to his column.

Like everyone else I looked up to, Frazier was a master stylist. He was less a reporter than a raconteur. He had a million stories. He seemed to know everybody, in New York as well as Boston.

I was quickly hooked on Frazier's stuff. He was, I still believe, the best daily columnist I ever read. His personal life, like a lot of columnists', was somewhat forlorn—born in South Boston, he graduated from Harvard in 1934 and then had a rather checkered career. He was a functioning alcoholic—semi-functioning, I guess would be a more accurate description. He wrote liner notes for jazz albums, worked for magazines including *Life* and *Esquire*. He had a collection of his magazine pieces published that didn't sell, despite not one but two plugs on Walter Winchell's radio show.

He was married briefly, had two sons, one of whom I later got to know when he was selling real estate on Nantucket.

Frazier never made big money, and was basically unemployed when Chris Lydon, another Southie–Ivy League guy who was then working for the *New York Times*, recruited him to come back to Boston and freelance for the *Globe's* Living pages.

I kept reading all these guys, and I convinced myself that if I could only get my foot in the door, in the same newsroom, I'd quickly be in the same league with them. I started trying to write longer pieces for the *Daily Tar Heel*. One Saturday I went out on a campaign swing with a guy named Pete Tripodi, the first UNC student to run for the state legislature.

Our first stop was at a general store near the Chatham County line. I knew the place pretty well, because it was near the trailer park I was living in. The store owner was the current state rep, a good old boy, and I hung back as Tripodi tried to size up his wily older foe. I don't think the statesman had a clue who his customer was, because he reached under the counter and came up with a cigar box. He leered at Pete Tripodi.

"Y'all ever see one of these?" he said to all of us, holding up a small wrapped package. "This here's what you call a French tickler—y'all got girlfriends, she'll sho 'nuff be thankin' you boys for buying one o' these."

I mean, the stuff just wrote itself. Tom Wolfe was right. All you had to do was hang around, keep your mouth shut, and take copious notes. It dropped right into your lap.

A couple of years later, after we were out of college, Tripodi got arrested for something or other, did a short bid in jail, and ended up going into a graveyard and killing himself. So I got another story out of that—I was learning how easy it was to recycle the same material, again and again and again.

I was on my way.

But before I could get a job at a real newspaper, I had to deal with a more pressing problem. When I went to Carolina I got so many extra credits from acing the placement tests that technically, by the start of my sophomore year, even though I was still only 18, I was already a junior.

That meant I would be graduating at age 20. That would not have been a problem—in fact it would have been a blessing, given the cost of college—except for one thing.

My number in the draft lottery was nine. That too would not have been a problem had I in fact registered with the Selective Service board in Franklin County, Massachusetts, my legal domicile. Nobody was being drafted anymore in Massachusetts, the only state anti-war Democrat George McGovern would carry in 1972.

But because I'd been worried about being busted for my fake in-state address at the YMCA, after I turned 18 in January 1970, I registered in Greensboro.

When I realized that I was still in jeopardy—the last Massachusetts resident who might still be drafted—I started dropping courses right and left so as not to complete my requirements.

But by the fall of 1972, the Guilford County draft board was sending me notice after notice to report for my pre-induction physical. I can't remember how many grandparents I had die that fall to keep the clock running.

But President Nixon had promised to end the draft, and all I had to do was hang on until January 1973. If I were smart enough to graduate from college at age 20, I figured, I should likewise be smart enough not to graduate from college at the age of 20.

So I dropped a course here and there, and I hung around Chapel Hill until May 1973. Now I was faced with another problem—unlike most of the new college graduates I'd be competing against for an entry-level job, I had next to no newspaper experience except at the *Daily Tar Heel*.

I hadn't spent my college summers interning. I had needed to make some money, and honestly, I had next to no interest in doing the kind of intern shit work that had been described to me. I also hadn't been all that impressed with the journalists, so-called, that I'd met. The professors at the J-school were decent people, but they were mostly fugitives from the copy desk.

Anyway, after graduation (which I skipped) I went back to the Colony Hotel in Kennebunkport—my fifth summer in the "hospitality industry." I saved more money, and after the season ended, I decided to see California for the first time. I drove out there with my girlfriend from Chapel Hill and spent a few weeks in Palo Alto, where one of my best friends from Deerfield was a senior at Stanford.

As the weeks dragged on in Palo Alto, I began putting together a list of newspapers to apply to—in both Massachusetts and North Carolina. As I expected, I got few replies, only two in fact—from the *Springfield Union* and the *Winston-Salem Journal*.

When I got back to my parents' house in Deerfield, I drove down to Springfield for my interview. After all, Tom Wolfe had started out there, and he'd done all right for himself. Not that I was thinking much about that, especially after the managing editor offered a job as copy boy for some pittance, maybe $100 a week.

"I wouldn't offer this job to anybody," he said. "The only person I ever offer this job to is somebody who's from around here, who can live at home, because that's the only person who could afford to take a job like this."

It didn't take me long to figure out I couldn't afford to take the job either, not if I had to live at home. I'd had enough of being a townie. Plus, the paper sucked.

3
JUST GOOD OLD BOYS

If I wasn't going to live at home and work as a copy boy for the *Springfield Union*, I only had one other option—the *Winston-Salem Journal*. The managing editor, Joe Doster, had been amused that on the same day he'd received very similar letters from both me and my girlfriend. So he sent me a letter in Palo Alto, saying, "When you two get back to North Carolina, give me a call."

So he had a sense of humor. I went to see him and he hired me. (My girlfriend got a job in Burlington.) The starting pay was $140 a week, the lowest among the four biggest dailies in North Carolina. But what were my alternatives? I rented a studio apartment off Peters Creek Parkway, behind Mr. Barbecue, across the street from a tiny AM radio station, WAIR, owned by a former Wake Forest football player.

The apartment was tiny, but the rental agent told me to look on the bright side: "Once you get a gal in here, boy, she's already in the bedroom."

That's the kind of place Winston-Salem was, very practical. I never minded living there. I liked the fact that there were all kinds of factories, where products people wanted or needed were manufactured—cigarettes (R.J. Reynolds Tobacco), beer (Schlitz), underwear (Hanes), doughnuts (Krispy Kreme). With those kinds of products, we always said that Winston-Salem was recession proof. The Twin Cities had their own big local bank (Wachovia) and even an airline (Piedmont), both long gone now.

17

Other big cities in North Carolina elected their city councils or boards of aldermen at-large to keep the black representation to a minimum. Not so Winston-Salem. They had wards. Sometimes, even in the 1970s, most of aldermen were black. Nobody batted an eye.

Reynolds had no factory unions—they'd broken the only serious drive by the Tobacco Workers back in the late 1940s, tarring them as Reds trying to stir up the black workers. After that, Reynolds kept the unions at bay by paying their employees whatever the unions at all the other cigarette companies could negotiate.

I was long gone by the time Reynolds was finally sold—remember the book *Barbarians at the Gate?* But scores of Reynolds factory hands became instant millionaires. It was a mostly benign oligarchy that ruled Winston-Salem.

The town fathers had an inferiority complex about not having a large local college, so they basically purchased Wake Forest University and moved it—lock, stock, barrel, and even its name—to Winston. It was Baptist and into the late 1950s, dancing was not allowed.

Like everywhere else in North Carolina, there were no bars serving mixed drinks, only bottle clubs, like the Twin City Club—no Jews, blacks, or women—where the *Journal*'s star columnist Roy Thompson could be reached every evening.

The *Journal* had been owned by a branch of the Reynolds family, but had since sold out to another family-owned Southern corporation.

Before its sale, the *Journal* had won a 1971 Pulitzer Prize for "public service" for some series about strip mining. As Alexander Cockburn of the *Village Voice* later explained, public-service awards were usually handed out by judges who didn't want to have to bother to read the damn series. Therefore, the more crap you could send the judges, the more likely you were to get the "coveted" Pulitzer, because it showed how serious you were.

I never heard a single word about what was in fact in the series, just that it had won the Pulitzer. It was always spoken of in hushed, reverential tones, like TV golf commentary at the Masters.

The rule at the *Journal* was that all new reporters had to spend their first month on the copy desk, to learn the paper's style, and to see if they could get along with everybody else. I don't know how it works now at the *Journal* or anywhere else—most newspapers no longer have copy desks per se. How can you have a "desk" of any sort when you don't even have a newsroom?

I did okay in what amounted to my tryout. The *Journal* had the usual copy desk crew of burn-outs, drunks, ex-sportswriters and, a closeted gay or two, all

18

of them bitter about their own lack of upward mobility, reporters with bylines and everything else.

The only complaint I recall that the lifer copy editors had about me was that I wrote my 7s in the English way, with a line through it, the way I'd done it for years, so as not to confuse 1s and 7s in my lousy handwriting.

One of the female copy editors, a spinster who during World War II had been a member of the WAVES—the female branch of the Navy—seemed to think it was some New England affectation. She gently chided me, "Howie, there are no Europeans in the press room."

When I graduated from the copy desk, I got a pay raise from $140 a week to $148.

The most important beats at the *Journal* were City Hall and the Forsyth County commissioners, both of which bored the hell out of me. I did some night police work, and also covered the Kernersville board of aldermen, one of whom was over 70 and liked to occasionally speak in a black dialect, much to the chagrin of his son, who was the mayor.

The first big story I got to cover was a Teamster strike against a local trucking company. One morning I got a call from the owner's daughter, who was also the company spokesman. The family had a St. Bernard, and the previous night, someone had grabbed the dog and hanged it from a children's swing set in the backyard.

It was the kind of story you can't learn about in journalism school. I was getting an education in a hurry.

There was a tiny unincorporated village near Winston-Salem named Horneytown. Nobody ever thought about Horneytown until the Horneytown Massage Parlor opened next to the Horneytown Baptist Church. The pastor went before the county commissioners and in great agitation told them that the sign outside the massage parlor read "Open 24 Hours—and that means all night!"

The *Journal's* Horneytown Massage Parlor stories got picked up on the national wires.

Our Congressman was Wilmer "Vinegar Bend" Mizell, a former National League pitcher who'd ridden into Washington on Richard Nixon's coattails in 1968. He was from backwoods Alabama, and it was widely suspected, at least among the Pulitzer Prize–winning swells at the *Journal*, that he was illiterate.

Eventually the *Journal's* Washington correspondent—which many mid-sized dailies had back in those days—conspired to get into his Capitol Hill office.

He then threw down an obscure bill or piece of technical legislation on his desk in front of him and asked Vinegar Bend to comment on it.

Vinegar Bend passed the test—he could read—but he couldn't overcome Watergate, and he was ousted in 1974 by a Democrat.

Probably because nobody else was interested in them, I got to cover both the local Ku Klux Klan and the Black Panther Party that operated out of North Winston.

Joe Grady was Grand Dragon—or whatever—of the local klavern. He was a recovering alcoholic, and he used to attend the aldermen's meetings to rail against fortified wine—"mixed drinks in a bottle." In his drinking days, he'd been arrested for exposing himself to the wife of a future state senator. Joe Grady was always between jobs. He used to say, "Howard, there's n-words, and there's white n-words, and if I don't get me a job soon, you can consider me a white n-word," although of course, he didn't say n-word.

One year on a Saturday night I covered Joe's annual cross burning out in the sticks. Like everyone else in Winston-Salem, he smoked, and he had a big lighter. Once it got dark and it was time to fire up the cross, he whipped out his lighter. The flames went right up the cross, but one side refused to catch. Our photographer had driven out for naught.

"Damn," Joe Grady said. "If that don't catch, I'm gonna cry."

I used that as the kicker for my story the next morning. Soon Joe was calling me with a warning.

"Howard," he said, "that quote don't help me none. I'm trying to keep this here organization under control, but there's a lotta hotheads out here want to get rid of me. I tell you, y'all gonna miss me when I'm gone."

Was Joe Grady appealing to me to act as a responsible community leader? Boy, did the Grand Dragon ever get a wrong number! But Grady did get into trouble with the grander dragons or whatever they're called when he went to bat for another one of my beats, the local chapter of the Black Panther Party.

It was run by a guy named Larry Little, who'd been rabble-rousing across the state since he was a teenager. I'd first seen him when I was a freshman at Carolina, during the post-Kent State disturbances in 1970. He'd driven down from Winston-Salem to deliver his usual denunciations of . . . The Man, Mister Charlie, crackers, honkies in general, etc.

He was speaking down on the South Campus and a couple of us drifted over to hear him speak. The only reason I remember it at all is because at one point

Little said something particularly incendiary, and one of the handful of students listening was offended and yelled out, "Boo!"

Larry Little didn't take no shit from no random ofays. He was not your father's knee-grow.

"Boo?" he yelled back. "Boo on you, motherfucker!"

It cracked us up, all us preppies who were watching the performance. It was Radical Chic, a few months before Tom Wolfe even published his piece of the same name in *New York* magazine.

Anyway, after I was sprung from the copy desk, I was told by the city editor to drive up to North Winston and introduce myself to Little and the boys—excuse me, wrong word there. There were always people coming and going, often young women with children. I never felt relaxed there, not because I was in any physical danger, but just because I knew I didn't belong. But no one ever called me a motherfucker or anything.

One of Little's deputies was Nelson Malloy Jr. He would later succeed Little as the ward alderman. By then he was in a wheelchair, having been paralyzed in a shooting involving party factions—crews, they would have been called, if it were organized crime.

The reason I mention Nelson Malloy Jr. is because of his father, Nelson Malloy Sr. Just like me, Senior worked at the *Journal*—as a janitor. I'd drive back to the *Journal* offices from North Winston after being with Nelson Malloy Jr. talking about "The Man," and I'd see his father emptying trash for The Man, in the *Journal* city room.

That was the thing about Winston-Salem—most everybody, black or white, was connected somehow or another to everybody else. It was an overgrown small town. Another thing different about Winston-Salem was the lingering influence of the early settlers of Salem—German Moravians. They were somewhat more tolerant, liberal, than the local hard-shell Baptists and no-nonsense Methodists.

Winston-Salem probably had more non-Anglo surnames than anyplace in North Carolina. One of the *Journal* editors was named Goodman—he was from one of the oldest families in the city. And one of the Black Panthers was Charles Zollicoffer—you don't get a much more German name than that.

Covering the Panthers led to my first interaction with the FBI. I was 23 when I got my initial write-up in an FBI 302, or 209, or whatever the number is.

One day I was making my rounds at Panther headquarters when Little casually mentioned that the FBI had been keeping tabs on the party. This piqued my interest, so I asked him how he knew this.

He explained to me that Charles Zollicoffer had a brother who was in the Army, stationed as I recall in Germany. One day the brother had been ordered into the office of his C.O. on some matter. The soldier had noticed his C.O. studying some documents on his desk that seemed to concern him. At some point, the officer got called out of the office and Zollicoffer grabbed the papers and stuffed them in his pocket.

Looking over them later back at the barracks, Zollicoffer realized they were copies of FBI files, indicating that the feds were keeping rather close tabs on him, his brother Charles, and the rest of the Winston-Salem chapter of the BPP. And the reports must have been widely circulated, if they had ended up at an Army base in Germany.

After Little told me the story, it may have been the first time in my brief career as a reporter that I asked a source, "You wouldn't happen to have a copy of those documents, would you?"

Larry Little did. I was excited, the city desk not so much. My bosses had no objections to running the story, they just didn't think it was a very big deal. I must have called the local office of the FBI for a "no comment," but I don't remember. Of course, I couldn't say where the reports had been obtained—that would have busted Zollicoffer's brother.

Every reporter had to write an "enterprise" story or two for the Sunday paper. So I wrote up the story about the FBI surveilling the local Black Panthers for the next weekend.

I was hoping it would make the front page, but no such luck. It didn't even make the local front. They threw it inside the A section, a not-so-subtle way of saying, nothing to see here folks, move along.

The FBI disagreed. I soon got a call from the local agents, asking me where I'd gotten the documents I'd quoted in the paper. They didn't deny anything—their names were on the files. They just wanted my sources. Naturally I refused to name them. I'd gone to journalism school after all. I'd even read *All the President's Men*—in hardcover. I told the city editor what the local agents had tried to do to me, and he shrugged. It just wasn't a big deal.

A couple of nights later, I was on deadline. Everyone was in the office, including some of the top editors. Suddenly, the two local agents were standing in front of my desk, asking me again who'd given me the documents.

Paper Boy

It seemed a calculated gesture, to get my bosses' attention. They obviously didn't understand the attitude of the management of Piedmont Publishing Co. They were more concerned about the latest zoning variances affecting the planned expansion of the trailer park in Tobaccoville, or the upcoming church social in Rural Hall, or when spring canoe rentals would resume on the Yadkin River.

I politely told the G-men I wouldn't tell them anything, and they left quietly. Again, my bosses never put the heat on me; they just plain didn't care. The Black Panthers weren't on their radar screen.

The next year, Congress started prying out the information about the FBI Counterintelligence program—COINTELPRO—and how much of it involved the BPP. Larry Little called me to make sure I'd seen the stories, which of course I had. But there would be no follow-ups in the *Journal*. Personally, for my own edification, I kept reading up on COINTELPRO, and I realized how the agents were taught to put everything in writing.

So I decided to file a Freedom of Information Act (FOIA) request to find out if I was in their files. A year or so later, I heard back from them—nothing in the files, they claimed. Every few years, I'd file another FOIA, and I'd always get the same response. Sometime in the 1990s, when I was getting along with my congressman, Marty Meehan, I asked him to see if he could pry out some information. He had no more luck than I'd had.

Finally, around 2005—30 years later—in some rogue outbreak of transparency, the FBI brass decided to start posting everything about their dark corners, or a few of them anyway. One of which concerned the Black Panther Party chapter in Winston-Salem.

It didn't take me long to discover the file the G-men had always told me didn't exist. There were a number of memos back and forth in the supervising Charlotte office, including this one from June, 1975, three months after I'd written the story:

"Charlotte had considered interviewing HOWARD CARR, reporter for the *Winston-Salem Journal,* and also contacting the publisher and managing editor for this newspaper. However, it is believed that this would result in possible embarrassment to the Bureau as well as further publication of the entire matter. In addition, these newspaper officials might seriously question our interest in view of the time lapse."

What I found most interesting was the note that the regional headquarters in Charlotte seems to have decided that the local agents should not question

To: SAC, Charlotte (157-6171)

From: Director, FBI (105-165706)-8-744

BLACK PANTHER PARTY (BPP)   PERSONAL ATTENTION
EM

▓▓▓▓▓▓▓▓ Copies of Special Agent LOWE's report were thereafter
disseminated to appropriate interested Federal agencies.

In the February 14, 1975, edition of The Winston-Salem
Journal, a local newspaper published in Winston-Salem, North
Carolina, appeared an article written by Staff Reporter HOWARD
CARR and entitled, "FBI Still Hovers Over Panthers, Members
Regarded as Possible Security Risks." CARR reported in the
article that an FBI report dated February 26, 1973, on CHARLES
ZOLLICOFFER, a member of the BPP, and written by ZACHARY T.
LOWE, an Agent in the FBI's Winston-Salem Office, had been
recently made available to the Journal and that the report
contained information furnished by three informants. CARR
also reported that the FBI file provided information concerning
CHARLES RAY ZOLLICOFFER's age, marital status, brothers'
criminal records, and other pertinent information.

On ▓▓▓▓▓▓▓▓▓▓▓▓▓▓▓▓▓▓ advised that the
February 26, 1973, report of Special Agent LOWE, referred to
in the February 14, 1975, newspaper article, had been furnished
to the newspaper reporter by unknown individuals associated
with the BPP and that the report had been obtained while an
unnamed individual or individuals were reviewing certain
undisclosed records. CE T-1 advised that it was unknown
whether or not the report was the actual report available in
the undisclosed records or a copy of that report.

On ▓▓▓▓▓▓▓▓▓▓▓▓▓▓▓▓▓▓ advised that BPP members
at Winston-Salem, North Carolina, had made the report of
Special Agent LOWE available to The Winston-Salem Journal.

On ▓▓▓▓▓▓▓▓▓▓▓▓▓▓▓▓▓▓ advised that CHARLES
RAY ZOLLICOFFER appeared to be the most knowledgeable BPP
member concerning the report of Special Agent LOWE, and it
was apparent from comments made by CHARLES RAY ZOLLICOFFER
that he had seen the report and/or had the report in his
possession.

2

1975: the FBI wanted to know how I obtained COINTELPRO surveillance documents
on the local Black Panther Party.

me. But they had—and they hadn't "memorialized" their visit to the *Journal*
city room.

In other words, the agents lied in their report. Why was I not surprised?

Much of the black community in Winston-Salem was rolling in federal
money that had flooded in everywhere during the War on Poverty. Welfare is
the ultimate drug. It's easier to kick heroin than a handout.

The local "anti-poverty" group was known as the Experiment in Self-
Reliance, which was exactly the opposite of what it was. In fact, ESR was an

experiment in total government reliance—nothing but handouts and the sort of "job training" that Tom Wolfe had skewered so deftly in *Mau-Mauing the Flak Catchers.*

The Panthers at least tried to stand on their own two feet. They were dissatisfied with the city's ambulance services in the black neighborhoods, so they decided to start their own. It was always a long shot, but it became a big story when Joe Grady went to an aldermen's meeting and announced that the Klan was supporting the Panthers, because the more that black people did for themselves, the fewer handouts they'd be demanding from white folks.

Pretty soon, there was a new grand dragon.

I continued working at the *Journal,* mostly general assignment, some politics. When Gen. William C. Westmoreland published a book, I was assigned to interview him at the book signing. He didn't much like my line of patter, and eventually he snarled at me, "People like you are why we lost the war in Vietnam."

I think he thought that was a knock. I didn't take it that way. One day I was sent over to the hotel across the street to interview Miss America—I couldn't even pick her out of the crowd in the lobby. As Roger Ailes later said of Gretchen Carlson, "Even Miss America has off years."

In that same hotel where I met Miss America, I interviewed ex-Georgia Gov. Jimmy Carter. I was not impressed. At the end of the interview he asked me for my address and a few months later I got a Christmas card from him.

More and more, though, I was working nights on the city desk. I was the assistant city editor. H.L. Mencken once compared becoming a city editor to getting one's sergeant's stripes. In other words, you were a non-commissioned officer, running the enlisted men, i.e., the reporters.

Being assistant city editor, which I was, at first without the title, meant I was back on the night shift, 4–midnight. I was working with my old mates on the copy desk, except my job was handling the locally written night side copy.

The fact is, though, that I was less an editor than I was a rewrite man. I would take badly written news copy and try to line-edit it into serviceable English. I quickly realized where this job could lead, or should I say not lead, if I didn't do something quickly.

The reality was, I was polishing other people's prose, and eventually they would be using their clips—that I had in fact written, or rewritten—to move up to better newspapers in bigger markets.

Meanwhile, I might still be stuck in Winston-Salem, working with the next generation of cub reporters. I might end up as a newspaper version of "Coach," that hardy perennial of the sports pages who is called by a reporter for a quote about one of his Pop Warner players from years past. The call comes after Pop's former player is picked in the first round of the NFL draft, and Pop proudly beams and says, "I always knew that boy was goin' places, by cracky!"

In August 1977, Elvis Presley died. It was big news, of course—the first time the TV networks ever blew away their usual dreary bureaucratic filler to lead the nightly news with a story viewers cared about. All I knew was that in 1956, Elvis had appeared at the old Carolina Theater on West Fourth Street, around the corner from the *Journal* downtown.

Roy Thompson, the paper's marque columnist, had covered it, and written a story that was still talked about, at least in our newsroom. All I needed was a few grafs from Roy and I could run excerpts from his wry column from 21 years earlier.

So I did something I never did—I called the Twin City Club and had Roy Thompson paged. I asked him to come back to the paper (it was walking distance) and knock out a quick column on Elvis. He blew me off. He didn't sound that loaded, he just couldn't be bothered.

I understood, it wasn't like Roy Thompson was going to toss off some scintillating prose and get a new job at a more prestigious newspaper. He was 54 years old. Roy had worked with Tom Wicker and he was still in Winston-Salem. There was nothing I could say to convince him to come back to the office for a half-hour or so.

I forget what I did with the Elvis story, whether I "localized" it or not. But what I remember thinking is that if I didn't get off my ass I could end up like Roy. Would I have my own bottle at the Twin City Club, assuming they'd embraced a new spirit of ecumenism and admitted Catholics, which I'd been told they hadn't always done in the past?

The Dixie Classic Fair (since renamed) was big in Winston-Salem. In 1977, when I had to assign a reporter to cover it, I realized that I was handling it, as either a reporter or an editor, for the fourth time. And I was only 25 years old.

I had to get out of the *Journal.* I'd interviewed here and there over the years, but either I hadn't been connected enough, or it was just a lateral move that didn't make any sense. But in 1977, another alumnus of the *Journal* named Bill McIlwain had been hired as the editor of the *Boston Herald American.*

Even at the age of 25, I realized I would have only a limited number of chances to escape from the newspaper Palookaville that I was stuck in, so I grabbed for the opportunity to flee. I figured it might be my only chance at the brass ring, or something close to it.

The managing editor didn't want me to leave—good rewrite men are always hard to come by. He asked me if I wanted to wait another year or so and then they'd help me get something at the *Globe*.

I knew better than to take him up on that offer. I knew it'd never be arranged, as Harry Chapin would say. A bird in the hand . . .

4
NEW KID
IN TOWN

It's hard to overstate how wretched a newspaper the *Boston Herald American* was when I started working there in January 1978. George Frazier, my late favorite columnist, had worked at the Hearst-owned *Record American* briefly in the 1960s between his stints on the *Herald* and the *Globe*. He said later that when he took the job, he'd known that the readers moved their lips when they read, but he hadn't known the editors did too.

That was in a piece he wrote soon after Hearst, the owner of the *Record*, bought the *Herald* in 1972. The *Herald* had been on life support after being stripped of its TV station, Channel 5. (In a final act of defiance of the FCC and Boston and everything else, the old owners signed off the air with an old war movie that delivered a blunt message—*Fixed Bayonets*.)

It was as if the paper, or papers, were cursed. The *Herald*'s ownership, at least according to Boston lore, had made a momentously bad decision during World War II. During the wartime paper shortages, newspapers shrank in size, and they had to decide which kinds of ads to continue printing. The *Herald* picked display ads—from department stores such as Filene's and Jordan Marsh—while the *Globe* opted for classified ads.

After the war, when the paper shortage ended, everybody got display ads back, but the *Globe* had a lock on the region's classified ads. Readers, even the old-line Yankees who'd been the *Herald*'s core readership for decades, began switching over.

Paper Boy

The *Boston Post*, long the dominant paper in Boston, folded in 1956. That gave the *Globe* a wider lane. Meanwhile, the *Herald* was fat and happy, living off the profits from Channel 5.

The *Record* was a Hearst newspaper, which meant that it was, *prima facie*, terrible. In his 1961 review of the W. A. Swanberg biography of William Randolph Hearst, A. J. Liebling in *The New Yorker* used the then recent merger of the *Record* and the *American* as his jumping-off point, laying out exactly how dreadful Boston's Hearst paper was, even by local journalistic standards, which had always been virtually nonexistent.

The *Record* had been printed in Winthrop Square. The editor on and off for many years was an old Hearst hand named Walter Howey. He had set up the tabloid *New York Daily Mirror* in 1924, supposedly in 10 days. From his career in the Chicago newspaper wars, Howey became the model for the fictional editor Walter Burns in the famous Broadway play and movie *The Front Page.*

By the time he returned to Boston, Howey was a full-blown alcoholic. One night in a rage he fired the entire staff on deadline and promoted a copy boy to editor. The copy boy had to wait until Howey passed out in his office, after which he went down to the paper's bar, the Blue Sands, and "rehired" everybody. (I got to know the ex-copy boy later at the State House; he'd become a flak for some state agency and later committed suicide.)

In the warm-weather months, pedestrians would sometimes be strolling by the *Record* offices when they would suddenly hear a stream of curses coming from the open windows on the second floor, followed by a deck of playing cards floating down. They were playing hearts—cut-throat hearts. It was the official card game of the *Record.*

Eddie Corsetti had been the overnight police reporter for the *Record.* One of his nightly duties was to stop by Howey's Beacon Hill townhouse after midnight and deliver him a bottle of elderberry wine and two packs of Spud cigarettes, the original menthol brand.

Howey's building had an elevator, and one day in the early fifties he drunkenly stepped onto it and didn't like the looks of a younger man who was already on it. Howey pulled out a knife and stabbed his neighbor. The case was later dismissed, and Howey died in 1954. But the *Record* lingered on.

In 1972, when Hearst bought the *Herald*, the *Record-American* moved from Winthrop Square to the much more modern Herald plant in the South End, at the intersection of the Turnpike extension and the Southeast Expressway.

It was a magnificent location for almost anything—as shown by the success of the upscale apartment complex that's since been constructed there, with a Whole Foods on the first floor, where the presses used to roar.

The *Record* had a much larger circulation than the *Herald*. The *Record* sold all day long. Hawkers frequented subway stops, Fenway Park, local taprooms. They were peddling tabloids with the next day's date—"Yesterday's news tomorrow," locals joked.

The real reason for the *Record*'s large circulation, despite its abysmal quality, was the fact that it carried the daily number—which in those days was referred to as "n-word pool."

Before the state lottery was started in 1972, everybody played the number. It was what made Mafia underboss Jerry Angiulo a multimillionaire.

For some misguided reason, Hearst decided to shift from a tabloid format to broadsheet. It made no sense, but then, nothing else about the newspaper did either. For some editions, the masthead said *Herald Traveler Record American*. Then they'd flip it to *Record American Herald Traveler*. Hearst had always called the Sunday paper the *Boston Sunday Advertiser*, but that name didn't survive the merger. I guess there wouldn't have been room on the front page for all the titles.

George Frazier described it, accurately, as "a Hearst hybrid beyond belief."

By the time I went on the payroll in January 1978, it was hemorrhaging money and circulation. The previous Hearst editor, Sam Bornstein, had just been put out to pasture. He'd been known as "Suntan Sam" for his frequent junkets to sunny places for shady people, as Graham Greene would say.

Suntan Sam insisted that all graft—say, free circus tickets to the Garden—go through him, because he used them as tips when he was out eating on the arm at Anthony's Pier 4 or Jimmy's Harborside. It was a firing offense for an intern to hold out on freebies. Every bit of graft was controlled by Suntan Sam.

At a Hearst newspaper, nothing was on the level. At Christmas, 300 Harrison Avenue resembled what Rome must have been like in 410 A.D. after the Goths sacked it. Minor functionaries—ex-cops turned lawyers, city council and school committee candidates, bail bondsmen, etc.—would appear in the city room, heads bowed, delivering graft for the local assistant city editors, who were often also officers of the newsroom's local union.

The usual tribute was a fifth of some blended Canadian whiskey. We all disdained the fruitcake that they offered. Eddie Corsetti's joke was, there were only four fruitcakes in the world, and they just kept getting passed around.

Paper Boy

The *Herald* was no longer an all-day newspaper, but the Hearst holdovers still held to the mentality of "the edition." McIlwain had brought in a few reporters and editors from his previous paper in New Jersey, the Bergen *Record*, and a handful of others, including me.

College boys, that's what the old Hearst crew dismissively called all of us. If I hadn't been on the Saturday-night shift, I'd have been totally written off by the old-timers as another hopeless dilettante.

The only strength the *Herald* still had were its photographers, especially Stanley Forman. You may have heard of Weegee, the great spot-news photographer in New York way back when. Joe Pesci later starred in a movie loosely based on Weegee's life.

Forman was the Weegee of Boston, only better. A Hearst man, he'd recently won two Pulitzer Prizes for spot news photography, one a young woman falling to her death off a fire escape, and the other of a long-haired South Boston anti-busing protester using an American flag to try to impale a black lawyer in a three-piece suit on City Hall Plaza. Forman cruised the city endlessly, listening to the calls from a bank of police scanners on the front seat of his car, waiting for the next spot news.

Most of the people in the newsroom were lifers from either the old *Herald* or the *Record*, although there were still a handful who'd started out on the defunct *Boston Post*, at one time the largest-circulation newspaper in the nation.

At the *Herald,* there were a lot of legmen, who'd never written anything. Most of them had started out as high-school interns, hired right off the street. Then they worked their way up, if you could call being a Hearst legman up. They phoned in everything for "the edition," usually to ex-*Herald Traveler* college boys.

One of the old Hearst rewrite men, Harold Banks, had gone to Boston Latin and Harvard with Theodore F. White, who went on to write the *Making of a President* series. Harold was a good guy, a chain smoker (most of them were) who had that hang-dog look of the permanently beat down. Years of toiling in the Hearst empire, especially for Suntan Sam, could do that to a man, even a Harvard man.

Both the *Herald American* and the *Globe* had "bureaus" all over the city, including at police headquarters, then on Berkeley Street. The press room was on the second floor. Some nights, the legmen would be playing hearts, and they'd get so drunk that they'd fall backward out the open window. In the winter,

31

the snowdrifts would usually break their falls. In the summer, if they were lucky, they'd topple onto the bushes.

At least one police-beat legman kept a collection of "clues" in his car. Call him Jocko. His trunk was like an arsenal, with untraceable weapons and other assorted "evidence" that could be left at any crime scene. If there'd been a rape-murder, say, he'd drop a bra near the scene and then phone the news into the edition, after which he'd call the cops. That way he had a beat on the other papers.

Headline: "Mystery Bra Found Near Death Scene."

Back then, a lot of bars had their own matchbooks. They'd be in big bowls next to the cash register and the toothpicks, or at the hat checks in the swankier joints. So Jocko maintained a huge collection of matchbooks in his car, including some from the handful of gay bars that operated more or less aboveground.

Say a murder victim turned out to be a "confirmed bachelor." If the killing remained unsolved, Jocko or one of the other legmen would eventually show up at the crime scene and drop one of those matchbooks from a gay bar nearby. On the street an hour later would be a screaming *Record* front page:

"Baffled Cops Seek Perv Link to Bay Village Slaying."

In the *Herald* newsroom, the lifers were still talking about this guy's greatest scoop, when an escaped killer named Rocco Balliro was surrounded in an Egleston Square walk-up with his moll and her infant child. He shot it out and somehow escaped.

But his girlfriend and her child were slain in the crossfire. A few days later, she was buried, and of course the cops had the entire cemetery staked out, in case Balliro made an appearance, like in a film noir B-movie. He was a no-show, however, and soon everyone had dispersed. Except for Jocko. He'd planned ahead by making a purchase of a bouquet of flowers that morning, in another town, and had removed anything that could identify its provenance.

The cemetery was deserted when Jocko stepped into a nearby phone booth and called Winthrop Square. He breathlessly informed the rewrite man that the police had just gotten a tip that a party matching Rocco Balliro's description had been spotted dropping off a bouquet of roses at the fresh gravesite of his girlfriend. As Suntan Sam and his minions excitedly replated the front page for the next edition, Jocko drove out to the graveyard, dropped off the bouquet, and drove back into the city.

That was Boston journalism back in the day.

Paper Boy

The old *Herald* holdovers had been working for Hearst for more than five years, but under Suntan Sam and his Hearst straw bosses, they'd never been fully integrated into the operation. The *Herald* guys were like prisoners of war, or trustees in a jail—they were permitted to do the shit work, but they weren't totally trusted because . . . they were doing time. They were wearing invisible stripes, like the title of the old Humphrey Bogart movie.

One of the old *Herald* hands was Joe Heaney. He was one of the funniest people I've ever known. Originally from Belmont, by the time I met him he lived on a farm in New Hampshire where he had a barn and boarded horses.

A lot of the sayings I've made my own over the years I got from sitting next to Joe Heaney, right across from the photo desk. If someone was drinking, he'd say, "He owed it to himself." If the guy was drunk, he'd say, "He got a bad ice cube." If the guy liked to drink, he'd say, "He will take a drink . . . under extreme social pressure."

If someone died, Joe would say, "He won't be down for breakfast."

Does any of this sound familiar from my radio show? Of course, I couldn't use some of Joe's *bon mots* on the air. Like, "He's up and down, like a bride's pajamas." Or, on Thursdays, asking whether the paychecks had arrived, he'd use the old military expression: "Did the eagle shit yet?"

I was just turning 26. I wanted to get along with everybody, because from what I could see, it didn't look like the *Herald American* was going to be a long-term gig. Taking the subway to work some days, I did my own personal audience survey on who was reading it—and the results were not encouraging. Scary, in fact, how old most *Herald American* readers were.

My guess was, some of them hadn't yet figured out that since 1972 there'd been a state lottery where you could play the daily number. A lot of them still called it the *Record*, or even the *American*.

I was living in a rented second-floor apartment in Somerville, the All-American City, as it had been called by *Look* magazine just before it went out of business. The blizzards that year started in mid-January, and they just kept coming. It seemed New England winters had gotten a lot worse in the years I'd been away.

Maybe there was something to all those global-cooling stories. . . .

When the Blizzard of '78 hit, my car was parked out on Powder House Boulevard. It was a Gremlin, and as I looked out of my second-floor window on Monday night, the only thing that I could still see visible above the snow was the radio antenna. It apparently offended someone's sensibility, so it was quickly torn off. There was just a mound of snow where my car had been. It looked like an igloo.

Tuesday afternoon, I borrowed a snow shovel from my landlord and spent hours digging out the space. Driving had been banned, but the media were exempt. So a few days later, I drove into the *Herald*. I didn't want to give up my space in Somerville, because the snow wouldn't be gone for months. So I dragged an empty 50-gallon oil drum up from my landlord's basement and rolled it into the space to officially claim it until the thaw, whenever it arrived.

That night after my shift I returned to Powerhouse Boulevard. The oil drum had been stolen, and my space was gone.

That's the kind of place Somerville was. I enjoyed living in the city, but it was like nowhere else I'd ever been, especially its politics. The former mayor would soon go to prison in a shakedown. He'd been given a federal job by Tip O'Neill, who was still terrified that someday he'd be knocked out by an Italian, as had almost happened (maybe actually did, before the votes were counted and recounted enough times) in his first congressional election in 1952.

The state senator had been born in Ireland. His name was Denis McKenna, and I always said he only had one "n" in his first name because he hadn't had time to steal the second one. He had three aides—including two aldermen, one of whom was his son, both of whom would be convicted of federal felonies. His third aide was a convicted truck hijacker out on parole.

One of the state representatives was a woman who'd been arrested in 1976 for biting a British sailor during the Tall Ships' visit to Boston. Her name was Marie Howe, but when she was arrested, she'd given her name to the Boston cops as "Rita Plunkett."

Her brother was on the city's board of assessors. They kept the official city records in pencil.

The other state rep was Vinnie Piro. His brother was an alderman, Peter Piro, who owned a print shop in Magoun Square, which was wall-to-wall buckets of blood. I had to drive slowly down Medford Street every Sunday morning when I was going home to my apartment in West Somerville, because the locals would come tumbling out of the gin mills after last call, brawling into the street.

There seemed to be a barroom on every corner. One day one of my friends from the Colony was coming in for a visit. He got lost in the deepest, darkest Somerville and called me from a pay phone for directions. I asked him where he was and he told me he was on a corner across the street from a bar.

Paper Boy

"If you want me to figure out you where you are," I told him, "you're going to have to be a little more precise than that."

One Friday morning at the *Herald* we heard on the police radio that there'd been a shooting in Magoun Square. The call had come from Piro Printing. There was a body inside. Sal Sperlinga, the political fixer of the Winter Hill Gang, had been doing his work release at Alderman Piro's print shop. The week before, Sal had ordered a junkie to get the hell out of Union Square, and the junkie had returned to kill Sal, which he did, first shooting him in the ass and then emptying his .32 into Sperlinga as he lay prostate, begging for mercy.

As I've told you, I was grateful for my Saturday night shift, because it gave me a chance to fit in as a non-college boy, despite my educational handicap. Living in Somerville in those pre-woke days didn't hurt my assimilation prospects either. Having the first name Howie was likewise a plus—the leading gangster in Somerville, the boss of the Winter Hill Gang, was named Howie Winter. We weren't related, but it made me seem less . . . foreign.

As I look back on my years in the Hearst empire, most of what I remember about the newsroom happened on Saturday nights.

The Saturday-night city editor was the aforementioned Eddie Corsetti, a legman extraordinaire. As the paper's senior police reporter, his nickname was "the Inspector." Also on the Saturday night shift was his son, Paul Corsetti, a Vietnam vet who also covered the cops almost exclusively. He too was a legman.

Unless some big story was popping, we spent Saturday nights at the photo desk, playing hearts, just like in the old *Record* days back in Winthrop Square.

I like hearts, I'd played the game a lot in Chapel Hill. It's a four-person game, each player getting 13 cards. There are two variations—everyone either passes three cards to the next player, or they don't.

At Chapel Hill, we never passed cards, because it tended to give an advantage to the better players. However, the Corsettis loved the whole ritual of passing cards—pushing them facedown to the next guy, smirking, as you dumped what appeared to be your worst cards.

Theoretically, it gave you a chance to screw the guy you were passing to, although it could often backfire, especially if you didn't know how to count cards or figure odds. The Corsettis were always trying to shoot the moon, that is, collect all the hearts as well as the queen of spades—the Cunt, as they called her.

Shooting the moon ended the game, and the winner collected a buck from each of the other three players.

Sometimes, in the middle of a harrowing moon shot, the phone would ring, and the copy boy—excuse me, editorial assistant, or e.a.—would timidly bring over a handwritten note to Eddie. I remember one night the kid came over with a note saying that there was a large fire going on in the heavily Hispanic city of Chelsea, much of which had been burned down a few years earlier.

"Eddie," he said meekly, "there's a huge fire in Chelsea."

Eddie grabbed the note, looked at it, crumpled it up, and threw it back at the college boy.

"Great!" he said. "I hope the rest of the city burns down and all the rest of 'em can fucking go back to Puerto Rico where they belong!"

One Saturday night I came in and Paul Corsetti was missing from the city room. I knew he didn't like to miss either the hearts game or *Love American Style,* but Eddie told me he was out in Dedham or somewhere, covering a botched robbery at a drugstore, with the two robbers shot dead. Harold Banks was gone for the night, so I took the call when Paul phoned in to "unload."

I asked him what had happened. It seemed like a big story on a slow evening, but Paul quickly disabused me of that notion.

"Just a couple of crows," he explained casually.

That's the way it was with black crime. Years later, when I was writing *Hitman,* I pulled the clips on Johnny Martorano's murder of three blacks, including two teenagers, during a January blizzard in Roxbury in 1968. In the Sunday *Advertiser,* the triple homicide had rated a mere one-column headline deep in the paper, with at most a six-paragraph, un-bylined story.

As late as the Charles Stuart murders in 1990, blacks were complaining that both Boston papers overlooked black crime. I remember the photo desk giving me a file folder full of gruesome recent crime-scene pictures, all of which had run in the *Herald.* I displayed them on a Channel 2 talk show to disprove the charges. It was just that nobody had paid any attention to them. Nothing had changed over 20 years.

As wretched as the *Herald American* was, it did have at least one advantage on the *Globe.* Just as the old *Herald* had lost its journalistic chops as it grew fat and lazy on the advertising revenues from Channel 5, the same process was beginning to repeat itself with the *Globe.*

The owners were gorging themselves on the millions they were collecting from their dominance in classified and display advertising. They never thought the glory days would end—no one ever does—until they do.

Paper Boy

The *Globe* had been owned and edited for generations by smug, imperious Yankee grandees—the Taylors and their liegemen, the Winships. As they begin to think themselves invincible and invulnerable, they stopped hiring what had been the lifeblood of the newsroom—blue collars, lower-middle-class guys from the neighborhoods.

This same phenomenon was unfolding in newspapers across the country. Suddenly, only college boys needed apply, and then only from the right colleges. It wasn't just the Internet that destroyed the newspaper business.

Woodward and Bernstein played a big part in wrecking the farm systems that had kept newspapers at least somewhat vital, connected to their working-class roots. After Watergate, suddenly, the less-bright scions of every trust-funded family wanted to become investigative reporters, and they were invariably hired over local street guys.

If you were a snot-nosed rich kid, not quite sharp enough to get into law or business school (medical school was obviously out of the question for anyone who ended up in a newsroom), then your father could just make a call to Mr. Taylor or Mr. Winship (there were multiples of both on Morrissey Boulevard) and get young Alexander (known as Sandy) onto the *Globe*.

True to their class right down to the fashion accessories, the *Globe* scribes often wore the *de rigueur* bow ties, which was why I later began referring to them as "bow-tied bum kissers." Another description I employed to advantage was "rump swab," a slightly less crude way of saying brownnoser.

As dominant as the *Globe* became financially, the banishment of the lower middle classes from the newsroom gave the *Herald* one small advantage. The *Globe* no longer wanted to get its hands dirty with the nitty-gritty type of stories that are, or were, the lifeblood of any real newspaper.

The *Globe* won a Pulitzer Prize in the early 1970s for its reporting on corruption in my future legal domicile of Somerville. After a long day at City Hall on Highland Avenue, some of the bow-tied bum kissers had repaired to a nearby low shebeen, and one of the swells had bellied up to the bar and ordered a "Dubonnet on the rocks."

The bartender, at least according to the story told later, did a double take and then yelled at the assembled Local 25 truck drivers and townie stevedores:

"Hey, anybody here know what the fuck a Dubonnet is?"

But at least those guys were in the bar. By the late 1970s, nobody from the *Globe* would have been caught dead anywhere near any place where the bartender didn't know what the fuck a Dubonnet was. And that left the *Herald*—and increasingly, me—an open path.

The *Globe*'s collapse of credibility in the city only accelerated after court-ordered school busing began in Boston in 1974. Like all good gentry suburbanites, the *Globe* was all in for busing. The federal judge who ordered it was from Wellesley, the governor came from Brookline, and the top *Globe* editors lived in Lincoln and Cambridge, respectively.

The *Globe*'s classist coverage was so one-sided that Whitey Bulger, of whom you will read much more later, once fired at the plate-glass windows on Morrissey Boulevard behind which the papers were printed. It wasn't the first or the last time he ever used an automatic weapon on the Boulevard—he and his hit crews killed at least two men on the road over the years.

Two incidents in the fall of 1974 showed just how wide an opening the *Globe*'s increasing detachment from the reality of city life had left for the *Herald* when it came to reporting the down-and-dirty news.

Rep. Wilbur Mills of Arkansas was the powerful chairman of the House Ways and Means Committee. He was also a falling-down drunk, and he'd become infatuated with a woman known as Fanne Foxe, the "Argentine Firecracker."

She and Mills had been stopped by U.S. Park Police earlier in 1974 after she did her shift as a stripper at the Silver Slipper. Fanne dove into the Potomac Tidal Basin. It was almost the end of Mills's career but he survived the November 1974 election, and Fanne Foxe was an overnight sensation at age 37.

She was booked into the Pilgrim Theater in the Combat Zone, an X-rated grindhouse that occasionally booked "burlesk" shows, as the management spelled it on their prominent marquee on Washington Street. On a Saturday night, Eddie Corsetti sent Joe Heaney and a photographer down to watch her show. In the middle of it, she suddenly introduced a surprise guest.

It was Wilbur Mills, drunk as a skunk, staggering around up on stage. Finally, he toppled backward into the theater's long-abandoned orchestra pit. After he climbed out, miraculously uninjured, he reeled backstage and conducted a "press conference" with one reporter—Joe Heaney.

The next day, it was national news. Until a copyrighted *Herald American* photo moved on the wires, the *Globe* steadfastly refused to believe it had happened, that they had been scooped by Hearst ruffians. Why hadn't they gotten a handout on it, the way they always did at City Hall or the State House? They were already getting spoiled by having everyone leak to them, to stay on their good side. Mills soon resigned from his committee chairmanship and never won another election.

The anti-busing disturbances were continuing throughout the city, but the epicenter of resistance was South Boston. One of the gathering places for the protesters was a gin mill on Dorchester Street named the Rabbit Inn. The Boston police, especially the fearsome Tactical Patrol Force, the TPF as it was known, were dispatched to keep order. Some mornings, the locals would throw rocks at the police, never a good idea, but especially not when the police were mounted. Horses frighten easily. Then the local thugs would run back inside the Rabbit Inn and out the back door before they could be apprehended.

Finally the cops had had enough. One Saturday night, a few weeks after the Pilgrim Theater headlines, the TPF staged an impromptu raid on the Rabbit Inn. They stuck tape over the numbers on their badges, and the first guy through the door slammed an unloaded throw-down revolver on the bar. Then the cops piled into the dive bar, after which they proceeded to beat the shit out of everyone. They then fled back into the night.

Eventually one of the maimed somehow managed to rise off the floor and stagger to the pay phone. The *Globe*, of course, was roundly despised, so there was only one media outlet to call—the closest one, just across the Broadway Bridge, the *Herald American*.

It was another big scoop for the *Herald*. But they were few and far between in those days. And many of them happened on Saturday nights.

One of the Saturday-night photographers was a second-generation news-paperman named Gene Dixon. If nothing was going on, and they had a fourth for hearts from the sports desk, I'd go out with Gene looking for photos for the edition. The Combat Zone was just a few blocks away, and if the cops were planning on rounding up a few hookers, we'd go out with them and take pictures of the arrests.

Then we'd go back to the *Herald*. I'd knock out a few paragraphs, a lengthy cutline basically, to illustrate Gene's old-time tabloid photos of garishly dressed "common nightwalkers," as they were called, in hot pants.

Sometimes Gene would make extra prints and head back down to Washington Street looking for the cops, to give them the photos of themselves with the freshly-lugged sex workers, to use the current terminology. He'd usually see the women back out on the streets before the cops.

Gene taught me a few tricks, such as never pulling up directly behind a car on Blue Hill Avenue. He explained that if some thugs came out and tried to pull you out of the car, you needed room to maneuver around and escape. I thought he was exaggerating, but he wasn't—gangster Stevie Flemmi's parents had been dragged out of their car in just such a brazen assault, I later learned.

Gene had started with Hearst as a kid right after World War II. He still wore a tie, because his mother had always told him he should always be well-dressed when he worked with the reporters, whom she described as "gentlemen." His first winter, Gene had an old prewar car with running boards. One frigid evening one of the gentlemen was so drunk that he pissed on the running board, and the urine instantly froze.

Until the next thaw, Gene had to pack fresh snow onto his running boards every evening so his mother wouldn't realize the kind of gentlemen he was in fact working with.

One night in the early seventies, Gene had been cruising the Zone with a young legman who had a thirst so great that it would cast a shadow, as used to be said of Brendan Behan. This night this "police reporter" spotted a woman of the evening he immediately took a shine to. He ordered Gene to stop the car, and jumped out of it, and began chasing her.

The hooker easily eluded the drunk Hearst man, but he was so unsteady on his feet that he tumbled into a large hole at a construction site. He was moaning and screaming in pain—he had suffered multiple broken bones in the fall—and Gene had to think fast after he called the ambulance.

Gene came up with a doozy of a story—his reporter/partner had spotted a pimp, wearing a wide-brimmed Superfly hat, working over the poor young girl, and had tried to intervene. The pimp had then pushed him into the pit. Suddenly the drunk legman was a hero. The story got picked up by the wires, went national. A few days later the legman was still lying in the hospital, in traction, all doped up, when the phone rang.

It was President Richard M. Nixon, calling to congratulate the young hero.

Another of the legmen was a toothless old-timer named Tommy Sullivan. I think he was from Charlestown. In the summer, he went to the Cape and "reported" from there. He basically picked up the *Cape Cod Times*, selected a likely story or two and phoned them in early to Harold Banks, or, if it was later in the day Saturdays, to me.

One Saturday night he had a story about a shepherd who'd put on a show at a fair or something. He was just reading quotes from the *Cape Cod Times*. Finally, just as a joke, I asked him, "What did the shepherd look like?"

Paper Boy

"What did he look like?" Tommy Sullivan said, and then thought about for a moment. "Why, he looked like . . . like a fucking shepherd!"

The yesterday's-news-tomorrow Hearst crew was hopeless, but the college boys (and girls) who'd been hired by Bill McIlwain in the immediate post–Suntan Sam era weren't much better. At least a couple had gone to either Harvard or the Columbia School of Journalism. In other words, they were as useless as tits on a bull, as Joe Heaney would say.

On my first day on the job in January 1978, I was sent down to the Blackstone Valley, on the Rhode Island line, to cover the deaths of two or three kids who'd been sledding on fresh snow that had iced over. They had skidded into the river and drowned.

I came back and wrote the story and handed it in to a female editor whom McIlwain had described to me as the best editor in America. She gave it a quick read and then asked me, "What was the color of the sled?"

Obviously, that was one of those "status details" that Tom Wolfe was so fond of. A novelistic touch to add some color, literally, to the story. But I had been writing off a police report. And anyone who's ever read an incident report knows that no cops, anywhere, are into status details, unless maybe they're trying to pin something on somebody, which was clearly not the case here.

I instantly knew that if she would ask such a question, then this woman had never had to routinely read police reports. And in 1978, if you'd never covered the cops, somewhere, you had never been a reporter, period. The next day I began making discreet inquiries and sure enough, I discovered that the best editor in America had never been "on the street."

Other than the chaos and incompetence in the city room, I had other headaches. Suddenly I was paying one-quarter of my salary for health insurance—the worthless newsroom union never fought for the younger members, because management had paid off the local's elected leaders with no-heavy-lifting desk jobs.

Every other newspaper in America was going to cold type, which is essentially reporters and editors setting type in the newsroom upstairs, rather than relying on blue-collar unionized tradesmen downstairs in what was called a composing room. The "hot" type was set on Linotype machines, which are now found almost exclusively in museums.

Cold type is a much more efficient and economical way of producing a printed newspaper. By 1982, the *Herald* was perhaps the largest-circulation daily left in the country that still relied on "hot type."

The reason was simple: A strike by the trade unions downstairs would have killed the already ailing *Herald*. In New York, the same kind of strikes had already put half the newspapers in New York out of business in the 1960s. And so the *Herald*'s back-shop unions with their obsolete technologies couldn't be broken, or even reformed.

Layoffs accelerated. Before holidays, the list of those assigned to work that day would be posted on the door of the coat closet in the newsroom. If you were scheduled to work, you considered yourself lucky—that you hadn't been laid off.

The last *Boston Post* survivor, who used to joke about how in that paper's final days the reporters had "dribbled" their checks to the bank, because they usually bounced, was laid off. An old *Herald Traveler* rewrite man was likewise cut. He went home and died in his sleep two weeks later.

A woman with a beet-red face who handled the TV listings, and who spent every lunchtime down at J.J. Foley's getting loaded, was let go. The overnight city editor, who used to pass out surrounded by a desk full of longneck empty Schlitzes, was likewise RIFed.

Finally, McIlwain was gone, along with almost all his blow-ins (except me). The new boss was Don Forst. He'd been on the city desk at the *Herald Tribune* during the Breslin-Wolfe-Dick Schaap glory days, then moved to *Newsday*, the Long Island tabloid. He'd also been one of the writers of the satire soft-porn best seller, *Naked Came the Stranger*.

Forst had been editing Hearst's dying afternoon daily, the *Los Angeles Herald Examiner*. He was a native New Yorker, diminutive, stylish dresser, a bit of a dandy. He was another guy who'd never worn out a lot of shoe leather as a re-porter, but he lived and breathed newspapers.

He took an instant dislike to the *Globe*, which made him Good People in my book. He hired a couple of *Globe* dissidents as his deputies, and soon he was shaking up the paper, as best he could, given the financial and union realities.

In the fall of 1979, a black student at Charlestown High was shot and sud-denly the riots of the just-ending anti-busing era were back, almost as bad as five years earlier. Forst gave me the assignment of cobbling together the daily lead story. In the mornings, to get a little color, I would head out to one of the city's public high schools—usually Charlestown, which was closest to Somerville. Then I'd head down to the South End to the *Herald* newsroom.

When I arrived in the early afternoon, I'd find the notes from all the legmen on my ancient manual Underwood typewriter. And usually on top of all their semiliterate notes (often cribbed from the live local TV news coverage they'd been watching from their favorite watering hole) would be a note from Forst, with a headline already written for tomorrow's front-page splash, with the question: "Can you stand this up?"

I always could. I had to. During the summer of 1979, the feds were auctioning off oil-drilling leases on Georges Bank. The auctions were taking place down in Providence in an old-style theater, the kind with a balcony, hard by I-95. The building was crawling with Texas oilmen.

I was sitting in the back of the auditorium when suddenly, from the balcony, somebody began dumping buckets of oil and dead fish down on the assembled oilmen. Then the assailants—you could see that they were hippies—bolted out of the theater, chased by a bunch of people—security, Texans, reporters. The hippies scrambled down the bank next to the theater and escaped into a Grateful Dead–type minivan headed north.

I made my way back into the theater and then down to the men's room, where the Texans were trying to clean themselves up. One of the local Rhode Island officials was profusely apologizing to them:

"Those damn hippies had to be from Massachusetts," he said. "Nobody from Rhode Island would do anything like that."

The auction broke up for the day and everybody headed over to the Biltmore Hotel to swap lies. I followed them, to get more color. A lot of them ended up in the bar, so I joined them, and struck up a conversation with a couple of the Texans. They were straight out of Central Casting—these were the days of *Dallas* and J.R. Ewing—and they were sucking them down and giving me quote after quotable quote.

I knew what they were saying might come back to haunt them, so I decided to give them good-old-boy aliases, Jimbo and Bubba, something like that. I didn't need to hang out long before I had more than enough material for my story, which I composed in my head as I drove back to Boston. I wrote a good story and Forst put it on the front page.

The next morning, I came into work expecting a pat on the back, but instead Forst's grim-faced middle-aged secretary somberly told me the boss wanted to see me as soon as possible. I walked in and Forst told me to sit down. He said that he'd had a call in the morning from a local lobbyist for the American Petroleum Institute who had accused me of making up the entire story, that no such people existed.

Forst was apologetic, but he asked me if I had any proof that Jimbo and Bubba were real people. I remembered immediately that they'd both given me their business cards, and that for some reason, rather than tossing them onto the front seat of my car when I got back to it, I'd put them in my wallet.

So I took the business cards out and handed them to Forst. He gave me a relieved smile, and said he'd call the flak immediately.

I didn't take it personally. I could understand anybody's skepticism about reporters. Whenever any of the old-timers drew the short straw to do a "man-on-the-street" story, it meant a long lunch at J.J. Foley's.

The only problem would be if the desk wanted some "art"—photos. Then you might actually have to go over with a photographer to the Common, or the Broadway station in Southie, to get a few inane quotes (and head shots) before heading over to the Quiet Man to wet your whistle. As Joe Heaney would say, we owed it to ourselves.

Columnists, of course, were even more likely to be . . . piping it, as they used to say in New York. The more smoothly the column read, the more likely it was to have been made up, piped. Especially if there were no last names, which was what had opened me up to suspicions when I got back from Providence.

As a Jewish lawyer's son and a "college boy," Forst was for some reason enamored of those Irish "street guys" from the outer boroughs like Jimmy Breslin and Pete Hamill. When he was in LA he hired Hamill's kid brother, Denis, then brought him along to Boston. As far as Forst was concerned, one-n Denis was a golden boy.

Someone on the Boston City Council decided to introduce legislation to require dog owners to leash their pets. It was a hardy perennial—at one such hearing, Dapper O'Neil had waxed rhapsodically about Roger, his late beloved German shepherd.

So Denis Hamill needed a quick Sunday column, and he decided to write on the proposed leash law in Boston. That Saturday night we were playing hearts when the first editions came up. Eddie Corsetti was trying to shoot the moon or something, but I glanced at Hamill's column, as I always did, just for laughs. Once after a gangland hit in the North End, he wrote a column quoting all the locals on Hanover Street talking about "button men"—which was a New York, but not a Boston, expression.

This night, I quickly noticed that Hamill was quoting everybody who lived in Chelsea. Interesting, because of course in New York where he was from, Chelsea is a neighborhood in lower Manhattan. But in Massachusetts, Chelsea is a separate city, and Boston's proposed leash law would have had no impact on Chelsea.

Yet all the people Hamill was quoting were concerned, and angry—at the mayor, Kevin White. The mayor of Boston, not Chelsea.

I leaned across the desk, handed the paper to Eddie and pointed out the problem. He glared back at me like I was one of the e.a.'s.

"What the fuck do you care?" he said to me. "Deal the fucking cards!"

Nobody else even noticed the problem, as I recall, or cared enough to say anything anyway. But the *Globe* had a much higher profile pipe artist, a guy by the name of Mike Barnicle. After George Frazier died of lung cancer in 1974, Barnicle inherited his column. From the sublime to the ridiculous, you might say.

Anybody who'd been in the business for more than 10 minutes could spot what Barnicle was a mile away. Like so many of these guys, he'd never been a news reporter. He'd spent Vietnam operating an elevator on Capitol Hill. But he'd write his columns as if he'd been slogging through the DMZ during the Tet offensive—never quite going full Da Nang Dick Blumenthal, but leaving the impression that he'd been in 'Nam, just the way he hinted that he was from Boston, rather than Fitchburg, and that his parents were first-generation Irish immigrants.

Once he replaced Frazier, Barnicle was quickly sued by the operator of a gas station on Blue Hill Avenue, whom he said had been tossing the n-word around. Barnicle learned his lesson. The last names largely disappeared from his column.

One Saturday I did a story about a fracas in Hyde Park at a Ward 18 Democrat caucus. It was the usual brawl of the era—Kevin White's payroll patriots versus the stalwarts of state Sen. Joe Timilty, his three-time opponent for mayor. After police cleared the hall, a revolver, with the traditional obliterated serial numbers, was found abandoned in the men's room.

I worked up a decent little story that Saturday night, actually tracked down Timilty, whose driver was the future mayor Tom Menino. I wrote the story on deadline, with lots of quotes and color. It got good play in the Sunday paper.

The next day the usual Monday Barnicle column appeared on the Metro front of the *Globe*. It was all about Hyde Park. He had all my quotes, unattributed of course. It wasn't plagiarism, but all he'd done was just rewrite my story, and nobody seemed to notice, or care. Of course by then Barnicle's M.O. wasn't exactly a secret.

Later, when it all came apart for Barnicle, there was a story told about one column he wrote about a guy being locked in a car trunk at a mall on the North Shore. I forget the details, but the next day, at the *Globe*'s morning editorial meeting, one of the younger bow-tied bum kissers mentioned what a great column it was, and shouldn't we do a follow-up, you know, call the police, interview the victim, etc.?

Everybody else around the table started laughing. The kid had thought Barnicle's column was real!

Jimmy Cannon, the great sports columnist for the (pre-Murdoch) *New York Post*, once wrote a famous tear-jerker column about Christmas in New York. It was a theme in New York newspapers that went back at least as far as O. Henry's *Gift of the Magi*.

I have no idea if Cannon's column was real or not, but guess what—maybe 20 or 25 years later, the exact same incident happened in Boston, and Mike Barnicle just happened to be there to record it.

The Patriots made the Super Bowl for the first time in 1986, against the Chicago Bears. The game was in New Orleans, and everybody from Boston was down there, including me, on expense account. You had to do a daily local-color column, which was easy enough, but even simpler for Barnicle. One day I picked up the *Globe* and there was a story about Earl Long, the late governor and younger brother of "the Kingfish," Huey P. Long. Barnicle's column had been lifted, practically word for word, from A. J. Liebling's book *The Earl of Louisiana*. I knew this because I was probably one of the few people in Boston who'd ever read Liebling's book.

Again, the Earl Long column wasn't exactly plagiarism, but it was damn close. Barnicle could have at least acknowledged his source. Instead, he made it sound like he'd turned up this marvelous material because he was such a streetwise guy with endless connections wherever he was, whether in Boston, New Orleans, or anywhere else.

By then, I didn't even bother to tell anybody. The *Globe* didn't care. He was what he was—a complete pipe artist.

A couple of years later, a *Herald* political columnist was coming back from the Iowa presidential caucuses. During a stopover at O'Hare Airport, he picked up a Chicago newspaper and read a column by Mike Royko. Two days later, Royko was on the Metro front of the *Globe* with a piece that bore an uncanny resemblance to what Royko had written 72 hours earlier.

Paper Boy

Once more, nothing happened. He led a charmed life. The same kind of protection Whitey Bulger was getting from the FBI, Barnicle was getting from his Yankee masters on Morrissey Boulevard.

He was also moonlighting on one of those then popular early-evening TV magazine shows, *Chronicle*, on Channel 5. He was their local-color "columnist," wearing a scally cap, talking out of the side of his mouth. One time he was feuding with the station management—over what, I can't imagine. Like the *Globe*, Channel 5 let him get away with everything.

Whatever the reason, station management wanted to scare Barnicle, so they brought me in to do a piece. Since I in fact worked on it, they gave me a producer's credit—not a big deal but just to show him that they expected a little more effort or something out of him.

Of course, that was my one and only shot at *Chronicle*. He got the message and came back and I never got any more calls.

Honestly, I resented the hell out of the guy. Maybe some of it was the Irish thing. As Dr. Johnson once said, "The Irish are a fair people. They never speak well of one another."

On the other hand, I have never been a professional Irishman, certainly not in the sense that he was. Barnicle was just such a phony, and he was standing in my way. Everybody who wasn't paying attention—which is always most people, anytime, on any given issue—thought he was a street guy from the city, that he was a Vietnam vet, an ex-Marine, that his parents were Irish immigrants.

Was it envy on my part? Of course it was. Sometimes, somebody's in your way and you just can't push them aside. Often it's because they're better than you are. In New York, Pete Hamill was always overshadowed by Jimmy Breslin (except when it came to having A-list girlfriends). Overall, though, the fact is that Breslin as a columnist was more accomplished than Hamill.

Sometimes you just have to learn to live with being in somebody else's shadow, a backup quarterback you might say. What grates more I think is when you know damn well you're better—and less of a fraud—than the guy who's taking the snaps in front of you.

Bob Crane had been the state treasurer since 1964. I called him "treasurer for life." He was a good guy, old-line Boston Irish, and he had great seats down the first-base line at Fenway Park. One year Crane had a primary opponent who might have given him a tough fight. Barnicle eviscerated the guy in the *Globe*, which in those days everybody read.

47

A few days later, he was sitting in Crane's seats with a Canadian cartoonist from the *Globe*. Another time, one of our gossip columnists spotted Barnicle shopping for socks—on Newbury Street. He bought a "cottage" down on the Cape. Every night he drove his BMW back to Lincoln, one of the most hoity-toity Yankee towns in the state. I called him the tough street kid from Lincoln.

Barnicle's second wife was a woman named Anne Finucane, a real do-you-know-who-I-am? kind of entitled broad. She spent her career, such as it was, carrying water for Irish millionaires. Around 1994, she was between her Hibernian-mogul gigs, and needed a recommendation.

Mike had always been tight with Kevin White—not only was Kevin White a wholly owned subsidiary of the *Globe*, but he also employed Mike's brother on the police department. One hand washes the other. . . .

Barnicle hadn't been quite so palsy-walsy with the next mayor, Ray Flynn. Flynn may not have been the sharpest knife in the drawer, but certain kinds of bullshit he could sniff right out, and Barnicle's bogus blarney fitted perfectly in that category.

Once, as a routine matter, the *Herald* filed a FOIA request for the mayor's phone logs. I can't remember if it was Ray Flynn or Tom Menino, but I think it was Mumbles. Anyway, after the initial stories about the inevitable calls to the mayor from developers and other assorted fat cats, the log was handed over to me for additional journalistic strip-mining.

I quickly discovered that a woman known as "Anne Finucane" had called the mayor's office.

Apparently the call was not returned, because on the next day's log, there was another call, this time from "Anne Finucane Barnicle."

Shortly thereafter, she was hired by the biggest local bank in the city. I just threw it into the overall column about the logs of mayor's phone calls from the Beautiful People, but it must have irritated Mrs. Barnicle. A day or so later, I was driving into work on the Pike when I got a call from Barnicle. Speaking calmly, he asked me, what was I trying to do to him?

I knew very well why he was calling. But as always in such situations, I merely inquired as to what he was talking about.

"You're married," he said. "You know."

Somehow Barnicle kept getting away with it. As the *Chronicle* gig was winding down, he ended up on one of those Point-Counterpoint gigs on the 11 o'clock news on Channel 5. This was the last gasp of those lame old TV "columnist" shticks that all the Boston stations used to have—an affable hippie or a pale imitation of Andy Rooney or someone like Barnicle pretending to be a street guy. A stereotypical, hackneyed walking cliché, in other words. A perfect fit for the tough street kid from Lincoln.

Barnicle was paired with David Brudnoy, a well-traveled radio talk-show host (and Channel 7 alumnus), a gay libertarian who would later die of AIDS. Brudnoy was Barnicle's counterpoint—not so much conservative counterweight as just not a complete pipe artist and phony.

Barnicle apparently used to go off the rails when he was live on TV, inventing even more outlandish boasts and tall tales than he did in his *Globe* column. We had no access to the videotapes, so we could never pin anything down. And Brudnoy, a gentleman to the end, never ratted out Barnicle, despite multiple entreaties by several of us. He wouldn't even pull the videotapes for us. What happened in Needham, stayed in Needham.

If "Bruds" hadn't protected him, Barnicle might have been taken off the board much sooner.

By the 1990s, everybody with any sense had figured out Barnicle's cheesy bluster, as *Boston* magazine termed it. The magazine had taken to running a periodic column, checking up on facts and names in his column. You can guess the results.

He thought he was up for a Pulitzer, but in fact his time was running out. The *Globe* had fired a black female columnist, yet another serial fabricator. People started asking, what about Barnicle? But all his sins were now cold cases, so he was okay, until the *Herald* ran a story showing that he'd been lifting jokes from a George Carlin book for one of his one-liner columns (of the type started by, of all people, Jimmy Cannon).

Barnicle claimed he'd never even read the book, but someone at Channel 5 finally flipped on him and turned over videotape of him promoting the book he'd claimed he never read.

But still he survived, even after the Boston *Phoenix* did a story about that A. J. Liebling column I'd noticed 12 years earlier but hadn't bothered to bust him on, because it had all seemed so hopeless.

All the pompous greedheads whose asses Barnicle had kissed so assiduously for so long went to bat for him, and he hung in for a while longer, until he was brought down, indirectly, by that most plebeian of journalistic institutions.

Reader's Digest.

For decades, *Reader's Digest* had had the highest circulation of any magazine in the nation. It sometimes seemed to be in every bathroom in middle

America—and for good reason. It had maybe 30 articles per issue, one to read during each morning bowel movement of the month.

Many of the magazine's articles were reprints of material that had appeared elsewhere. I knew this because they'd bought a few of my *Herald* pieces over the years. It was the easiest money I'd ever made—you didn't have to do any rewrites or legwork.

All they wanted was backup—to prove that the story was true. Apparently in their earliest days they'd learned the hard way that the *Boston Globe* wasn't the only newsroom teeming with pipe artists. Mike Barnicle was only the latest in a long line of journalistic grifters and flim-flam men.

Reader's Digest had picked up a couple of my columns on the annual reports of the Massachusetts Commission Against Discrimination (MCAD), the crazy woke stuff that nowadays seems so routine.

The fact-checkers called me and asked for my sources. I would just shove the printed report—by then well-thumbed and yellow-highlighted—in a padded envelope and mail it off to Chappaqua, New York. A month or so later I'd get a check for $1,500. Some months that money made all the difference to me.

As the Barnicle melodrama over the George Carlin plagiarism was playing out, it came to the attention of a former editor of *Reader's Digest*. Three years earlier, he'd read a touching Barnicle column in the *Globe* about two cancer-stricken young boys at Children's Hospital. The editor wanted to use the story to lead the next issue of *Reader's Digest* and had one of his fact-checkers call Barnicle.

Of course there was no documentation. Barnicle told one conflicting story after another. *Reader's Digest* called the hospital, and couldn't find even the slightest shred of evidence to back it up. The reprint was spiked, obviously, and forgotten, until the retired editor decided to do a story about it for the *Weekly Standard*. He called the *Globe* for a comment. By the time his magazine piece appeared, Barnicle was history.

He gave one final interview—to Brian Williams. Rather ironic in retrospect, wouldn't you say? Brian Williams interviews a guy who's just blown up his own squalid career making shit up, and what does he do? Williams just keeps making up his own shit, until he finally blows up his own squalid career by making shit up.

But all that was far in the future. Even then, though, in the late seventies, playing hearts every Saturday night in the city room with the Corsettis, I knew that if I ever got the chance, I could take Mike Barnicle or anyone else at the *Globe*.

But first, I was going to City Hall.

5
KEVIN FROM
HEAVEN

Barney Frank used to say that if you ran for the Boston City Council, only two things could happen to you and they were both bad.

Number one, you could lose.

Number two, you could win.

It's not quite so true now. There's always been some lateral mobility for ambitious city councilors—courthouse clerkships, "intergovernmental relations" jobs at local universities, etc.—but for decades nobody ever moved "up" in a political sense, the way Mayor Michelle Wu or Rep. Ayanna Pressley since have, as unfortunate as those promotions may have turned out to be for domestic tranquility and preserving the blessings of liberty, as the Constitution might have it.

I was sent to Boston City Hall in January 1980 as the *Herald American*'s third reporter. I still reported to the city room for my second shift Saturdays as Eddie Corsetti's reporter/rewrite man. But four days a week, I reported to the seventh floor at One City Hall Place.

The mayor was Kevin White, Kevin DeLuxe, Mayor of America, as one of our columnists called him. He was an ambitious second-generation city pol from West Roxbury, but he'd assimilated by going to Williams College and moving to Mount Vernon Street on Beacon Hill. He'd been elected secretary of state in 1960 at age 31. At the famous election eve rally at the Boston Garden, future president JFK had introduced him as "Calvin White."

In 1980, White was just beginning his fourth (and final, as it turned out) term as mayor. Third terms are almost always disastrous for executives—just ask Andrew Cuomo, or Michael Dukakis. And this was Kevin's fourth.

White had first been elected in 1967, after the previous mayor had been wise enough to call it a career after two placid terms. White, in a huge field, prevailed over Louise Day Hicks, an unassimilated, unapologetic daughter of South Boston at its most parochial, who'd already made the cover of *Time* magazine, much to the chagrin of the Boston Brahmin establishment, not to mention the Kennedys.

Even with the school-busing crisis still years away, the *Globe* was horrified at the prospect of her possible election as mayor. They had never endorsed a political candidate—their anodyne editorials reflected the conventional, disinterested wisdom of "Uncle Dudley," who was to the *Globe* what Eustace Tilley was to *The New Yorker*.

But a Mayor Hicks was unthinkable to the Yankee power structure. So Uncle Dudley took it on the lam, never to be seen again, and Kevin won.

He ran for governor in 1970 but lost (the *Globe* endorsed the Republican, a Yankee). He was briefly considered as vice presidential material by George McGovern in 1972 after the Thomas Eagleton disaster, but after Sen. Ted Kennedy's protests, McGovern ultimately picked a Kennedy in-law, Sargent Shriver, rather than a Kennedy wannabe.

Court-ordered busing began in 1974. Riots and turmoil engulfed the city. The middle classes fled by the tens of thousands. If you couldn't clear out, you would send your kids to live with relatives in the suburbs to finish high school there. (For example, future NFL star Howie Long, a native of Charlestown who ended up graduating from Milford High School.)

In 1975, White was running for a third term. He began to realize that all those Harvard types like Barney Frank whom he'd brought over from Cambridge to curry favor with the *Globe* counted for naught when it came to hand-to-hand political combat in the white ethnic wards. He was up against Joe Timilty, the city councilor and future state senator, the nephew of the former corrupt police commissioner who later became a bagman for old Joe Kennedy.

The 1975 election was a near-death political experience for White. He barely won, and he was chastened by his close call. The Barney Franks and the Bob Kileys were soon gone, replaced by street guys, many of whom had police records. They could straighten a thing out, as the old goombahs used to say. And that was all that mattered.

Paper Boy

That was City Hall when I arrived there in 1980. I'd been around somewhat, both in Winston-Salem and Boston. I'd covered riots, violent strikes, gory murder trials, etc. I thought I knew my way around the block, but I'd never seen anything like Boston City Hall.

After the 1975 fight, the mayor had set up an old-style urban political machine, with 22 ward "coordinators" (not bosses) and 255 precinct captains, probably 240 of whom had city jobs. At least two or three of the ward coordinators were ex-cons. Others would soon be jailbirds.

One ward boss later turned up on an FBI 302 report as a suspect in a significant organized-crime hit, although I can't vouch for its accuracy, because the source of the information was a Top Echelon FBI informant named Whitey Bulger.

Overall, City Hall was like a reform school, or maybe a halfway house—halfway back to the pen.

The mayor's top fundraiser was a former Mob lawyer from the North End. He married another of the mayor's top aides, which was very convenient because that meant they couldn't testify against each other. I learned so much about the law at City Hall.

The fundraiser and his wife eventually bought a townhouse in the North End from the city for one dollar. It made page one of the *New York Times*.

I remember Mayor White raging about that story the day it appeared—"You know they get the *Times* delivered at the Kremlin? It's supposed to be a newspaper for the whole world. What the hell must the Russians be thinking when they see a one-dollar townhouse in Boston on the front page?"

In the late 1970s, the federal government was shoveling out billions of dollars for "jobs" programs. It was called the Comprehensive Employment and Training Act (CETA). In Boston, the city used CETA money to set up something called the Youth Activities Commission (YAC). And any kid who wanted to basically do nothing could become what we called a YAC hack.

Most of the YAC hacks never got another real job, once they realized that they could finish life at home in their spare time and still get paid. That's what always happens. Once you go hack, you never go back. That was another life lesson I learned at City Hall. It was an extremely target-rich environment for reporters.

The problem for the *Herald* was that Kevin would always leak to the *Globe*, to keep on their good side. This was understandable, considering their financial clout (if not so much circulation dominance) in the city, but it was frustrating nonetheless.

Howie Carr

The only way the *Herald* could stay in the game at any level was to throw in with the opposition, such as it was. That was probably the most useful trick I picked up at City Hall—if there is a viable opposition to the powers that be, a reporter doesn't have to be in the satchel to the clique that's in power to be effective.

In fact, most of the time, in terms of generating good copy, it's better not to be kissing the ass of the ruling class. I know that concept runs totally counter to the reality of modern American journalism, which is 99 percent in the tank for the Democrat party, but it's the truth. Not that we had any choice about the matter at the *Herald*. Going anti-Kevin, which *ipso facto* meant going anti-*Globe* as well, was the only way for us to stay relevant.

As always, necessity was the mother of invention. I may not have won many friends, but I did learn how to influence people—well, readers anyway.

Under the city code, the mayor had virtually unlimited powers. All the City Council could do was squawk. But they did get to look at the official documents, especially budgets.

Early 1980s: Boston City Councilors, l–r, Freddie Langone, Dapper O'Neil, Joe Tierney.

Paper Boy

Nowadays, the City Council is a hotbed of wokeism, but in 1980, it was exactly the opposite. There were nine councilors, all elected citywide— five Irish, three Italian, and one Yankee (John Winthrop Sears, one of the many defeated mayoral candidates from 1967). My favorites quickly became Albert Leo "Dapper" O'Neil, another of those defeated 1967 candidates, and Freddie Langone.

Freddie was amazing. He was from the North End, and he walked to City Hall every morning. He was about to turn 60 and he'd already been around forever. His father Joe had a been a mobbed-up state senator who had run a funeral home (a common occupation for pols back then). Sacco and Vanzetti had been buried from the Langone Funeral Home.

It was all out in the open—when Beano Breen, the legendary Prohibition-era Irish gangster from Kerry Village (now known as Bay Village), was shot in the lobby of the Metropolitan Hotel, Sen. Langone rushed to Boston City Hospital to provide a blood transfusion. (Beano died.)

Langone was always a Curley man, until 1945, when Freddie came back from World War II and wanted to run for the Council. Even by 1945 standards, Freddie was a little rough around the edges, and Curley balked. So Joe defected, not that it mattered in that year of Curley's final landslide.

Freddie finally made it to the Council in 1961, when he replaced Kevin White's father Joe, who had suffered a stroke. By 1980 Freddie was a lifer, no more than 5'6", balding, a wet cigar, usually unlit, always sticking out of his mouth. He never finished much higher than sixth or seventh (you had to finish in the top nine to win), but he hung on.

He'd always been a Kevin White guy, as a reward for which his brother JoJo got to operate the family funeral home in the West End, on prime city property.

I never figured out why Freddie broke with Kevin the way his father broke with Curley, but it must have been acrimonious, because by 1980 Freddy was in an all-out political war against Kevin. The mayor was so pissed he had large concrete blocks placed at the entrance to the Langone Funeral Home parking lot. With no parking, business plummeted. Freddy's older brother Jojo, an ex-con who served on the Governor's Council (where he voted on pardons, commutations, and judgeships), operated the mortuary. The feud escalated.

At City Council meetings, Freddie would lounge back in his chair, removing the cigar from his mouth only long enough to denounce "the harmony clique," as he called the pro-White councilors.

He particularly loathed Chris Iannella, which I didn't understand until I picked up an old book called *Street Corner Society: The Social Structure of an Italian Slum,* by William S. Whyte. It was written in 1943 about the North End, by a Harvard sociologist who had moved into the North End to do his own firsthand research on the neighborhood.

Freddie hated the book—in his own memoirs he wrote that Whyte made it seem like "everyone was in the rackets." But even more than the book, he couldn't stand Chris Iannella, or "Chick," the moniker Whyte gave him.

"Chick" had been born in Italy and didn't move to Boston until he was 8. But he was ambitious, upwardly mobile, working in his uncle's store, always struggling against the neighborhood's Mafia influences (read: the Langones). He went to Boston College and then Harvard Law School. He was a "college boy." He married an Irish girl. And of course, he moved out . . . to Jamaica Plain.

That gave Iannella what all city pols dreamed of above all else—the double base, in this case, the North End and his new ward in Jamaica Plain. Plus, Harvard didn't hurt, nor did his marriage to an Irishwoman.

Two years after losing the 1967 mayor's race, Iannella ran for his old seat on the City Council. In an ancient urban political tradition, another candidate with a similar name got into the fight—Charlie Iannello, a former state rep from Roxbury who'd gone to prison for selling curb cuts or license plates or some such thing.

Jailbird Iannello figured he could cruise back into a cushy sinecure on Chick's coattails (or perhaps some more serious candidate put him into the fight as a straw to drain votes from the real candidate—another urban tradition, and not just in Boston).

Iannello started handing out bumper stickers, so Iannella responded with his own, that said "IannellA." Iannello laughed and put out his own new bumper stickers: "IannellO."

Iannella won, and was back on the Council. By 1980, he was 67 and just punching the clock. As city council president, he had a sink in his office. He used it for washing his socks. When a young lawyer was elected to the Council, Chris pulled him aside for an avuncular chat and asked him if he knew what the best thing about the job was.

The kid, from Brighton, was star-struck at being taken into the old war horse's confidence. He asked Iannella to tell him what the best thing about the job was.

"The parking spaces," Iannella said. "Do you know how much a parking space downtown costs?"

Chris Iannella, born in Italy, spoke perfect English. Freddie, born at Boston City Hospital, was a dems-dese-and-dose kind of guy. When he got angry, which was often, his grammar failed him. Once, he lost a vote to the harmony clique and exploded in rage:

"This time youse have pissed in my pants!"

Freddie would try his best to assist any constituent who called him, but he never bothered to adjust his language to the changing times. When White shut off the fire hydrants in Roxbury one summer, Freddie railed against the mayor.

"How are the little pickaninnies supposed to cool off now?" he thundered.

One night he was out walking on Commercial Street by the Coast Guard base. He was jumped by a couple of black Coast Guardsmen and stabbed.

"Don't youse tell me about them!" he would occasionally thunder, whenever some kind of racial issue was brought up. "They stabbed me!"

Whatever Freddie's reason for his falling out with the mayor, it certainly made my life easier. He couldn't give anything to the *Globe* because they were in the tank. They didn't like Freddie for the same reason they didn't like Louise Day Hicks—too Boston. So Freddie had to do business with the *Herald American.*

When computers started coming into general use at City Hall, Freddie demanded one. The mayor, logically assuming that none of the unwashed on the other side of the fifth floor would be able to master them, graciously had one installed in the Council offices. Soon Freddie would be camped in front of it, for hours on end, pausing only to relight his cigar or to call me or one of the other *Herald* guys to come down from the seventh floor to see what new outrages he'd turned up.

The city had been willed a marvelous old building on Beacon Street known as the Parkman House. It had been used for the offices of the Parks and Recreation department until 1968, when the head of the department decided to throw a party there on the Saturday afternoon of the most famous Harvard-Yale game, the one Harvard "won" in a 29–29 tie. (It was a big game at Deerfield too; listening on the radio we all cheered when Pete Varney, Deerfield '67 and a future catcher for the Atlanta Braves, caught the tying two-point conversion pass.)

Watching the game on TV, new mayor Kevin White immediately realized the potential of the Parkman House . . . as a mansion for himself. He evicted

Parks and Rec, sent the department back to City Hall, and spent hundreds of thousands refurbishing the mansion as just that—a mansion.

When Pope John Paul visited Boston in 1979, the mayor had hosted lavish parties at the Parkman House, which got a lot of attention. Freddie realized he had a huge target all to himself, and he proceeded to hold a series of some of the funniest hearings ever, anywhere, on the Parkman House.

The building was managed by a nice, polite twentysomething woman named Mary McFarland Piccolo, and she was not ready for the fractured-English third-degree from Freddie. He had all the invoices and bills—he asked exactly what was meant by "crudites," which he pronounced as "crud-ites." (As I would have; until I worked at City Hall covering "Mayor DeLuxe" I never knew how to spell "chauffeur" or "limousine" either. As I said, it was an education, in so many ways.)

He asked about the guest list after the concert on the Boston Common for the music group "Olivia, Newton and John." After the Papal Mass, Freddie was stonewalled again on the guest list.

"Did the Pope eat at the Parkman House?" he asked.

When she wasn't forthcoming enough, Freddie couldn't take it anymore.

"Who ate at the Parkman House?" he screamed at the frightened young blonde. "WHO?!?!? H-W-O-H?!?! WHO?!?!?!"

A few days later, Freddie's new computer was removed from the Council chambers per order of the mayor.

One of the *Globe*'s most politically connected columnists was a guy named Dave Farrell. He'd started at the *Herald*, where in the sixties he'd been a real nemesis of my favorite columnist, the late George Frazier.

Farrell could do some good work, but he was also . . . available, you might say. You would read his Sunday column—always terribly written, with clunky paragraphs and no transitions from one topic to the next—and try to figure out whose water he was carrying that day.

One day the *Herald* somehow got a tip that the mayor was about to announce a huge new series of post-election pay raises. Since we were in the same room with the *Globe* reporters, they overheard us, and told their bosses that we were about to scoop them.

It turned out, the *Globe* had a column that was slated to run the next Sunday—by Dave Farrell. That way the story would run, not on the front page, but in the opinion section—buried, in other words. But now they couldn't hold the Farrell column. This was before the Internet of course, so they had to send up a hard copy from the newsroom on Morrissey Boulevard.

When the *Globe* copy boy arrived with the Farrell column, which was now budgeted to run the next day, one of the *Globe* reporters came over to our side of the room and held up the column.

"You guys need to see this too," he said, "because it shows what we're all up against."

The column had been typed on sky-blue stationery, which was what the mayor's flaks used for their press releases. In other words, they had written Farrell's column for him—and he would have gotten credit for breaking the story of the pay raises. Most of the *Globe* editors, then as now, were so clueless that they didn't even comprehend the significance of the blue copy paper.

Nothing happened to Farrell, of course. The only way to get in trouble as a *Globe* reporter was to use a phrase like "fit of pique" to describe the mayor's anger about something or other.

A week or so later, Freddie called and told me to come downstairs, that he had something he knew I'd be interested in. The computer was gone, but he still had plenty of sources, one of whom was a short fat guy on his payroll named Tony who moonlighted taking photos for the mayor at the Parkman House.

Tony had a diary that the mayor's office kept up to date, recording the schedule of his upcoming photo shoots at the Parkman House. Freddie handed the diary to me, open to a day in the middle of next week.

The notation said: "Dave Farrell Lunch."

It didn't take long to figure it out. One of Farrell's sons was a military aviator, and he was about to get his wings. A proud moment for Dear Old Dad, and of course he would want his son to have the moment commemorated in the best possible way for a newspaperman—on the arm.

We took photos of the page, then returned the book to Tony, who took it back up to the mayor's press office. Then we filed a Freedom of Information Act (FOIA) request for the photo diary.

When we got it, the Dave Farrell Lunch had been erased, crudely, but as well as possible considering it had been entered in ink. We ran both pages side by side in the *Herald*. It was embarrassing to the *Globe*, I guess, but once again, Farrell wasn't fired or disciplined. (That would come later, for unrelated offenses.)

The problem was, financially the *Globe* had the *Herald* on the ropes, and they knew it. As the months went by, the *Herald* kept shrinking. More than ever, everybody in the city room closely studied the schedule for each upcoming holiday, to assure themselves they wouldn't be included in the next round of layoffs.

In January 1981, I got transferred to the State House. Normally, this would have been considered at least a bit of a promotion, but not in this case. The *Globe* had maybe six reporters on Beacon Hill, at least a few of whom were not foppish Ivy League legacies, and I was to be the *Herald*'s only guy. There was no way I could compete.

The governor was Edward J. King, the Irish Catholic ex-NFL player from East Boston. He'd knocked off the *Globe*'s favorite, Michael S. Dukakis, in the 1978 Democrat primary. The *Globe* was now engaged in a four-year jihad to restore normalcy, their normalcy. What was done to Ed King wasn't all that different than the railroading of Donald J. Trump all those years later.

I did the best I could, but soon I had other things on my mind. Don Forst had gotten the okay from Hearst to make the *Herald* a tabloid again, as the *Record* had been until 1972. I applied for a job as a columnist, which was what I'd always wanted to do anyway.

The paper converted back to the old *Record* tabloid format in the fall of 1981, and I became a columnist. Forst still called a lot of the shots on what I wrote about, but overall I had more freedom. I no longer had to worry about being scooped. I could work out of City Hall, or the State House, or any of the courthouses.

I was up and running quickly, because I knew exactly what I wanted to do. I'd studied and learned from the best. But despite my clips, I still seemed to be on what Fred Allen once called the treadmill to oblivion. Hearst remained a supremely lousy company to work for. As Joe Heaney used to say, working for Hearst was the journalistic equivalent of living in a public-housing project.

I'd bought a one-family house in Somerville, one street down Spring Hill from Howie Winter. It cost $47,000, which felt like all the money in the world to me. I wasn't even 30, and I had two kids. I needed some security, or at least less insecurity.

In the spring of 1982, the feds were trying the guys who'd fixed Boston College basketball games a couple of years earlier. The story would later become a small part of *Goodfellas,* the classic Mob movie.

Forst told me to go down to New York and cover the trial in federal court in Brooklyn. In retrospect, the highlight of the trial for me was witnessing firsthand the sentencing of Jimmy "the Gent" Burke—portrayed in the movie by Robert

DeNiro under a different name. Burke was in a prison jumpsuit, shackled by the U.S. Marshals.

During my week or so at the trial, I stayed in Manhattan with a woman who had gone to UNC with me and later worked for me in Winston-Salem. She was now a reporter at the *Daily News*—just as I had suspected would happen, some of the *Journal* reporters whose copy I'd painstakingly edited and massaged into some semblance of coherence now worked for better papers than I did, including at the *Washington Post* and the *Philadelphia Inquirer*.

Every day I'd cover the trial over in Brooklyn, an anonymous spectator while the federal prosecutors fawned over Lesley Visser, a former Boston College cheerleader who now worked for the *Globe*, still cheerleading for whomever she was ordered to. But I'd become inured to that kind of second-class journalistic citizenship in Boston.

One night, my hostess told me a great *Daily News* story about Michael Daly, a guy my age whose column in "New York's Picture Newspaper" that I'd been reading for a while.

He'd started out at the *Village Voice*, and sometimes shared a byline with Denis Hamill. (Do you see where I'm going with this?) I'd be working my ass off, doing what I thought was one stellar column after another in the *Herald*. Then I'd pick up a *Daily News* and see that Daly had come up with yet another, shall we say, unbelievable tale.

Being thoroughly familiar by now with the Barnicle-Hamill school of urban Irish-American columnizing, I had a pretty good idea what was going on. Plus, Daly was a rich college kid from Yale, which made it even more likely he was piping it.

A few months earlier, he'd been sent to Northern Ireland to cover The Troubles. Denis Hamill had likewise been writing endless blather about Bobby Sands et al. But when he got there, Daly just concocted a column about people and events that never occurred. The Brits called him out on it, and he was fired (although he later made a comeback of sorts—much like Barnicle and another later *Globe* fictioneer, Kevin Cullen).

After he was let go from the *Daily News*, a couple of the younger reporters, including my friend, were assigned to clean out Daly's desk. In it, they found scores of letters from *Daily News* readers, unopened, many of which included a few dollars for whoever the subject of that day's sob story was. Apparently, Daly at least felt guilty enough about making all that shit up not to pocket the money for himself.

My friend told me when they opened the readers' envelopes, the cash amounted to almost $1,000, almost all in dominations no larger than a $5 bill.

One night I got back from the courthouse in Brooklyn and my friend told me we were going to have dinner on somebody else's tab that night. The *Daily News*, like the *Herald*, was teetering on the edge of bankruptcy after a disastrous attempt to take on the *Post* with, believe it or not, an evening edition.

So ABC News' *Nightline* was putting some interviews in the can for the obituary for what was then the nation's largest tabloid when the inevitable occurred (it still hasn't happened, and a zombie version of the paper continues to be printed every morning, for whom, I've never been able to figure out). ABC News threw a dinner for the entire *Daily News* staff, to get most of their reporting done before the paper folded.

We went over with everybody else, and as the ABC producers were wrapping up the interviews, somebody remembered that the *Boston Herald American*, another dying tabloid, also had a representative in the free buffet line. So they interviewed me, and as I recall I said something like I'd been saying at J.J. Foley's for years. I expressed what I assumed I'd soon be telling the Boston TV stations:

"I always wanted the *Herald* to be the last newspaper I ever worked for. I just didn't figure it would be this year."

That *Nightline* dinner, I figured, was an omen, a message that I should get another job. And there was another portent for me that spring.

In 1980, I'd been approached by the editor of *Boston* magazine, the slick monthly, about writing a political column. His name was Terry Catchpole, and I knew his byline from the *National Lampoon*. Despite my apparently bleak career prospects in journalism, I was meeting a lot of the people I'd grown up reading, or reading about.

My columns in *Boston* magazine were well-received. They reached a different audience than those in the *Herald*—namely, *Globe* readers. I even got some nice mentions from the *Globe*'s magazine columnist—George V. Higgins, whose early organized-crime novels I'd always admired.

A. J. Liebling used to say of himself that he wrote faster than anyone who wrote better, and better than anyone who wrote faster. That's how I was coming to think of myself in terms of Boston journalism, as I now worked for both a tabloid and the slick city monthly.

Paper Boy

But no matter how good my columns were in either the *Herald* or *Boston* magazine, no one from the *Globe* called, or more accurately, returned my pleading phone calls.

One Friday in the spring of 1982, I was hanging out at City Hall. I had two paychecks in my pocket—one from the *Herald* and the other from *Boston* magazine. I walked across the street to the bank at 50 State Street and got into the always-lengthy (pre-ATM) lines. Finally, I got to the cashier and presented my larger *Herald* check to the cashier. She took a moment, checked her screen before giving me the news.

"I'm sorry Mr. Carr," she said, "but there appear to be insufficient funds in the *Herald*'s account for us to cash your check."

I considered the implications of that for a moment, then realized that I also had my $250 check from *Boston* magazine. I cashed that one and I was set—for the weekend, at least.

That was a message from God, or at least that's how I took it. And the message was: You better start looking for a new job, son.

6
DIRTY
LAUNDRY

By the summer of 1982, the "feisty" *Herald American* was on its last legs. I knew the *Globe* wasn't in the cards—after my *Herald* check bounced, I had made one last attempt to get the *Globe's* attention. I asked one of the guys at City Hall to make the proverbial discreet inquiries for me. He was given a quick brush off. They told him they "already had somebody like me." Meaning Mike Barnicle, the tough street kid from Lincoln. That infuriated me, but I'd gotten used to it.

So I went after a job in television news. I had no experience. I didn't even own a color television. But any port in a storm. Channel 2 had a local 10 o'clock news show, and anchor Chris Lydon was willing to give me a shot. He was a *Globe-Times*-Yale guy, but he was also from Southie, so he read the *Herald*.

So I had an opportunity. If I didn't have a column due at the *Herald*, I'd go out with Channel 2 reporter Janet Wu and shadow her as she worked her stories.

I figured *The Ten O'Clock News* would be my next job, as soon as the *Herald* went under. But Channel 7 had just changed hands, and after spending millions to wrest it away from its previous owner through FCC challenges, supermarket heir David Mugar was lavishing big money on his new toy. Channel 7 was looking for local reporters, and Mike Taibbi, the father of Matt Taibbi, who has now done such great work on Substack and on the Twitter files, suggested me.

The new news director was Bill Applegate, a guy who'd made his bones as a street reporter in Detroit during the race riots of 1967. He spotted me one

Paper Boy

Sunday night on an obscure talk show on Channel 56. I was on with the wife of the mayor's fundraiser, who owned that one-dollar townhouse in the North End that had driven Kevin White crazy.

I was just giving her the needle about it—by then the story was old hat, and we were circling one an other like the Roadrunner and Wile E. Coyote. We were on the clock, so to speak. But to Applegate it was brand-new local color, and the next day he called asking me if I wanted to come over and talk to him.

For a tryout, Channel 7 sent me out with a camera crew and a producer. Given my weeks of experience at WGBH, which of course I didn't mention, I knew the basic tricks of the trade, little things like cutaways and ordering B-roll and logging tape. Applegate was informed that I seemed to likely be a very quick study.

I can still remember the day I was hired at Channel 7. It was a Friday, just before Labor Day. At $50,000 a year, I doubled my *Herald* salary overnight. Channel 7 was the only TV station downtown, in Government Center, across the plaza from City Hall. I left their offices in a state of euphoria, a major load off my mind—namely, my future employment prospects.

I was practically skipping as I headed back toward City Hall, where I still had a desk, when I ran into one of the mayor's Dorchester ward coordinators on the plaza. He asked me why I seemed so happy, and I dodged the question—I didn't want the mayor calling up Mugar and demanding that my hiring be rescinded.

I started as a TV political reporter in September 1982, just before the statewide primaries. Dukakis won the rematch with Ed King, and John Forbes Kerry took the lieutenant governor's primary. I had a queasy feeling about the leftward *Globe*-Harvard-Brookline turn that state politics seemed to be taking, but I was too busy trying to master the rudiments of my new trade to worry much.

Television reporting isn't all that different than newspaper reporting, except for one thing—live shots. Newspapers have no live shots. I had trouble getting used to having to speak directly into the camera live from somewhere—the State House, City Hall, a crime scene. The anchor would "throw" it to me and I'd talk just long enough to get to the roll cue that told the director to go to the videotape package.

I was a real mess those first few live shots. One day, after a particularly disastrous live shot at City Hall the previous evening, I was eating lunch with my cameraman in a small downtown bar when the owner, who knew us, came up and started laughing.

"I saw you last night on TV," he said. "Boy did you suck!"

That was the bad news. The good news was that practically nobody was watching Channel 7, the perennial also-ran in the Boston market, the CBS affiliate. The legend was that 7 Bulfinch Plaza had been constructed on an Indian burial ground and was thus cursed to be forever at the bottom of the ratings.

The only time it had ever been number one had been for one brief spring rating book back in 1974, when the anchor was a guy named Chuck Scarborough.

The night Channel 7 finished number one, the station threw a giant party. News quickly leaked out that Scarborough was leaving to take a job as a news anchor at WNBC in New York, Channel 4. Upon hearing the news, one of our cameramen, crestfallen, approached Scarborough and asked him if it was true that he was bailing out.

"Charlie," Scarborough said, "in this business, you gotta fuck them before they fuck you."

Years later I mentioned that moment in my column in the *Herald*. Scarborough sent me a brief note telling me I'd gotten the exchange exactly right.

After Scarborough fled, the station reverted to form, spiraling downhill, with anchors in and out of the revolving doors at 7 Bulfinch Place. The sports anchor, Bob Gamere, quickly became known as "Two Beer" Gamere because of his propensity for getting into trouble at licensed establishments, sometimes in the men's rooms. (He later went to prison for kiddie porn.)

Another anchor was hired after the GM spotted him on Denver television and thought his dyed blond locks would be a turn-on for the female audience. On April Fools' Day 1980, the jokers in the newsroom decided to recycle some recent network videotape from the then current Mount St. Helens volcano and claim that the footage was from a sudden eruption in the Blue Hills just south of the city.

It caused a panic of sorts—somebody apparently was watching Channel 7 after all. The Blue Hills volcano became the Boston equivalent of Orson Welles's *War of the Worlds* radio show on Halloween 1938. Heads had to roll, and the assistant news director became the designated scapegoat.

There was always another designated scapegoat at Channel 7.

One year it would be a new news director and he'd repaint the set—earth tones, whatever those were, became very popular, very briefly. That wouldn't move the needle, so the news director would fire the anchor and bring in some new male model and/or anchor cupcake.

When that didn't work, the news director himself would be fired and the whole local TV news cycle would begin anew, with the set being repainted after which the anchors would be fired. . . .

As we used to say, if it's news to you, it's news to us.

If the news breaks, we fix it.

We're not happy 'til you're not happy.

One of the major investments of Mugar's well-heeled new ownership was in two television news readers well-known in Boston—Tom Ellis and Robin Young, the Dream Team, as they would become known.

The Dream Team turned out to be a nightmare in the ratings. The more money Channel 7 threw at the newscast, the lower the ratings dipped. For some reason the new owners wanted to have a local afternoon chat show. They squandered a huge amount of money buying the rights to the name *Look*—after the long-defunct, practically forgotten weekly magazine. It made no sense, but then nothing else did at Channel 7 either.

The genius producers began running a Zen/yoga-type segment as the nightly finale of the two-hour ratings black hole known as *Look*. If you had the lead story, your IFB—your earpiece—would be hooked up to the programming on *Look*, and all you would hear was "Omm . . . omm . . . omm . . . omm."

Whenever I would hear that chant or whatever it's called, I would know that across New England, whatever small number of viewers had been watching *Look* were now all grabbing their remote controls and switching over to one of the other 6 o'clock newscasts.

Bill Applegate, the news director who'd hired me, put up a giant banner in the newsroom:

"THIS IS WAR."

It sure did feel like one—World War II. It was May 1945, and we were the Germans.

As the fall of 1982 wore on, one Saturday all the "talent" was ordered to show up at some suburban farm for one of those treacly Christmas spots, showing the Seven "family" together, in this case on a quaint horse-drawn open wagon, wishing our miniscule audience Happy Holidays, or maybe Season's Greetings.

Applegate showed up and as he climbed up on the cart, everyone noticed his jacket—a red-and-gold San Francisco 49ers parka. Granted, the Patriots weren't "the Patriots" yet, but still, these sorts of feel-good shots—like the old Budweiser Clydesdale holiday spots—are supposed to establish your deep roots in the community.

Applegate shrugged. He didn't give a fuck.

By this time, though, there was major news breaking in the Boston media market. Hearst was finally getting ready to shut down the *Herald American.* So Forst took matters into his own hands and flew to New York to pitch Rupert Murdoch, the Australian owner of the *New York Post,* to buy the "feisty tabloid."

I'd been reading the *Post* since college, when I'd peruse back issues at the Wilson Library in Chapel Hill. It was liberal then, but quirky, and interesting. I liked Pete Hamill, whom Spiro Agnew had accused of writing "irrational ravings," which became the title of a collection of his columns. His younger brother, as I've already told you, was no Pete Hamill.

The *Post* was the last afternoon paper in New York, but it still couldn't turn a profit. So it was sold to Rupert Murdoch in 1976. It was his second newspaper in the United States. He started printing a morning edition of the *Post,* and soon he was selling a million copies a day. I started buying it every day at the deli around the corner from the State House.

It was so much fun to read, like the old *Daily News,* which had become stodgy and mainstream in a desperate bid to become, God help us, respectable and more like the *New York Times.* But no matter how high the circulation of the *Post* climbed, Murdoch couldn't get any decent department store advertising.

"Don't you understand, Rupert," one of the 34th Street executives supposedly told him, "your readers are our shoplifters."

But Rupert still wanted to buy the *Herald American.* At Channel 7, the statewide elections weren't competitive, so I was put on the *Herald* sale beat. It was another in my continuing series of educations. The two reporters I was competing against were Martha Bradlee of Channel 5, the wife of *Globe* legacy Benjamin Crowninshield Bradlee Jr., and Andy Hiller, a well-traveled New York native who worked for Channel 4.

Lucky for me I knew all the players on the *Herald* side, because Andy and Martha understood the TV racket a lot better than I did. Martha used to say, "We are not reporters, we are TV reporters. We are not in news, we are in TV news."

For a while we all did stories citing sources, no on-camera interviews with anyone who actually knew what was going on. Our narrations were covered with lots of B-roll of the *Herald* and *Globe* plants, the loading docks, delivery trucks, and so forth. The story didn't really ramp up until Rupert arrived in Boston to begin direct negotiations with the unions—he was insisting on major cutbacks in the newsroom and on the presses, among other places, cutting the crews from eight to two per press. It was the only way he would have any chance to turn a profit on the second newspaper in the city.

Murdoch set up his headquarters in a suite at the Marriott Long Wharf Hotel. So the three of us—Martha, Andy, and I—staked out the lobby. It quickly became the biggest story in the city. Soon the three of us were invited upstairs to Murdoch's suite by his minions to meet The Man himself.

I was introduced to him as the former lead columnist for the *Herald* who had left newspapers to take this new job in TV.

"You made the right decision," Murdoch told me.

One by one, the back-shop union bosses from the *Herald* were also making their way to the Long Wharf Marriott for face-to-face negotiations. Naturally, they couldn't say anything afterward. I would ask them, and they'd shake their heads sadly. I understood.

But one night, I absorbed another lesson in TV news, the hard way. The head of the pressmen's union—I believe his name was Henry Vitale—was leaving. Like all the rest he couldn't say anything. He came out of the elevator and I let him go.

But Andy Hiller started chasing Henry, with his cameraman in tow, screaming questions at him as he walked to his car out front. In terms of information, the hectoring was totally pointless. But it made for great video. After Andy's video appeared on the next newscast, I got chewed out by Applegate.

I tried to tell him that I'd spoken to the pressmen's boss myself, and that I had the exact same information as Andy—nothing. But, Applegate explained to me, that wasn't the point. The point was . . . good video.

Nobody ever out-chased me again, I can tell you that. I became the chasing-est guy in Boston TV news. I chased 'em into oncoming traffic, into courthouse elevators, down the subway steps, into the House chambers on Beacon Hill—you name it. I elbowed my way past beefy security guards, or at least tried to.

Murdoch was still demanding those concessions on manning the presses. So I heard that the *Globe* had decided to muddy the waters by demanding equal concessions, which obviously would have affected a lot more jobs than at the *Herald*.

One morning just for the hell of it, I called the publisher of the *Globe*. His name was of course Taylor, I think this one was Davis Taylor. I just wanted to be able to say in my next live shot that I'd tried to reach out to the *Globe* and that they had not returned my call. This was before cell phones, so I made the call from the newsroom before heading off to the Long Wharf.

Within moments, my phone was ringing. It was the *Globe* publisher himself, returning my call. For all these years, I had just been another one of the "muckers"—as George V. Higgins described the City Hall crew going after the mayor. But now that I could perhaps be utilized as part of the Taylors' campaign to give themselves a monopoly in the city, I had apparently become a respected member of the Fourth Estate.

Taylor politely informed me that of course the *Globe* was merely asking for the same concessions as Murdoch, no more, no less. I thanked Mr. Taylor for so graciously returning my call.

"Right-o!" he said, because . . . what else would he say?

As the days went on, as the deadline for the sale grew ever nearer, the negotiations became tenser. Murdoch threatened to sue the *Globe* for tortuous interference. I was now routinely chasing the union bosses as they left the negotiations. In the final couple of days, the three of us—me, Andy, and Martha—never left the hotel. We slept in the lobby. Martha Bradlee went to the gift shop and bought razors, toothbrushes, and toothpaste for me and Andy. We were touched.

"It's not for you," she told us. "It's for me."

By then, we had also equipped ourselves with small makeup compacts with mirrors so we could watch around corners in the conference rooms where some of the meetings were taking place. God forbid we should miss out on a good opportunity to chase and yell at somebody.

Late one night, after the 11 o'clock news, after being on stakeouts at the hotel all day long, my feet were killing me. I was on a couch in the lobby by myself, my shoes off. The pressmen's union guy that Andy Hiller had chased to such advantage wandered by. My cameraman was gone, and even if he hadn't been, chase video has a very short shelf life. I made no move to rise to greet him, just waved in recognition. My feet were throbbing and Henry Vitale must have noticed because he asked me what was wrong. I pointed down at my feet.

He shook his head.

"You should know better, Howie," he said. "You have to wear cotton socks, preferably white. Not those fancy socks you've got on. If you'd spent more time down in the press room, you'd know."

Rupert eventually gave the unions a final deadline—noon on a Friday in December. The clock ticked down. I remained at the Long Wharf with another reporter and two camera crews while the assignment editor sent a third crew down to the South End for the countdown at the *Herald*. Forst was already laying out a final front page.

"SO LONG, BOSTON."

Outside the hotel, I did my top-of-the-noon-newscast live shot—no more problems with stage fright now that I'd been doing so many every day I couldn't even keep count. I was speaking cautiously, though, because I couldn't be sure what was going on. Finally, I threw it to the reporter at the front door of the *Herald* about a mile away in the South End.

People I knew and had worked with were coming out of the old building, tears streaming down their faces, headed for Foley's to drown their sorrows. They'd been told by Forst that it was all over.

I watched the monitor, crestfallen. The *Globe* had won. Boston would now be a one-newspaper town, and what a newspaper. Suddenly, my relief reporter at the Long Wharf, a woman, rushed from the elevator into the lobby and then outside to where our crew was set up for the live shot. Running toward the camera, she yelled at me to tell the producer to throw it to us.

The *Herald* had been sold! The feisty tabloid had been saved! And we had it first, by a few seconds, so it didn't matter that much. But I'll always remember the photo in the *Herald* the next morning, with one of the editors in the newsroom jumping for joy as he got the word. He was watching Channel 7. I could tell by our "LIVE" chyron in the left top corner of the screen.

Murdoch came downstairs and did live interviews with all of us. I asked him if he was still planning to sue the *Globe*.

"It's rather a moot point now, isn't it?"

That night, his new *Herald* publisher called and told me I could come back to the paper now. I chuckled. The TV money was too good to give up. I went home to Somerville. My feet were still killing me, so I got a tub and filled it up with ice water and put my feet in it and cracked open a beer. My eyelids were getting heavy. I was planning to sleep all weekend.

Suddenly the phone rang. It was Bill Applegate, the gruff news director.

"Congratulations," he said. "Today you became a TV newsman."

I didn't know whether to laugh or cry.

7
DYING LIKE A DOG

There was a new U.S. attorney in town—William Floyd Weld, a Republican, nominated by Ronald Reagan. I'd met Weld during the Parkman House hearings. I forget who he was representing, but Freddie Langone pulled me aside and pointed at him with his soggy cigar.

"That's the guy that ran against Frank Bellotti for AG last time," he whispered with a chuckle. "Carried two towns. Two!"

Out of 351. Weld looked exactly like what he was—a trust-funded Yankee whose forebears came over on the *Mayflower*. Cuffs on his trousers, wingtips, white-shoe law firm. I was familiar with the type, so he didn't make much of an impression on me. But once Reagan was elected, he would be rewarded for his travails in Massachusetts electoral politics. Like Sen. George Washington Plunkitt of Tammany Hall, Weld had seen his opportunities and he took 'em.

The giant low-hanging fruit in Boston politics was still Kevin Hagen White. Once the *Herald* was sold to Murdoch, I was back on the City Hall beat. Weld may have appeared to be a fop, but soon his office was issuing a blizzard of subpoenas.

In his fourth term, Kevin had become totally imperious. He scorned everybody. In one interview, he dismissed the City Council, saying "Everybody but Freddie Langone is scared of me." This was not how to win friends and influence people.

Paper Boy

Kevin's father Joe White had given his son the kind of unassimilated kiss-me-I'm-Irish first name that most social-climbing harps shunned in those days. The Kennedys certainly did. Despite Kevin's unfortunate first name, the family was what they called lace-curtain or two-toilet Irish. Kevin was shipped off to prep school, and after that Williams College. He didn't make it to Boston College until law school.

He married into another Irish political family—his father-in-law, yet another city councilor like his father, had a classic Boston Irish moniker—"Mother" Galvin. Still, Mother's son-in-law liked to fancy himself a cut above traditional Boston Irish pols who talked out of the sides of their mouths. Early on Kevin moved to Beacon Hill, the ritziest and last real Yankee enclave in the city.

Kevin White never had a real job, but he lived like a potentate—like King Farouk, as Dapper used to say, dating himself as usual. White of course had a summer home on the Cape.

One of the *Globe* City Hall reporters was Peter Cowen. Like me, he was a UNC guy, and we got along well. He was from New York, and his father was a well-to-do stockbroker. One time his father told Peter to go to the big Brooks Brothers on Madison Avenue and buy himself a suit on the old man.

Peter struck up a conversation with the clerk and told him that he worked at Boston City Hall. The clerk was impressed, and mentioned that he too knew Mayor White, because he was a regular customer. That caught Peter's attention, because of course Brooks Brothers had a rather large store in Boston, on Newbury Street.

"It's odd, though," the clerk told Peter, "because the mayor always insists on paying cash."

Decades later, in Palm Beach, I ran into a guy working at The Breakers who recognized me from the old days at City Hall. He wasn't a YAC hack, but he'd lived in Ward 18, Hyde Park, on a corner—a prime location for a yard sign, in other words. A KEVIN yard sign.

After the 1979 election, his family had gotten its reward, a job for this kid, at the Boston Retirement Board, working under Louise Day Hicks, by then a rather pathetic, tragic figure, old and obese, mourning a thug son who had disappeared in 1978 in the Caribbean. The Retirement Board was in fact being run by Kevin's Dorchester ward boss, who had worked on her campaigns back in the day.

The guy at The Breakers, long since retired from the city, recalled his early days at City Hall.

"I could never really believe I had this great job," he said, "until one day the FBI came in—wearing those blue jackets with FBI stitched across the back. They had a search warrant. And they took out all the board records, everything. Then I knew—I was really at City Hall."

Yep, that's the kind of place City Hall was. Everybody seemed to be running their own scam, and mostly not very well either.

A gay city clerk was arrested for pocketing cash he collected from hunting, fishing, and marriage licenses to set up his young waiter boyfriend in a Back Bay love nest. Several members of the licensing board, which controlled liquor licenses in the city, were indicted for the usual shakedowns, sometimes after being praised by organized-crime figures on FBI bugs and wiretaps.

The feds were after the ward coordinator in Southie, Bob Toomey, who worked for Teddy Anzalone at the old convention center.

Anazalone was the old Mafia lawyer from the fifties, who'd gotten the townhouse in the North End for a dollar. The *Herald* morgue was full of photos of him walking into court with the old goombahs in their fedoras and Chesterfield coats. It was only natural that someone like Toomey, a Southie street guy, would be assigned to work with Anzalone, and that the feds would soon be all over both of them.

So Toomey staged a fake auto accident in Southie on a Friday afternoon, then filed for a disability. In those days, as I've mentioned, there were no ATMs. Banks were also restricted to one county—thus, if you lived in Middlesex County, Somerville, as I did, you had to be sure to get to your bank in Boston on Friday if you needed cash for the weekend. The lines were inevitably lengthy.

So this ward boss Toomey staged the accident. But then, before going to Boston City Hospital, he stopped by his local bank branch on Broadway and waited in line for 40 minutes to cash a check. Weld's feds got the surveillance video and then, when the hack was on the stand, the prosecutor asked him about the pain from the "whiplash" in the accident.

After outlining his agony to the jury, the feds produced the surveillance photos of him waiting in line, chatting away. Toomey was convicted, on every count, more than 20 of them. Each time he'd gotten a pension check mailed to him was another count of mail fraud—five years per.

On my live shots every night, before throwing back to the anchors, I would always say, "If convicted on all counts, Toomey could be looking at 130 years in prison."

Finally, one of the relatives came up to me outside the courtroom one morning before the trial resumed. He begged me to stop mentioning the 130 years every evening, for the sake of his wife.

"Every time you say that, she starts screaming," he said.

I stopped saying "130 years"—for a couple of nights anyway. Then I went back to it. I couldn't help myself.

Toomey's successor as ward coordinator in Southie started dipping into some of the city's federal urban funds. Among the improvements to his property, he built a backyard pool, but neglected to invite his neighbors' kids to cool off. The neighbors dropped a dime to Weld.

Another one bit the dust.

The city budget director was a guy from Brighton named "Squawker." Squawker was not a bad guy. He used to brief us reporters, off the record. He'd been a bad alcoholic, and had been fired from his city job years earlier. He'd been so destitute that he had to cash in his pension. Then he sobered up and Kevin rehired him.

But as time went on, and Weld's feds began tightening the screws, Squawker fell off the wagon. So he decided to go out on disability, because he didn't have enough years in for a traditional pension. He opted to fake a fall, on the ice. The only problem was, he said he slipped on the ice inside City Hall.

It made for good video, re-creating the "fall." Squawker was convicted and sent to prison. When he got out of Club Fed, he was hired by a local dog-track owner. Squawker was a good numbers guy, so it made sense to have him in the counting room. And of course the track owner was politically connected, had to be, because the legislature controlled the number of racing days annually granted to each track.

"I like hiring cons," the owner told me later. "It's a cash business, right? So you always have to worry about stealing. Your average jailbird understands he's gonna be watched like a hawk. That means I don't have to keep an eye on any of them so much, since they know they're always under suspicion."

The feds figured that if they could flip Teddy Anzalone, they could finally get to the mayor. But first they had to bag Teddy. I was hunting him myself, in a different way, along with all the other TV crews in the city. We needed some video of him, and he was an elusive character. He'd learned something from his Mafia clients—he knew how to spot a tail.

But we had to get him. It was a real pain to have to talk about this sinister Anzalone every day, with no video except some ancient black-and-white newspaper photos snipped from the actual papers. If you don't have good video, it's harder to sell the story to the producers.

At night, I'd move around the city with a cameraman, to any receptions held by the mayor or "times" thrown by members of the Council's harmony clique. I was stalking Teddy. It was mostly on me because nobody else knew him personally.

Finally, one night at City Hall, there was a wine-and-cheese reception in the lobby. I walked across the plaza from Channel 7 and entered the Hall with my cameraman, as unobtrusively as possible. After all these weeks of tracking, I finally spotted my quarry—a slight, dapper, late-middle-aged Italian lawyer in a proper yet stylish pinstripe Brooks Brothers suit.

I whispered to the cameraman to just roll for as long as possible. And he did. The money shot was Teddy raising a glass of red wine to his lips. We used those few seconds of video so many times that finally his wife came up to me somewhere and begged me to stop running that same old B-roll.

"Everybody's starting to think Teddy's an alcoholic," she said. "They never see him on TV when he's not sipping that wine."

In the spring of 1983, Kevin White was playing a cat-and-mouse game with the entire city. Would he or wouldn't he run for a fifth term as mayor? Finally, he bought time on Channel 7—the least-expensive station because we had the lowest ratings. His announcement would run at the end of the 6 o'clock newscast.

Six months after buying the *Herald,* Murdoch was trying to make a splash with his new paper. So it was a big deal when one of the few holdover *Herald* columnists got the scoop on the mayor's plans. Or so he thought. This guy had been making sport of the mayor for years, but somehow Kevin gave him the exclusive over the *Globe.* Or so the *Herald* thought. The front-page splash on the morning of Hizzoner's announcement was:

WHITE WILL RUN

Except he didn't. He'd just scammed the columnist who'd been laughing at him all those years. At 6:55 Kevin DeLuxe, the Mayor of America (as the columnist had dubbed him) announced his retirement from politics.

He who laughs last . . .

So Boston had a mayor's race. And I absorbed another bad beating from Andy Hiller. The three top contenders were City Councilor Ray Flynn, a slick West Roxbury pol named David Finnegan, and a black state rep from the South End, Mel King.

It seemed likely that King would make the final election, and it was even more obvious that whichever white candidate got into the final—Flynn or Finnegan—would prevail in November.

Late in the preliminary campaign, Andy Hiller of Channel 4 staged a live 6 p.m. debate on City Hall Plaza between Flynn and Finnegan. Finnegan had just started running a radio ad pointing out that Flynn, who was now running as a "populist," sort of an anti-Kevin man of the neighborhoods, had once been an avid anti-buser. In Finnegan's ad, Flynn was described as a "chameleon."

During the live debate, Flynn suddenly began yelling at Finnegan: "You called me a lizard!"

It was great TV. I'm not even sure it changed the dynamics of the race— Flynn won. But the newest Channel 7 news director, a guy by the name of Jeff Rosser, was all over my ass. I had to stage my own follow-up Flynn–Finnegan debate the next night, and of course there were no sparks. Nothing happened.

The J.J. Foley's crew 1984: Channel 7 photographer Charlie Sullivan, Mayor Ray Flynn, and me.

This occurred just as I'd thought I was doing a little better as a TV reporter. With all the scandals at both City Hall and at the State House, I spent as much time as possible outside the newsroom—out of sight, out of mind, which was the only way for me to survive, because of this new news director, Jeff Rosser. He'd been Andy Hiller's boss at Channel 4.

Rosser cared nothing about news. He was a big blond guy who'd gone to Brigham Young, although I don't think he was Mormon. He had a giant "Y" class ring that I used to stare at when he was berating me for, among my other faults, a smirking disrespect for politicians I would be interviewing live. He also hated my five o'clock shadow, as well as the fact that I occasionally would do a live shot with the top button on my shirt unbuttoned and my tie askance.

One Monday I broke a political story at the State House, even ahead of the newspapers. I strolled back down Beacon Hill to the station and into the news-room, for once feeling good about myself. One of Rosser's coat holders suddenly materialized and told me, with averted eyes, that the boss wanted to see me.

Uh-oh. I walked in and Rosser yelled at me to sit down. I had no idea what was wrong until he began pointing at my face.

"What's that . . . that thing . . . on your lip?"

It was a cold sore, a fever blister, just a hereditary problem I've occasionally suffered from my entire life. It hurt, but I hadn't even considered not coming to work.

Rosser's face contorted with rage. He was beet red. He looked a lot scarier than I'd just appeared on the shot from the State House. He turned his attention to the three giant TV sets in front of him that he used to monitor "news."

He pointed at a taped post-game interview from the Patriots locker room on another station. Steve Nelson was the team's star linebacker, and it looked like he'd just been in a barroom brawl. His face was all bruised and cut up.

"You look worse than him!" Rosser sputtered. "What were you thinking of, going on TV looking like that?"

My hand reflexively went to my upper lip. I knew it didn't make much sense to ask him if he'd liked my story.

"You are never, ever to come to work looking like that again," he said. And I never did, but by then I was on my way out of Channel 7 anyway.

Naturally I wasn't the only object of Rosser's ire. Petty tyrants like Rosser always have a long shit list. It makes them feel important. Berating underlings proves they're getting the job done. And I was a mere street reporter.

Rosser despised one of our weekend anchors named Bill O'Reilly, who had been picked up off the waiver wire from CBS News. To this day, people who remember the old days at 7 Bulfinch Place still sometimes ask me, what was Bill O'Reilly really like?

I always answer: You've watched him on TV, right? Then you know what he's like. Because with O'Reilly, what you see is what you get.

And if you want to understand what O'Reilly could be like, check out those bootleg videos of his meltdowns on YouTube when he screws up a pre-taped intro or something. Not that his temper tantrums are any worse than those of liberals like, say, Lawrence ("Stop the hammering!") O'Donnell of MSNBC.

In a newsroom, as in most workplaces, it pays to be a go-along-to-get-along kind of employee. O'Reilly never got that memo. He quickly alienated most of Channel 7's cameramen by instructing them—often in brusque terms—how to light and frame their shots. He did not suffer anyone—fools or otherwise—gladly.

He lived in a rented apartment in Harbor Towers, a high-rise complex on the Waterfront near the station. At the time, he was not married. There's an anecdote told about him that one night he and somebody else—I hesitate to use the word "friend" for anyone who knows O'Reilly, even those who like myself get along with him. Anyway, O'Reilly and this other guy went out together with two blind dates. Small talk has never been O'Reilly's forte. For one thing, he didn't drink.

After about an hour of listening to get-acquainted small talk from his date, or so the story goes, O'Reilly abruptly stood up at his chair in the restaurant, pulled a couple of twenties out of his pocket, tossed them on the table, and announced to the woman:

"I'm sorry, but I just can't take any more of this. You are the most boring person I have ever met in my life."

And then he walked out.

O'Reilly was soon gone from Channel 7. He landed at Channel 5, of all places, where he was soon known among his coworkers as "Bill O'Really?" He attended graduate school at the almost-Harvard Kennedy School, then drifted back into national television.

Some TV critic (back in the days when newspapers still had TV critics) once wrote that although he always liked to say he's from Long Island, O'Reilly's real hometown was "Television News." I concur.

But this is how much O'Reilly hated Jeff Rosser: Before he began his wildly successful nonfiction *Killing* series with Martin Dugard, O'Reilly wrote a couple of novels. At least one was a *roman à clef* titled *Those Who Trespass,* about the brutal world of television news.

The plot concerns an embittered (Irish-American) newsman who becomes a serial killer dispensing rough justice to the vile, unprincipled monsters he has encountered in local TV news, and who have fucked him over.

Jeff Rosser, or maybe even two versions of Jeff Rosser, is brutally murdered in *Those Who Trespass.* I enjoyed reading those gruesome passages almost as much as I'm sure O'Reilly enjoyed writing them.

O'Reilly describes Rosser—whose fictional name is Lance Worthington, as "a sleazy weakling . . . (who) lacked the basics required of a news manager. He had never covered news in the field. He didn't recognize a good reporter from a hack. And he was obsessed with research, so other people were always telling him what direction the news should take."

That sums up most of the suits in television "news." The only difference is, it describes Rosser-Worthington even more so.

O'Reilly's alter ego—Shannon Michaels—begins ridding the planet of all his coworkers in TV news, one by one. First Shannon offs a slimy lecherous reporter—think Matt Lauer, who would follow us at Channel 7 a few years later. Then he knocks off an imperious female from HR—now I'm visualizing Jeff Zucker's gal pal at CNN. Next to go is the research director whose polling has discerned that O'Reilly, er, Michaels, has a low "Q" rating.

Finally, it's Rosser's turn, and as O'Reilly slits his throat, he whispers to our news director:

"It's a cutthroat business you're in, Worthington."

The owner of Channel 7, David Mugar, had long since gotten rid of the station when he died in January 2022 at the age of 86. In his obituary, a *Globe* reporter quoted what Mugar had said after he sold Channel 7, under duress, 30 years earlier.

"It's a cutthroat business," Mugar had said, sadly. Didn't we all know it?

Hunter S. Thompson once described TV news as "uglier than most things." That's accurate, I would say.

"It is normally perceived," Thompson wrote, "as some kind of cruel and shallow money trench through the heart of journalism industry, a long plastic hallway where thieves and pimps run free and good men die like dogs, for no good reason."

That was me, dying like a dog. I was under contract, and not even one of the big ones either, at least compared to the Dream Team's or even O'Reilly's.

Paper Boy

The assignment editor was a great old news hand named Chuck Gordon, and he did his best to keep me out of Rosser's sight.

Sometimes there were tasks that I was better suited for than anyone else. As the Kevin White era at City Hall was winding down, the thievery and chicanery inevitably ramped up.

A relic of James Michael Curley's mayoralty, which ended in 1949, was his old, ornate desk. Somewhere along the line, it disappeared from City Hall. The rumor was that Mayor White had stolen it, taken it either to his home on Beacon Hill or perhaps to his Cape Cod retreat in Bourne.

One day I drove down with a cameraman to the mayor's "cottage" and we peered in all the windows, looking for it. We couldn't find it, but we did see a miniature replica model of downtown Boston—something like the Boston Redevelopment Authority would have had built for a press conference. The little Lego-like skyscrapers were mostly on their sides, as if someone had slapped them aside in what the *Globe* forbade its reporters to call a fit of pique.

Only one of Governor Curley's nine children survived, an ex-Jesuit priest named Francis Xavier Curley. He'd been a teacher at the Jesuits' Cheverus High School in Portland, where he used to appear in his classes drunk in the mornings. Treasurer Bob Crane had hired him after he left the priesthood, and he was always around in the Saltonstall Building for a comment on our ongoing search for the missing desk.

Frank Curley would look directly into the camera and say, "Give it back, Kevin!"

There were other things to occupy my time as my time at Channel 7 wound down. I still lived in Somerville, in one of those single-family homes that made up a mere 12 percent of the All-American City's housing stock.

One day I got a hysterical call to come back to my house—there'd been a break-in, a burglary, by the local yutes. It wasn't the first one either. I had a garage out back that I didn't use and they'd been stashing stolen goods inside. This day, I rushed back to Somerville with my cameraman, in the Channel 7 Ford sedan, and met a couple of cops who had answered the 911 call. In my neighborhood, you didn't see many males in coats and ties, especially during business hours. Not unless they had a court appearance scheduled.

The cop, a plainclothes detective, asked me what I was doing at the scene of the crime. I told him I was the owner of the house. The cop's eyes narrowed, and he pointed at my cameraman, a hulking bearded guy in work clothes—standard TV photog garb, in other words.

"Then who is that guy?" he asked.

"That's my cameraman," I said.

"Your cameraman?" he said. "What does that mean?"

"I work for Channel 7," I said. "I'm in TV news."

"You're in television," he said, incredulously, looking around the wretched, trash-filled street. "And you fucking live here?"

I'd begun asking myself the same question, although I figured my days on the gravy train would be over as soon as the second, final guaranteed year of my contract was over.

Nothing was getting any better at Channel 7. It was one cluster-bleep after another. They hired an unemployed British anchorwoman named Angela Rippon. She must have been big in London because for a week or so after she was hired none of us had to buy any drinks at our local watering hole across the street from the Langone Funeral Home.

Every paper on Fleet Street sent over hacks to dig up dirt, or something, on Angela, and they were all competing with one another to get the scoop. The only way they knew to operate was to spring for drinks all around. It was okay by us. We made up all kinds of shit for them, and they lapped it right up, like we were lapping up their booze.

Angela was soon gone.

They had a sportscaster from St. Louis named Zip Rzeppa. One year he made the wrong prediction on the Super Bowl, and at 11 he began his sportscast by saying, "Boy, do I have egg on my face!" Then he picked up an egg and cracked it on his forehead and then did his report with the yoke dripping down his face.

Zip was soon gone.

In 1983, the United States lost the America's Cup in yachting for the first time in 132 years. Channel 7 sent a crew down to Newport, and somehow they found Dennis Conner, the losing skipper, and tracked him down, like he was some City Hall hack fleeing a grand jury appearance at the courthouse in Post Office Square. Conner just kept walking until the female reporter said:

"Well, Skip, look at it this way, you can just go out and win it back . . . next year!"

At which point, Conner turned around and snarled at her: "You don't know what you're talking about!"

The reporter came back all excited and thought it was a big scoop. The 11 o'clock producer had to gently explain to her that the races are only held every four years.

The same reporter got an interview with Marvin Gaye when he was in Boston for a concert. She again rushed back to the newsroom all excited about her interview, in which Marvin had explained all the forces, cosmic and otherwise, that were conspiring against him.

Again, the 11 o'clock producer had to explain to her . . . what's goin' on . . . namely that Marvin Gaye had had a snootful of Bolivian marching powder and had long been totally *non compos mentis*.

That reporter was soon gone. Ditto, Marvin Gaye, shot by his own father.

At the *Herald American,* we had all gotten into the habit of not bothering to introduce ourselves to incoming editors, on the sound theory that they'd soon be out the door, so why bother? I quickly discovered that was likewise a wise policy in the TV world, or at least the Channel 7 world.

In July 1983, the station hired a new sportscaster named Jim Kelly, from parts unknown. I regarded him warily, partly because he acted like he was slumming being in Boston, or maybe just Channel 7.

I knew I should have introduced myself and welcomed him to our fair city, etc., but something just told me, don't bother. Sure enough, he was gone by October. When I just now looked Kelly up on Wikipedia, there was a citation saying that the *Globe* reported that he'd been fired. But he told the *Philadelphia Inquirer* he'd quit. I remember it the way the *Globe* wrote it up.

By then I knew it was only a matter of time until I joined Angela and Zip and O'Reilly and Kelly on the unemployment line. But I needed the money so I figured I'd hang in as long as I could, at least until my guaranteed two-year contract ran out.

In the meantime, I was getting to observe firsthand just how depraved the television culture was, and not just in the newsroom either. It wasn't exactly *Mad Men,* but the medieval tradition of *droit du seigneur* persisted.

Like the ancient feudal lords, the top male executives expected to have their way with their female subordinates, the younger the better. One of the bosses had an endearing question for young women he was interviewing for sales jobs: "Are you a swallower or a spitter?"

Same thing was going on in radio, as I would later discover. Probably most places, for that matter. It later turned out that the top editors in the woke newsroom of the *Globe* kept a "fuckability" list of the local female e.a.'s. Nobody was ever fired for that. It was apparently as accepted a *Globe* tradition as plagiarism, making up stories, or wearing bow ties.

Meanwhile, as my time in television was winding down, it was a plus to live in Somerville, because the feds were now rounding up all our local politicians, and who better to cover it for Channel 7 than somebody from the neighborhood.

The feds had inserted an undercover FBI agent into Somerville, a guy claiming to be a businessman looking for all kinds of permits and licenses and so forth from City Hall, with plenty of cash to hand out. It was like shooting fish in a barrel.

The former mayor of Somerville, who'd been given a hack federal job by Tip O'Neill to remove him as a potential challenger (he was Italian, which petrified Tip), was bagged for trying to shake down developers. The state senator—Denis McKenna—was targeted and was supposed to be bribed at a sit-down at his house at 9 a.m. But the undercover G-man was met at the door and told that the statesman was unavailable for a meeting.

He was drunk.

The big fish, at least from the feds' perspective, was state Rep. Vincent J. Piro. Vinnie was a former high-school basketball star, where he first made news during the old Tech Tourney at the Boston Garden. In front of a full house, Vinnie unmercifully kicked an opposing player who'd been knocked to the floor by one of the other Highlanders.

Two-on-one is Somerville fun. That was one of our old sayings. Another old saying was that in Somerville math classes, the future politicians learned how to add . . . but never how to divide.

The undercover fed was named Jack Callahan. As usual, the FBI utterly botched the case. None of us would find out until much later, but Callahan was from Dorchester. Why would they send an undercover operative back to what might as well have been his hometown?

Plus, Callahan had a rather checkered past, like so many of these bent G-men. We would discover all that stuff later. The first stories were just that Vinnie had been recorded taking cash from the fed in return for racing dates that had to be approved by the legislature. Then, a couple of weeks later, Vinnie had called Callahan back, and had returned the cash, claiming it was "all a fucking fantasy."

There was only one problem for Vinnie: the feds had of course recorded the serial numbers of all the bills, and when the money was returned, some of the bills were different. In other words, Vinnie had been spending the money, "greasing a few guys," as he put it so colorfully when he was recorded on Callahan's wire.

The perhaps apocryphal story about why he returned the payoff in marked bills came out later. After accepting the money, or so everyone in Somerville came to believe, Vinnie had taken his girlfriend to a Bruins game, where she had spotted Callahan and waved at him. Vinnie was surprised that she would know this new guy in town. He asked how she happened to recognize hm.

Vinnie's girlfriend told him that no, he wasn't from out of town, he was from Dorchester, and that the last she'd heard, he was in the FBI.

When I asked him about the rumor, off the record, Vinnie vehemently denied everything.

"Number one," he said, "I don't have a girlfriend. Number two, who the fuck goes to Bruins games?"

I believed number two, but not number one.

This Somerville corruption probe should have been a boon to my career, or at least saved my job at Channel 7. I personally knew everybody who'd been targeted. What made it even more interesting was that one of the feds' chief targets, the drunken state senator, Denis McKenna, was not running for reelection.

This saddened me, because I always mourn the passing, in whatever form, of a guy who can provide me with a good story anytime I need one on a slow news day. Denis McKenna was one of those guys.

In my *Herald* columns, I'd always mention how in his State House office was hung a pair of praying hands like you can buy at a Stuckey's in South Carolina. I'd always say that underneath the hands was the inscription: "Let us prey." Not pray, prey.

I mentioned how many times he'd flunked the bar exam after graduating from night law school.

"He never could pass the bar," I would write, "because there was one on the way home."

Senate President Billy Bulger once mentioned at his St. Patrick's Day breakfast in South Boston how he had been on a recent junket—"if it were Dukakis it would have been a trade mission"—to China.

"We were told not to drink the water," Bulger said. "So I drank beer in the morning, beer in the afternoon, beer in the evening. I felt like Sen. McKenna."

There was a young female senator from Methuen, Sharon Pollard, who was overweight. One morning, at a hearing, McKenna told her, "Honey, if you lost 30 pounds, you could be Miss America."

He hated George Bachrach of Watertown, a "reformer" who would later become embroiled in a scandal involving the Teamsters. Bachrach had defeated one of McKenna's drinking buddies, plus he was from New York, or, as McKenna put it, "that well-known billionaire area, the state of Upper New York."

One of McKenna's State House aides was, like his indicted son, also a Somerville alderman. His name was Francis P. Bakey. I still remember Bakey's amazed reaction to finally being lugged. I had run into him in Union Square after his arraignment.

"You have no idea," he told me, "what it's like to pick up your own indictment and read, 'The United States of America v. Francis P. Bakey.'"

Like many alcoholics, Sen. McKenna was a master at hiding his stashes of booze. In the study at his home, he had a tall desk that he worked at, as much as he could ever work. When he died, workmen arrived to move the desk, and when they did, hundreds of empty nip bottles tumbled down from behind the back of the senator's desk.

When McKenna announced his decision to retire, the state Senate seat appeared to be Vinnie Piro's for the taking, at least until his attempted extortion indictment. A reformer, Sal Albano, then jumped into the race, but "Fat Sal," as Vinnie called him, was still the underdog. Vinnie's lawyer was Bob Popeo of Mintz Levin, originally from East Boston. Popeo got along well with me and another reporter covering the trial, Frank Phillips of the *Herald*.

Frank, who had formerly worked for the *Lowell Sun*, was from the Bird family of Walpole—old-line Yankee, with a huge mansion on the ocean in Osterville around the corner from the hoity-toity Wiano Club, where Ted Kennedy had famously once ridden a horse up the front steps. His wife's family had their own mansion, on Nantucket.

In other words, Frank Phillips had almost the same *Social Register* pedigree as the U.S. attorney, William Floyd Weld, as opposed to me and Popeo. We both had the exact same pedigree as most of the defendants in all the political corruption cases out of Somerville and Boston.

Somehow, just before the trial began, Phillips and I both obtained transcripts of the FBI-recorded meeting where Vinnie gave the bribe back to the undercover G-man Callahan and said taking it had just been a "fantasy."

It was exculpatory, up to a point. Of course, we didn't have the official transcripts—they were under seal. What we had were . . . copies.

Frank was running with the story for the morning *Herald*, and I was going to break it as that evening's lead story on Channel 7. I'd called the U.S. attorney's office for the pro forma "no comment." I was in the editing suite, putting together the final story, making sure all the chyrons were correct, since most of the narrative would be quotes from the FBI transcripts. The phone rang, and when I picked it up I heard the whining voice of Mark Wolf, an assistant U.S. attorney, an entitled Ivy League rich kid from Weston.

Wolf immediately began threatening me with some unspecified payback if we put the story on the air. I shrugged, hung up, and we ran the story. It was one of those rare evenings when I got to sit on the set with the anchors, instead of doing a live shot on the street from parts unknown.

The next morning, I showed up at the courthouse in Post Office Square to cover Vinnie's ongoing trial. I was minding my own business when Wolf, a pudgy, balding little guy who bore more than a passing resemblance to Rhode Island Mafioso Bobby DeLuca, except that DeLuca was more personable, stormed up to me.

"Where do you live?" he snarled. "Do you still live in Somerville?"

I nodded. "Everybody knows that," I said.

A few days later, a letter was delivered to my Somerville address—from the Internal Revenue Service. I had suddenly been selected for a . . . random . . . audit. I took the letter to the courthouse with me that morning, and when I got to the courtroom, I approached Vinnie's lawyer, Bob Popeo. I pulled the letter out of my pocket and handed it to him.

"Guess what I got yesterday," I said, and Popeo smiled. He pulled a letter out of his pocket.

"Guess what I got yesterday," he said. It was the same letter. Of course, Francis Bird Phillips did not get such a letter. In the halls of justice, the only justice is in the halls.

Popeo told me not to worry, that he would handle it. He sent off two identical scorching letters to the IRS, demanding to know how we'd been picked for their "random" audits. There was no response, not even a form follow-up letter dropping the probes. The IRS went dead silent. Just to cover my ass, I had my accountant send them a letter saying we would be glad to cooperate, just let us know what they wanted.

No response.

Every night, after the trial, Vinnie would do live shots with me and the reporter from Channel 4, Shelby Scott. One night I'd be first; she'd get him first the next night. As I recall, Channel 5 didn't have nearly as much interest in the case—it was all just too tawdry.

Naturally the judge had instructed the jurors to disregard all media coverage, but every morning when they filed into the courtroom, they'd all be smiling and nodding in Vinnie's direction. He cut a rather impressive figure in those live shots, taller than either Shelby or me, more fashionably attired. And most assuredly no five o'clock shadow.

Just before the Democrat primary, a mistrial was declared, and Vinnie won easily. In those days, in Somerville and even more so in Medford, the other city in the district, it was not such a bad thing to be on the Democrat primary ballot while under indictment.

Still, in the end, Vinnie lost to Fat Sal, who ran on stickers and amazingly won. Again, it was sad to lose as colorful a character as Vinnie Piro. But by then, though, I was onto new quarry, in another contiguous north-of-Boston city where a criminal record could in fact be what Rush Limbaugh used to call a résumé enhancer—Chelsea.

How corrupt was Chelsea? A few years later, Whitey Bulger would tell his FBI agent Zip Connolly that Winter Hill had had to pull out of the city—the overhead was too high, because there was so many politicians demanding to be paid off. Chelsea's municipal government was finally placed into receivership after several mayors in a row were convicted of felonies, mostly shakedowns of local contractors and vendors.

James Mitchell had been a city councilor. He was a Dapper O'Neil type, only not smart enough to understand and accept his limitations. As mayor, he had succeeded a corrupt Mike Dukakis hack and soon found himself in way over his head at City Hall.

He stopped showing up for "work," which Chelsea voters could understand. But when he didn't show up for the Chelsea High School graduation, the Americans who hadn't yet fled the city began circulating recall petitions.

In the summer of 1984, Mitchell summarily fired the city treasurer and the longtime chief of police. I went over to City Hall with a camera crew and utilized all the local-TV news techniques I'd learned from Andy Hiller.

I strolled into the mayor's office, camera rolling as I asked to speak to the mayor. I was rebuffed. I then set up shop outside the mayor's office, did a live shot for the noon news with B-roll of my courageous confrontation with the mayor's secretary.

The mayor was, I knew, a hothead. Sometimes in TV news you need only light the fuse and eventually there will be an explosion . . . of great video. You just keep the camera rolling. His office, as I recall, was on a mezzanine of sorts. The stairway was open. So I staked out his office, with a cameraman hanging somewhat back. It was a perfect angle for what happened next.

Eventually, Mitchell stormed out of his office in a rage, his face beet red and his fists clenched. He began screaming at me, calling me a "first-class phony," among other things. I kept my cool—by now I well understood that my role in this little melodrama was to stand there and take it. If I responded in kind, I would forfeit the coveted victim status. The videotape would just be of two assholes screaming at one another. The viewers would be confused as to who to root for.

The mayor stomped back into his office and slammed the door. I stuck around, of course. This was one of those days when two cameras would have been better than one, just in case. It wasn't long before we heard a commotion downstairs and saw an old lady carrying a large pocketbook coming toward the stairs, yelling loudly.

It was the fired police chief's elderly mother, enraged, screaming, "I'm going to get him! I'm going to stab him."

She climbed up the stairs onto the landing and then got wobbly before finally keeling over. She didn't pass out, though. She was just dizzy, or faint. My cameraman ran up as she lay on her back, thrashing.

"I'm going to kill him!" she kept screaming. I peeked into her open purse and saw a huge pair of shears. She wasn't kidding. My cameraman got footage of the scissors and we kept rolling until the ambulance arrived and she was taken away on a stretcher.

It was a big story. The next morning it even made the top of the front page of the *Globe*—in those days that was a big deal, as hard as it may be to believe today. I was identified by name and channel, with the correct quote from the mayor—"first-class phony."

I thought maybe I'd saved my job (and the third, $63,000-guaranteed, year of my contract). But the Chelsea headlines didn't do me any good. Rosser had finished whacking all the anchors from the previous regimes, so now he was going after the reporters. And I was at the top of the Hit Parade.

I started talking to Murdoch's new managers at the *Herald* about getting my old column back. I knew I'd have to take a pay cut, but there didn't seem to be any way around it. I'd still have my monthly column at *Boston* magazine. Before I got my job at Channel 7, I'd been teaching a course or two every semester in introductory journalism at Boston University. I figured I could go back to that part-time job to make up the deficit I was facing.

In the meantime, I was going through the motions. One day I got a memo to schedule a time to meet with the station's "make-up consultant." This was Jeff Rosser's idea of journalism. I dutifully appeared and a frowning, middle-aged woman studied me, shaking her head. Finally, she leaned in close to my face and announced her verdict.

"We're going to have to do something about your beard," she said.

It's not that I had a heavy beard, she said. It's just that it was rather dark, especially against my fair skin. Black Irish, I suppose you'd call it. I thought to myself, what exactly was I supposed to "do" about my beard? Electrolysis?

One day I picked up the local Quincy afternoon paper and read that I was going to be fired. I'd heard about people finding out they were going to be dumped by reading it in the paper, but it's one of those things you never figure will happen to you.

I went into Rosser's office and asked him if it were true. He said yes and I asked him why he hadn't had the courtesy to tell me directly to my face.

"If you'd asked," he said, "I would have told you."

Which of course would be like hearing that there was a murder contract out on you and then going to the Doghouse on Prince Street, or the South Boston Liquor Mart, to ask Jerry Angiulo or Whitey Bulger if he was planning to clip you.

I called the *Herald* and told them I'd take the job. My contract at Channel 7 wasn't renewed for the third and final year. I became an at-will employee. I gave my notice to Rosser's deputy, a black guy who I got along with, and he asked me to work through New Year's to cover for everybody else's vacations. I asked him if he was kidding.

My last day I was planning to do nothing, but Rosser had other plans. He ordered me out on some State House story about an audit of the MBTA by state auditor John Finnegan, the older brother of David Finnegan, the unsuccessful mayoral candidate who had called Ray Flynn a lizard.

I'd always gotten along with Finnegan, an urbane, easygoing lawyer from Dorchester. I told him it was my last day and that I was going back to the *Herald*, and he told me something about newspapers that I've always remembered.

When he started out in politics, Finnegan said, every morning he'd wake up and rush out and pick up the newspapers and go through them. And if he'd see his name in any of them, he'd be happy.

"Now," he said, "I do the same thing—I wake up and go through the papers, and if I don't see my name—then I'm happy."

I understood exactly what he meant. That was another lesson I learned at 7 Bulfinch Place.

That afternoon, the writer at the Quincy paper who'd broken the story of my firing did another piece about my departure. To illustrate it, she used my official station photograph, pointing out that even though it was a posed photo by a professional photographer, I still had a trace of . . . you guessed it, five o'clock shadow. The fact that my tie was slightly askew was also noted. What did I care? Every knock a boost. . . .

My final Channel 7 live shot was down at a Red Line station in Quincy. No guests, just me, introducing a package with videotape of Finnegan talking about his report, at a semi-deserted subway stop. At the top of the 6 o'clock newscast—I was going out with the lead story. I recalled the final movie that the old owners of the *Herald Traveler* had memorably run after they lost Channel 5 back in 1972—*Fixed Bayonets.*

It was clear to me what Rosser was up to. He was hoping I'd throw a nutty at the top of the show, scream and yell and throw down my mic. If he got really lucky, I'd swear too. Act like Mayor Mitchell, like an asshole. That way, Rosser could say to Channel 7 owner David Mugar (and to the *Globe*), "See, I told you so!"

It happened occasionally in local news back then. The black weekend sports anchor at Rosser's old station, WBZ, had done it one Sunday night in 1978, ripping off his lav mike and storming off the set. I'd been watching—it was must-see TV. *Fixed Bayonets* indeed.

But I never even considered torching any potential future I might have in TV. I played it straight. That night I ended up being late for my own farewell party around the corner from the station. But I did a flawless live shot, although I didn't bother to shave. I wanted to leave Rosser with something to remember me by, even if it was only my five o'clock shadow.

8
NEW
SENSATION

When I went back to the *Herald* in 1985, there was a wide-open lane in the Boston media for . . . reporting with an attitude, both in print and in television.

After World War II, in the absence of any serious competition, the *Globe* had prospered, but it was still at best a lazy, mediocre newspaper. It was run by trust-funded suburbanites for trust-funded suburbanites.

Now more than ever, the *Globe's* mission was afflicting the afflicted and comforting the comfortable.

The old blue-collar crew of *Globe* newsmen were being supplanted by the weak-chinned scions of the upper classes. On St. Patrick's Day, Billy Bulger would joke that if you wanted to get anyone from the *Globe* after business hours, you had to dial "1"—for long distance, because none of them lived in Boston.

I'd always been a big fan of Jimmy Breslin, who'd bounced around from one dying New York newspaper to another over the years. As Tom Wolfe pointed out in *The New Journalism,* "Breslin made the remarkable discovery that a columnist could actually leave the newsroom and do real reporting."

Out on, you know, the street.

I'd known all that in my first run as a *Herald* columnist, but I realized that being in television news for two-plus years would make me a better columnist. Now I better understood how news was produced, how the media could be massaged. I saw everything in news more clearly.

Paper Boy

I'd only been gone from the *Herald* for a little more than two years, but in January 1985 I returned to a whole different newspaper. For one thing, "*American*" was gone from the name, not because Rupert Murdoch hadn't yet been naturalized, but because it was a reminder of the abysmal Hearst legacy, like the defunct *Journal-American* in New York and the soon-to-be-defunct *Baltimore News American*.

The word *American* on the masthead of a newspaper branded it as a Hearst rag, much like *Examiner*—as in *San Francisco Examiner* or *Los Angeles Herald Examiner.*

The paper's old address in the South End, 300 Harrison Avenue, had become One Herald Square. The wags would call it One Wingo Square, after the circulation-building game that Murdoch splurged on.

In the newsroom, it was all new faces. The Corsettis were gone, so were all the old legmen and equally ancient rewrite men. Stanley Forman, the three-time Pulitzer Prize winner who had called me a "rat fucker" one night during the sale to Murdoch, had himself left for a TV cameraman's job at Channel 5.

Stanley and I would nod at each other and smile whenever our paths crossed later. No hard feelings—it was all in the dim past, like Walter Howey's drunken reign over the Hearst hacks in Winthrop Square back in the fifties.

I'd always been the youngest reporter/rewrite man in the city room, even when I had more than four years in. Now that I was back, at age 32, I was among the oldest of the ink-stained wretches. The editors were youngish old Murdoch hands, like Joe Robinowitz, a Texan from Rupert's first American paper, in San Antonio, and Les Hinton, who decades later would take the fall in the hacking scandal at the *News of the World* in London.

I was eager to hit the ground running. As always, I had a lot of scores to settle. Finally, it seemed like I would have something I'd never had anywhere else—somebody who had my back. Plus, I felt like I was at the top of my game. Television news dominated all media, no doubt about it, and now I had direct experience in it. I knew firsthand how it worked—and didn't work. And I had people in the TV newsrooms that I could go to for the raw videotapes that the local stations often never used, except for the year-end blooper reels played at the Christmas parties.

I'd already seen what could be accomplished if you had unlimited access to video. During my years at Channel 7, I'd continued writing a monthly political column for *Boston* magazine. It wasn't so much that I needed the $250 per column. I just had to keep my hand in print, especially once Rosser arrived on the scene and I needed new clips to show the new Murdoch crowd running the *Herald*.

Boston magazine was now being run by Don Forst, and he gave me free rein.

In 1984, when I was still at Channel 7, Elliot Richardson, the hero of Watergate, returned to Massachusetts after 15 years in Washington to run for the Republican nomination for the U.S. Senate. He was the favorite to win the GOP nomination against Ray Shamie, a conservative businessman who had been the sacrificial Republican lamb against Ted Kennedy in 1982.

I figured it would be a good *Boston* magazine column to ride along with Richardson on the campaign trail one Saturday. The day was set up by a guy in his campaign who'd been one year ahead of me at Deerfield.

In the car was El-Yacht, as he was known, his driver, me, and a second reporter, Margot Hornblower from the *Washington Post*. We drove around all day, hitting the Republican towns where he'd address small knots of crusty old-line Republican primary voters. Margot Hornblower would be taking notes furiously, as I'd be drifting around on the outskirts of the crowds.

I was searching for those status details, such as when he referred to the Copley Plaza Hotel as the Statler, which had been its name when he was elected state attorney general in 1966.

The Democrats' Senate candidate was John Forbes Kerry, the lieutenant governor. Richardson was soon telling us about how ironic it was that Kerry, the bluest of Brahmin bluebloods (at least on his mother's side), was trying to portray Richardson as some out-of-touch Yankee when his actual background was from a family of solid but hardly Brahmin upper-middle-class physicians.

El-Yacht didn't say anything derogatory, but it was fascinating to me to hear him speak so honestly about another Yankee. I guess he figured he was among his own kind. I was from Deerfield, and Margot's maiden name was Roosevelt.

The inside-baseball Yankee stuff bored Margot, just as the standard campaign boilerplate she was going after meant nothing to me. Finally, she pulled me aside and asked what the hell I was doing if I wasn't taking notes on the important stuff?

I explained to her that as a TV reporter, I had access to videotape of all of Richardson's standard press conferences and stump speeches, and that I was doing a magazine piece. I think she dismissively muttered something about "New Journalism," but I just shrugged.

Six weeks later, my piece came out. El-Yacht came across as an out-of-touch fossil. My friend from Deerfield became *persona non grata* in the campaign. Richardson was crushed in the GOP primary by Shamie, and I got a short note at Channel 7 from Margot Hornblower on *Washington Post* stationery:

"Now I understand what you were doing."

I tried to do the same kind of story with Rep. Gerry Studds, the Cape Cod congressman who had just been outed for having sex with an underage male page he'd gotten drunk on a European junket. He was more guarded, for obvious reasons, than Richardson.

Studds was a bad guy, as I knew from his unceremonious departure as a teacher from St. Paul's School in Concord, New Hampshire. One of the other reporters at Channel 7 was a St. Paul's alumnus who told me how Studds had mysteriously vanished from the campus mid-semester back in the sixties. Of course, this would not be confirmed for more than 40 years, long after his death, when St. Paul's released its official report on sexual abuse down through the decades. And later Studds would be named in a civil lawsuit brought by some of his victims.

As a prep-school master, Studds ran a dormitory, and he had a custom of running his floor's meetings with everyone in the nude. He also liked to drive his "boys" off campus and then come on to them.

After his dismissal from St. Paul's, he decided to get into politics. In 1970, he almost knocked off Rep. Hastings Keith, a Republican graduate of Deerfield Academy. Keith held off Studds—like most of the St. Paul's boys in the front seat of his car—but the political trends were clear. Keith took the hint and retired, and Studds won the seat in 1972.

Studds was a sanctimonious prig, in addition to being a pederast. It wasn't nearly as amusing hanging out with him as it had been with El-Yacht (I missed Margot too) but I wrote the column anyway. Didn't think it was much good, but I guess it was politically correct, let's put it that way.

Much to my surprise, in the spring of 1985 I won the National Magazine Award for my "incisive and elegant reporting." (You could look it up in the *New York Times* archives.)

The magazine got to keep the strange plaque, although I don't know what's become of it, because I am now one of *Boston* magazine's World's Worst People. No problem, though. It's like being ripped in the *Globe*—if nobody's reading it, who cares?

As a columnist for the magazine, I was annually drafted to take part in *Boston* magazine's biggest yearly feature—the Best & Worst Awards every August. We used to have a lot of fun putting them together, especially the worsts.

I remember one French-themed suburban steakhouse—Le Beeftique or some such name. It got the worst steakhouse award—Le Pits was our description.

At the height of the feds' City Hall investigation, two retired Boston hacks with journalistic pretensions (or maybe just protection rackets) were targeted by the grand jury. We invented a new category: Best & Worst Newspaper Columnists under Investigation by the Boston Retirement Board.

There was no extra pay for those awards duties, just free food and booze during the deliberations, such as they were. The real plus side was that you could do favors for your friends. That taught me yet another important lesson, a corollary to the one I already knew—that no good deed goes unpunished.

What I learned from Best & Worst was that if you finagle something like a "Best" award (or an internship, or a freebie, or any other good deed) for somebody, they will assume that it came to them, not from some mere mortal doing them a favor, but from . . . God, as a reward for their own greatness, or goodness, or something.

Even if a winner knew that I was their only possible connection to getting taken care of (and if you won in certain categories, say, any kind of best food or specialty shop, it could mean quite a lot to your business), you couldn't necessarily expect any thanks, or even an acknowledgment.

Which was only to be expected, I suppose. The bigger problem was that the people who got the "worst" awards suddenly turned into Sherlock Holmes or Columbo and began relentlessly hunting down whoever had so unfairly screwed them over.

Eventually, the magazine did away with the "Worst" awards. They were costing Herb Lipson, the tight-fisted owner, too much in advertising dollars. After that revenue-based decision, I don't think the awards themselves were ever as popular again. The subscribers to the magazine obviously enjoyed reading the barbs as much as we had enjoyed writing them.

I kept writing the political column for *Boston,* but my real focus now was on the *Herald.*

The new *Herald* reporters were mostly locals, some of them former *Globe* interns who hadn't made the cut for whatever reason. The police reporter was Kevin Cullen, from the Holyoke *Transcript.* I'd met him when I was still at Channel 7. Sen. Paul Tsongas, stricken with cancer, had announced he wasn't running for reelection, and had leaked the story to his old friend from Lowell, Frank Phillips, who was at the *Herald* by then.

Anyway, after the leak Tsongas wasn't doing any interviews, but we all tracked him down somewhere and staked out the location. We were all pissed that he was playing favorites, and we wanted to bust him, cancer be damned.

I was afraid, though, that he'd just screw out the back door and leave us— leave me—holding the bag. Not what I needed when I was on the ropes with the Channel 7 suits. So while everyone else stayed out in front of the building, I went around to the back of the building. There was a huge trash barrel that I knew could block Tsongas's exit. I tried to push it in front of the back door but it was too heavy for me.

I ran back to the front of the building and told Cullen to come with me, and together, we pushed the barrel in front of the door, blocking his attempt to leave. He had to come out the front door and give all of us a comment.

After that, I figured Cullen was okay. He certainly talked a good game. Anyway, at the new *Herald*, the reporters were good, and so were Murdoch's new editors, although I missed Forst. After that brief detour to *Boston* magazine, he would resurface at the new but short-lived *New York Newsday*.

Finally, the *Herald* had computers. They'd gotten rid of all the old linotype operators, years or decades after every other major newspaper. Harry's King of Draft, their hangout at the corner of Berkeley and Harrison with the Narragansett beer sign out front, would never be the same again.

With Kevin White no longer mayor, Boston City Hall wasn't nearly the volcano of breaking news that it had been. In Napoleon-like exile, he was now a professor of sorts at Boston University, ensconced in a townhouse on Bay State Road that was plush by any standards unless perhaps you'd been living at the Parkman House for years—on the arm.

Ray Flynn was the new mayor. I'd gotten to know him pretty well, somewhat from City Hall but more from J.J. Foley's. Ray would take a drink under extreme social pressure, as Joe Heaney would say. And during busing it was tough for Flynn to drink in Southie—too parochial, too thugged up, too nasty in general.

Foley's was just across the bridge, but in nobody's neighborhood. It was to Boston, or at least to white Boston, our Boston, what Switzerland traditionally was to Europe. An oasis of neutrality. It was a DMZ.

You could watch people kill themselves with booze at Foley's. I remember Paul Ellison, an anti-busing city councilor, who went to prison for larceny of public funds. He got out and by the age of 47 had drunk himself to death in Foley's dark back room—the Berkeley Room, as we called it.

The Foleys served anybody who walked through the door, and judged no one, lest they be judged themselves. Nobody came armed, in any sense of the word, to Foley's. Except for the cops of course, which was mostly a good thing.

Ray Flynn was a typical Foley's patron. He was old-line Southie. He'd been a good basketball player at Providence College and even had a tryout with the Knicks. He was a shooting guard, the same kind of athlete as he was a politician—liked the jump shot a lot, not so much offensive rebounding. His hoop nickname could have been "the Pedestrian," because he never drove.

Flynn had been in the old 240-member state House of Representatives, before it was reduced in size to 160.

Pols like Billy Bulger and Kevin White, who'd gone to law school, looked down on Ray as a ham-and-egger, as they called street pols. The "two-toilet Irish" scorned him as the sort who couldn't afford to wake their deceased loved ones at the neighborhood funeral home. They'd bring the departed's casket home and put it in the front room, the parlor, and pass beers to one another across the bier.

Flynn came from a family of longshoremen. Every morning at dawn longshoremen had to "shape up" for work on the docks. Billy Bulger wrote later about how desperately he wanted to leave that kind of life behind him.

In *The Last Hurrah*, the novel by Edwin O'Connor, the James Michael Curley–like mayor said that as a young man, he'd wanted a job where he could wear a suit—but not the chauffeur's cap that came with it.

Ray had at most a couple of suits. That was more than me, but then I was a reporter. I could afford to dress badly, like a plainclothes cop, because I was representing a large organization with clout behind it. Politicians are expected to dress better than cops or reporters.

Ray didn't have a driver either, just a shitbox station wagon. It made an impression, mixed I would say. Decades later, I remember Mayor Marty Walsh laughing about his predecessor's car as he recalled Raybo behind the wheel putt-putting down Savin Hill Avenue.

In his final term as mayor, Kevin invited Ray to the Parkman House occasionally, and offered him books, as if he never read. Billy Bulger just basically disdained him.

I remember when Freddie Langone was running for mayor, he couldn't believe that he was a mere asterisk in the polls while Ray was headed for the runoff.

In the Council, Freddie had always had to explain everything to Ray—very slowly. Ray wasn't a details guy, at least when it came to legislation, either on Beacon Hill or City Hall.

In addition to liking his beer, Ray liked to run, and he became one of the early non-smoking zealots. It was a good issue, especially among the kind of people who otherwise might recoil at his pedigree—think Beacon Hill Civic Association.

So Ray put in a resolution to ban smoking on the Council floor. It was aimed primarily at Dapper and Freddie, but it would also have affected Joe Tierney, as well as several of the beat reporters. Flynn's anti-smoking proposal got some headlines in both papers.

One of the *Herald American* reporters, a young old-timer, you might say, who liked to do as little work as possible, decided to "advance" the story of Flynn's proposed ban on smoking before the actual vote.

He drifted into the Council chambers in the morning, when the lights weren't turned on and no one was around. He lit up a cigarette, took a few puffs, and then walked over to Ray's desk and began flicking the ashes all over it.

After spreading the ashes all around, he went back upstairs for an hour or so, then wandered back down after the lights had been turned on for the afternoon meeting. He took a quick look, then rushed into Ray's office and told him he had something to show him in the Council chambers.

Ray saw the ashes all over his desk and flew into a rage. That afternoon he was thundering at certain unnamed parties who had no consideration for anyone else and hadn't they ever heard of the dangers of secondhand smoke? Dapper and Freddie and Joe Tierney were all glancing at each other, puzzled, wondering what the hell Ray was so agitated about.

All of us reporters watched, trying not to burst out laughing, just like when we were kids in church. But a lot of days at the City Council were like that. The point is how easy it was to put one over on Ray.

Like Dapper, he had no checking account, but he did have six kids. When he announced for mayor, I was wondering to myself what he would do to support his family when he lost, which I and everyone else assumed he would. Would he go back to his old job as a probation officer?

What nobody realized was that after all these years of Kevin White's imperious rule from the Parkman House, the voters were ready for someone who didn't put on airs. After the you-called-me-a-lizard! debate with David Finnegan, Raybo won easily.

Now City Hall was full of neighborhood guys—not wiseguys and ex-cons, like Kevin's army, but real people, many of whom had until recently been punching a time clock or carrying a lunch box.

They would be getting into their own scandals soon enough, but it would take them a while to find their crooked footing. The makeup of City Council had been changed too—instead of nine at-large city councilors, there were now only four, with nine district city councilors.

It was a totally different place. Dapper had barely hung on—in the final days of the '83 fight, knowing Dapper was struggling, Kevin White had given him money, because, like all of us, he appreciated the Dap's entertainment value. Freddie was gone—he would have lost in the new Eastie-North End district to one of Kevin's wired-in precinct captains, Bobby Travaglini, the future president of the state Senate.

As a consolation prize, the city gave Freddie a good location for a bake shop, in the redeveloped Haymarket, just a few feet from City Hall. It should have been a gold mine, but Freddie hung around at a front table, stinking up the place with his cigar and complaining to whoever would listen about whatever was on his mind. Hemorrhoids, as I recall one morning. Freddie's venture into the hospitality industry didn't last long.

Dapper was adrift, at least for a while. He no longer had Freddie to lean on during budget debates. The Council now included several women—"the Andrews sisters," Dapper called them. There was a new openly gay councilor, David Scondras. He and Dapper did not hit it off.

Luckily for me, Mike Dukakis was back at the State House to make up for the fall-off in news from City Hall. In 1970, the Duke had been the Democratic candidate for lieutenant governor when Kevin White had unsuccessfully run for governor. From his own defeat in 1978, he had absorbed the same unfortunate lesson in bare-knuckle politics as his 1970 running mate—the Duke was determined never to be out-hacked again.

Dukakis's new hacks-only-need-apply administration was made to order for me and the new *Herald*. Now we had the entire state to investigate. Plus, what made it even easier was that so many of the politicians at the State House, Democrats and Republicans alike, detested Dukakis. He was too smug, sanctimonious.

At City Hall, I'd been able to work a handful of city councilors and a few bureaucrats here and there, but it was a small universe of leakers to extract material from. On Beacon Hill, though, there were still a lot of Republicans. And both branches of the legislature had competing Democratic factions, all leaking against one another.

Until 1978, the House had had 240 members. It had been just too messy and raucous, or so it was believed, by the goo-goos—good-government types. Few legislators had offices, or phones—they used banks of pay phones outside the House chambers.

Turnover was high, and many of the defeated reps had few prospects in the declining Massachusetts economy. Some remained at the State House as "court officers"—they held open the doors for their former legislative colleagues. Some of the court officers supplemented their modest incomes by taking bets.

Other erstwhile lawmakers were employed at what were basically taxpayer-funded almshouses for the unemployable—the Legislative Service Bureau, the Legislative Research Bureau, and so forth. There was an office in the basement that had been set up after World War II to pay the bonuses to the returning veterans. In 1980, it was still in operation, after a fashion.

The percentage of ex-cons may have been a little lower than at City Hall, but the waste, fraud, and abuse was above and beyond anything Kevin White could have imagined. The State House was a target-rich environment for a "feisty" tabloid newspaper like the *Herald*.

Except for the pay, working for a Rupert Murdoch tabloid was everything I'd always dreamed of. As for the money, the cliché was that Rupert liked to get a dollar's worth of work for a quarter.

I was no longer in the union. I had an "exempt" contract, not a lot of money of course but I did have a good expense account. And I not only had the *Boston* magazine column, for the next few years I alternated part-time gigs between two of the local TV stations—Channel 2, the local PBS station where I'd sort of interned in the summer of 1982, and Channel 56, a Gannett-owned independent down on Morrissey Boulevard next to the *Boston Globe* building.

Again I was so near . . . and yet so far.

I like to think I did some good local TV news for both Channels 56 and 2. Good is a relative term, of course. And in this case, by good I mean entertaining, or at least "momentarily adequate," as Rod Serling once said of his work, in a real understatement, obviously.

Too bad that both stations—or at least their newscasts—are long gone, because I'd enjoy rewatching some of my greatest hits. I was basically doing my newspaper column on video, but not those old-line "editorials," or Andy Rooney–type so-called curmudgeons just sitting at a desk.

I would go out and do real reporting, with an edge, an attitude. On my good days, I mean. I still remember Kurt Vonnegut Jr.'s fictional character (or alter ego) Kilgore Trout, the science fiction writer. Someone told him once that 90 percent of science fiction was crap, and Trout responded with a shrug, "Ninety percent of everything is crap."

With TV news, it's closer to 98 percent, my product most assuredly included. Still, I did have some good outings. Of course, many tricks that I could employ in my newspaper columns didn't translate well on TV, such as telling stories about the old days, or listing salaries of entire families on public payrolls.

As a columnist, my days in the paper were Wednesday, Friday, and Sunday. I never wanted to be caught flat-footed for my Wednesday column. So some Mondays I'd head over to the Suffolk County courthouse in Pemberton Square, across Cambridge Street from City Hall, and just hang out in the first session of Boston Municipal Court.

Some days I'd get a column; other times I'd just soak in the vibes. For instance, watching a perp with a dozen or more aliases, all of which would be read into the record. Or some dirtball wearing the tee shirt he'd been arrested in Friday night, emblazoned with the words, "I love every bone in your body—INCLUDING MINE!"

In court, I might run into some lawyer, or more likely a court officer, who would tip me off to something I could use down the road.

Often, subjects that made good columns in the *Herald* could also be turned into interesting TV stories. For instance, every few months the Boston Police Department would do a roundup of johns over the weekend in the Combat Zone. They called it Operation Squeeze.

The johns would be brought in and they would sheepishly tell the judge how they just happened to be lost, not in the Zone, but in the Downtown Crossing area, and they needed to ask for directions, and the first person they happened to see just happened to be the statuesque young woman in hot pants who invariably turned out to be an undercover female police officer. The johns usually represented a good cross-section of the male population. One day the cops even arrested a 90-year-old. That column of mine rated a tease the next day on the *Herald* front page.

I would sit in the gallery, watch and take notes on their incoherent ravings, and then follow them out to the elevators after they had their cases continued. Few of them would ever say anything, and I quickly realized the chases would make even better television than newspaper columns.

So I returned to my Channel 7 chasing-the-perp ways, with a camera crew. I'm not saying I was advancing the march of human progress, but it was amusing—chewing gum for the eyes, as Fred Allen used to say of TV.

Later on I even made a segment out of Operation Squeeze for my radio show. I would get a list of the johns from the police or the district attorney's office, and I would call them and offer them a choice: they could come on the air and I would identify them as "Mr. X" and they could tell me what happened, or if they didn't want to go on the air, I would identify them, by name and the city or town they lived in.

Very few wouldn't agree to come on the air.

Yes, I know, that was cruel of me to humiliate horny guys, but what the hell. Worse things are done every day to better people. That's the way I justified it in my own mind, anyway.

Some days there would be a story in one of the papers about an elected official who was jammed up about something or other. I would take a cameraman with me and we would just barge into his office. This wasn't a job for everyone, naturally.

One day, working for Channel 2 (where two-man crews were still the norm, a cameraman and a sound man), I told my crew we were going up to an office building in Downtown Crossing. It was the headquarters of one of those dumping grounds for ex-legislators.

The boss was a guy named Ditto Dan Foley, the former Senate majority leader from Worcester.

Ditto was accurately described by another Boston reporter as "a hot-tempered moron." It was said that Billy Bulger picked his number-two guy by giving an IQ test at the start of every session to the Democratic caucus. Whoever finished dead last would get the job. That was a joke, sort of.

Shakespeare wrote, "Uneasy lies the head that wears the crown."

But Billy Bulger slept like a baby—who wouldn't, if the guy behind you was Ditto Dan? He was one of those just-happy-to-be-there guys, like Chris Iannella for whom the parking space at City Hall was all important. Ditto's was under the arch at the State House, one of the primo spots—in other words, protected from the cold and precipitation, and just a few feet from the entrance.

After John Kerry was elected to the Senate, the lieutenant governor's space was up for grabs, and Kitty Dukakis, the alcoholic first lady of the Commonwealth, grabbed it. But one day someone beat her to it, so she just parked in Ditto's. Ditto arrived and, well, you can imagine the reaction of a hot-tempered moron who just happened to be—drumroll, please—the majority leader of the Massachusetts State Senate.

He double-parked, blocking the top of Mount Vernon Street, and stalked into the State House. One of the first cars behind him was from Channel 7, with one of my cameramen behind the wheel. He recognized the vanity Senate license plate and just sat stewing in his car for a while, awaiting Ditto's return.

When Ditto finally came back, with one of the Duke's coat holders in tow with the keys to move Kitty's car, my friend was not in a good mood. The assignment editor had been screaming at him over the two-way radio, asking him why he was running late for his next assignment. As Ditto finally returned to his Oldsmobile, my friend honked his horn to get Foley's attention. Then he jumped out of the station car and got into Ditto's face.

"Who's the asshole who just left his car double-parked here in the middle of the street?"

Ditto's face, always "ruddy," as the cops say, grew beet red.

"Who are you calling an asshole?" he screamed.

"Is that your car?" asked the cameraman, himself a bit of a hothead.

"Yes that's my car," Ditto sputtered.

"Then I guess I am calling you an asshole!" They almost came to blows, right there under the arches.

These were—and still are—the kinds of pressing issues that are the focus of life at the State House. In the next primary, some pretty boy took Ditto out, a guy who promised to be a "reformer" and then immediately went into the tank for Bulger. (As Billy used to say on St. Patrick's Day, "Show me a reformer and I'll show you someone who won't be back.")

The problem for Ditto was that after a lifetime of gainful unemployment, he now needed a job (which was not to be confused with "work"). So Bulger appointed him the boss of something called the Legislative Research Bureau. Mainly they researched the bars in the area. (Locke Ober downstairs was probably a little too pricey).

The other hack holding pen for ex-hacks, the Legislative Service Bureau, was on the fifth floor of the State House. Being off-site, the Research Bureau was the holding pen for the less presentable erstwhile statesmen. In addition to Ditto, there was a one-termer from the North End and one or two other ex-rep reprobates, forgotten but not gone.

On the elevator upstairs to Ditto's lair, I gave my crew instructions they never got from anyone else at the "nonprofit."

I told them to be prepared for some pushing and shoving, but that they should keep rolling no matter what. That's job one for any TV cameraman, obviously, at least if you don't work for a "nonprofit." But since it was WGBH, I figured I had to point out the obvious to them. They were somewhat surprised but seemed cool about it. It was going to be our little adventure. We got inside and as soon as I announced myself, the hacks scattered like roaches in a dark tenement kitchen when you flip on the lights.

We roamed through the offices, getting video of the usual nonsense, but for once, Ditto and the boys were smart enough not to mix it up. I had thin gruel at best. But then we arrived at their little kitchen and I saw an open box of doughnuts and crullers. Bingo!

The cameraman was a black guy, and I told him to get some tight shots of the pastries. I said this very loudly, with a sneer in my voice, because I wanted to make sure Ditto and his hench-hacks could hear me. In return for their no-heavy-lifting jobs, the payroll patriots were willing to take a lot of shit, but being made sport of over their doughnuts—that sort of provocation would not stand!

Ditto and a couple of them stormed into the kitchen and began pushing us out, down the hall, toward the elevator. I played it deadpan, identifying myself as being from WGBH (hah!) and calling him "Senator." They were rough with us, huffing and puffing, but no punches were thrown. Now I was getting exactly what I needed. I didn't want a fight, I wanted video.

When the elevator doors finally closed on us, my camera guys were pleased. This was something out of the ordinary, a day to remember. The white sound guy asked me how I had known there was going to be trouble.

"I had a hunch," I told him.

As the elevator door opened on the ground floor, the black guy chuckled.

"You know something Howie?" he said. "I know I'm black, but when it comes to Channel 2, you're the affirmative action hire."

My *Herald* column gave me more notoriety than being on a couple of semi-obscure late-night TV newscasts. But all these years later, I more clearly remember my television "columns," maybe because I always had to go back to the station and log the video and the sound cuts, and then give directions to whoever was in the editing suite.

There were public resources available that the *Globe* either refused to use, or hadn't figured out how effectively they could be employed. Divorce records, for one thing. Most of the files were public record. One ex–state senator was running up huge bills, spending wildly on his new girlfriend. I found this out because he had the same name as one of my radio engineers, and one month my guy got the ex–state senator's bill by mistake. He almost keeled over when he saw the balance.

I made a call to the estranged wife's lawyer and was told the bills had been filed as an exhibit. I went to the courthouse in East Cambridge, pulled the file and discovered the credit card bills, along with a motion by the politician's lawyer to impound them, lest a reporter discover them. The motion had been denied by the judge.

I photocopied the bills and wrote a column about the senator's champagne and floral expenses in New York. The next time I stopped by the courthouse I checked the file again, and the pol's lawyer had put in a new filing—a copy of my *Herald* column about the credit card bills.

Another time I got a tip that the wife of a state rep who was a plumber had accused him of taking a shit in the kitchen sink in the family home just before it was sold. I got the public document—which meant it was fair game, and I couldn't be sued—and then I called the state rep for a comment.

"Please," he begged. "You know me, Howie. You know I'd never do something like that."

Indeed I did. But, the complaint was public record. And I was giving him a chance to deny it. I wrote the column. The rep was defeated for reelection.

Drunk-driving arrests got ever juicier, as cops came to the same realization that I had—that once something was in a public record, it could be used for . . . whatever.

Gradually, more and more of the laconic *Dragnet*-like OUI incident reports were replaced by narratives that were good enough to read on the air, and that was exactly what I began doing. A solon would be ordered to count backward from 100, going down by seven each time.

Then the cop would record the response: 100 . . . 93 . . . 83 . . . 84. . . .

Even better was when they'd be asked to recite the alphabet, backward. Not a single legislator—I called them "solons," a Joe Heaney word—could ever pull that off.

You could always call the reps after they were bailed out the next day. If I called them twice and they didn't answer, I would write that they hadn't responded to "repeated" calls. But sometimes they were so hungover, or so stupid, that they picked up.

Once I got a guy from Worcester County who, after he was lugged, had pissed on a state trooper's boot. I caught up with him by phone the next afternoon and the poor slob explained to me how his life had fallen apart since his election a few years earlier.

"When I got to the State House," he told me, "I thought everybody was my friend. I'm not like you guys from Boston."

He thought I was a Boston guy, just because I could walk and chew gum at the same time. That's how dumb he was, below average even by Beacon Hill standards.

The more I tore up the people who had previously been off limits to reporters, the more information I got. Every day I'd sort my mail into two piles—letters with return addresses, and all the others that were sent anonymously. That second pile always got read first. That's where the dirt would be.

Everybody needed a nickname. Some caught on, some didn't. Sometimes I'd try to come up with them myself, other times the readers would pin the names on my targets. There was a corrupt senator from Milton who always changed his vote. One of my regular sources named him "Multiple Choice Joyce."

There were families of aspiring politicians who tried to mimic the Kennedys, right down to the hair, the rumpled suits, the affected Yankee accents of JFK. They were all over the state—the Markeys of Malden, the Creedons and Lawtons of Brockton, the Timiltys. The same guy who came up with Multiple Choice Joyce came up with the perfect description for those clans—K-Mart Kennedys.

I took credit for all the nicknames. Sometimes they were mean-spirited. A 400-pound House speaker became "D-Papa Gino's." I nicknamed one of Dukakis' coat holders with acne scars as "Scarface." His sister was a judge named Del Vecchio. I dubbed her "Let 'em Go" Del Vecchio.

I even had *Globe* sources. They were already starting their dreadful series of "affirmative action" hires that have continued to this very day. One day

I got a tip about a surly black lesbian who was basically refusing to do any work, knowing that she could never be fired due to her status in multiple protected classes.

A *Globe* reporter faxed me—yes, faxed!—an internal memo on her gold-bricking. I quoted it in some column or another, and as a kicker said, "Keep those faxes coming!"

Little did I know what would happen next. The *Globe* grandees were so angry that somebody had ratted out one of their sacred cows that they began going over every fax machine the paper owned, trying to figure out who'd sent me the information.

They ended up firing a young reporter, a decent kid I barely knew. And I certainly didn't realize he'd been the one sending me the dirt, because if I had known, I never would have mentioned, even inadvertently, how I came by the information. But that's how angry the *Globe* was about any sort of criticism.

Especially by the likes of me.

As far as I know, though, that was the only time I have ever burned a source. I love people who give me information, and even if I didn't, I would never flip on them. It would be bad for business.

For a few years after the last Winship retired to the Yankee redoubt of Lincoln, the *Globe* ran through a series of hopelessly incompetent editors. They finally did the unthinkable and promoted an Irish lifer. He didn't last long either. When he was shown the door, that Hibernian hoper gave an interview in which he said, "Nobody ever mentions Howie Carr when they talk about the *Globe's* problems."

I wish I could find the exact quote. I'd like to frame it and hang it on my wall, or at least tweet it out.

Sometimes, when kicking the ass of the ruling class, television could be more effective than print.

For instance, the most exclusive Yankee club in the city was the Somerset on Beacon Street near the top of the hill. A complaint was filed with the Licensing Board, demanding that their liquor license be pulled because of the Somerset's obvious discrimination against anyone who couldn't trace his lineage back to the *Mayflower*.

I set up my camera outside the club at lunchtime and videotaped all the swells coming in for lunch. I would loudly ask them to allow me to join them for a watercress sandwich with the crusts cut off, or maybe some finnan haddie.

I made sure my viewers got to see their archaic outfits—the cuffed trousers, the button-down collars, the wingtips, the patched elbows on their suit coats, the straw boaters (it was summer). Some of them tried to shoo me away. I told the story, from *The Proper Bostonians,* about an evening after World War II, when a blaze broke out in the club kitchen. The local fire company stormed up the front steps on Beacon Street but found their entrance blocked by an ancient Jeeves-like footman.

"I'm sorry, gentlemen," he said, "but this entrance is for members only. You must use the servants' entrance around back."

Another day for Channel 56 I followed up a *Globe* story about an ex–state senator who had been handed a no-show hack job after being defeated for reelection. He foolishly agreed to sit down for an interview. He was so nervous that he literally began sweating as I was questioning him, and the perspiration showed up on the videotape.

Another day, another ex–state senator got busted in a no-show job—he didn't even have a listed number for his post-election-loss "literacy program."

I called him and set up an interview—he was still delusional enough to believe he could resurrect his political career. When the camera was set up and he was seated, I asked him what the hell was going on and he stammered out something, then turned away from me and began speaking directly into the camera.

"I want to assure everyone who is watching this," he said, his voice cracking, "and everyone who is not watching this—"

Sometimes the reprobate reps didn't translate into good TV, but they still provided great newspaper copy. There was an ex–state rep from Dracut named Nick Lambros. After being convicted of a misdemeanor count of bribery, he lost his House seat by three votes. He then demanded a recount. During the proceedings, Nick was puffing on a cheap cigar when he made a statement I've always remembered.

"One thing you have to understand about my people," Lambros said. "They're very fucking stupid."

The great thing about people like Nick Lambros is that just because they were defeated, it didn't mean they went away. Where were they going to go, after all?

So Nick retreated to the Dracut Water Supply District, of which he was not only a commissioner but also superintendent. The town got its water from the nearby City of Lowell, and soon Dracut's bill began dropping by hundreds of thousands of dollars a year.

Somebody eventually put a surveillance camera inside the pump house, and guess what—Nick Lambros was going in at night and turning off the meter. We began calling Lambros "Nick at Nite."

I lifted a line from a *Lowell Sun* columnist—"Vote Lambros and get your water—hot!"

But Lambros still picked up the phone when I called. So I asked him about the day he'd talked about how very fucking stupid his constituents were. What kind of cigar were you smoking, Nick?

"Philly Blunts, that was my brand. It was the cheapest smoke I could find."

I asked him if he'd been stealing more than $500,000 a year in water from the City of Lowell for more than five years.

"Not really," he said.

This kind of journalism isn't exactly rocket science. You just keep your eyes open, take phone calls from anonymous sources, and then follow up with a few more calls yourself. The reps would dime each other out. For a *Boston* magazine column, I listed the 10 Dumbest Legislators.

I asked one of my sources—a former rep—how stupid one of his colleagues was.

"How stupid is he?" the ex-rep said. "He's a fucking Elk."

Technology was also starting to make my life easier, and not just with those drunk-driving police reports. Fax machines made it possible for me to get depositions from lawyers without having to drive downtown.

I still remember the first time I noticed that at the end of a deposition the affiant signs a statement saying his testimony is true—under pains and penalties of perjury. I kept reading that over and over in the happy realization that I could print anything in the deposition and not have to worry about any pushback.

Each medium reinforced the others.

One day I was out grabbing sound for a quick Channel 56 man-in-the-street, about Gov. Dukakis's then nascent presidential ambitions, and I saw a middle-aged woman walking toward the Green Line entrance, scowling. I asked her what she thought of Michael Stanley Dukakis.

"He's a henpecked wimp!" she snarled.

Another day I was at the State House for some silly press conference and, near the end of it, Gov. Dukakis said as an aside about his wife Kitty: "I don't know about the pillow talk at your home, but I go to sleep at night with Kitty's advice, counsel, and urgings ringing in my ears."

My cameraman just happened to be rolling. We used that sound cut for years, often butting it with, "He's a henpecked wimp!"

One time I was accused of assault after one of my stories ran on Channel 56. I'd confronted a Republican state committee member from Somerville whom I vaguely knew. I forget what we were after him for, but he was pissed. There was another GOP grifter named John Lakian whose campaign for governor in 1982 had disintegrated in a blizzard of lies. He'd claimed a "battlefield promotion" in Vietnam, and when he said he'd gone to Harvard, his wife had corrected him in front of a *Globe* reporter. She had pointed out that although Lakian had gone to school in Cambridge, it wasn't Harvard that he attended, it was the Cambridge Center for Adult Education.

A decade after that memorable gaffe, there were unfounded rumors that Lakian was about to buy the *Herald*. As my cameraman rolled, the GOP state committeeman began screaming at me:

"When Lakian buys that paper, you're going to be fired," he screamed. He was an old Yankee—swamper, I guess you'd have called him, because he certainly wasn't a Brahmin. "You know, Somerville used to be a nice place, until you bastards moved in and ruined it."

I beat that assault rap in Cambridge District Court. The judge was an old state rep from Lowell.

Another day, I did a story on the open race for John Finnegan's job as auditor after his decision to retire. The Democrat candidate was Rep. Joe DeNucci, from "Da Lake" in Newton, a former middleweight prizefighter, another dems-dese-dose type of guy.

I grabbed DeNucci on Beacon Hill as he was leaving the House chambers and he reluctantly agreed to do an interview.

"I must have rocks in my head for talkin' to you," he said. We made good use of that sound cut on television and radio for years.

It was entertaining TV, which is to say, fun TV. It also increased my . . . cachet, as a print reporter, to have the TV gigs. And it kept me sharp, working in what was, for better or for worse, the dominant medium.

The money wasn't great—$250 for each piece on Channel 56, the same as I earned for my monthly column in *Boston* magazine. But I needed the dough after the pay cut I'd taken when I was fired from Channel 7. I got along with the Channel 56 management too. At one point, they wanted to do an in-house promotional spot for me and they needed a politician to react in anger to my reports.

I asked Dapper O'Neil to help me out and he agreed. At one point, he had to get so angry that he would break a glass—a fake glass, obviously, a prop from Jack's Joke Shop—by squeezing it so hard. But there was a problem with the fake glass—it had chemicals in it or something—and when Dapper broke it, it burned his hand, not badly, but the general manager wanted to make it up to him somehow.

So he gave Dapper two Celtics tickets—we were the Celtics' TV station, at the height of the Larry Bird era. The GM's name was Walsh, and he was from Dorchester, so the Dap figured he could be honest with him. He looked at the tickets with disdain.

"What the hell do I care about African handball?" he sneered at Walsh. But I pointed out to Dapper how coveted they were, and he ended up giving them to the dishwasher at Amrhein's.

Later, they had a roast for Walsh, and they needed a funny video to break up the night, so I again recruited the Dap and we went out and did a *Dragnet*-style spoof of searching for Walsh. I cut in a lot of video of bums pissing on the Common, which we would occasionally grab for laughs while waiting for our next marks to wander by for a man-in-the-street interview.

Waste not, want not—those are words to live by and I always tried to find a way to "repurpose" any videotape that was available. Sometimes I wouldn't have time to go out with the crews to shoot new B-roll, so the stuff on the cutting-room floor came in handy.

By 1989, the organized-crime busts by the feds (other than the FBI of course) had finally begun, and one day the G-men lugged the Mafia crew that hung out at Heller's Café in Chelsea. It was right under the Mystic Tobin bridge. I told a female photographer to go over and get me an establishing shot, slowly panning down from the bridge to the entrance of the bucket of blood.

I was waiting for her when she came back to the station—I was using pre-produced chyrons of the text of the indictment and breaking it up with mug shots from the *Herald* morgue and needed some new video to mix in with the black-and-white stills. I asked her how it went and she smiled without saying anything and motioned me back to an editing suite where she inserted the tape for both of us to watch together.

The first time, she panned off the bridge to the entrance of the bar. Then she repeated the pan. On the third time, as she panned down to the entrance, a guy was standing at the front door, his back turned to the camera. He pulled down his pants and mooned her.

More laughs for the Christmas blooper reel!

The problem was, product like mine was expendable. It was only a matter of time until I got hit in a Gannett budget cut, and I did. I went back to Channel 2 for a few months, until I ran into a different problem. But by then, I was already on my way to my next career move.

9
"LADIES AND GENTLEMEN, THE BEAT GOES ON . . ."

I first listened to Jerry Williams when he went onto WBZ nights in 1969. I was a freshman at UNC suffering some culture shock from being back down South. So I got into the habit of listening to the clear-channel 50,000-watt Boston station on my new six-band Panasonic radio that I was so proud of.

I'd always loved radio, but I wasn't like Rush Limbaugh, dreaming of becoming a broadcaster even as a child. Like every other teenager, I just enjoyed Top 40 radio. It was all AM radio back then, and I tried to find different stations to listen to after dark. It's called DXing.

At Deerfield in the daytime, I listened to WHYN in Springfield and WPTR in Albany. After nightfall, I'd go back and forth, up and down the dial—WABC in New York, WKBW in Buffalo, WLS and WCFL in Chicago, CKLW in Detroit/Windsor, WPOP in Hartford.

But I never listened much to talk radio—not that there was all that much of it—until I started following Jerry Williams, formerly Jerry Jacoby of Brooklyn.

Born in 1923, he'd been a ratings monster in the sixties on WMEX in Boston, at 1510 on the AM dial, but I never heard him there. I was too young, and

WMEX didn't reach western Massachusetts. I started listening to Jerry during my freshman year at Chapel Hill. I was homesick for New England, and I'd listen to both Jerry and the overnight guy, Larry Glick, who'd sometimes call pay phones at truck stops in places like Pensacola.

In Kennebunkport, where I worked summers, I listened to the Boston rockers—WMEX, which had a north–south directional signal, and WRKO, the Top 40 giant, formerly the flagship of the old Yankee network, which my aunts would always listen to in Portland, and which had been a real snooze fest. Top 40 was great for riding around in a car, obviously, or hanging out in the dorms. But sometimes you wanted something different, or I did anyway.

My job at the Colony Hotel in 1970 was in the Marine Room bar. Nights, I'd be washing glasses. I'd bring my radio into the room back of the bar and tune in to Jerry Williams. This was after Kent State, and his show had taken a hard anti-war turn.

One night he got a call from a World War II veteran from Worcester who was all bent out of shape by the anti-war demonstrations that had been convulsing the nation.

Jerry goaded him. He was a master of drawing a caller out. The guy sounded like the title character "Joe" in the then current movie about a hard hat (Peter Boyle) hunting down hippies. Or maybe Archie Bunker, who was still months away from his *All in the Family* debut on CBS. Finally, Jerry's caller said he didn't give a damn about hippies, and that he was going to organize a "hard hat brigade" of World War II vets to fight in Vietnam.

For the rest of the summer, it was a recurring gag on the show. Whenever the calls lagged, Jerry would ask "Joe" to call back and tell him how the recruiting was going for the hard hat brigade.

In the fall of 1972, back in Chapel Hill, I was watching Walter Cronkite one night and he mentioned that at a Democratic campaign rally that day, Sen. George McGovern had played the tape of a call made by an emotional Vietnam vet to a "Boston radio talk show host."

I knew instantly who it was. I felt the same kind of secondhand fan's pride I would feel later when George Frazier, my favorite *Globe* columnist, made Richard Nixon's White House Enemies List.

Wherever I went, I always had the radio turned on, either in my car or wherever I was living at the time. In Winston-Salem, I not only listened to the radio, I covered the local AM-FM scene. It was one of my beats. I was given a tour of the new computerized FM country station, WTQR—the future of radio, as it turned out, for better or for worse. I did a story about the local dollar-a-holler religious station, where all the time slots were for sale, except for Sunday mornings at 11, when they couldn't give the time away.

"Nobody wants to be on then," the GM explained, "because only the damned are listening then. Everybody else is in church."

I'd never thought of that before.

Back in Massachusetts and working for the *Herald,* I occasionally went on the radio as a guest. For awhile the *Herald American* had an evening show on WITS, which was WMEX with new call letters. It had taken the name of the *Daily News'* show on WOR in New York—the Bulldog Edition. Peter Lucas, the *Herald's* political columnist, was the host most nights, and I was his number-one fill in. It was fun. Hell, it was radio.

As for my own personal listening habits, like everyone else I soon abandoned WRKO, the Top 40 AM rocker of my youth, for WBCN, the Rock of Boston. The music was migrating to the FM dial, and all the AM rockers I'd listened to in my youth were switching to talk.

In 1981, WRKO flipped, and in the afternoons, they brought back Jerry Williams from his days wandering around the country since he'd left WBZ. Always attuned to the zeitgeist, Jerry quickly zeroed in on Mayor Kevin White.

It was only a matter of time until I got the call. It was quite an honor, being in the same studio with one of the heroes of my youth. George Frazier was dead, I'd never take a bounce pass in the Garden from Havlicek, I wouldn't be roaming the outfield at Fenway with Yaz. But now, I was in a studio with Jerry Williams.

He was short, and wore boots that seemed to have lifts in them. He was pudgy, he was cheap—but Jerry was a goddamn radio genius. Sometimes I've wondered how much money he could have made if he'd come along 30 years later. Howard Stern was good, but how good could Jerry Williams have been?

Kevin White quickly realized he was being destroyed, four hours a day, from 2 to 6. Jerry had a Kevin impersonator, who went on and on about bein' mayah of the Shitty of Boston. Finally one day in 1982, just before I was hired at Channel 7, the impersonator went too far, and somebody had to take the fall. Jerry's loyal producer drew the short straw.

I wrote what I thought was a measured column about it, but apparently it wasn't measured enough for Jerry. He went on screaming tirades about me, and I figured my radio career was over almost before it began.

Paper Boy

In the summer of 1988, the Democratic Party was about to nominate Gov. Mike Dukakis as its presidential candidate in Atlanta. Everybody in the Boston media was there—newspapers, radio, and television. As usual, I was working for the *Herald* and Channel 56. One of my jobs was to keep a count of all the hacks on the state payroll who were taking the week off.

I'd just stroll around Peachtree Street or hang out in the hotel lobbies, soaking in the hack ambience. Every morning, I'd call back to Boston, where Eric Fehrnstrom, a young State House reporter who would someday work for Mitt Romney, would take down the names I'd seen the previous day. Then he would head across the street to the comptroller's office, where he would get the most up-to-date salaries, after which he'd call me back and I'd insert them into the next day's column.

(It's so much simpler today, when you can just go online and see anyone's salary—or pension—history.)

The *Herald* was sharing a suite with the *New York Post*, which Murdoch had sold earlier that year, after the Fat Boy controversy (which I'll get to later), so that he could retain his new TV station in New York. I was just sitting around when Jerry Williams's producer showed up, introduced herself, and asked me if I'd like to go on the radio show on WRKO that afternoon.

Absolutely! Jerry basically asked me what was going on and I read off a list of Dukakis's payroll patriots that I'd seen that morning. It was a very lengthy list. Jerry held me over for a second segment. It was such a hit that I was invited back the next day. My first exile from talk radio was over.

The entire Massachusetts delegation was ensconced in a single hotel, and they were passing the afternoons lounging by the pool. So one afternoon I grabbed one of the *Herald* photographers and we did some "sneaky stuff," as we used to call it at Channel 7. We took photos of everyone we could—including Joe DeNucci, who again must have had rocks in his head to get caught like that.

Next morning, we had the photos in the *Herald* on a double truck, with the headline "Hacking Around in Atlanta."

When I got on the plane back to Boston Friday morning, I noticed DeNucci was also on the flight. If looks could kill . . .

Back in Massachusetts, a lot of people mentioned what a good job I'd done in Atlanta. But most of them didn't mention the *Herald* or Channel 56. They talked about my afternoon reading of the hacks' names and their salaries on Jerry's talk show.

I ran into Marty Meehan, the future congressman, then a coat holder at the State House. He was a Lowell guy, that's how I knew him. His father Buster worked in the pressroom of the *Lowell Sun*, then a very solid newspaper, where Frank Phillips and others had gotten their starts.

Marty mentioned how I'd made him famous in Lowell by outing him as a delegate and listing his salary at the Secretary of State's office. I nodded and said, yeah, the *Herald* sold well in Lowell.

"Not the *Herald*," Marty said with a smile. "They heard you on the radio."

When Dukakis left the convention in Atlanta, he had a 17-point lead in the national polls. It was not a good feeling, knowing that the likely next president of the United States detested me and had publicly described me as a "nut cake" and a sociopath. When he nominated one of my Deerfield classmates for a judgeship, in the interview the Duke had pointedly asked him, "What did you people do to Carr at Deerfield?"

Fortunately, the Duke thought it was a Massachusetts election—once he'd gotten the Democrat nomination, it was all over. As George H. W. Bush criss-crossed the country, the Duke vacationed in western Massachusetts.

Even when Bush came to Boston and went on a boat tour of Boston Harbor, to show how incompetently the Duke had handled the federal court-mandated cleanup, Dukakis did next to nothing in response.

Meanwhile, at the *Herald*, we got our marching orders from the Murdoch organization—the paper was to be all anti-Dukakis, all the time. The Duke had been calling Massachusetts a "national model," and sure enough it was, for waste, fraud, and abuse.

Per Rupert's orders, it was all hands on deck for the *Herald* to stop Dukakis. One day in October I decided to throw a changeup and write about a local Massachusetts race. I told the editor, Ken Chandler, that I needed a break.

"Well, okay," he reluctantly said, "just don't make it too long."

I was nervous right up until the election. There were rumors that Bush was going to be busted for an alleged extramarital affair and taken out *a la* Gary Hart, but it never happened. In the end, Dukakis was blown out. He lost 42 states. The next night he was back in Brookline. He would lose his Secret Service protection the next day.

He was spotted in the Star Market on Beacon Street in Brookline, pushing a shopping cart, by himself, trailed by his Secret Service detail. Kitty had ordered him to do the shopping, after he'd been dogging it all year. It was the most embarrassing photo of him since he'd ridden around in the tank in Michigan, or maybe when he returned from the campaign trail to Perry Street and Kitty had made him cut the postage-stamp-sized lawn, with his ancient rotary push mower, while wearing his pressed suit pants and wingtips.

In other words, he was still a henpecked wimp.

The late Governor's Councilor Sonny McDonough had always said, "Lame duck is my favorite dish," meaning, it's easier to roll a politician on his way out, who's either not running or has been defeated for reelection. Soon Dukakis was a lame duck. The state was in shambles. The third term, as always, had become a disaster, and a fourth wasn't in the cards.

One day in the spring of 1989, I wrote a column about Sen. Ed Burke of Framingham. He was one of two Burkes in the Senate—Burke the Lesser and Burke the Least, as I called them, after the fashion of the two St. James's, the Greater and the Lesser. It was a Catholic reference.

Sen. John Burke (the Least) was from Holyoke. He later became a court officer, fetching coffee for judges in the 413 area code.

Ed Burke (the Lesser) was married to the personnel director of the Massachusetts Water Resources Authority (MWRA), the state's newest hack agency. It was very convenient for all concerned, and we would soon learn that some of Whitey Bulger's cocaine dealers had been hired for less-than-arduous work at the MWRA after the traditional nationwide searches.

I wrote a column about Burke the Lesser and his lovely bride, and soon thereafter, his opponent in the next election showed up at an event in Framingham and began passing out copies of the piece to the assembled voters.

Burke, who was quite tall, must have been feeling the heat, because he physically assaulted his political foe, and began throttling him. It was just another night in Lame Duck Land until a columnist for the local newspaper in Framingham, Ron Doyle, decided to write a column about the attack.

Doyle said that it was Howie Carr who had driven this extinguished, er, distinguished public servant over the edge. But, he added, it could just have as easily been done by Jerry Williams or Barbara Anderson, the Marblehead woman who ran the state's leading anti-tax group, Citizens for Limited Taxation (CLT).

In fact, Doyle wrote, in this lame-duck world of Massachusetts politics, Mike Dukakis was no longer calling the shots. The three real governors, he wrote, were Williams, Carr, and Anderson.

I don't think he meant it as a compliment, but that's the way we three took it. We had just been promoted. That Tuesday afternoon, Barbara and I went over to WRKO studios just outside Fenway Park, and the first meeting of "The Governors" was convened.

It became a weekly two-hour segment on the Tuesday afternoon show, from 4 to 6. Jerry would ask if we had any new business and, guess what, we always did. I would routinely mention the previous Sunday's Hack Family of the Week in the *Herald*, with salaries. Sometimes I would go over a list of names and ask Jerry if he would like to guess whether they worked in the public or, as I put it, the Dreaded Private Sector.

Barbara would mention pending bills, or referendum drives to cut taxes or some other anti-Dukakis initiative. Those two hours—4 to 6 Tuesday afternoons—became the highlight of my workweek. It became fun to go to work again, the way it had been like covering Freddie Langone's Parkman House hearings at City Hall.

The other exhilarating part of what became "The Governors" was the reaction. It absolutely drove the powers that be crazy. Soon there was a drumbeat of criticism, decrying the sudden lack of "civility" in Massachusetts politics.

Some of it was blamed on "tabloid" journalism (as if there were more than one tabloid in Boston), but mostly it was blamed on us. Most of the barbs came from the columnists at the *Globe*, a dreary lot indeed, none close in talent to the late George Frazier but all utterly full of themselves, the latest incarnation of those paralyzing snore-mongers Tom Wolfe had written about in *The New Journalism*.

Williams was dismissed by the bow-tied bum kissers as an "entertainer." He always took that label as a dismissive insult. He wanted to be taken seriously, whatever seriously meant. I tried to tell him that he should take it as a compliment, that they wouldn't be writing about him if he weren't having an effect.

One of them described Jerry and me as using "McCarthyite" tactics, a tired cliché, nothing more than a way of saying they disagreed with our politics, so we must be evil, i.e., like Joe McCarthy. I'd grown up hearing from my father and my uncle Ray that McCarthy wasn't nearly the ogre that he'd been made out to be by his enemies. Later on I found out that the Kennedys, including Bobby, felt exactly the same way. Maybe it was an Irish thing.

Finally, the *Globe* decided to do a story, or actually a series, on "The Governors." Every knock a boost. We didn't care. If anything, it would only increase my cachet at the *Herald*.

Paper Boy

By this time, I was also back working one day a week for *The Ten O'Clock News* on Channel 2. Chris Lydon, the anchor, seemed to like having me around, but I wasn't so sure about the rest of them. Public television was never a good fit for me. There was another problem—Channel 2 took a lot more time out of my day than Channel 56 ever had. Everything was . . . slower. It took maybe twice as long to go out and get the tape and then come back and cut it.

What can I say? It was, and is, a nonprofit.

Still, I didn't want to give it up—I still thought any TV news experience made me a sharper columnist (and now radio host). But it was now fourth on my list of priorities, after the *Herald*, WRKO, and *Boston* magazine, where I still had the monthly political column.

The *Globe* had assigned a bunch of younger reporters to go after us. This was a way for the little rich kids who'd just blown into Massachusetts to make their bones, I suppose.

I wasn't that worried, because I'd realized that as far as the corporate media were concerned, I was an Untouchable, in the Indian, as opposed to the Chicago, meaning of the word. I was . . . unclean. Under no circumstances would I ever be hired by the *Globe* or any other "reputable" organization. I carried the mark of the beast, as written in the Book of Revelation. I had rejected "the Word."

The series would begin on a Sunday. For a few weeks, I would drive down to the self-service gas station on Route 2A in Acton, where I had moved after fleeing Somerville. I'd check out the pile of Sunday *Globe*s. Nothing, until one weekend I got there and perused the front page. I quickly scanned the headlines and concluded that once again, they'd put it off. But then my eyes returned to one headline:

Poisoned Politics

So that's what we were—poisoned politics. Or had we poisoned politics? They didn't lay a glove on us—they were, after all, *Globe* reporters, legacies, pampered pukes. The only thing I can specifically remember was a description of me as having "a chip on my shoulder the size of Texas," which I suppose was sort of true.

The *Globe* said we had been "instrumental in either creating or aggravating the poisonous climate" of state politics. Some, the *Globe* said, making it clear that it included itself in this high-minded group, considered us "overrated egotists who pander to a constituency of narrow-minded cranks."

Well, as long as it was nothing personal.

Like the administration of their hero, Mike Dukakis, the *Globe* always had a lot of nationwide searches. Thus, Taylors followed Taylors as publishers. In the editorship, Tom Winship Jr. succeeded Tom Winship Sr. In the British sense, *Globe* peerages were hereditary, rather than lifetime, at least for the Yankees at the top of the masthead.

At the time, the political editor was Benjamin Crowninshield Bradlee Jr., the son of *Washington Post* editor Ben Bradlee, who'd made his journalistic bones covering up the assorted scandals of John F. Kennedy, including his first marriage (which was not to the future Jackie Onassis).

As a reporter, Bradlee *fils* customarily wrote some of the longest, most meandering leads I'd ever read. Obviously, he'd never spent much time watching straphangers read newspapers on the subway. On the Orange Line, you learn fast that the quickest way to lose a reader's attention is to write an impenetrable lead sentence.

Little Boy Blue Bradlee was also married, but not for long, to my old TV-news pal, Martha Bradlee, soon to reclaim her maiden surname of Raddatz.

In those days, "The Governors" were sometimes included in polls with other state politicians, because that's what we were. I remember comparing my numbers, before and after the four-part series, and my unfavorable numbers had gone up 20 points. But so had my favorability ratings. So basically, the *Globe* had just introduced me to a huge new number of people who'd never heard of me previously, and while four days of solid vitriol from the *Globe* made half the population dislike me more . . . it also made the other half of the population appreciate me more.

The only problem for me was that the series emboldened the *Globe* to come after Channel 2, which was run by a very *Globe*-like crew of blue-blood suburbanites. Before, Chris Lydon had once introduced one of my pieces—maybe the scuffle with Ditto Dan Foley's crew—by saying that if any of the viewers had read or heard about me and were offended, "then now is the moment to avert your eyes."

One of the *Globe* columnists was David Nyhan. He had just written a campaign hagiography of Dukakis (currently available at your favorite used-book site for $1.53). None of the *Globe* people liked me, obviously, but some tolerated me, or at least detested me less than some of the others.

Nyhan was shocked, shocked that some shanty Irish mucker like myself would be permitted on public television, i.e., *their* television. He wrote an entire column suggesting the crowd who supported Channel 2 should withhold at least some of their contributions as long as my "below-the-belt journalism" was permitted on *The 10 O'Clock News.*

I think he mentioned only withholding some token sum—perhaps a quarter—but the threat was clear, not to mention unprecedented. I was gone from Western Avenue very quickly. Nobody likes getting fired, of course, but anyone who's been fired more than once knows that some sacks are more painful than others.

It was odd to me how obsessed the Irish on Morrissey Boulevard all seemed to be with aping (I don't know any better word to use) their Yankee bosses. Nyhan had led the charge to get rid of the Jewish editor who succeeded his hero Winship, who lived in Lincoln, the uber-Yankee town where "street columnist" Mike Barnicle had moved as soon as he made the grade as a *nouveau riche* Beautiful Person.

The editorial page editor who followed a Yankee dowager from Cambridge named Cabot was another professional Irishman named Marty Nolan. He was so successful in his social climbing that his second wife was actually a Weld, as in Gov. William Weld, not to mention the old financial firm, White, Weld.

Nolan liked to point out that I'd gone to Deerfield Academy, as if that made me, I don't know, a phony or something. It was pointedly mentioned in *Poisoned Politics* that my parents were "staff" (as opposed to faculty). I guess I wasn't the only one who had noticed the *Upstairs, Downstairs/Downton Abbey* angle to my life.

In *New York* magazine, Pete Hamill once described the colonization of Gaelic Ireland by the English. He wrote that there was always a certain type of Irish who were, basically, collaborators, or quislings. Whenever the native population would take up arms against their English masters, that crew of Irish would flee to the nearest castle, and the armed protection of their Protestant English masters.

Thus, they became known to those subsisting in the peat bogs, still speaking their native Celtic tongue, as "castle Irish."

That's how I regarded them at the *Globe*—castle Irish. People are no longer taught that there were other kinds of minstrel shows beyond blackface. There was Pat & Mike, the Irish tosspots. For a while in the 1980s, the *Globe* owned a monthly golf magazine, which once ran a knee-slapper about how the Irish who worked replanting turf on the golf courses had to be instructed "Sod Side Up."

Uncle Dudley didn't catch the slur. Nor did anyone else at Affiliated Publications. Their loyal retainers—Pat & Mike—didn't care if their kinsmen were the butt of ethnic slurs.

A few weeks after the *Globe* series, the *Washington Post* sent Howard Kurtz up to do a story on me. It started with me on the air at WRKO doing a reading from the previous Sunday's Hack Family of the Week, on my old nemesis, Ditto Dan Foley of Worcester, and the rest of his gainfully unemployed family.

I mentioned Ditto, the hot-tempered moron, his brother the Senate door opener, another brother who was a "senior assistant deputy superintendent" somewhere, a daughter at UMass who was "director of administration and external affairs," a nephew who was a part-time guard at the Worcester jail, etc., etc.

Total: $344,338 a year.

Ditto was asked to comment: "I have nothing to say about his so-called journalism."

Kurtz also got a comment from Bradlee, who harrumphed about *Poisoned Politics*:

"The effect of the series was to say enough is enough," he said. "Some people are saying it's high time the *Globe* stood up."

Such has always been the white man's burden in Massachusetts. Someone must stand up to the Fenian rabble, and Little Boy Blue Bradlee was up to the task of putting us back in our place. Not unlike back in 1834, when his ancestors burned down the Ursuline Convent in Charlestown.

Anyway, Nyhan whacked me at Channel 2, but he got his comeuppance a few years later. He was chatting up a future editor of the *Globe*, Brian McGrory. McGrory got his job the old-fashioned *Globe* way, because he was somehow related to spinster Kennedy groupie Mary McGrory, a political sob sister for a couple of different Washington newspapers.

Anyway, WASP wannabe Nyhan asked the younger "hoper" McGrory if he could join his fellow Pats & Mikes in a pickup basketball game.

McGrory said no, his wife wouldn't approve, and Nyhan sneered that McGrory was "pussy whipped." It was one of those classic gaffes—the unfortunate telling of an inadvertent truth. Much hilarity ensued, with Nyhan eventually forced to issue what *The New Yorker* called a "groveling" apology.

A few years later, in 2001, Nyhan "retired" at age 61, the same year Nolan took the pipe. The *New York Times* had bought the Boring Broadsheet in 1993 for $1.1 billion, then spent an even more preposterous $300 million for the still more dreadful *Worcester Telegram*. The Ochs-Sulzberger clan didn't have the same bemused tolerance for the endles drunken Pat & Mike–style minstrelsy as the Taylors.

In 2004, though, Nyhan and all the rest of the Dukakis-era rump swab were looking forward to a restoration of sorts—when John Forbes Kerry would reclaim . . . well, something.

But it was not to be, and Kerry's drubbing was a devastating blow to the geriatric coat holders at state-run media's crumbling edifice on Morrissey Boulevard. Even Hunter S. Thompson would kill himself in February 2005, after the Super Bowl, when he realized that with Kerry's loss, he had no new asses to kiss.

Nyhan didn't even make it to the Super Bowl. A few days after W's second inauguration, he was clearing the snow at his manse in Brookline (like all his social-climbing ilk, he claimed to be from "Whiskey Point," as if he were still somehow a man of the people).

On this wintry day, Nyhan wore himself out shoveling snow, rather than his customary Democrat bullshit. He stumbled back inside his mansion and "took a heart attack," as I would always write in those columns of mine about Democratic hacks that so enraged him. Nyhan was DOA. Like Hunter S. Thompson, he'd kissed his last Democrat ass.

And I was my usual Timex-watch self. I took a licking and kept on ticking.

10
THE DAP

More than any politician I've ever known, Albert Leo "Dapper" O'Neil was *sui generis*—one of a kind, unique.

I first met him when I was assigned to City Hall in 1980. One of the other *Herald American* guys was introducing me around before a meeting, and when we reached Dapper, he looked at me with a sneer.

"And where do you live?" he practically yelled.

"Somerville," I said.

"Somerville?" the Dap said, suddenly deflated. "You know, I was going to say something snide, but now that I know you're from Somerville, I just have one thing to say to you. I pity you!"

Later I realized that was one of his shticks, asking people where they lived. If you weren't from Boston, and couldn't vote for him, you became a prop in his act. I remember Lenny Zakim, for whom the bridge is now named. He came to a City Council hearing one day. Dapper immediately sniffed him out—it was probably his New Jersey accent—and asked Zakim for his address.

"Franklin Street," he said. It's downtown, with office buildings.

"Franklin Street?" Dapper snapped. "You don't live on Franklin Street pal. I'm asking you, where do you live?"

Newton, Zakim admitted. The Dap looked over at the press and nodded in triumph.

"Newton!" he said. "Well, let me ask you this, Mr. Zakim. How do you like our restaurants?"

I'd been reading about Dapper for years. George Frazier once wrote that O'Neil could only be nicknamed "Dapper" in a city where buying a suit of clothes with two pairs of pants was considered the height of fashion.

Born in 1920, Dapper grew up in Roxbury. His hero was James Michael Curley, his fellow Roxbury Irishman. After Army service in World War II, he returned to Boston, living with his mother who was a cashier in a lunchroom on Dudley Street. He tended bar at Meldon's, a workingman's watering hole in Roxbury. By night he poured Green River whiskey with Pickwick Ale chasers. By day he used his GI Bill benefits to attend Dr. Delbert Moyer Staley's School of the Spoken Word on Bay State Road.

The older Kennedy boys—Joe Jr. and the future president—were both trained there. So were the two Irish Democratic governors out of Roxbury—James Michael Curley and Maurice Tobin (as well as an Irish state rep from Roxbury named O'Connor who went to federal prison for income tax evasion in 1971).

Dapper O'Neil poses with a photo of his hero, Mayor James Michael Curley.

Dapper said Dr. Staley, who ran his school from 1905 until 1957, educated his students in how to, among other things, walk with both authority and dignity, and even more importantly, how to e-nun-ci-ate.

Dapper first ran for state rep in the early 1950s, against the previously mentioned rogue Charlie Iannello, who also ended up in prison. Dapper lost but in his City Hall office he kept fliers from that campaign, featuring a photo of himself with his fellow Staley School grad, Jim Curley.

I later read that in his final years, Curley charged young candidates $300 for an endorsement and an accompanying photograph. When I asked him about it, Dapper angrily denied that he'd been charged by the mayor, for whom he'd campaigned as a youth.

One of Dapper's most-treasured possessions was an LP of some of Curley's most familiar orations—another late-life income generator, along with an autobiography he wrote to cash in on his final burst of fame after *The Last Hurrah* was published and became a bestseller. For the title, Curley used a variation of the fictional mayor's final words—*I'd Do It Again.* Last time I checked, it was a collector's item on sale for $143 on my favorite used-book site.

Dapper was widely regarded as the ultimate old-school politician, but the fact is, he ran for office repeatedly in the fifties and sixties yet never won . . . until television became the dominant medium and he could show off all those techniques he'd learned from Dr. Staley.

In 1962 he was the driver for Democratic gubernatorial candidate Endicott "Chub" Peabody, JFK's Harvard College '39 classmate, a football All-American who was said to have played too long without a helmet. The other joke about Chub was that he had three towns in Massachusetts named after him—Endicott, Peabody, and Marblehead. Sometimes a fourth was added—Athol.

After Chub won, he promised Dapper the job of chief secretary—meaning, patronage. But the Dap was a bit too raw for that sensitive position, so Peabody quickly exiled him to the Boston Licensing Board, which controlled liquor licenses in the city.

It was a perfect fit for the Dap. He was soon defending his . . . constituents . . . against the slings and arrows from the local newspapers. Even as an appointed official, Dap was already using a pickup truck and a bullhorn to harangue his foes. When the *Record American* undertook a series against the Licensing Board, Dapper took his truck to Winthrop Square and challenged the managing editor, Eddie Holland, who had a Chinese girlfriend, to debate him.

"We'll do it in Chinatown, Eddie," he yelled. "Because I know how much you like that sweet and sour!"

In 1967, Dapper ran for mayor. Hey, it was an open seat. Why not? With the black migration transforming his old neighborhood of Roxbury, one of Dapper's slogans was, "We work. Why don't they?"

It was the Summer of Love, and not just in San Francisco. The hippies were camping out on the Common. Dapper took his sound truck and bullhorn to Tremont Street, stood up in the back and hurled bars of soap at the hippies.

"When I'm elected," he bellowed, "all you birds are going to get a good bath—and a shave!"

He finished eighth, with less than one percent of the vote. He never won any race for anything other than the City Council—he ran and lost for Suffolk County sheriff three times. So he went back to the Licensing Board, but in 1970, his term was about to expire.

The Republican governor, Frank Sargent, was an amiable Yankee from Dover who had succeeded John Volpe when he quit the Corner Office to become Nixon's first secretary of transportation. After Dapper's antics, "Sarge," as he was known, was not inclined to reappoint him. He just wanted to get reelected, and he'd already picked his running mate, an ethnic obviously—Rep. Marty Linsky from Brookline.

As a member of the Licensing Board, by law Dapper received Boston police reports of all incidents within a certain number of feet from any licensed establishment in the city. Dapper pored over the reports carefully every morning, just as he did the paid obituaries in the morning papers, to decide which wakes he'd be attending that evening. Dapper took a street-level approach to politics.

So imagine Dapper's surprise—his glee—as he was studying the daily BPD reports in his office at City Hall and noticed that District 4 police the previous night had pulled over a car driven by Linsky. His companion: a convicted prostitute. Linsky told the cops he was just giving her a ride.

The way the Dap told the story, he then went to Sarge or one of his people, and waved the BPD report in his face. Dapper smelled seven more years of job security but Sarge was outraged by Dap's attempted shakedown.

A couple of days later, the prostitute story was leaked to the papers, and Linsky was dropped from the ticket and replaced by Donald Dwight of Holyoke, a Deerfield graduate 20 years ahead of me. Two years later Linsky ran for

Congress against Whitey Bulger's old patron Robert Drinan, lost, and eventually got a job at, where else—the Kennedy School at Harvard.

Dapper wasn't reappointed to the Licensing Board, but he wasn't unemployed long. He'd run for the City Council in 1969, finishing tenth, just below the top nine candidates who were elected. But in the fall of 1970, City Councilor Louise Day Hicks won the congressional seat John McCormack had held for 44 years. When she resigned from the Council to become the new Congresswoman, the Dap was sworn in as her replacement.

He would remain on the Council for 29 years—until January 2000.

As counterintuitive as it might seem, his shtick was absolutely made for TV. Dapper spoke in sound bites. He never bothered to master the intricacies of the city budget the way Freddie Langone did, but the fact was, under the city code, the mayor had all the power anyway.

In the mornings, the Dap would attend hearings—at the Licensing Board, which he still dominated as if he were its chairman, or the Zoning Board of Appeals, etc. If the hearing was contested, he would bring two envelopes with him, one in favor of whatever the proposal was, the other opposed.

Dapper would check out the size of each faction, and most often make his decision based on which group was larger—with more potential votes in the next election.

Then he would head down to his office on the fifth floor and check out the obituary pages and plan his itinerary for the evening. One night for a *Boston* magazine column I tagged along with him on his nightly rounds. We hit a Chinese wake in Kenmore Square—"Let's go in and grab some dimes," Dapper said, after the Chinese custom of wrapping dimes in wrapping paper for the mourners to take. We hit a wake at the Langone Funeral Home, in the West End near City Hall.

One of the old connected Italians who knew Dapper from his Licensing Board days doddered up to Dapper and complained about his replacement, a good-looking female lawyer who wasn't as amenable, shall we say, to compromise.

"Dapper," he rasped, "we gotta get ridda that douchebag on the board."

I still remember that because I mentioned it for the column in *Boston* magazine, and it got Dapper in a jam for a moment, because he didn't defend his successor. Another time, on a Friday afternoon, I needed a few items for the *Herald American's* Sunday notes column, "Pols & Politics." I walked downstairs and asked Dapper about his campaign for the board of the Massachusetts Municipal

Association against some Yankee dowager from the North Shore. I told Dapper I wanted a quote.

"I'll bury the broad," he helpfully said.

A couple of weeks later he called me up and asked me if I'd written something about the race. I reminded him of my visit to his office. He remembered and then he told me the selectwoman from Hamilton or Wenham or some such place was using the quote against him in the campaign. He didn't give a shit, he just didn't remember saying it. He lost.

When Don Forst took over the *Herald*, he wanted to meet with so-called community leaders. Even Dapper. He invited him to our building in the South End, at the intersection of the Mass Turnpike extension and the Southeast Expressway. From Forst's office, you could see the cars headed south.

Sitting with his top editors, New Yorkers recruited from the *Globe*, Forst asked the Dap what they could do to make the *Herald* a better newspaper, to better serve Boston.

Dapper stood up, theatrically, as always. He strolled over to the window and pointed out at the southbound traffic.

"What can you do?" he said. "All-a you can go out there and get on that fucking highway and go back to New York where you belong!"

Wherever he went the Dap packed a gun, a .38-caliber Police Special revolver. He had a shoulder holster. Billy Bulger used to joke about him at his annual St. Patrick's Day breakfast.

"Don't you feel safer, knowing that Councilor O'Neil is armed and at large." Pause. "He's a city councilor at large. At large. In more ways than one."

Dapper was one of the few pols in Boston who didn't feel obligated to attend the annual standing-room-only slobberfest at what I dubbed Halitosis Hall, lifting a line from the British satirical magazine *Private Eye*.

One year I asked Dapper if he was planning to head over to Halitosis Hall on Sunday morning.

"Are you kidding?" he said. "Who wants to go somewhere where you can't piss for four hours?"

One night in the 1970s, after being reelected, he was driving home to Roslindale on Washington Street, under the then elevated Orange Line. He noticed a light on in a trailer that belonged to one of the losing Council candidates. Dapper pulled over, took out his gun and made a citizen's arrest on a burglar who had several outstanding out-of-state warrants on him.

Howie Carr

Another night, the Dap was eating out with a buddy of his at Amrhein's in the Lower End in South Boston. It was spring, and it was still light as Dapper and his buddy left the restaurant. Outside, they were confronted by a guy with a knife, who mugged them, then took off running toward the Broadway station.

Dapper pulled out his gun and ordered the mugger—whose name was something like Eddie Linberger—to stop. When he didn't, Dapper shot him in the back, wounding him. On the way to Boston City Hospital, in the ambulance, Linberger writhed in pain and asked the EMTs:

"Why'd he shoot me? All I wanted was his money."

A year or so later, it looked like Dapper had gotten lucky. He was a Democrat, of course, but he loved Ronald Reagan, and endorsed him, even accompanying him on a swing through Bristol County. That had included a campaign stop where the Dap had scoped out Nancy Reagan and then turned to the accompanying reporters and said:

"Not a bad tush, for an old broad."

Dapper was tired of the Council—"the Munsters," he called them, after the old 60s black-and-white TV comedy show whose reruns he watched every afternoon in his fifth-floor office overlooking City Hall Plaza. He wanted to be the next U.S. marshal—a plum patronage job controlled by the new president.

Reagan was game to reward his loyal Democrat supporter, but Dapper had to clear one final hurdle—a background check by the FBI. A couple of months later, Dapper got the bad news. His pal Dutch couldn't give him the job. The background report was that bad. Dapper was devastated, so he decided to find out who'd ruined his chances for a dream job. Like all the people dubbed the Worst by *Boston* magazine, Dapper began a manhunt for those who had screwed him.

He even filed a Freedom of Information Act (FOIA) request for the actual report. Normally, he would have scorned such a reform as a tool of "the social-planning liberal do-gooders." But now it would come in handy.

The day the FBI sent over the report, Dapper called me and I went downstairs to see him. He was raging in his office, pacing back and forth under the framed photograph of James Michael Curley, shouting random obscenities. His two female secretaries, who would later sue him for workplace abuse, were cowering in fear.

As I walked in, Dapper was holding up one of the pages in the FBI report to the overhead fluorescent light. He was trying to read the names of the people who'd been interviewed by the feds. Their names had all been redacted—blacked out.

132

Dapper figured if he held up the pages to the light, he could somehow read the names that had been removed.

I explained to him that these weren't the originals, these were copies. There was no way we could figure out who had ratted him out to the G-men. He unleashed another wave of obscenities before finally giving up, going back to his desk and lighting up a Kool. Then he went back to reading what these anonymous character assassins had said about him.

He read from the report: "O'Neil is well-known in the community as a reprobate."

Dapper looked up at me. "Reprobate? What the hell is a reprobate?"

He kept turning the pages until finally his eyes lit up. One of the social-planning liberal do-gooders apparently had forgotten to tell the feds to redact his name. Now Dapper had someone he could go after. His name was Eddie Linberger, the jailbird he'd shot in the Lower End. He was still in state prison, as a parole violator.

I wrote my column, with Linberger's name included. The next morning, I was back in Dapper's office when one of his secretaries timidly approached his desk.

"Councilor," she whispered. "There's someone on the phone wants to speak to you." Dapper looked at her curiously. Usually whoever called was put right through.

"Well, who is it?"

"It's Ed Linberger. He's calling collect from the prison."

The Dap jumped up from his desk. "Ed Linberger!" He took a deep breath, composed his thoughts as his face again turned a bright crimson in rage. Finally, he spoke again. "You tell that bearded fucking little weasel I don't take collect calls from bearded fucking little weasels." She started backing out of the office as Dapper thought of something else.

"No wait," he said. "Tell him that I plan to see him again—at his next parole board hearing."

The Dap was a triple-threat pol—great on television, great in print, even great on the radio. Years later he was in the WRKO studio with me and we were doing an hour or two about all the bums who'd overrun the city, squatting under bridges and on the Boston Common. I had one of my interns out on the Common, reprising my old man-in-the-street gig, only now it was bums in the street.

Dapper listened in on the headphones to one drunken wino who was slurring his words. Then he leaned into the microphone and growled at my intern.

"Ask him where he's from!" Dapper told him. Now he was reprising one of his old shticks—what's your address, pal?

The guy said Brockton or some such place. Dapper banged the table and said, "I knew it!"

He leaned into the mike and barked an order at my intern. "Ask that bird where he gets his check delivered."

And the answer was, of course, the package store on the corner.

The last time Dapper ran for sheriff he was going up against a clean-cut career bureaucrat who'd never run for office before. It was an open seat. The Dap called me one day and told me he'd gotten a great deal on his radio ads—he was only paying five bucks a spot. I was amazed. I asked what station was selling him five-dollar spots.

"WROL," he said, naming one of Boston's daytime-only AM stations. "It's for *The Irish Hour* on Saturdays. Everybody listens to that show, you know."

Everybody who voted for Dapper, that is. All the state reps endorsed his opponent, and the guy raised enough money to buy TV spots. The *Herald* let the goo-goos—the Good Government types—pull out all the wacky pictures of Dapper over the years. They ran print and TV ads of Dapper promoting his record, *The Irish Belly Dancer*, posing in a trench coat and a Borsalino hat, waving a gun, etc.

Dapper lost.

He had a girlfriend—"my Helen," he called her. They'd been going together or so he said, for 50-some odd years. I never met her. He claimed to be quite the ladies' man. He once confided to a *Herald* editor—one of Forst's guys whom he'd told to go back to New York—that he had a foolproof way of finding out how serious a woman was.

He said he'd pick up a "broad" in a bar, offer to drive her home. Once they got inside, he'd say he was thirsty and ask for a glass of water.

"While she's in the kitchen, I take my pants off. When she comes back, either she's happy or she tells me to get the hell out. If she throws me out, I got time to get back to the bar and try to pick up another one."

A lot of Irish guys in those days had girlfriends but never got married until their mothers died. It was a cultural thing, I guess. One of my uncles in Portland was like that. But Dapper's mother had died in the early sixties, and he never popped the question to "my Helen." Instead he fled Roxbury, along with most of the rest of the white population. He moved into a third-floor apartment on Washington Street just outside Roslindale Square.

He never owned his own home. Like Ray Flynn back then, Dapper never had a checking account. Maybe it was a Depression-era hangover, or just old-line shanty Irish.

Mayor Curley's last surviving son, Frank Curley, a former Jesuit, used to say that his father had always told him never to put his money in a bank.

"I shouldn't even have to explain to you why," the governor told him.

As for Dapper, when he relocated to Ward 18—"God's country," he called it—he lived with his widowed sister Gert and his beloved German shepherd named Roger.

Was Dapper gay? I don't know for sure. If I had to guess, I would say, yeah, he probably was. I didn't care. He was just a guy who was fun to be around, and great copy.

He was always in the public eye, out every night at the wakes and in the barrooms, but ultimately he was a lonely guy. I remember one Sunday with my two older daughters, stopping by his third-floor apartment in Roslindale that he shared with his sister Gert, and my two kids eating ice cream while wearing Dapper's wide-brim gangster hats.

Later, I got a call one morning from a distraught Dapper. His voice cracking, he told me Gert had died. I expressed my condolences as best I could, but I wondered, why was I among the first people he was calling?

He would drive around the city in his big American sedan, with the vanity license plate "Ole Dap" and a bumper sticker that said "Liberals: An American Cancer."

Wherever he went, the Dap provided good entertainment—and copy—for anybody tagging along. That was usually me. One day he was doing a meet and greet with a community group in Charlestown near the projects with a couple of other city councilors. An obese, aging, toothless female townie started giving Dapper some lip. He endured her abuse for a while, but she kept interrupting him as he was trying to chat up more amiable voters.

Finally, he turned around to face the hag. He got right in her face.

"Listen," he said, "like my father used to say, I'm not in the shit business. I don't give it and I don't take it. And I'm sure as hell not gonna take any shit from a big fat fucking project rat like you."

Dapper then turned to Steve Murphy, a younger city councilor.

"Hey Steve," he yelled, pointing at his tormentor. "Watch out for this one! She's a real fucking piece of work."

He had another line to describe old ladies who publicly disputed his perorations, although he never used it in public. Later, with his friends, he'd shake his head.

"Imagine her out and about giving me the business at her age," Dapper would say. "She ought to be home, praying for a happy death."

Another one of his trademark lines, when asked how he'd do in the next election, was, "They won't be countin' my votes tonight, they'll be weighin' 'em."

He used to complain that the district councilors, especially in the light-voting black wards, got paid as much as him. But as time went on, his vote totals began to drop. Everyone's did; Dapper's just went down faster.

I used to go out with him when he needed signatures to get on the ballot. It was a good column of course, but as the years went by, the voters' reactions to Dapper changed. He was less likely to have a volunteer with him; at the end, fellow councilor Steve Murphy had to send out his aides with the Dap.

The old-timers who used to reminisce with Dapper about the old days drinking dimeys at Meldon's became few and far between. First it was, "Dapper! You knew my father!" But as the years went by, when he was at, say, the Roche Bros. in West Roxbury, more and more often then twentysomething would tell him, "Dapper! You knew my grandfather!"

I began to see the handwriting on the wall.

One early fall Sunday afternoon, at the Brighton Day parade, Dapper was in a rented truck with a bullhorn. The crowd was sparse, and they did not look like Dapper voters.

"Buenos dias!" the Dap would yell. "Welcome to our country, amigos!"

He put the bullhorn down and turned to me. "I wouldn't mind if I only had to learn three or four new languages, but this is getting ridiculous."

Another day, at the Dorchester Day Parade, he was recorded muttering something about how Fields Corner was looking more like Saigon every day.

The first lesbian elected to the legislature was Elaine Noble. After the size of the House was reduced, rather than run against Barney Frank in the Beacon Hill district, she went to work at City Hall for Kevin White. Both Dapper and I got to know her, and we got along with her fine. She had her problems with the feds, but who among us didn't?

Paper Boy

Years later, she moved to Cambridge (as did the first gay city councilor Dave Scondras). She decided to run for the City Council (as did Scondras later). It was different across the river. The progressives, called the Cambridge Civic Association, ran their own slate of candidates, and Elaine didn't pass muster. She gave an interview to the local Cambridge weekly and was asked, in passing, what she'd learned at Boston City Hall.

Elaine said that she'd met a lot of people she usually wouldn't have associated with, and that she'd discovered that just because you didn't always agree with somebody politically didn't mean they weren't decent human beings. She singled out two: Dapper and me.

Seemed like a harmless enough observation, but not to the Cambridge Civic Association. The next week, in the *Chronicle*, they ran a huge ad about Elaine Noble and her association with what they called THE WORST OF THE GOOD OLD BOYS.

By the 1990s, I was mostly working out of the radio station. I was no longer within walking distance of City Hall. I still hung out with Dapper when he was getting signatures, and on election days, but we didn't spend much time together anymore.

Eventually, his health started failing. The Kools and the brown water were catching up with him. He had a stroke or something like it and lost 50 pounds. Then he began having trouble walking. For a while he had to move into a nursing home—outside the city limits.

By 1999, he was barely able to function as a city councilor. But he still insisted on doing standouts, which mainly showed everyone just how fragile he'd become. The end came when Michael Flaherty Jr., a scion of an old Bulger-connected South Boston family, decided to run for City Council as an at-large candidate.

Everyone in Wards 6 and 7 got the memo—give Baby Flats "the bullet," meaning just a single one of their four votes for at-large councilors. If Flaherty got the bullet, that meant nothing for anybody else, even Dapper. Losing all those Southie votes was crushing for the Dap's reelection prospects.

On election night, just before my show ended at seven, I got a call from Steve Murphy, the city councilor from Hyde Park and one of the guys who'd been getting the Dap his signatures. He told me it looked bad and that I should get over to City Hall ASAP.

I arrived around eight and ran into Mayor Tom "Mumbles" Menino and City Council President Jimmy Kelly. Dapper was sitting in his office, surrounded by a few of the real old-timers, toothless tigers from D Street and Meldon's. We shooed them out and sat down.

Dapper was trembling. He knew the three of us weren't there for a celebration. We tried to tell him that it was okay, that everyone still loved him. It wasn't like the losing scene in *The Last Hurrah,* when the Curley-esque mayor continues holding out hope. As soon as we'd seen the numbers from Southie, everyone knew it was all over, Dapper included.

"You didn't change, Dapper," Jimmy Kelly told him. "It was the city that changed."

The mayor told him he'd get him an office, that he could still come to City Hall every day, just like always. Dapper just sat there, now maybe 80 pounds lighter than in his prime, his shirt collar several sizes too big, no more Kools to smoke. Tears rolled down his cheeks.

"What am I going to tell my Helen?" he kept saying.

Menino kept his word and gave him a little office downstairs. But the Dap went to it less and less often. He could no longer get up the steep outside stairs to his top-floor apartment in Roslindale.

By the fall of 2007, Dapper was 87 and in a nursing home in West Roxbury. I got a call from Steve Murphy and he told me that if I wanted to say goodbye, now was the time. I met Steve there one afternoon and we went up to see him together. Dapper was in tough shape. He had a roommate, and he was complaining about him—same old Dap in that way at least.

Dapper felt forgotten, and after we left Steve and I discussed how to make him feel, well, not forgotten. I started writing a column but I was having a real problem coming up with a lead, which as I've told you is the most important part of any newspaper story.

Finally, I remembered the scene from Edwin O'Connor's novel *The Last Hurrah,* when the Curley-like mayor is dying. One of his old comic-relief coat holders, Ditto Boland, comes into the hospital room with tears in his eyes.

The mayor smiles wanly and says, "Ditto, how do you thank a guy for a million laughs?"

That's how I started the column—"How do you thank a guy for a million laughs?"

In the next few days, the Dap got scores, if not hundreds, of letters, notes, and cards. Even Billy Bulger sent one. It was the least I could do for Dapper—after a million laughs.

A few weeks later, he was dead. I still miss him.

11
The First
Family

My family was for John F. Kennedy for president in 1960. At least my father's side of the family—the Irish side. My mother's side, I'm not so sure. I do know that my grandmother, Letha Hamilton Sutton, who loved me dearly, voted for Herbert Hoover in 1928. My mother explained that "Dan," as we called her, cast her first vote for a Republican that year because he was running against Gov. Al Smith, who was both "wet" and Catholic.

The fact that JFK was Catholic was why my family was for him, of course, like millions of others. Catholics were supposed to vote for JFK because he was Catholic, and Protestants were supposed to vote for him to show they weren't prejudiced against Catholics. Kind of like 2008, only then it was a half-black Democrat instead of a Catholic that all the guilt-ridden virtue signalers were supposed to vote for.

I was in the fourth grade at Palm Beach Public when JFK was inaugurated. If he was in Palm Beach for the weekend, as he often was during the season, my mother would take me and my brother to Mass in West Palm Beach, at St. Ann's, because our regular parish, St. Edward, would be overrun with tourists.

My father never talked about it until years later, but he knew the Kennedys very well, having been in Palm Beach at The Breakers since 1927. The Kennedys owned their own oceanfront mansion, in the North End, but they wouldn't have been welcome as guests at The Breakers.

The problem for Joe Kennedy was that he was, at bottom, if not a gangster, at least a racketeer. His father-in-law, Honey Fitz, the former mayor, would often spend the day in The Breakers' lobby, just like his political arch-nemesis, James Michael Curley. Neither Fitzgerald nor Curley could get a room in The Breakers, but as I've told you, the lobby was like a train station—a public place.

Later, when I was working at Channel 7, during a sit-down with Teddy, I mentioned my background. He laughed and told me how he'd learned to drive as a teenager—by driving his grandfather down to The Breakers every morning to sit in the lobby.

Given his driving record, I figured discretion was the better part of valor. I said nothing.

Until the early seventies, The Breakers was a seasonal hotel—open from just before Christmas until around St. Patrick's Day. That was "the Season." And the help, most of whom lived in the hotel, on the lake side, without ocean views, signed up for "the duration," as they said during World War II. Unless you got sick, you stayed to the end of the season.

Just before World War II, the way my father told the story, there was a beautiful young woman working in one of the shops off the lobby. The shops have always been there, they still are. My mother worked in a couple of them just after World War II. Anyway, before Pearl Harbor, one day in the middle of the season, this attractive young woman came up to my father and asked him if he could give her a ride to the train station in West Palm the next morning. He was one of the few Breakers employees who had his own car.

My father was surprised. This was at the end of the Depression, and this woman had a decent job. If she walked away from it, she wouldn't be hired again in any of the other winter resort hotels either in Florida or in the summer ones up and down the East Coast.

My father asked her if something was wrong. The woman said yes, as a matter of fact there was. Did he know a man named Joe Kennedy, who'd been working as something or other in the Roosevelt administration? She said the patriarch had been "chasing her all over town" and "wouldn't leave her alone."

My father drove her to the train station in West Palm Beach the next morning and never saw her again.

This was the Kennedys' Palm Beach. This was where Joe Kennedy had begun his affair with Hollywood star Gloria Swanson—by raping her at the old Royal Poinciana Hotel on Lake Worth.

Paper Boy

Palm Beach was as segregated as any town in America. Blacks were not allowed to buy property on the island. In nearby Lake Worth, there were no public schools for blacks—segregated or otherwise—until after World War II.

It has been said that Palm Beach was JFK's real hometown, not Boston.

So I knew something about the Kennedys. But like most Americans, I had no real idea of just how depraved they were. I remember in college hearing from a female student I knew about one of her friends who had worked for Ethel Skakel Kennedy—whose family had also been banned from The Breakers, after drunkenly trashing their rooms. The Skakels had an even worse reputation than the Kennedys. Remember Michael Skakel?

After Bobby's assassination in 1968, Ethel used young nannies to raise her brood of kids, and Teddy was often lurking about. One day, this young nanny who my friend knew, was down in the basement, retrieving some toys for the children, when she heard something behind her. She turned around and there was Teddy, weaving slightly, a drink in his hand, his swimming trunks down around his ankles.

She ran screaming up the stairs.

Years later, when I returned to Massachusetts in 1978, I understood that the *Herald* wouldn't be getting too many scoops from the Kennedys.

When Teddy was first running for the Senate in 1962, at the age of 29, JFK had brought a couple of *Globe* editors to the White House and negotiated, in the Oval Office, about how to release details of Teddy's Harvard College cheating scandal.

Would the "scoop" be played above or below the fold on the front page, in which paragraph, and with a headline how many columns wide?

The *Globe* was also the paper that had made Teddy seem like a martyr after Chappaquiddick, saying he had "wandered in a daze" for hours after putting the blonde in the pond.

No, the *Globe* had the Kennedy ass-kissing beat all wrapped up.

I knew it was bad—both the Kennedys and the *Globe's* coverage of them—but I had no idea how deep the levels of sycophancy went. The Kennedys acted like they owned the whole state, maybe because they just about did.

The state treasurer was Bob Crane, a World War II veteran who'd been a state rep from Brighton, the guy who gave the Red Sox tickets to Mike Barnicle. Crane had scored his dream job in 1964 when the previous treasurer, a high-school classmate of his at Boston English, had given Crane a heads-up before he resigned to become chairman of the Turnpike Authority.

Crane soon arranged to have the six-year term limits (three two-year terms) abolished, as well as having the terms extended from two to four years (at the same time the terms of all the constitutional offices were lengthened). Treasurer was the only job he'd ever wanted, and he had no intention of giving it up.

In 1978, Bobby's oldest son, Joe, was 25, basically a dissolute hippie, who hadn't even been able to get into Harvard. He needed a job. Teddy took him to the State House for a sit-down with Crane and gave the old warhorse the bad news—he was out. Joe needed an office from which to launch his political career, and treasurer was it.

Crane was shocked. In 1960, he'd almost lost his House seat to a write-in candidate because he'd been out of state working for JFK in the primaries. In 1968, he flew to Indiana, on his own dime, to campaign for Joe's father Bobby.

Crane was the most loyal of liegemen, and now the lords of the manor were telling him that he was through.

It took me years to figure out why the Kennedys figured the treasurer's job, among all the others they could have simply claimed by divine right, was theirs for the grabbing. They didn't care about why Crane and all the rest of the state politicians so appreciated the power of the Treasury—control of the state pension system, the patronage in the new state lottery, and all the rest that would fall to Crane in the years ahead.

No, as far as they were concerned, it was just an entry-level job, as the Senate had been for Teddy.

Back in 1954, a clerk in the Gillette factory in Southie considered the popularity of the state's young junior senator and figured, what the heck, he'd run for state treasurer. His name was John F. (for Francis, not Fitzgerald) Kennedy. All he needed was the name, and the initials, and he had the job until those pesky pre-Crane term limits kicked in and he had to run for governor in 1960, the same year the real JFK was at the top of the ticket. Treasurer John F. Kennedy lost. (For years afterward, candidates named John Kennedy kept running for the job—I wrote about the phenomenon in *Kennedy Babylon, Vol. 2.*)

Eighteen years later, the Kennedys figured the job of state treasurer and receiver general still belonged to them. Joe could simply claim it, just as Teddy had taken his brother's Senate seat, after two years of a seat-warming mayor from the North Shore who'd gone to Harvard with JFK.

Paper Boy

The Kennedys were like the Mafia: What's ours is ours and what's yours is ours.

Crane was stubborn, though, and he told Teddy and Joe that he wouldn't go without a fight. The Kennedys finally backed down. Joe had to wait until 1986, when House Speaker Tip O'Neill retired from Congress after 34 years. The Kennedys figured that seat was theirs by hereditary right as well—Jack had served as the district's congressman for six years before Tip stepped in for his fleeting 34-year interregnum.

The more I watched the Kennedys, the more I concluded that to them, life was a movie. They, and only they, were the stars, the names above the title. Everyone else in the world was an extra.

And it appeared that most of the voters in Massachusetts were just happy to be in their crowd scenes.

Every summer, the Kennedys would invite the "working press" in Boston to a big party some Saturday afternoon on the lawn at the compound in Hyannis Port. The ink-stained wretches were granted a *noblesse oblige* opportunity to rub elbows with a drunken Teddy and lesser (but equally loaded) members of the clan. I never went, but it was disturbing to see how many of my coworkers had those stars in their eyes.

Until 1980, I never did much reporting about any of the Kennedys. But then Teddy decided to run for president. Under Kennedy rules, the White House belonged to them. Everyone else, Democrat or Republican, was an interloper. The years since 1963 had been but another interregnum, a regency (a word that seems especially appropriate, since Teddy was "the world's oldest juvenile delinquent," as I would soon be calling him).

Down in New York, Rupert Murdoch had bought the *Post* from Dolly Schiff, and even though he wasn't even a U.S. citizen yet, he was already flexing his political muscles. He threw in with Jimmy Carter, and the *Post* went after Teddy in a way he was not accustomed to, to say the least.

He'd been back on his heels since the beginning of the campaign, when he couldn't coherently explain to Roger Mudd on CBS why he wanted to run. (Again, much of this is covered by my books, *Kennedy Babylon, Vols. 1* and *2*.)

Using Fleet Street rules (or lack thereof) the *Post* began rounding up Teddy's girlfriends. It didn't take long for Murdoch to draw blood. One of the best tomcatting stories they turned up involved Teddy's affair with a woman named Lana Campbell, "the Countess."

It was nasty stuff, but in those pre-Internet days the lurid tale needed wider circulation than the *Post* could deliver, especially in New Hampshire, with its first-in-the-nation primary coming up. So the *Post* set it up with Forst, and I was called down from City Hall to do the *Herald*'s interview with the Countess.

I reclaimed my old city-room desk, next to the men's room. When the appointed time arrived, the phone rang. One of the *Post* editors introduced himself and then said, "I have the Countess for you, Howie."

In Boston, we knew all about the girlfriends. The *Herald* wanted to know about the drugs. I ran down the usual list of contraband. Finally I got to LSD.

"We took LSD together, the Senator and I," she cooed, in an accent I couldn't quite place. "And then we made beautiful love together."

Teddy limped to the convention, but his campaign was on life support even before I was introduced to the Countess.

In 1986, House Speaker Tip O'Neill announced he would not seek an 18th term in Congress. Joe Kennedy was in the fight before he could even sell his mansion in Mansfield to his pedophile brother Michael and move into Uncle Jack's Boston-Cambridge-Somerville district. I joked that if the moving van broke down on the way up from the South Shore, Congressman Joe Moakley of South Boston might find himself in a primary fight.

Over the preceding few years, the family retainers who were still around and hadn't drunk themselves to death (like Kenny O'Donnell) had been busy trying to prop Joe up as some kind of disinterested altruistic philanthropist. They had set up a racket called Citizens Energy, which sold cheap foreign heating oil from Venezuela. It was incorporated as a nonprofit, so every winter, Joe got what seemed to be unlimited PSAs on the local TV stations, bundled up and dragging a fuel-truck hose toward some nondescript three-decker in a working-class neighborhood.

If you wanted your cut, all you had to do was dial Joe 4 Oil.

I think the first time I ever met Joe was on a Saturday afternoon in the early eighties when he was doing a Citizens Energy photo-op and I was still at the *Herald American*. I had to ask him about something bad that had happened to his younger brother David, not his later overdose death in Palm Beach but maybe his arrest at the drug house in Harlem where he was known as "White James."

Whatever, I figured he was the guy to go after in 1986—to turn into a punching bag, a cartoon villain. I was soon hitting him so hard and so often that one of his opponents said that if I'd been saying about his family what I'd been saying about Joe's, he'd have punched me in the nose.

I knew most of the other candidates in the fight from the State House. Some were less loathsome than others. A couple had just drifted into the state from New York—an increasingly troubling phenomenon, not because all New Yorkers are bad, but because the ones who come to Massachusetts and go into politics have a bad habit of trying to take over everything here. And don't get me started on the later blow-ins from Illinois—Deval Patrick, Ayanna Pressley, and Michelle Wu, among others.

In 1986, every candidate not named Kennedy was doomed. Once he moved into his uncle's old district, Joe started street campaigning in the North End, which Tip had cut out of the district years earlier, because of his legitimate fear that a decent Italian candidate could prevail by weight of sheer numbers. Just as he didn't know the district's new boundaries, Joe didn't know much about anything else, as it turned out. I suggested that in a live debate, one of the other candidates should grill him on, say, the order of subway stops on the Red or Green Lines.

I knew a guy who was in politics in Medford, which is just north of Somerville, but was not in the O'Neill district. On primary day 1986, this guy was working a precinct in Medford, and he told me that all day a steady stream of old ladies came into vote, but then angrily returned to the wardens complaining about how they'd been given the wrong ballot, because they couldn't find "that nice young Kennedy boy" on it.

Joe was of course elected to Congress, and soon I was getting tips about his "Do you know who I am?" moments with lesser mortals, such as ticket agents at Logan Airport. One day I was flying somewhere and one of them recognized my name and said, "Keep up the good work. You don't know the half of it."

Meanwhile, his uncle Teddy was increasingly out of control. He had ballooned to upwards of 300 pounds, and was wandering around the Cape shirtless. (See the photo on page 1 of *Kennedy Babylon, Vol. 2*.) As Joe Heaney liked to say, "He looks like he's been sucking on a helium gun."

I began referring to Ted in print as "Fat Boy."

Summer was always the worst time for the Kennedys. I used to write about how it wasn't officially summer on Cape Cod until one of the Kennedys had driven onto the sidewalk in Hyannis.

One day in the summer of 1987 we got word that Teddy's boat had run aground in Falmouth. He'd radioed the Coast Guard that he was two miles southwest of Hyannis Port. In fact he was 10 miles away when the Coast Guard located the *Mya*.

In those days, newspapers still employed police reporters who made routine calls every morning to assorted first responders. Unwisely, the local Coast Guard station house released all the very Teddy-esque details—on the boat they'd found two men (Teddy and some unidentified pal), five scantily clad (as we always referred to them) young women, and approximately 500 empty cans of alcohol, mostly, but not all, of the cylindrical and aluminum 12- and 16-ounce variety.

As soon as the story moved across the wires, I got on the phone to Woods Hole or wherever, and fleshed out enough for a column. It was just another day on the Cape Cod Kennedy beat, but Teddy must have gone crazy, because a day or so later, I got a call from the same Coast Guardsman I'd talked to.

He was speaking on an official line—I could tell because I could hear that beeping that indicated that it was being recorded like any other 911 call. I felt sorry for the poor bastard. It was clear he was making these calls under duress, and that he was just going down the list of every reporter he'd talked to that morning.

It must have been humiliating, but what was the alternative? Clearing ice floes in the Bering Straits in January?

So I had to write another column, which was almost nothing but his quotes. I broke up the paragraphs with "BEEP," indicating the recording going on.

There was always another Fat Boy column. One Friday afternoon, he was at the airport in Washington and went to a pay phone to record a statement for Massachusetts radio stations (some of them used to have actual news departments). Teddy would do just fine reading the faxed copy until he got to the word "renegade."

Then he would go all Foster Brooks. Regno, renegno, regneno . . .

Finally he gave up in frustration and ran back into the airport bar to wet his whistle. Hey, he owed it to himself!

That became the lead item in our Sunday "Pols & Politics" column.

I guess it was assumed Teddy was a big boy and could take it, because I never considered that he might try to take revenge on us. We had a circulation at the time of maybe 360,000, compared to the *Globe*'s half-million or so. But ours was mostly blue-collar, old-line Massachusetts, the same one-third to 40 percent of the state electorate that always voted against him, the size of the "renegade" vote depending on the year and the relative sordidness of his latest scandal.

Sometime around Christmas 1987, the *Herald* started getting unusual reports of a rider attached to a budget bill in the U.S. Senate that would have apparently affected only one man—Rupert Murdoch. Basically it would have prohibited him from owning both a newspaper and television station in the same metropolitan market.

This happened just as Murdoch was establishing what would become the Fox Network. He had just bought Channel 9 in New York. Earlier he had purchased Channel 25 in Boston. Obviously, some powerful interest or interests were trying to put the screws to him, big-time. Since the television stations were worth so much more than the "feisty" tabloids that he loved, Murdoch had a big decision to make.

Murdoch was always a big fan of newspapers. He would sometimes call his editors to congratulate, or criticize, their front-page news judgment, sometimes on such relatively arcane matters as story placement above or below the fold (the same subject that had obsessed JFK when plotting how to break the story of Teddy's expulsion from Harvard for cheating). He would also critique his editors on such matters as the type size a headline warranted, or the number of columns it should be stripped across.

Newspapers, after all, were where he had gotten his start, running his late father's newspapers in Australia, then moving into the United Kingdom and buying *The News of the World* from the Carr family (no relation, obviously).

In the eighties, he would fly into Boston at least once a year, usually around Christmas, to host a sumptuous dinner at one of the local steakhouses for the newsroom brass, including the "contract," that is, nonunion workers, like me.

As it became obvious that he was moving the organization in a different direction, i.e., TV, Murdoch would always assure that whatever his empire evolved into, there would always be room for us ink-stained wretches, because the basic need would always be for product, i.e., news. And newspapermen were the best to provide it.

That was true, at least up to a point, and it made us feel better, up to a point, as Evelyn Waugh would say in *Scoop,* the classic Fleet Street novel. In fact, it was becoming more and more obvious where Murdoch was directing the corporation's resources.

By the end of 1987, we were worried about the *Herald*'s future. It was perhaps making a little money, but expenses were high. The previous year, after only two years of ownership, Murdoch had sold the *Chicago Sun-Times* and bought a local television station. We figured the handwriting was on the wall, his reassurances notwithstanding.

It turned out, the budget-bill rider targeting Murdoch had been attached in the Senate at the behest of Teddy by Sen. Ernest "Fritz" Hollings of South Carolina. He was an old segregationist who as governor in the sixties had actually begun flying the redesigned new state flag, which included the old Confederate stars and bars, at the state capitol in Columbia.

Many years later, in 2015, after the Dylann Roof hate crime in Charleston, Gov. Nikki Haley, a Republican, was blamed for the flag flying over the Capitol. The media had no interest in which governor had in fact put the flag up, because it was an embarrassment to Democrats.

We quickly learned that Hollings's rider was in fact payback for the treatment Teddy had received from both the *Post* and the *Herald,* and specifically because of my "Fat Boy" columns about him.

The *Herald* assigned reporters to stalk Kennedy, seeking comment. Finally, one night, as he was getting off the DC shuttle at Logan, one of our reporters confronted him and Teddy admitted he'd caused the anti-Murdoch rider to be attached to the budget bill. Hundreds of jobs were at stake at both the *Herald* and at the *Post*—blue-collar, union jobs, the kind Teddy claimed he cherished.

If Murdoch sold the papers, the new owners might not have deep enough pockets to keep them in business over the long term. Fat Boy could not have cared less.

After Teddy admitted his role and national media began making mention of how angry he was about my coverage, I wrote a column in the *Herald* that began:

"Was it something I said, Fat Boy?"

It may have been the best lead that I ever wrote. By this time Jerry Williams had a weekly show on Channel 25, and in addition to the First Amendment issues at stake, which he did believe in, he sensed an opportunity to win a few brownie points with his TV boss. Jerry loved being on TV, even more than most "talent" in the media.

A few days after railing against Kennedy on Channel 25, Jerry was on WRKO blasting Ted Kennedy's attempts to put the *Herald* out of business. Apparently, Ted was being driven to an appearance on the Cape, and was listening to the show. He was drinking in the car, or seemed to be, because once he called into the show and was put on the air, live, he began slurring his speech more and more.

"I don't have to listen to your dribble," he told Jerry. Not drivel, but dribble.

Then Teddy went after Rupert Murdoch, only he called him "Rudolph" Murdoch. It was amazing radio, and it went on for more than 20 minutes.

In the end, Murdoch sold the *New York Post*, buying it back years later after the developer he sold it to went into bankruptcy. He couldn't afford to part with his new television station in New York. But there were fewer obvious well-heeled potential buyers in Boston for the *Herald*, and Murdoch didn't want to give Teddy the "W." So he sold Channel 25, buying it back years later for tens of millions of dollars more than he'd sold it for.

I've always appreciated how not only did I not get fired, but no one, from Murdoch on down, ever said anything about how much money my columns cost the company. Not that I had done anything wrong, of course, but a lot of corporations—most in fact—would have blinked. Yet I never worried for an instant.

It's different now, of course. Just ask Tucker Carlson. But Rupert is 92 years old. His sons are woke. And the Deep State is so much more powerful—and unapologetic—than it was back in 1987. If it happened today, I'd probably be thrown under the bus, just like Tucker. At the very least, I wouldn't be writing about "Fat Boy." I'd be riding the pine.

A few months after the *Herald*'s near-death experience, a new Kennedy appeared on the scene—Patrick, Teddy's 21-year-old son, a student at Providence College. Not the kind of school you'd expect to see a Kennedy attending, but Patches had had to leave prep school because of his cocaine problem. Providence College was the alma mater of Sen. Chris Dodd, Teddy's drinking companion at La Brasserie in Washington and every other damn place up and down the East Coast.

At the time, one of the sensations of broadcast television was Morton Downey Jr. He had a syndicated talk show that was taped daily in Secaucus, New Jersey. The format was basically . . . professional wrestling.

His father was the Irish radio tenor, Morton Downey Sr., a good pal and occasional business partner of the old man, Joe Kennedy Sr. They shared a code word for Jews—"Canadian geese." The Downeys had had a summer place in Hyannis Port as well, and Mort Jr.—his real name was Sean—grew up with the Kennedys. He was Teddy's age.

Mort was a complete wild man. After his radio station in Sacramento fired him, he was succeeded by Rush Limbaugh. He bounced around and ended up in New Jersey, with this crazy kind of show that I'd seen before, in the sixties, with Joe Pyne. Like Pyne, he was a chain-smoker (both would die of lung cancer, as would Rush Limbaugh) and his show featured brawls, both in the audience and on the set.

I forget how I met him—maybe through his producer, another Massachusetts guy—but I soon ended up on the show. We hit it off—I enjoy the company of wild men and the entertainment they provide. When he came to Boston, he wanted to get together. I told Bob Crane, the state treasurer, and he got very excited. I think he liked the show, but he appreciated Morton Downey Sr., an Irish tenor like himself, even more.

Bob Crane and I ended up meeting Downey and his producer for breakfast at the old Ritz Café. It was like being back on the sound stage in Secaucus. As we found out later, he was in Boston because he was, shall we say, courting a young college girl, or trying to anyway. The producer whispered to us that the previous evening Mort had given her a $10,000 ring, which she'd taken, then at the first stoplight bid him adieu and jumped out of the limousine.

But Downey didn't care. He told Crane and me that he was coming up on his seventh anniversary. Crane and I looked at each other. We had no idea what he was talking about.

"Seventh anniversary of my bankruptcy," Mort explained. "Now I can file again."

As I got to know him a little more, though, what I most enjoyed were his stories about the old days in Hyannis Port in the forties and early fifties. Old Joe would hang out with the boys and share his wisdom. He sternly warned them to avoid Jack's mistake of getting married on a whim to a twice-divorced Protestant socialite in Palm Beach. He even told them how much it had cost him to cover it up and save Jack's nascent political career in January 1947.

That was the first time I'd ever heard the story of JFK's first wife, Durie Malcolm. Is there much doubt now that she was married to JFK? (As I was researching this book, I came across information that it appears one of her two daughters by one of her later husbands—she had five all told—eventually married the brother of future Gov. William F. Weld of Massachusetts. It's a small world.)

What was even more fascinating was what Mort said about how Joe had his sons' political careers plotted out. The plan was for Jack to stay in Massachusetts and eventually run for the Senate, which of course he did.

Then Bobby would run for the Senate in New York, which he did.

Finally, the plan for Teddy was to become the senator from Rhode Island.

"Sure it's small," Joe told Downey. "But it has two Senate seats, just like New York or Massachusetts. And it doesn't cost nearly as much to get elected down there."

Apparently, the Rhode Island option was never totally abandoned. After Patrick entered Providence College, it was decided to run him, at age 21, for the state legislature. The incumbent was another Irish Catholic, a loyal Kennedy Democrat named Jack Skeffington, the same last name as the fictional mayor modeled after James Michael Curley in O'Connor's *The Last Hurrah*.

Like Bob Crane in Boston, Skeffington had campaigned out of state for Bobby Kennedy in 1968. It meant no more to Teddy than Crane's loyalty had. Skeffington, a funeral home director, didn't go down without a fight.

As I've mentioned, sometimes I come up with a nickname that sticks, other times I just lift one that somebody else comes up with but doesn't want credit for. In the case of Patrick Kennedy, I tagged him with the nickname Patches, after the 1970 single from Clarence Carter.

Patches is the son of a man who's been beaten down, and as he's dying, Dad makes a final plea to his boy:

"Patches, I'm dependin' on you son/To pull the family through/It's all left up to you."

Some people didn't get it. Why would anyone leave anything up to . . . Patches? If you were relying on Patches to pull the family through, wouldn't that just mean you were . . . doomed?

Well, yes, exactly. That's why the moniker worked. Like the ugliest Mafia hood in East Boston, whose nickname was "Hey Good Lookin'." Irony is a powerful tool.

Thus, he became Patches.

One afternoon in the summer of 1988, Patches was on a Providence radio station, taking calls when someone phoned in and asked him about his campaign headquarters, and the cross streets around it. Patches didn't have a clue.

It made for both a good column and a few funny segments on Jerry Williams's radio show. Once Patches defeated Skeffington in the primary, I knew I had another recurring cartoon character Kennedy for my own personal comic book.

The *Providence Journal* in those days wasn't the hollowed-out shell of a newspaper that it is today. Like so many other American broadsheets, especially in

The Kennedy "bum" magnet, a reference to the two "bums" headed out to sea—and at sea.

state capitals, it aspired to serve as a . . . paper of record. That has always been a formula for both dreadful tedium and a craven avoidance of reporting on the questionable behavior of the powers that be.

Patches was soon drunkenly stumbling around in the State House. He had neither the intelligence nor the patience to learn the legislative ropes. In addition, he had severe substance-abuse problems.

Patches alienated the entire legislative leadership with his demands for what, I can't even remember now. I just wanted tape of his idiocy, for both the newspaper and the radio.

Since no one at the *Providence Journal* was interested in the obvious entertainment angle, I soon found myself the recipient of occasional deliveries of videocassettes of his performances, sent anonymously to the *Herald* from Providence. They didn't come all that often, because he seldom showed up for the formal legislative sessions, during which they debated and had votes. But I got them often enough, and I kept them around.

The same year Patches launched his sad career, in 1988, Teddy was running for reelection. His opponent was a young Republican newcomer named Joe Malone. Kennedy would only agree to one debate—a half hour, on a Saturday night, on Channel 5, a Democratic-controlled outlet. His hands shook uncontrollably, and it was another fest of malapropisms. He referred to "crop-killer bullets," among other gaffes.

Even Teddy had to endure such indignities as televised debates . . . and appearing before newspaper editorial boards. I showed up for his meeting with the *Herald* that year. I asked him if he'd ever taken illegal drugs. He denied it. Then I asked him another question that had two parts.

"That's actually then two questions," he said, his hands shaking.

"It's happy hour, Senator," I responded.

He looked up at the clock in the room and shook his head.

"Not quite yet," he said. "It's only 4:45."

Never argue with a Kennedy about happy hour, I guess.

He was reelected easily, of course, even as Mike Dukakis was spanked by George H. W. Bush. I suspect Teddy wasn't that displeased about the outcome. As Gore Vidal said, "It is not enough to succeed. Others must fail."

I knew a fundraiser from the Merrimack Valley named Nick Rizzo. He was ex-Sen. Paul Tsongas's top money man, and he would later go to federal prison for embezzling millions from Tsongas's account during the 1992 presidential primaries.

One day in 1989 Rizzo invited me to meet him for lunch at the Algonquin Club on Commonwealth Avenue. He brought with him Michael Kennedy, Joe's younger brother. He'd run New Mexico for Dukakis. It was a futile effort—gun control was not a winning issue in New Mexico.

Michael lived in Marshfield, in the house Joe had sold him when he moved to Boston to run for Congress. His wife was the daughter of Frank Gifford, the New York Giants immortal who'd become an announcer on *Monday Night Football*. That was the first time I'd ever met Michael Kennedy, who would become a fixture in the *Herald*'s coverage a few years later.

On Easter weekend 1991, Teddy flew to Palm Beach for his "traditional Easter weekend"—meaning an epic drunk. He was particularly interested in trying out a new watering hole, Au Bar, just off Royal Poinciana Way.

By Easter Sunday, the cops in Palm Beach were looking for his nephew, William Kennedy Smith. A young single mother from Jupiter (from the family that had owned Channel 7 before I worked there) had told cops she'd been picked up with Smith and his uncle and cousin, Patrick "Patches" Kennedy. Back at 1095 N. Ocean Blvd., she said, she'd been raped by Smith.

The *Herald* as usual scrambled all hands on deck. This was a made-to-order story for any tabloid, but particularly the *Herald*. It was payback time for our recent near-death experience. Teddy ducked the press for a while, but finally decided to meet the Boston press on an early spring Friday afternoon on the MIT campus in Cambridge.

It was another memorable press conference. I rolled tape and then just transcribed his incoherent babbling. He called the victim "a girl," and said she'd stolen his 99-year-old mother's urn, which he called a "yearn."

Shockingly, after all these decades of looking the other way, the Palm Beach cops were finally going after the Kennedys. They took depositions from everybody involved, including the family servants, one of whom was an 80-year-old kitchen maid named Nellie McGrail. She described at some length how every morning she had to squeeze all the family's oranges by hand, because Rose was too cheap to buy a power squeezer. She had to perform her kitchen duties between her kidney dialysis treatments.

We took the depositions and added up what all the help said they'd served Teddy on that Good Friday—which is, remember, the holiest day of the year on the Christian calendar. We tallied up his entire booze intake that day—wine, daiquiris, more wine, Scotch.

It added up to at least two dozen drinks throughout the course of Good Friday. His son Patrick and his nephew Willie had returned to the mansion after a night of bar-hopping and were asleep when he woke them up for another run back into town to Au Bar.

Once the Kennedys got there, visibly drunk, Teddy quickly got into an argument with a young woman who for some reason had accused him of being intoxicated. Teddy then returned home after Patrick and Willie had picked up women. He vanished briefly, then reappeared on the mansion's lawn clad only in an Oxford dress shirt, without trousers, or as I quickly put it, using my European History 101 knowledge of the French revolution, *sans culottes.*

The depositions provided me—and everyone else at the *Herald*—with an endless stream of stories, items, and columns all summer. Whatever lingering myths remained of Camelot were laid to rest—and I do mean laid.

Paper Boy

As part of discovery, the Kennedys had to produce their credit card bills. We got a bar tab from Chuck & Harold's on Royal Poinciana, the gin mill nearest to St. Edward. Teddy and Patches had gone to the 11:30 service, a high Mass.

It was packed and there were no seats when they arrived a few minutes late. So Teddy found himself standing in the back of the church on a hot spring morning. He soon developed a powerful thirst, and Teddy, as I often said in my columns, never got the memo from the old country song about how drinkin' doubles don't make a party.

What made Milwaukee famous had made a loser out of Teddy, as Jerry Lee Lewis used to say.

So father and son fled to Chuck & Harold's, pulled up a couple of bar stools, and began drinking brunch. I looked at the bill and saw that Teddy had ingested two or three Bloody Marys, which was only to be expected.

What surprised me was what Rep. Kennedy had ordered—Long Island iced tea, which calls for six or seven different liquors. The problem was, Patches already had an acknowledged drug problem—he'd been a cocaine addict as far back as prep school. A parent can't tell his child how to behave, of course, but shouldn't Teddy have understood that it might not be a good idea for his son, a supposedly recovering cocaine addict, to be guzzling Long Island ice teas— before noon?

When the trial began in December, the *Herald* sent a whole team of reporters and photographers down—spending the kind of money that would be unthinkable now. We were booked into The Colony, and had a couple of rented cars. Again, it seems like another age.

Even Jerry Williams was broadcasting from the island—he owned a house in Palm Beach where his estranged wife lived. There wasn't room enough in the courtroom for all the reporters, but the trial was being carried live on cable TV. I had to appear on Jerry's radio show every afternoon.

Jerry was 68 years old now, but he seemed older. Spending time with his estranged family was likely quite stressful, especially after the stories earlier in the year about his relationship with the 23-year-old woman who he'd gotten a job for in the Treasury. (More on that later.)

We were doing the afternoon show from 2 to 6 from a bar called E.R. Bradley's, after the town's old-time gambling czar. It's now the location of a fusion-style restaurant in the Palm Beach outpost of the swank White Elephant on Nantucket, which is around the corner from the mansion that used to be owned by John Kerry's second wife's first husband's trust fund.

Back then, though, the future White Elephant South was about as close to a dive bar as Palm Beach could, or would, tolerate.

One afternoon, Jerry and I were pretty much by ourselves in the bar, with a WRKO producer who'd flown down from Boston, when suddenly Jerry began having problems.

He would do time checks, and in those pre-Internet days, he needed an actual clock to know when to break. So he had a small digital clock set up on the table next to him. I was sitting across from him, but I could see the clock. He was okay the first hour, but after the 3:30 hard break, we came back at around 3:35. Jerry looked at the clock and said, "It's now . . ." He stopped for several seconds. "It's now 5:42."

Obviously, something was wrong. I tried to take over, and he just sat back. On the next break, I called his producer back in Boston and told her to call his wife, who was about seven or eight blocks away, and tell her to get over to E.R. Bradley's to get Jerry out of there. When we came back, I took over and Jerry just sat there, slack-jawed. I had no idea how sick he was. I began to wonder what I'd tell the media if he had to be hospitalized, or even died.

It turned out that he hadn't had a stroke, just an aneurysm, but he was through for the week. The next day, the on-site producer set me up poolside at The Colony, where a lot of us were staying during the trial.

The Kennedys' PR operation wasn't nearly as smooth as it had been in New Frontier days, but they still knew a few of the old tricks, like having somebody out in front of the cameras every morning at the courthouse in West Palm Beach before the trial resumed. Every day a different member of the family would serve as that day's designated Kennedy.

One morning I was standing with Al McNaughton, a cameraman I'd worked with at Channel 7. Eunice Shriver was the Kennedy du Jour, and she was looking tough, very tough. Do you recall the old horror movie, *Bride of the Mummy*?

After she finished and was walking inside, Al turned to me and said, "Do you think Sargent Shriver cheats?"

After the main scrum of reporters had broken down their equipment and headed upstairs to the courtroom, the plaza was commandeered by Steve Dunleavy, the Murdoch hand who'd left Australia to work at the *New York Post*. He'd also ghostwritten the best-selling tell-all book about Elvis Presley, *Elvis: What Happened?*, which sold more than three million copies after the King's death in 1977.

Paper Boy

When he died, Rupert Murdoch touchingly called Dunleavy "the greatest reporter of his generation." Rupert also said he left behind scoops "littered" everywhere he went, and that was certainly true, the part about the litter anyway.

In West Palm, Dunleavy had assembled a crew of what were in effect old-style legmen. Dunleavy himself would work the bars all night, and every morning, hungover, he'd assemble his legmen—mostly seedy-looking *National Enquirer* types now bivouacked in nearby Lantana.

He'd pull out a huge wad of bills and begin peeling them off, barking out orders to one henchman after another about the sort of tabloid fodder he was looking for that day, for all the Murdoch titles in the United States, the UK, and Australia.

In addition to writing his column for the *New York Post*, Dunleavy was one of the reporters on *A Current Affair,* Murdoch's gossipy pre-Internet evening magazine show. Somehow—with some of Rupert's cash, most likely—he got a sit-down interview with Patches's Au Bar pickup, Michelle Cassone. She would be variously described as either an "heiress" (by the tabloids) or as a "waitress" (by Teddy's mainstream-media rump swabs).

What Dunleavy didn't tell her as the cameras started rolling was that he had also obtained a photo of Michelle in a position of, shall we say, love, performing what would still be known for a few more years until *Lawrence* v. *Texas* as an "unnatural act."

She demanded Dunleavy turn over the XXX-rated photo and when he haughtily refused, she lunged for it. They grappled with one another, not lovingly, for more than a minute. Finally she bit him. You can still see the video on YouTube.

It was like old home week for me in Palm Beach. I interviewed Steve Brill, who'd been one class ahead of me at Deerfield. Now he was running Court TV. The host of the biggest local radio talk show was Jack Cole, another alumnus of Channel 7 in Boston.

Cole had been anchoring one night as the station ran a news story about how to keep a blaze going in your living room fireplace. It was no more or less inane than any other story on any other local TV newscast, but somehow it really grated on Cole.

When the story was finally, mercifully over the director switched back to Cole on the anchor desk. He was glaring at the camera.

"We'll be back with more of this alleged news in a moment," Cole said, but he wasn't. He was pulled off the set during the break and never reappeared. It was just another night at 7 Bulfinch Place.

Like so many other New Englanders, he was now reinventing himself in Florida. And after Dunleavy's horseplay with Michelle Cassone, Cole came up with his own little song about her, which is also still available on YouTube.

It was party time for everyone in the press contingent, especially Murdoch's Brits. The only day I ever saw them observe the slightest bit of decorum was one Sunday when the Kennedys attended Mass at St. Edward.

For me, it was like 1962, when JFK was president and I was 10 years old. At the arrival of the Kennedys—among them Congressman Joe Kennedy— I assumed the Murdoch hands, if not the cameras, would follow them in. But for some reason, they seemed reticent. Nobody wanted to go inside the church vestibule.

Finally, I volunteered. What the hell, or should I say heck, I'd been confirmed in that church, at the tender age of 8. We had a huddle, and I told the cameramen that at the end of Mass, I'd see which way the Kennedys would be departing, either through the main entrance on North County Road, or out the side door on Sunset Ave.

I went in late and sat down in the pew behind where they were sitting, and drifted off into the same kind of daydream/coma I was always in as a kid at Mass. The only difference was, Msgr. O'Mahoney had gone on to his eternal reward.

Another thing had changed. Now, near the end of the Mass, everyone turns to other churchgoers around them. They say, "Peace be with you," and shake somebody else's hand. So when Joe Kennedy turned around and extended his hand he saw . . . me.

He was not pleased. I assume he was even less pleased a moment or so later when I abruptly left the pew and went to the back of the church and waited for the end of the Mass so I could alert my fellow Murdoch hacks to their exit.

Which I did.

It was fun being back in Palm Beach, on an expense account no less. We ate well, partied at night, and generally had a great time. The trial itself was anti-climactic. The victim testified, but all I remember (like most people) is the fact that her face was covered on the live television coverage with a blue dot.

The supposedly outstanding local prosecutor, Moira Lasch, turned out to be a complete bust. She questioned Teddy under oath, but when it was all over

I wrote as the lead to my column that Teddy had to be thinking to himself as he left the witness stand, "I had to go on the wagon to get ready for *this?*"

Lasch was even worse with Willie Smith, who had been dubbed "Sluggo" in the *Herald*. The judge hadn't allowed his prior bad acts with women to be presented to the jury, although we had already printed the depositions from his alleged victims.

She couldn't even lay a glove on Sluggo when he took the stand in his own defense. When he admitted he'd had sex—consensual sex, he claimed—with the blue-dot woman twice in less than half an hour, she did a double take and sneered at him:

"What are you, a sex machine?"

Smith's lawyer was Roy Black, from Fort Lauderdale. He later married one of the jurors in the case. Unlike Moira Lasch, who'd had to maintain a grinding schedule of other court appearances in the months leading up to the trial, Black had had unlimited time—and unlimited funds.

It didn't take the jury long to acquit Sluggo. The family went out to celebrate, and the rest of us flew home.

After Au Bar, Teddy slowed down a little, although he did resurface for the 1992 primary election in Massachusetts. Chester Atkins, a Yankee stiff from Concord, had worked his way up to chairman of Ways and Means in the state Senate. He was the typical Yankee rich kid, born in Geneva, Switzerland. We called him the Swiss Guard.

Like so many Yankee politicians of both parties at the State House, he inexplicably worshipped Billy Bulger. In 1984, the congressional seat in the Merrimack Valley was open, and Chester went up against Sen. Phil "Sooky" Shea of Lowell, whose main claim to fame was that he'd once fought in the Golden Gloves. In Lowell, that made you Mr. Big.

Like Chester, Sooky did what he was told to do by Bulger. But in 1984 Sooky wasn't on the team. So in the congressional primary he took to calling Chester "Billy Bulger's butler." It was a great putdown, but Sooky was hopeless. In one of those TV debates, Atkins accused him of ducking some vote, and Sooky recoiled in mock horror.

"Why you know that's not true Chester," he said. "I wasn't hiding. I was sick and home in bed hallucinatin'."

Hallucinatin', recuperatin', what's the difference? Atkins won, but the Swiss Guard would always be vulnerable to any ethnic candidate out of the Merrimack

Valley. He won four terms before he ran into Marty Meehan, an old acquaintance of mine from the State House.

Naturally I was with Marty, for every reason. So was everyone else in the Valley. He took a three-term limit pledge, which I thought was foolish, and told him so. He shrugged. He would deal with that broken promise when it came time . . . to break his promise.

The primary wasn't even close. By the final weekend, Atkins didn't even show up for a big parade in the district. He knew it was all over. On the day after the primary, there was a "unity breakfast" in Lowell. Teddy was never on top of his game before noon, and now he was only getting worse. That's always the way it is with drunkards as the years go by.

Teddy arrived at the old Speare House and he walked upstairs into a banquet hall with all the grandees of Fifth District Democracy. The walls were completely covered with signs that said "MARTY MEEHAN."

After the customary greasy breakfast, Fat Boy stood up and, after a few burps and farts, began delivering the standard post-primary we-must-unite bloviations.

Teddy talked about what a great congressman the Valley was about to elect, how he had known him forever, and how he came from a wonderful family, etc., etc.

Only one problem: He kept calling Marty "Andy Meehan."

He kept bellowing out his name, "Andy Meehan! Andy Meehan!" Apparently, he never once noticed any of those signs around the room.

That was Teddy Kennedy in the early nineties, an overstuffed empty suit, as he was so well described in *The New Republic*.

He was running for reelection again in 1994, and for a moment it looked like he might in fact lose to Mitt Romney, the multimillionaire businessman and son of George Romney, the former Michigan governor. Mitt was everything Teddy wasn't—sober, faithful, trim, articulate, well-groomed. Joe Kennedy II, continuing an old family tradition by acting as campaign manager for the older family patriarch, denounced Mitt for his . . . religion.

That was Joe Kennedy. As they say about baseball pitchers, million-dollar body, ten-cent head.

Meanwhile, there was an open congressional seat in Rhode Island, and naturally Patches jumped into the fray. It was a typical Patches comedy of errors, which I covered in *Kennedy Babylon, Vol. 2.*

Paper Boy

One day I got a call from a young Washington reporter for the *Weekly Standard*, the magazine Bill Kristol had founded after the Clintons ousted his boss, Vice President Dan Quayle. He'd briefly been added to ABC "News" with George Stephanopoulos as a kind of Point–Counterpoint dynamic duo. In retrospect, Kristol was a patsy, which probably explains why he's since lost his mind. Steffie, a shameless Democrat shill, is now making north of $15 million a year to parrot the party line. Kristol, on the other hand, is little more than a Twitter troll, not even rising to the level (financially, anyway) of a Lincoln Project grifter.

The *Weekly Standard*'s reporter's name was Tucker Carlson. He wanted to use Patches's stumbling and bumbling in the legislature for his piece, and the boys in Providence had told him I was the unofficial keeper of the Patches Kennedy video archives.

I met Tucker in the press gallery at the State House and handed over the tapes. He did a good job with the story and has since confirmed what I've always agreed with Rupert Murdoch about, that in terms of journalistic training, there is no substitute for print. Which is yet another reason why it's so unfortunate that most print media have largely ceased to exist.

The next Kennedy scandal involved Michael Kennedy, whom I'd met with future felon Nick Rizzo at the old Algonquin Club after he ran New Mexico for Dukakis in 1988. I still remember how he'd said he knew the state was lost when George H. Bush began running TV ads stressing the Duke's squishiness on the Second Amendment. The only other subject I recall discussing with Michael Kennedy were the "ritual crucifixions" of the Hermanos Penitentes Catholic confraternity that I'd long read about. They supposedly take place up in the mountains on Good Friday every year.

Michael was another one of the Kennedys with an oversized libido, although I didn't know it at the time when he and I were discussing the Bill of Rights and Catholic sects.

He had followed in older brother Joe's footsteps—taking over Citizens Energy, the oil "nonprofit" that had been set up to provide some accomplishment for Joe before he began his political career. With Joe in Congress, Michael started paying himself big bucks. Once the GOP took over Congress again in 1994, Joe decided to temporarily give up politics and return to Massachusetts.

Joe wasn't running for reelection in 1996, figuring he'd be elected governor in 1998, by acclamation I guess. But then word of Michael's affair with his underage babysitter began leaking out. I didn't do any of the heavy lifting on this scandal. The *Herald* had a gossip column, the "Inside Track," and most of the reporting was done by Gayle Fee and Laura Raposa.

Even by Kennedy standards, it was a sordid tale. First Michael took the baby-sitter, then he seduced her mother. The father was a big Democrat contributor. It turned out Michael was a full-service perv. In his car—a convertible, of course, another family tradition—he kept stacks of pornographic magazines and books.

One of the primary sources against him was his cousin, Michael Skakel, who himself would eventually be convicted of bludgeoning a female teenage neighbor in Connecticut to death with a golf club. (The conviction was later overturned.)

In 1998, Joe tried to follow through with his plan to run for governor, but he couldn't get out of the gate. I had never thought I'd see a Kennedy floundering at the local, Massachusetts level. At the time I was writing occasionally for the *New York Press* run by Russ Smith. (His brother's holding company now owns the *Herald,* among many other once formidable, now ruined titles. The *New York Press* was a sort of downtown conservative weekly alternative to the *Village Voice.*

I still remember writing a story about Joe Kennedy's campaign for Russ Smith. By now you know my belief that a good enough lead can carry an entire piece.

My lead was: "It must suck to be Joe Kennedy."

I used lines from my radio show that I couldn't even work into the *Herald*. I mentioned the Kennedy family's favorite ice-cream flavors. For Michael, statu-tory grape. For Joe, who had crippled Pam Kelley in a 1973 Nantucket Jeep ac-cident, fudge cripple. For Patches (who at that time didn't seem to have a steady girlfriend), tutti frutti.

As the years went by, the family's power and influence slowly waned, both here and elsewhere. One of my producers went to a yard sale and for a quarter or so bought a couple of cheap framed photos of JFK and Jackie, obviously from the immediate post-assassination period when they were considered earthly saints.

My producer had taken off the backs of the frames. He showed me what he'd found inside. Behind the photos of the First Family—likely clipped from the *Record*—were photos of two young children—most likely grandchildren of the old-timers who'd decided the pictures of the martyred Kennedy and his widow deserved greater prominence than those of their own grandchildren.

But that era was coming to an end. There were still the occasional head-lines about drugs, drunk-driving arrests, drownings, plane crashes, and abortive attempts to run for office in Massachusetts and New York. I still made sport of the family on the radio, especially their increasingly inarticulate speech. (See the chapters on four of them in *Kennedy Babylon, Vol. 2*.)

The family trust was broken up and everything was sold off, including even the mansion in Palm Beach on North Ocean Boulevard that I called "Comfortably Numb by the Sea." The old man Joe had bought it in 1933 for $110,000. In 1995 it was sold for $4.9 million. In 2015 it changed hands again, for $31 million, and just five years later, during the COVID-19 flight from New York, Comfortably Numb was sold again—this time for $70 million.

Joe Kennedy had always known how to turn a buck on anything—penny stocks, racetracks, movies, bootlegging, etc. Now his descendants were just living like the old Yankees Joe had so disdained—off their dividends, increasingly digging into the capitol to pay for their dissipated and indolent lifestyles.

Teddy died in the summer of 2009. My listeners always text in on the anniversary to say, "Teddy observes another year of sobriety." His son Patches, in his final term as a congressman, came drunkenly up to Massachusetts to endorse the Democrat candidate in the special election to replace him in January 2010.

Her name was Martha Coakley. He called her "Marsha." She lost to a Republican state senator.

In 2012, Joe's son, Joseph P. Kennedy III, was elected to replace Barney Frank in the House. He wasn't a bad kid—the Kennedy had been just about bred out of him. My daughter Charlotte and I had dinner with him and his wife. When my mother died, he sent me a touching sympathy note. He called me a "happy warrior," a sobriquet I have never aspired to.

Like Teddy with Patches, Joe was depending on young Joe to pull the family through. My son it's all left up to you . . .

In 2014, my daughter Charlotte graduated from Deerfield Academy. One of her classmates was Conor Kennedy, Bobby Jr.'s son and the boyfriend, briefly, of Taylor Swift.

One of the traditions at Deerfield is a big post-graduation party for all the cool kids in the senior class. Mine was held at Malkin's in Manhattan, an East Side gin mill that catered to underage preppies, owned by a closeted gay who was later stabbed to death by rough trade.

Charlotte called me one night and told me excitedly that the Class of '14 had picked the location for their party—Conor was going to throw it at the Kennedy compound in Hyannis Port. What could possibly go wrong?

The party was cancelled, and during Christmas 2016, Conor became the first Kennedy of his generation to be arrested, after a barroom brawl in Aspen, Colorado, where his pedophile uncle Michael had killed himself skiing into a tree almost exactly 19 years earlier.

Rep. Joe Kennedy ran for the Senate in 2020 against incumbent Sen. Ed Markey, the original K-Mart Kennedy, who had been in Congress since 1976. He was so out of touch that when Tom Brady won his fifth Super Bowl in 2017, Markey took to the floor of the Senate to congratulate "the Boston Patriots," which they hadn't been since 1970.

It was assumed that at the age of 74, Markey would call it a career. That's what liegemen are supposed to do, after all. But like Bob Crane in 1976, Markey refused to go. He recruited Alexandria Ocasio Cortez to campaign for him in the woke districts. As always, Markey stumbled and bumbled but he still outworked young Joe, who spent the summer of 2020 trying to set up a national presence.

Caroline & Max Kennedy under arrest Barnstable MA 8-20-2017
"I'm drunk... I know that!"
www.howiecarrshow.com

My most recent Kennedy magnet: the 2017 arrest of Max and his daughter in Hyannis Port.

Paper Boy

His plan was obvious. The young senator would run for president in 2024, at the age of 42, just about the same age as his great uncle in 1960. The campaign would be about passing the torch to a new generation.

But it was not to be. In the Democratic primary, Markey crushed young Kennedy by a 55–45 margin, a landslide for all practical purposes. Markey won by 150,000 votes. Kennedy's only real strength was in the faded working-class towns around the state, like the one where my producer bought those two framed photographs.

The ultimate irony: the Kennedy dynasty in Massachusetts was finally ended by . . . a K-Mart Kennedy.

12
THE BROTHERS BULGER

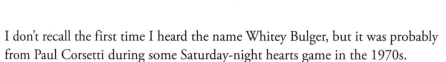

I don't recall the first time I heard the name Whitey Bulger, but it was probably from Paul Corsetti during some Saturday-night hearts game in the 1970s.

It was an interesting, retro name—"Whitey." Like Whitey Ford, left-handed Hall of Fame pitcher for the New York Yankees. But mostly I knew it as a Hollywood name for the gunsels working for assorted Mr. Bigs in gangster B-movies and old radio detective shows. There had been a "Whitey" in the Bowery Boys movies, and later a different younger Whitey was one of Beaver Cleaver's pals.

But I don't think I'd ever personally known anyone named . . . Whitey.

Just across the Broadway Bridge from the *Herald* were several buckets of blood, the bloodiest of which was Triple O's, named after the three O'Neil brothers, one of whom was an obese, acne-scarred money-launderer for Whitey. During the race riots after Martin Luther King Jr.'s assassination in 1968, Kevin O'Neil had been arrested and charged with murdering a black motorist on D Street. He beat the rap after hiring as his attorney a young state rep named Billy Bulger.

Triple O's was originally known as the Transit Café, and it had been owned by Donald Killeen. After his gangland murder in 1972 (more on that later) the license had somehow been transferred to O'Neil. As a convicted felon, Whitey couldn't own a liquor license (nor could Dillon, the Whitey-like hitman in *The Friends of Eddie Coyle* by George V. Higgins). There was always trouble at all those Southie dive bars, especially ones in the Lower End.

166

Even by Southie standards, though, Triple O's stood out. In 1981, a wiseguy named Louis Litif had been murdered upstairs there (as we would discover later). His body was found in his wife's car in the South End outside Mafia boss Larry Baione's laundromat—a coincidence, as it turned out.

It was an interesting case, another "unsolved" murder in Southie, and it caught the attention of Paul Corsetti. All clues seemed to point back to Triple O's, Whitey's barroom in the Lower End.

At the time, Paul was enjoying his Andy Warhol-esque 15 minutes of fame. He had just refused to tell a judge who a source was for one of his stories—I can't remember what it involved—and he had spent a few days in the East Cambridge Jail.

It was a big story—a big TV story, which was all that mattered. For that brief moment in time, everybody recognized Paul Corsetti.

Now Paul was back on the police beat, making inquiries about the late Louis Litif. One day in the city room he got a tantalizing call, offering him a few tidbits unknown even to the police. The anonymous caller said he had much more inside information about Litif. Paul was told that if he wanted to find out exactly what had happened, he should appear that night at a bar down in Quincy Market.

Paul dutifully showed up and sat down at the bar. Soon a slight but well-built middle-aged man appeared and pulled up the next bar stool. He looked at Paul, did an exaggerated double take, and then announced, "Say, aren't you . . .?"

"Yeah," Paul said, nodding. "I'm Paul Corsetti."

The guy tried to make small talk, like a fan, until finally Paul told that as much as he'd like to chat with him, he was waiting for someone.

"You're waiting for me, motherfucker," the guy snarled. "I'm Jimmy Fucking Bulger."

Whitey then pulled a piece of paper out of his pocket. He read off the address of Paul's house in Medford, then the make, model, and license plate number of his car, and most ominously, the address of where his young daughter was dropped off for day care every morning.

Then Whitey got off his stool and stalked off. The next morning, Paul showed up in the city room wearing a holster with a gun. Everybody was taken aback, until we heard the story. Paul first went to the Boston Police Department, where he was told that the cops "liked" Whitey for maybe as many as 50 murders, but that there wasn't anything they could do.

Paul's next stop was North Margin Street—North End headquarters of Larry Baione, the number-two guy "In Town," as the local Mafia was known. Baione would soon be recorded on an FBI bug at his social club calling Whitey and his partner Stevie Flemmi "beautiful fucking guys who can straighten a thing out"—in other words, hitmen.

This day, Baione told Paul much the same thing as the Boston police—that as much as he'd like to help, there was nothing he could do about such a beautiful fucking guy.

Paul kept working his sources, and it turned out that Whitey was less concerned about his own guilt in the Litif murder—which would be impossible to prove—as he was about his brother getting mixed up in his travails. Paul put out the word that he had no interest in politics—he was, after all, a police reporter, Eddie the Inspector's son. Paul sought only a good organized-crime story.

He ended up with a story of sorts—as with so much else, we wouldn't know the half of it until decades later. Litif, as it turned out, had been on the Hit Parade because he'd murdered another wiseguy in Southie, without getting Whitey's blessing.

This had happened in, where else, a bar. So Litif then shot the only witness, the bartender, and apparently made the bartender's body "do the Houdini," as the Westies in New York used to say when they disposed of one of their victim's bodies.

Whitey's paid FBI agent Zip Connolly was contacted and tried to use his G-man clout to obtain a life-insurance payout for the bartender's family, even though the body had never been found (and still hasn't, for that matter).

The story about Litif's unsolved murder was quickly forgotten. But everyone in the Boston media would long remember the threats made against Corsetti, about how brazen the Senate president's brother had become.

In Southie, the scope of Whitey's mayhem was somewhat understood, but even more frightening was the number of disappearances. People who crossed Whitey just . . . vanished. Still, a lot of this scuttlebutt never made it across the Broadway Bridge.

In Southie, many people didn't even dare to mention Whitey by name. I learned this at City Hall. But the Corsetti story was the kind of advertising money can't buy, and Whitey's name vanished from the public prints for years afterward.

Outside Southie, Whitey was a rather enigmatic figure. I remember later at Channel 7, trying to find a mug shot of Whitey. There weren't any—at least none were being circulated. An ex–state cop who worked on our assignment desk finally came up with a grainy state police photo from the Lancaster Street garage surveillance, which at the time none of us knew anything about.

Looking down at something in his hands, his receding hairline combed straight back, Whitey looked like Lon Chaney Jr. in an old *Wolfman* movie.

Billy Bulger was of course much better known. He was the president of the state Senate, a Beacon Hill lifer. He'd first been elected to the House at age 26, in 1960. He'd succeeded future congressman Joe Moakley in the state Senate in 1970. He became Senate president in 1978, after the prior occupant had been forced to resign in a scandal involving a $1,000 check.

The most fascinating thing about Billy Bulger, though, was Whitey. Years later, I got his military records from the FBI. While stationed at an Air Force base in Montana, Whitey had been charged with the rape of a teenaged girl. He was on the verge of being court-martialed, and his superior officer told him that with a dishonorable discharge, he wouldn't be able to get a decent job in civilian life.

"What I'm going to be doing when I get out," Whitey Bulger told his CO, "it really doesn't matter what kind of a discharge I get from the Air Force."

According to his records, he also dropped the name of his congressman, John J. McCormack. Even at an early age, Whitey knew how to skillfully play every political card he'd been dealt.

A diminutive, blue-eyed blond, Whitey became a "tailgater," stealing cases of whatever he could off the back of delivery trucks. Razor blades from the Gillette factory in Southie were a perennial favorite. He supplemented his income turning tricks as a gay male hustler. His most famous mug shot, which the FBI gave me much later, was taken on St. Patrick's Day 1953, after he rolled a drunk in Bay Village. He is wearing one of those big Borsalino hats that were *de rigueur* among wiseguys back then. He started doing odd jobs—maybe even a hit or two—for a gay Southie gangster named Hank Geraghty, who operated out of a Texaco station in Andrew Square.

Then Whitey started robbing banks. He studied hard, trying to master his new trade. He made sure that everyone who walked into the bank was dressed alike, just like in black-and-white film noir movies. When the crew robbed a bank in Melrose, Whitey scheduled it just as a freight train made its daily run through the center of town, blocking any pursuit from the police station, which was on the other side of the tracks.

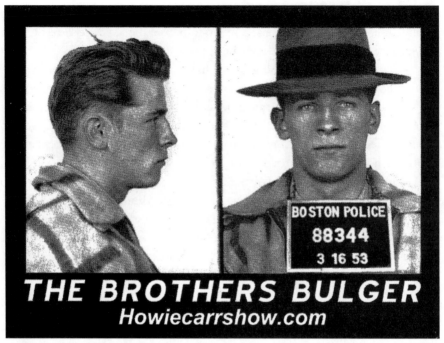

A gift from the FBI that became my most popular magnet ever.

Whitey's bank-robbing spree lasted long enough for him to even go on the lam with a girlfriend, a dress rehearsal for the trek he would undertake in late 1994. But eventually he came back to Boston. He dyed his hair black, but somebody ratted him out, and he was arrested in Revere by an FBI agent from Belmont named H. Paul Rico.

Whitey was convicted in federal court in Boston in 1956. He was sent to a series of federal prisons, including Atlanta, where he volunteered for the experiments the CIA was conducting with LSD. Later he tried to parlay his early LSD "trips" into an excuse for his antisocial behavior—like Alice Cooper, he'd been such a sweet sweet boy 'til they got ahold of him.

Then Whitey got shipped out to Alcatraz, "the Rock," the real résumé enhancer of his prison years. In the early 1960s, he ended up at Leavenworth. He had few visitors beyond Hank Geraghty, his old boss (and maybe more) in the small-time rackets of South Boston, and Will McDonough, a young sportswriter from the *Globe* who had managed Billy's first campaign for state rep in 1960.

McDonough was covering the Red Sox, and whenever they were on the road playing the A's in Kansas City, he would rent a car and drive out to Leavenworth.

Finally, in 1965, Whitey was released, after nine years in prison. The congressman from South Boston was still John McCormack, and he was now Speaker of the House. Like almost everyone in Southie, McCormack had connections to the element, and in his case, they weren't tenuous. As a young lawyer in the 1920s, he'd represented some of the Wallace brothers, who hung out on Gustin Street and thus became known as the Gustin Gang.

In addition, his brother, Edward "Knocko" McCormack, was a colorful figure in Andrew Square, the proprietor of a block-long bar and the man who controlled the snow "buttons" in Southie.

(After a blizzard, if you produced a "button," you would be paid at City Hall for a day of shoveling. In the Depression that was a big deal. Tip O'Neill wrote about snow buttons in Cambridge in his autobiography.)

The kingpin of Southie crime during Prohibition had been one Dan Carroll. He'd been a Boston cop who was fired during the Boston Police Strike of 1919. From then on, he kept a picture of then Gov. (and future president) Calvin Coolidge on his desk, as a reminder of the inadvertent favor he'd been done when he'd been fired from his low-paying job as a cop. He'd been forced to go into the rackets, which in his case proved much more lucrative.

When he died of natural causes years later, his obituaries in the Boston papers all described Carroll as a "sportsman," the journalistic shorthand of the day for "successful racketeer," along with "boxing manager."

I mention this only because Dan Carroll had a brother—Ed Carroll. He became the state senator from Southie. In other words, the Bulgers—Whitey the gangster and Billy the politician—were not unique in Southie history.

I knew none of this at the time. Other than the Bulgers themselves, and a handful of old-timers in the Lower End, I'm sure no one did. But everyone was about to get a crash course in the Bulgers—especially me.

Whitey's nine years in prison turned out to be a good career move. He missed the entire so-called Irish gang war between the McLaughlins of Charlestown and what became known as the Winter Hill Gang of Somerville.

During Whitey's years in prison, Billy had done his best to make sure his brother got every break. Billy was tight with John McCormack, the congressman whose name Whitey had dropped to his Air Force superior officers in the fifties. McCormack was very close to J. Edgar Hoover, the FBI director whose budget

McCormack shepherded through Congress every year. The McCormack-Hoover connection would come in handy later for both Whitey and his own personal FBI agent, John "Zip" Connolly.

Whitey was 36 when he was released from the prison in Lewisburg. He needed a job, so he used Billy's address when he applied to be a night custodian—janitor—in the Suffolk County courthouse in Pemberton Square. These days it's hard to explain what it was like in those public buildings back then. I told you about the "court officers" at the State House—the joke was that there were more door openers than doors.

In the school department, for instance, the unions had negotiated "heat days." Any day when the temperature went above 95 degrees or thereabouts, everybody was sent home. Boston was a very hot city in the summer, I can tell you that.

The courthouse may have been one of the last public buildings in the nation with elevator operators because . . . jobs.

As for the night crew of janitors, those were no-show, or at least seldom-show jobs. Some cleaning was done, after a fashion, a very desultory fashion. But say there were ten janitors on the payroll. Maybe . . . two or three, tops, showed up at the courthouse on any given night.

The guy in charge of the hiring was John E. Powers, the former state senator from South Boston. He'd been the first Democrat to become senate president since the Civil War, back in 1957. He had been the favorite to win the election as mayor in 1959, but was taken down by a well-timed series of gambling busts. One occurred in East Boston, in a building with a giant Powers for Mayor sign on the roof.

Every paper in the city ran front-page photos of the cops dragging out bookies—shocking stuff indeed!—with the Powers sign on the building's roof delivering a not-so-subtle message. Cardinal Cushing delivered an election-eve peroration about the need for moral men in public life, and Powers was defeated by John Collins in a major upset.

It was always assumed that Billy Bulger had gotten Whitey the no-show job. Later, however, in a crazy, drunken, typewritten letter written before his death in 2003, in addition to pleading with the judge in crooked FBI hitman Zip Connolly's corruption trial not to send him away to prison, Will McDonough took credit for getting Whitey his first post-Leavenworth job.

Whatever, the no-show job gave Whitey a claim to legitimate income for the parole board or probation officer. And it didn't put a crimp in the time he needed to reconnoiter the changed landscape of the Boston underworld.

Whitey was soon taking bets on afternoon greyhound racing at the local tracks like Wonderland and Raynham—the dogs were a lucrative racket back in those days, just like numbers, before the state lottery was started in 1972.

Whitey told people later that he went back to robbing banks after getting out of prison. He also went back to killing people. For years, I would get letters at the *Herald* from people, with photocopies of old clippings from the newspapers, inquiring about unsolved murders in South Boston and Dorchester. They'd ask me, was their father/uncle/cousin/whatever another victim of Whitey?

How could I know? Anyone who was with Whitey tended to end up dead, sooner or later. Or, if you were lucky, just in prison.

The top guy in the Southie rackets back then was Donald Killeen. He owned that bar in the Lower End, the Transit Café, about a block from the Broadway T station, that would soon become Triple O's. One of his brothers had been murdered in the North End years earlier, and another was in Donald's crew. But the Killeens had the traditional organized-crime problem—young guys coming up, hungrier and faster.

In Southie, these were the Mullens, who took their name from the corner they hung on—the corner of O and East 2nd Streets, named after a military veteran named Mullen.

In his book with Nathan Glazer, *Beyond the Melting Pot,* future Sen. Daniel Patrick Moynihan wrote that the Irish had been largely displaced in New York organized crime because bookmaking and other rackets were not trades for heavy drinkers. I used that quote once in the *Herald* and was accused of making up anti-Irish slurs. But it was a real quote, and a legitimate observation, as was proven by the gang war in Southie.

It began at the Transit Café, the Killeens' bar on West Broadway, when Kenny Killeen bit off the nose of one of the Mullens, Mickey Dwyer, a future MBTA bus driver, and then shot him several times. Not seriously wounded, Dwyer ran off to another watering hole and rounded up some Mullens who returned to the scene of the crime.

The Killeens had fled but the war was on.

To give you an indication of just how inbred and incestuous Southie was in those days, one of the Mullens was Paulie McGonagle, later murdered by Whitey. He had a brother named Donald, a legit guy who made the mistake of borrowing Paulie's car one night. Whitey and another couple of Killeens spotted it and opened fire, killing Donald McGonagle.

There was a third McGonagle brother, Robert. He was a Boston firefighter and he was married to a dental hygienist named Catherine Greig. After his brothers' murders by Whitey, the third McGonagle brother died of a drug overdose. And Robert McGonagle's widow, Catherine Greig, became Whitey's girlfriend. She was arrested with him in Santa Monica in 2011 after 16 years as a fugitive.

Talk about a small world. Here's another example. One of the Mullens was a guy named Dennis "Buddy" Roache. One night in another bar on West Broadway, he was shot and paralyzed by Whitey and Billy O'Sullivan, another of the Killeen thugs who also had a no-show state job, like Whitey.

Buddy Roache's brother was a young Boston cop named Mickey Roache. Years later, Senate President Billy Bulger would demand that the new mayor, Ray Flynn, appoint John "Zip" Connolly as the new Boston police commissioner.

Flynn balked, because it was widely known (at least in Southie) that Connolly was in fact a crooked cop, on Whitey's payroll. Instead, he picked Buddy Roache's brother, Mickey. Billy considered such *lese majeste* a provocative act, and the city's legislative needs often languished in Bulger's legislative limbo for years afterward.

Everyone in this demimonde was somehow connected to everyone else in one fashion or another. One of the city councilors was Joe Tierney, who would later run for mayor, and whose daughter Maura would do well in Hollywood. Tierney was from Southie, although he'd later moved to Hyde Park. So he had the old double base that was so important for winning citywide elections back then.

One of Joe Tierney's brothers was a . . . door opener in the state Senate. He worked for Billy Bulger, in other words. There was a third Tierney brother—who was murdered, shot in the back, in a random shooting in Southie.

One Saturday night in the *Herald* library (the "morgue") I was looking through a clip file on an old Southie murder from the Irish Gang War days in the sixties. I found a letter, handwritten in the elegant old Palmer style of both my aunt Mabel and (as I later discovered) Whitey Bulger.

It was from the mother of the slaying victim. She had apparently written to all the city's newspapers saying that she would greatly appreciate no longer seeing her son's name being mentioned as a victim of the "gang war," because he wasn't. He had just happened to be in the low shebeen when a real hoodlum, one Billy O'Brien, gunned him down in a drunken moment.

All this was just sort of expected in Boston, like blizzards in the winter and the occasional hurricane in late summer. People got shot. Nobody asked questions, certainly not at the *Globe*, especially after Paul Corsetti's travails became common knowledge.

One of the never-to-be-touched third rails of Boston politics and the media became the relationship between Whitey and Billy. The good brother–bad brother theme is an ancient one in fiction, but it wasn't a perfect fit in this case. And after Paul Corsetti, nobody wanted to be first to break the taboo.

In 1985, just as I was returning to the *Herald*, the federal racketeering trial of Boston Mafia underboss Gennaro "Jerry" Angiulo was about to begin. The feds had bugged the "Doghouse"—his headquarters on Prince Street in the North End—for several months back in 1981.

It had taken them more than a year to transcribe the tapes, but in addition to being totally incriminating, they were comic gold. When Jerry got the word one morning that one of his loan shark victims was dead, he started screaming, "He can't be dead! He owes me twelve thousand bucks!"

Later a couple of *Globe* old-timers did a book—mostly about how the intrepid FBI had planted the bugs. I thought to myself at the time, wouldn't it have been a much more entertaining book if they had just printed the gangsters' conversations verbatim, with a short introduction before every section?

The feds had transcribed everything, and before they played each one in court, they'd pass out copies to the jury and to the press. It was the easiest work I'd done since the Parkman House hearings at City Hall.

I'd write a column and the next day Angiulo would start screaming at the *Herald* reporters, Shelley Murphy or Kevin Cullen, about me.

"You tell Carr to lay off that Irish milk!" He hated the Irish, which we well knew from the tapes. "Tell Carr to come see me when he sobers up!"

One recurring theme on the Doghouse bugs was Whitey Bulger. Day after day they talked about him. He owed them a lot of money. He could find out more about what was going on in state courts than Jerry. He did hits for In Town.

I began to think that maybe the Curse of Paul Corsetti was wearing off—that everyone could write about Whitey again. Then I heard that the *Globe* was maybe working on a series on both brothers.

It seemed more like a column for *Boston* magazine. And I had an ace in the hole. Chris Lydon, of Channel 2, had done an interview with Kevin White after his third and final victory over Joe Timilty in 1979. During the cutaways, Kevin had been in a reflective mood, and he described the source of Senate president Billy Bulger's power.

"If my brother threatened to kill you," Kevin said, "you'd be nothing but nice to me."

On videotape, he went on to say that during the 1975 fight, during busing, when everyone in Southie was backing Timilty, he'd been working out at a South Boston health club at night, and leaving, he'd realized that Whitey might take him out.

"He was crazy enough," the now-former mayor said, "even then."

I wrote the column and suddenly I started hearing stories. Whitey was pissed, that's what everyone said. I was told by the *Herald*'s gossip columnists that they'd heard maybe I should stay out of Southie, as if I spent a lot of time there anyway. I'd only been to Triple O's once, on a Monday night pub crawl with Andy Hiller and another media guy. It was not the kind of place you could just drop into.

The joke about Triple O's was, the first shot was on the house. After that, you had to use your own bullets.

I didn't take the stories that seriously at first. By then I was working at Channel 56 two days a week, on Morrissey Boulevard, next door to the *Globe*.

Once again, so near, and yet so far.

To get to Channel 56 from the *Herald*, I had to drive by the South Boston Liquor Mart. That was the package store that Whitey had basically extorted from a local hustler named Stippo Rakes. Everybody knew who it belonged to, even if not on paper (because a convicted felon like Whitey couldn't own a package store, just as he couldn't be the owner of record at Triple O's).

The local Southie pols liked to have their signs in the front window of the Liquor Mart during election season. Their presence represented Whitey's blood-stained imprimatur.

One morning a *Globe* photographer was driving into the city past Whitey's store when he noticed a crew from the city's Department of Public Works at the Liquor Mart installing parking curbs in front of the package store—a city crew!

The photographer pulled around, parked his car in an inconspicuous spot on a side street, and then took some photos of the city crew doing work at the liquor store of the most notorious gangster in the city, whose brother just happened to be the most powerful politician in the state.

Seemed like a good story. He turned in his photos and then delivered another set to an FBI agent he was friendly with downtown. But the next day no pictures or story appeared in the *Globe*. No one said anything to the photographer. It was *Globe omerta*—silence. A couple of days later, the photographer drove by the Liquor Mart and saw a new crew—a private crew—tearing up the work of the DPW crew.

How do I know this? Because years later, the photographer testified in federal court during the first hearings into FBI corruption. The story, which didn't get nearly the attention it should have, just proved how in the satchel both the *Globe* and the FBI were with the Bulgers.

Whitey was rightfully concerned about law-enforcement bugs installed by cops who weren't on his payroll (and there were some). So in the warm weather, he would stand outside, just outside the store, and hold court, often with another serial killer, his partner Stevie Flemmi.

Being on television twice a week, I was recognizable. Pretty soon, Whitey knew me, and my car. As I drove through the rotary on my way from the *Herald* to Channel 56, he would glare at me. It was not a pleasant experience.

I remembered an old paperback I'd read about another local hitman, Joe Barboza. He said the easiest guys to hit were creatures of habit. If you stuck to the same routine every day, left home at the same time, slept in the same place every night, had coffee at the same Dunkin' Donuts every morning, you were the type of person who'd eventually get caught flat-footed.

I decided Barboza knew what he was talking about. I stopped hanging out in bars, even Foley's. It was too close to Southie. I tried to drive home a different way every night. Some nights, when I'd be leaving Channel 56, I'd want a road beer or two—I owed it to myself, as Joe Heaney would say. The nearest liquor store was the South Boston Liquor Mart, but that was out of the question, obviously.

So I would take a left on Preble Street, just before Whitey's, and I'd head into Andrew Square, where I'd grab a couple of 16-ounce Ballantine Ales. I thought I was being, for lack of a better phrase, street smart.

The anchor at Channel 56 was Jack Hynes, a good guy whose father had finally defeated James Michael Curley for mayor back in 1949. He'd worked at Channel 5 and then moved over to Channel 56. He lived in Southie and sometimes bought a bottle of wine or two at the Liquor Mart.

One day I arrived at the station and Jack motioned me over to his desk. I walked over and he whispered to me that he'd had an interesting conversation the previous night at the Liquor Mart. The guy—whom he hadn't recognized—asked him why I never came into the store, since I was in the neighborhood all the time.

Jack was no dummy. He said he had no idea. Which was when the guy said, well, you know, Howie stops off in Andrew Square some nights, so how come he don't come into our store?

Jack was kind of surprised to be hearing this, given his status as not only a well-known media celebrity, but also as the son of a former mayor.

Then the guy told Jack to pass a message on to me.

"Tell Howie if he ever comes in here we got a fresh dumpster in the back just waiting for him. It'll be another Robin Benedict."

Robin Benedict had been a Combat Zone hooker who'd been murdered and presumably dismembered by one of her johns, a Tufts University professor. Her body had never been found.

After that, I was watching my back full-time. The good news was, the *Globe* had finally gotten around to publishing their series about the Bulger brothers, strongly suggesting that Whitey was a rat for the FBI. That took some of the heat off me—Whitey had other people to hate now, including one of the FBI agents he'd been bribing, whom he correctly blamed for leaking to the *Globe*.

But why did Whitey hate me so much? Others in the media were likewise beginning to tentatively tip-toe around the question of the Bulgers and their connections to the city's power structure.

All the reporters at the *Globe* who weren't Irish or Italian—and that was most of them now— would never be menaced. They had their rich parents, their trust funds, they were legacies. But people like me, or Paul Corsetti, or even later Kevin Cullen—we were little more than knock-around guys. Nobody would miss us, really, if we turned up missing. Especially if you worked for the *Herald*.

One additional problem I had was my visibility—a newspaper column and a TV gig. Plus, I was in Whitey's neighborhood all the time. I was not out of sight, out of mind.

The larger problem for me was that I was going after his little brother Billy. Whitey took that really personally. In 1970, when Billy was first running for the state Senate, an obscure candidate had tried to raise the issue of Whitey in the primary campaign. Whitey had considered killing the guy, as came out at the congressional hearings in 2003.

With my digging into salaries and hack families, and my TV crew at the State House, I was getting under Billy Bulger's skin. I would stake out the Senate chambers, and he would refuse to come out until I ran out of time and left.

He would look around and say to whoever was there, senators or reporters: "Has the savage gone yet?" Other times, I found out later, he preferred to use a Latin word to describe me—"excrescence."

Meaning, an abnormal outgrowth, something very ugly.

One time a new State House cookbook was being published. A ceremony was scheduled in the Hall of Flags. I knew Billy would be there, so I hid behind a pillar with my cameraman until he appeared. I sneaked up behind him and said, "Mr. President, what's your favorite recipe?"

He turned around, thought for a second and then said, "Roast reporter!"

Then he chuckled, very satisfied with himself. But I was ready with my own comeback.

"Really?" I said. "I would have thought it would be strawberry shortcake."

His smile evaporated. He turned and walked away, muttering over his shoulder: "Observe my back."

He hated being the shortest guy in the State House—about 65 inches high, as I always put it. He had a guy, his top aide, Eddie Phillips. His only qualification seemed to be that he was even shorter than Billy. Eddie Phillips's house is where Billy went to take the call from Whitey after he went on the lam in 1995.

(Whitey wasn't much taller; he wore lifts in his boots because, as he told the other guys in the gang, he had to carry a knife in his boot because as an ex-con he couldn't get a permit to legally carry a gun.)

During Dukakis's presidential campaign in 1988, Frank Phillips, who had by then gone over to the *Globe,* called up a judge whose budget had been decimated because he hadn't hired the son of one of Billy's cronies.

Dukakis was terrified of Billy Bulger and had done nothing to protect the judge. So Frank asked the judge what he took of Dukakis running to become the leader of the Free World.

"How can he stand up to the Russians," the judge said, "when he can't stand up to a corrupt midget?"

From then on in my column, that was Billy Bulger's name. The Corrupt Midget. That was on first reference. After that it was "the CM."

There was a guy who'd been in the old McLaughlin gang. His name was Francis X. "Gaga" Murray. I never met him, but he used to leave letters for me on Sunday mornings at the front desk of the *Herald.* He was a funny bastard who had survived several shootings in the 1960s. When he'd been on the lam from

Winter Hill (which was often) he hung out in Hot Springs, Arkansas, when it was still Owney Madden's town.

Years later, Gaga wrote a crazy e-book about the Boston underworld, and credited me with creating what became the myth of Whitey Bulger.

"Guess who puts his name in the newspaper? Howie Carr. He was after Billy Bulger. Howie Carr hated Billy Bulger. . . . There was no way catching him. Howie Carr wanted to make a name for himself. 'Whitey the killer.' 'Whitey could punch this guy out.' 'Whitey could do this, Whitey could do that.' Instead of the truth."

Gaga also said I never told the truth about Whitey being gay. That wasn't true. I was the first one to publish the photo of Whitey in his Village People cowboy outfit, taken down in Provincetown. The FBI gave me that photo.

But Gaga was right about the fact that Billy Bulger was a lot more fascinating character with his mysterious, sinister serial-killing brother behind him. The ties

THE BROTHERS BULGER
Howiecarrshow.com

Another FBI gift, a "Village People" photo of Whitey taken in Provincetown that I made into a pink magnet.

between politics and organized crime were just so . . . in your face. And I had that beat all to myself.

"Howie Carr MADE Whitey Bulger," Gaga said. "BIG MAN in Southie. Dorchester. And everywhere else. Even in Walpole. Guys was running around: 'Whitey's my brother-in-law.' 'Whitey's that.' If only they knew the truth!"

Gaga also mentioned what everyone who had been paying attention knew— Whitey hadn't been around when the real wet work was going down, in the Irish gang war between 1961 and 1965.

"Whitey wouldn't have lasted in our circle. Too much a movie star. When Whitey left Alcatraz, we were gone. He had a lucky run. Nobody was around to stop him. He went up against small guys."

True, I would say. But whatever else you say about him, Whitey (or some version of himself) has been portrayed on the silver screen by Jack Nicholson and Johnny Depp. In its own way, that's something. Maybe not much, but better than nothing, I guess.

The *Globe* series on the two brothers finally came out, years later. In it, Billy said of Whitey, "There is much to admire." That took the heat off me. Whitey turned his attention to Kevin Cullen, another guy from "the neighborhood." He blamed one of the FBI agents he'd been paying off for leaking to the *Globe*. That G-man was later promoted to director of the FBI's training academy in Quantico. That's the FBI for you.

In the summer of 1990, the feds finally came down hard on Whitey's cocaine operation. The *Globe* had long insisted that Bulger had "kept the drugs out of Southie." As you would expect, the head cheerleader was the tough street kid from Lincoln, Mike Barnicle. He called Whitey "Jimmy," as if they'd grown up in the projects together. He once wrote that the only words the brothers shared were at Thanksgiving when one or the other said, "Pass the gravy."

It was an early Friday morning when the cops began rounding up Whitey's 50 drug dealers. Zip Connolly, preparing to retire to a hack job at state-regulated Boston Edison, was beside himself, worrying that Whitey—er, Jimmy—would be arrested.

He wasn't, but by mid-morning, dozens of his dealers were being brought into the old federal courthouse in Post Office Square for their initial court appearances. I was there with our court reporter, and the *Globe* had two reporters as well, one of whom was Elizabeth Neuffer, who would later die in a car accident in Iraq in 2003 while working as a war correspondent.

This was one of those occasions where everyone had to cooperate, because there was just too much to handle otherwise. So we divided up the arraignments and headed downstairs.

When we compared notes later in the afternoon, we realized that almost all of Whitey's cocaine dealers had jobs in the public sector—they were hacks, in other words. One was picked up while he was sleeping through his overnight shift at the city DPW yard on Frontage Road. Another had a job at the Mass Water Resources Authority (MWRA), where the personnel director was the wife of the state senator from Framingham whom I had slammed in the column that led to the beginning of "The Governors" on WRKO.

When one of the younger dealers was lugged in the Lower End, he began screaming, "I'm a working man!" He too had a hack job.

Everything I'd been writing about hacks—and which the *Globe* had been denying for years, while attacking me for even daring to report it—was proven true. I wrote a column calling Whitey's crew "the hack gang." The feds had a press conference saying that the arrests put a lie to the *Globe*'s abject fictions that Whitey had kept the drugs out of Southie.

The arrests elevated the governor's race to a new level. The Republican candidate was William F. Weld, the former U.S. attorney. The Democrat was John Silber, the president of Boston University, a very conservative Democrat (I voted for him in the primary). The problem with Silber was that he was endorsed by Billy Bulger. Bulger had made sure he'd gotten the necessary 15 percent at the Democratic state convention in Springfield to get on the ballot.

Weld ran a TV ad in which Whitey's face morphed into Billy's. It was a brutal campaign. Many of Weld's political operatives had worked for him at the federal courthouse, and had access to the wiretaps that the feds had recorded of Whitey's drug dealers. We knew about a lot of the tapes, had even heard some of them.

As the election neared, Weld was lagging in the polls. For one thing, Silber seemed more conservative than the patrician Weld, supposedly the last Yankee ever to be valedictorian of his graduating class at Harvard College, in 1966.

Silber would say whatever popped into his head. He speculated why so many foreigners from "the tropical climes" were ending up in Massachusetts, on welfare. He did not suffer fools gladly. At one event, I went up and introduced myself and told him I had once been one of his instructors at BU, in journalism. He looked me up and down. He knew very well who I was.

"Journalism?" he said. "I just hope it wasn't journalism ethics."

Silber was a tough guy, very intelligent, and he'd always had to overcompensate for a withered left arm. He was from Texas. Billy always did better with people who weren't from around here. He could hit them with the old blarney, tell them he never watched television and quote Juvenal (in English of course). They'd invariably swoon.

And Billy returned the favor to Silber, tongue-bathing him with one slobbering tribute after another.

"He'll be inaugurated in January," Billy would say. "In February, we invade Rhode Island."

It was an orgy of self-congratulation. Silber seemed to be well on his way to victory, until he did an interview with Natalie Jacobsen, the anchor-madonna of Channel 5. Local television news was at its pinnacle, and Silber couldn't bring himself to just smile and nod at her inane questions. (During the 1988 presidential election, she'd referred to the Dukakis campaign as "we.")

In that single interview with "Natalie," as everyone familiarly called her, Silber's innate nastiness was revealed for all to see. Those of us who taught at BU knew what a martinet he could be, even if we had voted for him in the primary. It's okay to have a chip on your shoulder—God knows I've always had one, as the *Globe* pointed out—but you shouldn't let strangers see it. They might get the wrong idea, or the right idea.

As they used to say in Hollywood, self-pity is not good box office.

Just before the election, Weld's people asked me to do them a favor—cohost a night out with Weld for the boyos at Foley's. We'd play "whip out"—$200 cash from each of us, to buy as much beer as that would pay for. The goal was to make Weld seem like less of a patrician stiff. On Beacon Hill, they used to say, "A gentleman never drinks before 5 o'clock, and he never drinks east of Park Street."

J.J. Foley's was more than somewhat east of Park Street.

The local television stations all gave it great play. It was the least I could do, not so much to help Weld, who in my book was just okay, but to foil the Bulgers, who weren't.

On election night, it quickly became clear that Weld was going to win and become the first Republican elected to the governorship since 1970. I was doing coverage on WRKO with Jerry Williams and my old pal the state treasurer, Bob Crane, not a bad guy, as Jerry always said.

Every break, Crane would step out of the studio and call the State House for the latest returns. And every time he'd return, another Democratic state senator would have gone down to defeat. It was a total wipeout. The Republicans were even ousting entrenched hacks far down the ballot in obscure county fights, like register of probate in Middlesex County.

It was exhilarating. Dukakis had called me a nutcase, told me personally he never read my stuff. And I was winning.

Jerry, Crane, and I were mostly talking among ourselves, reading the wire copy that was brought in by newsman Jon Masters. I was only one of the four in the studio who wasn't a World War II vet. Almost 40, I was still the youngest guy in the room.

Late in the evening, we got a call from an older man who wanted to ask me a question, about, of all things, Deerfield.

"What would Mr. Boyden think of you, Howie," he asked, "if he knew what you'd been doing all this year?"

1990: Buying a round with GOP candidate William Weld at J.J. Foley's—a photo op for the 11 o'clock news.
Source: AP Photo/John Cetrino

Paper Boy

It was a good question. What would the headmaster think? The Quid was always one for decorum. He was endlessly exhorting us boys to finish up strong. As I've told you, the school motto was "Be Worthy of Your Heritage."

Had I been worthy of my, you'll pardon the expression, heritage? Chasing hack pols through the city, hanging out in courtrooms as drug-dealing gangsters were dragged in front of judges, in handcuffs, and finally working behind the bar far east of Park Street?

Maybe it's not the way Frank Boyden would have played it, but on the other hand, he loved and cherished the old Massachusetts. Born in 1879, he'd grown up listening to the stories of Union veterans of the Army of the Potomac. I'd seen the photos of Boyden campaigning back in the mid-50s with Christian Herter, one of my all-time favorite governors, just based on his official portrait hanging in the State House. In it, he is smoking a cigarette. (Now that I think about it, I wonder if Herter's portrait has been cancelled.)

I assumed the caller was, like me, a Deerfield boy, much older and probably Yankee, but still someone much like myself.

"What would the headmaster say?" I said, trying to compose my thoughts. "I'd like to think he'd say . . . you did what you had to do, and that ultimately, you made things better. A little better, anyway, maybe."

Later on, after he'd been run out of the presidency of the University of Massachusetts with what is now a $272,000-a-year pension, Billy Bulger gave an interview to *Boston* magazine. He said that back in 1990 he'd considered suing "this nut"—me. The writer said Billy Bulger and I had such similar backgrounds and temperaments that "they could be brothers themselves."

I don't think so.

The CM also described my M.O. as a reporter, not inaccurately:

"He's got all kinds of people who come in through the back door, doing business with him, telling him things about people that might embarrass someone, and that's fine, that's a way of doing business."

That's how newspapers used to operate, when they meant something to people, when you had to read at least one every day. But as we all understand, those days are long gone.

Of all the things Billy said about me over the years, I most remember his words at the congressional hearing in 2003. Someone asked Bulger to address all the stories about him and his brother, and who or what exactly had created the situation that he now found himself in, under oath, under scrutiny on live television in the twilight of his career.

Billy Bulger obviously wanted to blame me for his downfall, but it wasn't the right occasion to denounce "the savage" or "excrescence." So when he was asked who had brought him to this sorry pass, he paused for a moment to consider how to word it precisely.

"It comes," Billy Bulger finally answered, "from the tabloid talk-shot stuff in Boston and it was concocted there."

So Gaga was right all along!

13
"GOOD MORNING, NEW ENGLAND!"

WRKO had a solid lineup. By 1990, I was the number one fill-in, but I couldn't break into the starting rotation until 1993, when the midday host, Gene Burns, made a poor career decision to take a job at WOR in New York.

I lobbied for the midday job and got people to call on my behalf. Jerry Williams was dead set against any promotion for me. I was like Brutus, as far as he was concerned. I had that lean and hungry look. He was pushing 70, but seemed older. As I've mentioned, he was running around with a dim-witted young woman in her early twenties. He'd even taken her down to the Cape with Barbara Anderson and me when "The Governors" were making an appearance somewhere. We were in a limo, and it was a very long ride.

Jerry had gotten Bob Crane to give her a job at the Lottery, which he controlled. Bob was always an easy touch.

But after 26 years as treasurer, Crane had decided to retire at age 64. The new treasurer was a young Republican, Joe Malone, who'd been heavily touted by Jerry. Now Jerry wanted his young gal pal taken care of. She got a promotion at the Lottery, and one of the older women who'd been passed over filed a grievance with her union.

Everyone was going to be deposed, maybe even me. It was going to be very messy. To protect myself, I leaked the story to Frank Phillips, who was now at the *Globe*. It was embarrassing to Jerry. Rather than endure a lengthy arbitration, with everything guaranteed to be leaked to the papers, his friend quit. Suddenly Jerry, rather than the taxpayers, was on the hook for her expenses.

The weekly "The Governors" show continued, but it wasn't the same. Our guy Bill Weld was in the Corner Office, and Billy Bulger was hobbled by the fact that 16 of his 40 members were now Republicans. At the station, Jerry and his producer were always snarling at me, as if I were somehow responsible for the indefensible situation he had found himself in, a reformer outed as a sugar daddy.

As my Aunt Mabel used to say, there's no fool like an old fool.

The Federal Communications Commission (FCC) was getting ready to deregulate radio, which would mean that large companies could expand their footprint—the number of stations they could own in any market. And with that added money coming in, the aggregators could expand . . . and expand . . . and expand, with money borrowed from Wall Street hedge funds.

Over time, the deregulation would create havoc and eventually wreck the entire radio industry, as so often happens with any industry unfortunate enough to be "reformed" by the government.

But in the early 90s, it just meant that the would-be radio moguls were too busy gobbling up their competitors and moving into new markets to actually manage their existing properties. The owners of WRKO brought in a blustering blowhard by the name of Dick Penn to run the cluster.

Eddie Andelman, a legendary sports talk-radio host in Boston, used to dismiss recycled baseball lifers with his own invented one-word phrase: "good-baseballman." Dick Penn was a "goodradioman." Just bouncing from one market to another, always fucking things up, leaving every place worse than he'd found it. He might as well have been a nomadic local TV news director.

One day around Christmas 1992 he came into my office waving the November ratings, which had just arrived. He was stunned at the drop in WRKO's p.m. drive ratings from the October levels.

"And I checked—it happens every year," Penn said. "I'm going to have to do some research into this. The ratings go down every November! There's a problem here."

I asked him if he'd ever heard of Daylight Savings Time. He had. I patiently explained to him that every year DST ends in the first week of November. Then I asked him if he'd ever studied the coverage pattern for WRKO. Of course he hadn't done that, because that would have required . . . effort, thought, study, research—in short, work.

I told him that WRKO had a north–south directional signal, 50,000 watts. That meant it was weaker in the western suburbs, even in the western neighborhoods of the city, like Brighton and Allston.

Per FCC regulations, the daytime pattern ends at sunset, and suddenly, WRKO cannot be picked up west much beyond Kenmore Square. That, I explained to him, was the problem, a big problem. You couldn't pick up WRKO's signal in perhaps a quarter of the SMSA—standard metropolitan statistical area.

"Oh," he said.

And yet I was the newspaper guy who didn't know anything about radio. No, I'd just listened to it my entire life. But that was the rap on me on WRKO, among many, because Jerry and the rest of the "goodradiomen" didn't want me in the starting lineup.

Nonetheless, when Burns moved on, I replaced him, but with a major impediment. I got to do two mid-morning hours by myself, but in the third and final hour of my show, I was paired with an English woman who'd never lived in Boston. After the 60 painful minutes with me, she then did two hours solo. She seemed to have one, and only one, observation on the Colonies:

"In America, so many of the men consider their guns to be extensions of their penises. . . ."

How profound. My third hour with her was dreadful. At noon, I walked out the door and 90 percent of the audience departed with me. Jerry had somehow convinced management to hobble me but good, but he'd also gut-shot himself. Gene Burns had always left him with a sizable lead-in, and I would have, but Victoria Jones left Jerry with almost no listeners when he went on the air every afternoon at 2.

I was still writing three columns a week for the *Herald*, so I didn't have a lot of time to hang out at the station, schmoozing. The people who didn't like me were at the office all day, undercutting me, sniping, backbiting.

Besides the new idiot station manager Dick Penn, they brought in a new program director who was nicknamed, appropriately enough, Junior. His main job was telling Dick Penn how nice his tie looked that morning. Junior's assistant was Jerry's producer, who whispered everything Jerry said about me to Junior, who whispered it to the station manager.

Early on in my radio career somebody told me that almost everybody in radio was a C student. That was a charitable assessment, I discovered.

I liked to start my show by saying, "Good morning, New England." Jerry started his show by saying "Good afternoon, New England." He complained to his producer, who complained to Junior, who complained to the station manager. I was told to stop saying it. Instead I began, "Good morning, six-state region."

I wasn't all that concerned. I figured my ratings must be pretty good, and the sales staff liked me, especially one—a 27-year-old woman I'd started going out with after I separated from my first wife. I was living in a rent-controlled apartment in Harvard Square. Soon my name was splashed in paint on the wall of a building on Memorial Drive—the owner was a small landlord who railed against rich liberals living in rent-controlled apartments.

Number one, I was far from rich. Number two, if there was going to be rent control, my landlord preferred tenants like myself, who were too busy working all day to keep dragging him into Housing Court with bullshit complaints.

My new girlfriend and most of her colleagues wanted me to do their live reads, which is the mark of success in radio. If the advertisers want to buy time on your show, that's good. If they want you to read their ads, that's even better, because it means they think that you, personally, can sell their stuff, because the audience trusts you.

As Jerry Williams always said, "Never forget that we're not in the radio business, we're in the advertising business."

Meaning that radio, all media in fact, exists first and foremost to sell products or services—through advertising. Good programming is what attracts a large audience. That's why a manager tries to put on the best programming he can, to draw the largest audience that will buy the largest amount of whatever your advertisers are selling. Good programming is nothing more than a means to an end, and that end is sales.

I understood that. That was one reason I never could quite figure out why Jerry hated it so much when somebody, usually in the *Globe*, referred to him as an entertainer. So what?

I knew some people at the station didn't like me, but after you work awhile at places like City Hall or the State House, on the visiting team so to speak, a few boo birds in the cheap seats don't bother you too much.

I could handle the glares and the backbiting, just for the extra money I was finally making. Financially, I was finally beginning to get my head above water again.

Divorce is tough, especially in a no-fault state like Massachusetts. It's totally stacked against men. I always say, the way the law works here is, if she catches you with somebody, you owe her a million bucks. If you catch her with somebody, you owe her a million bucks.

Once I got the three-hour weekday gig in late 1992, I figured I was back on my feet again. I was even starting to think about looking for a new apartment—my fifth-floor unit didn't have heat, which is not a good thing in the winter. It also didn't have a parking space, which in Harvard Square is even worse.

But just as I was starting to think I'd survived a couple of years of near-destitution, I was called into Dick Penn's office one Friday morning after my show and fired. I was stunned. Here I'd spent all this time mastering the radio business, and just like that, suddenly, it was over.

The owner didn't like me. It was as simple as that. That's an understatement, as I would later find out. It had nothing to do with the show—I had by far the best program on the station, and I had the ratings to prove it. The owner later blamed it on Penn, but ultimately it was his call to order the hit.

I still had a contract, but I'd been signed to a short-term deal. Before long, I would have to live on my *Herald* paycheck, which wasn't enough, not nearly.

They also got rid of my semi-cohost, and hired a fat slob who'd just been fired from a station in Los Angeles, Tom Leykis, a radio cliché out of *WKRP in Cincinnati.* That hurt—Leykis was a complete buffoon.

The winter-book ratings came out a week or so later and guess what—the station that had just fired me owed me, in addition to my regular salary under my contract, another $4,000 in bonuses. I had the only decent numbers at WRKO.

I called up somebody in management and demanded my bonus money. They didn't put up a fight and about a week later, Penn himself got whacked. As spring turned into summer, the assistant to the owner telephoned me and asked me if I wanted to do fill-in work on WRKO.

Nah, I said. Fill-in work was not in my contract. Just keep sending me the checks, I said, or I'll be seeing you in court.

Leykis had no ratings. Jerry's were lower than whale shit as well. Channel 7, my old employer, had bought a "legacy" AM station, WHDH. It had been the Red Sox flagship station during the Impossible Dream season in 1967.

Like almost all AM radio stations, WHDH had fallen on hard times, and Channel 7 had picked up the signal for practically nothing. But they couldn't do anything with it, just as they couldn't make a go of the TV signal. So they sold it for short money to the owners of WRKO, who decided to convert "full service" WHDH into the second talk station in Boston.

Guess who the afternoon guy would be? Yup. Not only was I going back to the same company, I was going back to 7 Bulfinch Place, because it was decided that it would probably be wise to separate me from the crew at now-flailing WRKO who'd stabbed me in the back.

I would be going head-to-head against Jerry Williams.

Jerry was not pleased with my return. I owned afternoon drive from day one. It was 1993, and the Boston City Council elections were on. As I've mentioned, the first gay city councilor was a guy named Dave Scondras. He was a bad drunk. One night, as the election neared, he got drunk, very drunk, and began calling 911, looking for a deputy superintendent who'd once run for the Council himself. He'd lost his phone number.

Scondras was totally wasted, slurring worse and worse as the recorded calls continued. But he kept phoning. Finally, the female dispatcher started yelling out to her supervisor, "It's Scondras again!"

The supervisor finally took the phone and told him, gently, that he shouldn't be calling 911, that it might even be considered a crime to be calling, drunk, again and again. Finally Scondras gave up, said "Okay!" and hung up.

Somebody made a copy of the calls and gave the tape, not to me, but to the *Herald*. But what could a newspaper, even a tabloid, do with such a tape in that pre-Internet era? So I got the tape, and my producer cut it up, complete with a musical bed. We played it, in segment after segment, call after call, all afternoon, just before the election.

Two weeks later, Scondras was narrowly defeated for reelection.

By then, I was crushing Jerry in the ratings. My lead-in was this new syndicated guy named Rush Limbaugh. Jerry's lead-in was Tom Leykis. One day Leykis devoted his entire four-hour show to a discussion of . . . dog shit. Hey, it beat doing show-prep work.

Now it was Christmas. The company was having a Christmas party, open bar for all the stations in the cluster, which meant both my new station and WRKO. The GM of WHDH, who like everyone else in radio at 7 Bulfinch Place was an exile from the mother ship, insisted that everyone from WHDH wear tuxedos. That way we would distinguish ourselves from the also-rans at WRKO.

None of us drank anything. I don't remember much memorable happening, and we all left early. We'd made our point. We were a team, down to the uniforms. Then the next morning I got some very exciting news—an early Christmas present.

Tom Leykis was under arrest at the Area 1 precinct, next to the Channel 7 building. He was charged with beating up his (second or third) wife in a drunken assault at their rented apartment on Beacon Hill after the Christmas party. According to the police report, Leykis had attacked her with a lit log from the fireplace.

In my career, I have tipped the *Globe* off to very few stories. For the first time since Jerry Williams's girlfriend was hired at the Lottery, I dropped a dime again when Leykis was lugged.

The *Herald* got the first tip, then Frank Phillips at the *Globe.*

What could I do to finish off WRKO once and for all? That was my next question. As the leader in Boston talk radio (at least until the fall ratings came out), WRKO had a deal with a big cell phone company. You could call in for free to WRKO. In those days, that was a big plus. I decided to put an end to that perk once and for all.

I called a female columnist at the *Globe*—the same woman whose apartment I'd stayed at in New York while covering the *Goodfellas* trial in Brooklyn.

I told her about the unspeakable incident of domestic abuse, and the circumstances that led up to the horrific assault. I informed her where the archfiend was locked up, and told her that she might want to inquire about the cell phone provider's corporate policy about subsidizing wife-beating drunkards. I didn't have to draw her a diagram.

In a jolly Yuletide mood, I strolled into 7 Bulfinch Place and took the elevator up to the third floor. I sought out one of my producers, Virgin Boy, as we had dubbed him. I gave him the name and telephone number of the radio reporter for the *Los Angeles Times.*

I wanted the bad news for Leykis out quickly, so he wouldn't have a chance to spin some preposterous yarn as he desperately sought to flee back to his old market. Sometimes you want to give a defeated foe a chance to escape, but under different circumstances it behooves you to destroy all his means of retreat. I wanted to demolish every bridge Leykis could flee on, not that it was anything personal, you understand.

Then I got a phone call from the owner of the two stations. Remember, this was the guy who just a few months ago had engineered my firing, out of spite. He'd always had me over a barrel of one sort or another. Until now. Now he seemed nervous.

"Howie," he said, "have you heard what happened to Tom Leykis?"

"No," I said. "Gosh, Steve, I hope it's nothing bad—after all, Christmas is only two days away."

He told me what had happened. Leykis had apparently hired a lawyer and made bail. He was off the air, of course, and out of the rented apartment he'd shared with his latest wife on Beacon Hill.

"Oh my goodness," I said.

"Listen, Howie," he said. "You have to promise me one thing."

Of course, I said. After all, I thought to myself, you've treated me so well, Steve, in so many ways.

"Please," he said, "don't tell the newspapers. You wouldn't call the papers, would you?"

"Steve," I told him, "you have my word, I will not call the papers about this."

He seemed relieved. The story was on both front pages the next day. The cell phone company cancelled its deal with WRKO. Other advertisers followed suit and bailed out. Of course, I couldn't mention Leykis's crime on the air—he was, after all, a colleague. But I did slip up a few times and let callers get through who asked me about Leykis's behavior.

"All I know is what I read in the papers," I would say in my most unctuous tones. "I understand he mistook his wife for a Duraflame log."

A few weeks later, the ratings for the fall 1993 book came out. In their biography of Jerry Williams, *Burning Up the Air*, authors Steve Elman and Alan Tolz described what happened next:

"Jerry was aghast. Howie Carr had 5.3 percent of the listening audience. He had 2.4 percent, one of his lowest shares ever on WRKO."

It was all over. I had won. Management began planning for a transition. They bought a struggling little 5,000-watt AM signal that the Celtics had been operating as a sports station without success. The word was that they would move the pitiful sports format to AM 850, WHDH, my signal, which was 50,000 watts, and then combine the strongest programming of the two talk stations on WRKO.

Jerry knew he was on the ropes, but he figured he had an ace in the hole for the spring 1994 ratings book—his "sex survey." For a week, every June, he would open the lines and ask the listeners to call in and tell him their sex secrets. It couldn't have been any more low-brow—"The Governors" had always taken that week off—yet it was amusing in its own way.

Jerry thought maybe he could at least come close to me, and hang on even in some diminished capacity. But after all these years, the sex survey was as exhausted and spent as its creator. The fact that Jerry was now 70 made it seem even more like dirty-old-man radio than in the past.

On Friday, June 17, 1994, as Jerry began the final day of his final sex survey, O.J. Simpson, just indicted for the murders of his wife and Ron Goldman, jumped into Al Cowlings's white Ford Bronco. The famous slow-speed chase was on.

At Channel 7, we were monitoring the helicopter live shots on TV in real time. I was doing the play by play. As I was later told, Jerry's calls began drying up. Soon, his lines were empty—for the sex survey! By 4 or 4:30, he shut it down and began talking about the white Bronco.

Jerry Williams was finished.

A couple of months later, the radio shakeup was officially announced. I was going back to WRKO, in afternoon drive. My lead in: Rush Limbaugh. Jerry was demoted to a two-hour mid-morning slot. On my last day at WHDH—the final day of that famous station—I gathered up all the journalistic plaques they'd garnered over the years, put them in plastic trash bags, and dragged them downstairs. I set up shop outside 7 Bulfinch Place.

I did the show live, and invited commuters on their way to North Station to stop by Channel 7 and pick up some journalistic awards. Most I sold for a dime, the larger ones for a quarter. It was a gag—we donated the money to some charity—but I was also making my own little statement about journalism.

In the words of an old front-office man for the New York Yankees, as quoted by the late Jack Zanger in *The Jocks,* "To hell with newspapermen, you can buy them for a steak."

Ditto for almost everybody else in the media.

When I got the afternoon shift at WRKO, I figured I'd eventually give up my column in the *Herald.* But it didn't work out that way. For one thing, I needed the money. I had two children born in 1994—Irish twins, as they say—and another born in 1996.

My new wife and I bought a house in Wellesley, across the street from Dana Hall School. The nearby campus made it almost like being back in (a less rural) Deerfield, but what I most liked about the house was that it reminded me of 45 Kenwood Street in Portland. The third floor was a bonus, and so was the screened-in porch overlooking the town's brook path.

The media were already beginning to change. The Taylors were gone from the *Globe.* The *New York Times* had gone on a $1.4 billion spending spree in New England. They were buying newspapers! What would they do next, lay siege to One Wingo Square with catapults and battering rams? Rupert Murdoch knew better, despite what he'd told us at the annual Christmas parties. By the 1990s, Rupert was wisely getting out of the regional newspaper business.

In 1994, he unloaded the *Herald* to his publisher and longtime deputy Pat Purcell. More significantly, he sold Purcell the plant, at the intersection of the Southeast Expressway and the Turnpike Extension.

It was tolerable working for Purcell, until everything started going south almost 20 years later. What eventually transpired wasn't Purcell's fault. We didn't know it yet—nobody did—but newspapers were doomed. So was everything else in media, but how could you know before it happened?

I'm not a total Luddite when it comes to technology, but I'm not exactly on the cutting edge either. I had a flip phone for way too long, just to give you one example. But the first time I realized something was changing was in 1997. The *Herald* had cut some deal with AOL—remember them?—and every Sunday I had to write a piece that was posted onto what was called their Boston page or some such thing.

It wasn't what I would call a column per se, I just had to jot down a few thoughts and email them to somebody, I don't even remember whom. One Saturday night in August 1997, Princess Di was killed in a traffic accident in Paris. I've never been a big fan of the royal family, so her death meant nothing to me. But since it was dominating the news, I dashed off a few hundred words that essentially boiled down to: "Who gives a shit?"

It was posted and that AOL site suddenly got hundreds, maybe thousands, of angry replies. I wasn't going to get "cancelled," of course. All my listeners knew the contempt in which I held the "royal" family. They were nothing more than welfare chiselers as far as I was concerned. The Windsors were of such little interest to me that I don't believe I'd ever bothered to write anything about them before.

What impressed me most about the reaction to my Princess Di column was that it could create so much response, so immediately. Obviously, something was going on here.

A few months later, a much more significant event showed me just how quickly everything was changing. *Newsweek* magazine, then still a real thing, had confirmed that President Clinton had been having sex with a young intern at the White House, in the Oval Office.

Clinton, though, was a Democrat, and thus a member of a protected class. *Newsweek* spiked the story—professional courtesy and all that. But then some random guy obtained the story, and posted it online, on a website called The Drudge Report, owned and operated by one . . . Matt Drudge.

A few years earlier, probably no one would have ever seen Drudge's scoop. But then Bill Kristol, long before he succumbed to Trump Derangement Syndrome, went on one of the Sunday morning chat shows and began talking about this spiked *Newsweek* story and how it was available on the Internet.

Now that impressed me. Amazing enough that it appeared that the president of the United States had obstructed justice—lying under oath about it during a deposition in a different sexual-harassment lawsuit. But what was even more astonishing was the fact that some random civilian had used this new technology to bust state-run media for trying to protect one of their own, to wit, a Democrat.

The next day, Monday, I went with the Monica Lewinsky story for all four hours of my show. It was a huge day. I could feel the excitement crackling in the air. Would Clinton be forced to resign in disgrace, as a Republican would have been? Or would he Ted Kennedy it out? (In retrospect, the answer seems obvious.)

At 7, the WRKO night show hosts came into the studio. Two wealthy, uber-privileged liberal women from New York—*Two Chicks Dishing,* they called their show. I'm telling you, WRKO was like a train station, the way all these shows came and went.

The two women were shocked that I had devoted my entire show to . . . blow jobs. They didn't see it as a big deal. One of them was even a lawyer, and she thought nothing of the fact that a member of the bar, Clinton, had been caught lying under oath in a civil deposition, even one involving sexual harassment.

That year, 1998, turned out to be a great year for talk radio. On the rapidly declining AM band, it was ever more difficult for me to prevail in the ratings. But in 1998 I was number one in both the spring and the fall books in radio's prime demographic, persons 25–54.

That year was also when the local owners of WRKO, having bought a bunch of stations around the country after the deregulation of the media, cashed out. They sold everything to CBS radio.

Since CBS already owned several stations in the market, it would now have to divest itself of some of the Boston properties. As an AM station, WRKO would be among the first to be jettisoned, and I would soon be working for yet another new ownership, my third in less than a year.

And then Mike Barnicle was finally forced out at the *Globe*. As the consummate brown-nosing ass-kisser that he was, he had lately been sucking up to Don Imus. Imus was a white-knuckle drunk, the morning-drive shock jock on WFAN, the CBS-owned sports-talk station in New York City.

Barnicle had been basking in his New York exposure, but it didn't save him in the end.

Barnicle's firing, after all those years, made my day, to say the least. A local TV station came into the studio to record my reaction, and I lit up a cigar—the photo that used to top his piss-poor column included a cigar because he was, you know, a man of the people.

Then I wrote the kind of column of one-liners that had initially gotten him into his final jam. One of the throwaway lines was: "Don Imus will be 103 years old when his son graduates from high school."

I doubt Imus even saw my Barnicle-is-dead one-liner column, but somebody—I wonder who—told him that I'd said that he would be dead before his son graduated from high school.

So one morning soon after Imus went on the air and started ranting about what I'd allegedly said, he finally blurted out, "I'll live long enough to see his wife blowing Riddick Bowe—again!"

I didn't hear it, but later in the day someone told me about it, rather sheepishly, as if it was bad news. It surprised me, at first, because I couldn't recall saying any such thing. But then I decided to listen to what he'd said, on tape. That's when I heard the magic word "again."

That meant the I-man—Don Anus, as Howard Stern called him—was saying my wife had already fellated Riddick Bowe, the sometime heavyweight boxing champion of the world.

My wife was not a public figure under the standard definition of *Times* v. *Sullivan*, the landmark Supreme Court libel case from 1964. Don Imus could have gotten away with saying I'd given Riddick Bowe a blow job, because I am a public figure, but not my wife.

The only possible problem was that my wife would be suing my employer— CBS Radio. So what? I had a contract. It took us about two seconds to decide to file suit.

I called Alan Dershowitz, because he'd already sued Barnicle and won an out-of-court settlement after he was falsely accused of making a sexist, anti-Asian slur in Harvard Square. Dershowitz handed the case off to another lawyer.

Before we filed the complaint, I wanted to check to see if I'd ever actually said anything remotely like what Imus had accused me of saying. The way I usually figure these things is, even if I don't recall saying anything, if I had been thinking it, even just to myself, there was at least an off-chance I had blurted out something on the air. When you're live on air four hours a day, it's impossible to remember everything you've said.

But I'd never even thought about Imus being dead before his son graduated high school. It hadn't even occurred to me. Still, I wanted to make sure. I paid one of the station interns to listen to a week's worth of my shows, and he confirmed that I'd said nothing remotely like what Imus had been told I'd said.

CBS settled quickly. Their lawyers knew they didn't have a leg to stand on. At the time, CBS was a major radio company, and I doubt they even knew that I was on their payroll. As I said, even under the new rules of deregulation, the FCC wouldn't allow CBS to own both their own stations in Boston and those of Atlantic Radio. It would have amounted to a virtual monopoly in the market.

So they spun off some of the stations, including WRKO, to a company out of Philadelphia called Entercom, which turned out to be by far the worst corporation I ever worked for.

For starters, Entercom's management knew absolutely nothing about programming. In all the years that I was indentured to them, I'm unaware of a single success the company had in programming anywhere. In a few cases, they didn't screw up something they inherited, but mostly they had the reverse Midas touch.

Everything Entercom touched turned to shit.

The owner of the company was Joe Field, a lawyer who'd bought an FM station in 1968 and parlayed it into a nice little holding company. But then he turned it over to his son, David Field, a spoiled rich kid.

It's a variation on an old joke, but it applies to David Field. How do you make a million dollars in radio? Give a billion dollars to David Field.

Since 1994, as I mentioned, WRKO had owned another station, the sports-talk WEEI, a 5,000-watt AM signal formerly owned by the Celtics. They couldn't make a go of it, so the signal was moved to AM 850, my old station, which had 50,000 watts.

My "team," if you could call WHDH that, had won the talk-radio war in Boston. When I moved back to WRKO, Jerry Williams was on his last legs and the sports station was for all intents and purposes bankrupt.

But suddenly the management—first American, then CBS, and finally Entercom—began transferring most of WRKO's assets over to WEEI, starting with the Red Sox games, which were a big deal back then.

I had a fill-in, Gerry Callahan. I'd known him from his days covering sports at the *Lowell Sun*. After he came over to the *Herald* he was sometimes called "Howie Carr in short pants," because he had an . . . attitude. At least I didn't have to worry about Callahan being hired by the *Globe*. He had the same racial handicap as me. Too Irish, way too Irish. Unlike me, in fact, Callahan was FBI—full-blood Irish.

The new management decided to give Callahan his own show—on WEEI, with another Channel 7 refugee, sportscaster John Dennis.

That was okay, but it quickly became clear that Entercom loved sports, and hated talk radio. David Field was a big-time lib. He loved humanity, even as he treated his employees like shit. I once read a story about an old hand on Fleet Street advising his son about the newspaper business:

"Never work for a liberal employer, dear boy. They'll sack you on Christmas Eve."

So true. And in my case, they wouldn't even fire me, as much as I begged them to. That's how bad Entercom was.

As for WEEI, if you've never listened to sports talk radio, you haven't missed much. The best one-word description I ever heard of the entire format was "Shillville," coined by one of the local TV anchors. All the local teams were "we."

At the start of every season, all the hosts would make their predictions. The Red Sox were going to the World Series. The Patriots were going to the Super Bowl, the Bruins would win the Stanley Cup. The Celts were going to hang another banner from the rafters.

Guaranteed. Always.

When Tom Brady arrived, WEEI, the entire station, developed a kind of 24/7 homoerotic undertone. Some of the jock sniffers were practically throwing their panties at Number 12. On my show, I used to occasionally do one-man parodies of Boston sports talk.

Host number one: "I want to have Tom Brady's baby!"

Host number two: "I want to have Tom Brady's twins!"

Host number three (usually a part-time sidekick ex-jock): "I want to have Tom Brady's triplets!"

When Twitter came in, I started tweeting out after every Patriots' loss, parodying the slobbering way WEEI covered the games.

"Going in, I thought WE would win, but then THEY lost."

The most infuriating thing of all was, if the local teams did do well, WEEI's ratings went up, despite how dismal most of the entire station's lineup (outside of morning drive) was. And my ratings would go down. The jock sniffers strutted around like they were Number 12. Once after the Red Sox won the World Series, a couple of Shillville sycophants climbed onto one of the duck boats that were in the team's victory parade.

WEEI was handed everything by Entercom's clueless management. All our assets were dismantled and transferred to WEEI. WRKO was picked clean, for the benefit of Shillville.

Consider one of the longest-running features of my show, the Chump Line.

It developed from a one-time Howard Stern stunt. His show didn't start in Boston in morning drive. In the beginning, on the old WBCN, he was on DB—delayed broadcast. One night, I was driving home to my rent-controlled apartment in Harvard Square listening to a tape of Stern's show from that morning.

He had just replaced some local yokel in Rochester. Apparently the guy had a loyal following, and his fans deluged the station manager, leaving hundreds of messages on the GM's voice mail.

So Stern decided to play some of the taped calls, which were often crude but invariably funny. Sometimes Stern would interrupt the calls to answer his critics directly.

It occurred to me that it might be a good feature—every day. Just set up a number, tape the calls as they came in and play them back, as a regular daily feature at a regular time. We could call it . . . the Chump Line.

A few days later, it was up and running. The Chump Line quickly became one of the most popular segments on my show, every afternoon after the top-of-the-hour 5 o'clock news break.

Then we bought WEEI and suddenly everyone and everything at WRKO was an afterthought. The afternoon jock-sniffer show decided to start their own voicemail message service—the Whiner Line. That was okay, I guess, but a couple of months after lifting my idea, they began claiming that they had in fact been the ones who'd come up with the concept, and I'd copied them.

Where did I go to get my reputation back?

WRKO was suffering the traditional death of a thousand cuts. It started slowly, with minor changes, like losing our "street team" of interns. No great loss in and of itself. But then outside advertising was ended—no billboards, bus-backs, TV spots, etc.

The jock sniffers complained that WRKO's studio was better than theirs, so we were evicted, banished to one that was the size of an old-time phone booth, and that smelled like a bus station. Our best salesmen figured out what was happening and began to transfer over to the sports side, WEEI. Our news department, not that it was worth a damn, was eliminated.

In 2003, the morning team at WEEI was talking about the escape of a gorilla from the Franklin Park Zoo in Roxbury. Somehow the hosts brought up the METCO program, which allowed inner-city Boston high-school students—but only blacks, no whites need apply—to go to suburban high schools in the lily-white suburbs.

Then they started speculating on whether the gorilla was trying to flee the city, and one of the hosts called the primate the "METCO gorilla," and the other one said he was headed toward Lexington.

You can imagine the reaction. The hosts were suspended, and soon everyone in the cluster who was on the air had to take . . . sensitivity classes.

The roundup of the usual suspects of course included me. I hadn't done anything, but I had to go to Diversity University. It was just another indignity. It was bad enough that I was on a second-class station owned by a fourth-class company, but now I had to pay the price for a fuck-up by the jock sniffers.

I went to the first session, where some pampered affirmative-action grandee in a $2,000 suit was telling me—me!—to confront my white privilege. During the first break, I called a few people and told them to start calling me on my cell phone, which I neglected to mute.

After about four phone rings, and my loud exits from the Star Chamber, the presiding Rev. Bacon—he of "steam control" fame in Tom Wolfe's novel *The Bonfire of the Vanities*—told me maybe I should just leave. I agreed.

A day or so later, Entercom suspended me from my show for a week, without pay, for insufficient white guilt. We had a union, which was generally worthless, but I called our local's business agent anyway to vent about the injustice of it all.

He came up with a great idea—the union would file an official grievance over my suspension with Entercom. As part of discovery, we would demand to know just how much money Entercom had paid the "community advocates" at METCO for steam control to put the gorilla issue to rest.

Management freaked out. They couldn't let those numbers get out there. Rev. Bacon must have really rolled them for some big-time "steam control."

The empty suits told the union they'd made a mistake suspending me and that as far as I was concerned, all was forgiven.

Soon after I'd returned to the air, the imbecile general manager—his name was Tom Baker—came storming into my office, threw a check on my desk, and walked back out without saying a word. It was the money Entercom had stolen from me by suspending me for no reason.

Next, the SMSA—the standard metropolitan statistical area—was changed, taking in even more cities and towns west of Boston. This was crushing to WRKO, and especially to me, with our flawed signal. Now, when Daylight Savings Time ended, I lost 40 percent of my audience at sunset—which by December was about 4 o'clock, one hour into my show.

The station became more and more of an afterthought to the Entercom suits, who on their best days couldn't have managed a one-car funeral.

Two station employees or hosts were convicted of murders involving poison. The program directors came and went, making ever more stupid programming decisions until they were shown the door, to be replaced by yet another goodradioman.

Finally, what was left of WRKO was turned over to WEEI's program director, Jason Wolfe, who was known to one and all as "Coffee Boy."

Meanwhile, on Beacon Hill, one House speaker after another was being convicted of assorted felonies. The second one of three (a fourth was merely an unindicted co-conspirator) was hired after his obstruction-of-justice conviction as the morning-drive host at WRKO.

I had a closer connection to this speaker's crime than I did to the others. I had been an actual witness to his crime—he had lied under oath, in a federal courtroom in Boston, to an appeals court panel that included former Supreme Court Justice David Souter.

His name was Tom Finneran. After his conviction, I dubbed him "Felon" Finneran.

I had been covering the hearing. I was sitting next to him, trying to bait him. He'd been waiting to testify, reading a pocket-sized biography of Winston Churchill, as if being busted in a tawdry gerrymandering scheme was somehow the equivalent of the Battle of Britain.

Finneran's risible excuse for his string of preposterous lies under oath was that he been under the influence of drugs—Advil. From then on I referred to him as "Advil-addled."

As in "the Advil-addled Felon Finneran."

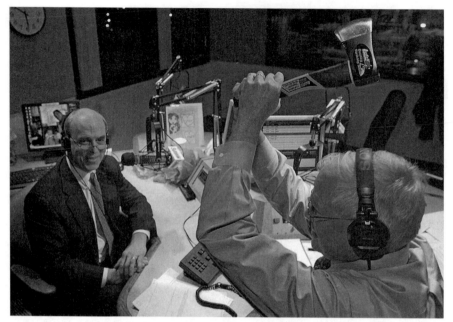

Doing a crossover with Advil-addled Tom "Felon" Finneran before he was axed from WRKO.
Source: Photo by John Wilcox/MediaNews Group/Boston Herald via Getty Images

It was an absurd decision by WRKO to put a crooked hack on a station that was supposed to be the voice of the taxpayers, but . . . Entercom happens. That was how I explained every disaster that occurred. I just told my listeners:

Entercom happens.

The owner's woke son, David Field, jock sniffer that he was, tried to put it in sports terms when he spoke to me about the hiring of a corrupt Democrat criminal. He said Finneran would have plenty of inside information on politics, just like the ex–Red Sox players (including Dick Radatz and Rico Petrocelli, both good guys) who were at one time or another on the WEEI roster of on-air personalities.

I tried to explain to Field that as far as WRKO's audience was concerned, hiring Finneran would be like hiring a key member of the hated New York Yankees—say, manager Joe Torre—to be your color guy.

My warning wasn't heeded. Finneran was hired and the morning numbers cratered from their previous level, which was already lower than that whale shit I'm always mentioning. I ordered polo shirts with the logo, "I am not a felon."

When asked about it by management, I explained that I wanted to avoid any confusion between the drive-time hosts at WRKO events.

Finally, the inevitable happened—an also-run FM signal was flipped to a talk format. Nature abhors a vacuum and WRKO was managed so wretchedly that it offered a tempting target for a new competitor. The same fate would soon be suffered by Shillville's sad sycophants—FM competition.

The new FM talk station, however, was as unlistenable as WRKO. It wouldn't have represented a threat, except for the only thing that mattered. It was on FM. It didn't matter that it had strictly Grade B talent—Imus's syndicated show anchored their morning drive, which said it all. The only thing that mattered was the signal, especially in the expanded SMSA.

By this point, less than 20 percent of the radio audience ever listened to the AM band, and those listeners skewed old—the 80-to-death demographic, as the joke went. One night I was driving with my older kids in the western suburbs—where WRKO's signal was weakest—and one of my daughters asked me, "Is this shortwave radio, Dad?"

Would that it were. After sunset, Radio Moscow had better coverage of the Boston metro than WRKO.

It was just one damn thing after another. Next, Entercom got the radio rights to the Boston Celtics. I didn't care one way or the other. Like most people, I hadn't listened to basketball play-by-play on radio since Johnny Most's departure from Celtics' broadcasts in the early 1990s.

But one January day, the pipsqueak program director of WEEI, and now WRKO, came up to me and told me that the first couple of hours my show would be preempted in Boston on the following Monday, the Martin Luther King holiday.

Why? I asked. Coffee Boy explained to me that, well, the Celtics weren't all that much of a draw, and they might drag down the WEEI afternoon show's ratings. So we just figured we'd put them on WRKO. On my show, in other words, because who cared about WRKO?

I was having a run of bad luck at the *Herald* too. The Internet was starting to catch on, and circulation was dropping. The editors were fired and the old Murdoch hand that replaced them decided to bring back . . . Mike Barnicle.

His comeback didn't last long—just long enough to put a dent in the *Herald*'s credibility as a news source. But I began referring to myself on the radio as the paper's "nonfiction columnist."

My luck, though, was about to change, thanks to Whitey Bulger.

14
"A WASTE OF OXYGEN"

Willard Mitt Romney is not one of my favorite politicians these days, but he did help me, however indirectly, to finally get a book contract in 2003.

In 2002, eight years after losing the Senate fight to Ted Kennedy, he came back to Massachusetts as a hero after saving the Winter Olympics in Salt Lake City.

The acting governor was a young Republican woman, Jane Swift, a plus-sized former state senator from Berkshire County. She'd become governor the previous year, after Paul Cellucci bailed out to become President George W. Bush's ambassador to Canada.

Cellucci had needed a female running mate in 1998, and Swift was available. After losing a congressional race in 1996, she'd been given a desk (but more significantly no telephone) at a far-flung inland outpost of the state hackerama known as the Massachusetts Port Authority.

She had young twins and a much older basically unemployed husband whom I always described as a "blueberry rancher." She reveled in the perks of the governorship, such as taking a state police helicopter home to Williamstown on Thanksgiving Eve 2001.

In my column and on my show, I made her the latest cartoon character in my political menagerie. I learned much later that she had one of her coat holders go down to the *Herald* loading docks every midnight before my column appeared to pick up a copy of the paper. He would then telephone her wherever she was and read to her what I'd written about her.

When *60 Minutes* decided to give her one of its traditional slobbering wet kisses, I was selected to wear the black hat. I would be the heavy, the bad guy. Every *60 Minutes* piece needed a villain. *60 Minutes* isn't journalism, it isn't even close. *60 Minutes* is cheap melodrama, Democrat soap opera.

That's why they've never minded making shit up. It's also why their audience has almost totally drifted away—even those shut-ins who still watch network television have figured out that *60 Minutes* is a complete grift.

But in 2002, it still had some viewers. So when Morley Safer described me as a "radio hitman," it pleased me greatly. Every knock a boost.

Jane Swift was going to lose, badly, in the fall elections of 2002. When Mitt triumphantly returned to Massachusetts after rescuing the Winter Olympics in Salt Lake City, one of his pals paid for a poll of Republican primary voters in the state.

In a theoretical Republican matchup, Mitt was ahead of Jane Swift—61 percent to 11. She dropped out, and Mitt went on to win first the nomination and then the general election, over another female former state senator, a Democrat, a second-generation hack who had been elected state treasurer.

Meanwhile, Billy Bulger was no longer president of the Massachusetts state senate. In 1996, a year after his serial-killing brother Whitey fled his impending arrest, Billy had been appointed president of the University of Massachusetts. He'd been taken care of by his new best friend, Gov. Bill Weld.

Bulger was now making more than $500,000 a year. He was also stuffing the payroll with his cronies, at much higher pay, and with even less heavy lifting, than he had offered them either at the State House or at the MBTA—Mr. Bulger's Transportation Authority.

The problem for Billy was that Mitt Romney still dreamed of the presidency, which had eluded his "brain-washed" father back in 1968 when he was governor of Michigan. The stories about Whitey's serial-killing reign of terror had already begun to come out, on the public record, in the pre-trial hearings for Whitey's fellow gangsters in the federal courthouse on Northern Avenue.

Those horrific crimes, aided and abetted by multiple FBI agents in the Boston office, came to the attention of Rep. Dan Burton, the chairman of the U.S. House Committee on Government Oversight and Reform.

Burton, a Republican from Indiana, was horrified, especially by the corruption among the Boston G-men. He vowed to get to the bottom of it. He talked to his Democratic colleagues from Massachusetts, and they urged him on—they'd been bullied for years by Billy Bulger. He especially reveled in lording it over them during the congressional redistrictings every decade, which are overseen by the state legislatures.

In Massachusetts, that meant the Corrupt Midget.

Shortly after Romney's victory in November 2002, Burton announced that his committee would be holding a congressional hearing in Boston on FBI corruption. He subpoenaed Billy Bulger, and through his flaks, Bulger leaked to the press that he would defy the subpoena and not show up.

It was outrageous, even by Bulger's high-handed standards. Romney, the governor-elect who would soon be appointing the board of trustees at UMass who controlled all hiring and firing, announced that he would not tolerate any state employee defying a lawful order to appear before a congressional committee.

In December 2002 Billy appeared in a drafty courtroom in the old federal courthouse in Post Office Square. Along with the rest of the Boston press, I was sitting in the jury box. Chairman Burton asked his first question and Billy immediately invoked his Fifth Amendment protection against self-incrimination. He cited a 19th-century court ruling about witnesses who found themselves in "ambiguous circumstances."

A month later, Burton was no longer the committee chairman—a victim of those silly term limits that always seem to backfire. The new chairman was another Republican, from Virginia. But he was a graduate of Amherst College, and Billy Bulger tried to work that angle, as if Amherst and UMass-Amherst had anything in common besides a zip code.

Burton kept the heat on, though, and in June 2003 Billy Bulger flew to Washington to testify. I flew down too—in a small private jet owned by one of our advertisers on WRKO. It was trade.

There was a line to get into the hearing room. I was waiting just behind Jon Keller from Channel 4. When we got inside, for some reason Keller suggested we switch seats. I didn't care, so I agreed. C-SPAN was covering the hearing, gavel to gavel, and all the big TV stations in Boston were picking up the feed.

I wrote about that hearing in detail in the first chapter of *The Brothers Bulger*—in which I detailed Bulger's obfuscations and endless memory failures. He'd been immunized, which meant that he could only be prosecuted if it could be proven that he lied. His attempts to "forget" everything turned out to be a complete disaster for him, from start to finish.

Paper Boy

This type of arrogant stonewalling has since become standard operating procedure at congressional hearings—at least among Democrats, who appear immune to punishment of any sort. But at the time it still seemed astonishing that someone in such a position of authority could display such a cavalier disregard both for the truth and the law.

As badly as Bulger did, his performance was a gigantic win for me, because of my seat directly behind him, two rows back. Whenever he said that to the best of his recollection, he did not remember, I would throw my head back, roll my eyes, or, occasionally, hit my forehead with the palm of my hand.

At first I didn't even consider the fact that I too was on camera, at least not until the first break. Then the *Herald* cameraman asked me if I knew what was going on back in Boston. I didn't, so he told me.

Washington 2003: I had the perfect position behind Billy Bulger at the congressional hearing.

The *Herald* switchboard was being deluged with calls demanding . . . something. On the commercial channels, the network anchors were first identifying me and then asking their viewers to stop calling the station, because they couldn't do anything about my juvenile antics.

The photographer filled me in on all this. I laughed and told him, "They ain't seen nothing yet."

After we came back into the hearing room, Bulger was back to his lame memory-challenged routine. Now, when he could not recall, I grabbed my throat, or stuck out my tongue, or both. I was hamming it up for the folks back home.

At one point, in his questioning, Burton got a bit confused about Whitey's relationship with one of the supporting players in the story. So during the next break, I went up to Burton and spoke to him, politely correcting him. The error was insignificant, but I wanted Billy Bulger to see me instructing the chairman.

Bulger stared at us. He was very, very pissed.

At the lunch break, I left. I had my afternoon radio show to do. We adjourned to one of the conservative think tanks and I did my four hours. Then I wrote my column. It was another 15 minutes of fame.

A few days later, I got a call from a literary agent I knew, and soon I had a contract to write a book on the two brothers. The advance was $100,000, out of which I had to pay a freelance editor. Maxwell Perkins wasn't coming through that door. It was all on me.

The Brothers Bulger was not an easy book to write, and not just because I was a novice. Over the years, I'd written one complete novel—I called it *Number Six*, about a cynical local television newsman who stumbles into uncovering a scandal at City Hall.

I don't remember the name of my main character (I hesitate to call him a hero) but I do remember that I had him doing the occasional meet and greets in front of his starstruck fans. Such events had been common during the glory days of local television news—the talent got a few hundred bucks for an appearance fee and maybe scouted out some potential new talent, meaning girlfriends.

At the end of his station-sanctioned events, my fictional TV newsman would emotionally invoke the sacred mission of his station's newscast—which bore more than a passing resemblance to the Channel 7 where Bill O'Reilly and I and so many other lovable losers and no-account boozers had toiled. At the end, he would recite the memorable engraved inscription above the Dartmouth Street entrance to the Boston Public Library:

"THE COMMONWEALTH REQUIRES THE EDUCATION OF THE PEOPLE AS THE SAFEGUARD OF ORDER AND LIBERTY."

I thought that was a rather droll touch on my part—I'd certainly known people in the local TV rackets cynical enough to try to scam viewers into believing that they gave a shit about the original mission of the BPL. But I realized *Number Six* was a non-starter—"no commercial potential," as Frank Zappa used to claim that the record suits said of the Mothers of Invention. I never even attempted to sell it.

But a book about the Bulgers seemed like a real shot at the main chance.

The difficulty would be writing it as a dual biography. Plus, I needed new material—if not the full "untold story," as it were, then at least some new "untold stories." Fortunately, I got a break when the FBI reached out to me. They were embarrassed, as well as they should have been, by what had been going on since Whitey went on the lam in December 1994.

By now, his partner Stevie Flemmi had flipped, and told the feds that he and Whitey had had six Boston G-men on the pad. Two had already been indicted for murders in Oklahoma and Florida.

The four guys who'd been framed by the FBI for a gangland hit in 1965 in Chelsea were about to get more than $100 million in their wrongful-imprisonment lawsuit. Of course, two of them had already died—in prison.

To make amends as best they could, the FBI set up what they called a Violent Fugitive Task Force—a VFTF—to at least go through the motions of tracking down their former paymaster and co-conspirator. They were working out of the old Coast Guard building on Northern Avenue. They had reports, which ultimately didn't turn out to be true, that Whitey had become interested in the Internet, and that he was keeping up with topics that interested him—including the latest on Boston organized crime, and yours truly.

The feds proposed that I set up a website that might get his attention. They would monitor the traffic, and maybe catch him. It sounded like a good idea to me. We called it *Whitey Watch*. The feds didn't exactly have a lot of IT-savvy people on the job, so I brought on a former radio engineer I'd worked with, and the feds paid him, but not me.

Every Thursday we'd post a whole new narrative on *Whitey Watch*. It was fascinating to observe people checking it out in real time from all over the world. There was one person who got on in the United Kingdom almost as soon as the new material was posted. That was tantalizing, because there had been at least one somewhat reliable sighting of Whitey in Piccadilly Square.

It didn't pan out.

Another time, on a holiday weekend, we had multiple hits from a Motel 6 or some such place in the Midwest. The feds scrambled agents on that one.

The best thing about *Whitey Watch* as I was writing the book was that the FBI would turn over to me new, previously unseen material on Bulger. Sometimes I'd just use old mug shots—which I'd been stockpiling for years from various law-enforcement sources—but other times they would turn over a treasure trove of material to me.

For instance, when FBI agent Zip Connolly retired in 1990, his friends held a retirement dinner for him at Joe Tecce's. It was videotaped, and when Whitey went on the lam in late 1994, he left his copy behind at his condo in Quincy.

The tape was maybe an hour long. It was full of all kinds of tidbits. I had my producers cut it up and we put 10- or 12-minute cuts on *Whitey Watch* every Thursday for weeks. No one had ever had this stuff before.

It came in handy when I was writing *The Brothers Bulger*, providing all sorts of detail that had never been revealed publicly. The FBI gave me Whitey's military records from the Air Force in the early fifties, when he was dropping the name of future U.S. House Speaker John McCormack (whose letter of recommendation to J. Edgar Hoover in 1970 on behalf of Zip Connolly was read at Zip's farewell dinner—another revealing bit of previously unknown Boston underworld history).

The FBI also gave me what has become the iconic mug shot from his arrest by the Boston police on St. Patrick's Day 1953. He's wearing one of those big gangster lids. I think he'd probably been rolling drunks, quite possibly closeted gays. That was another of his little rackets that no one ever talked about.

I had the original mug shot, probably the only one in existence. There was only one problem. Someone had put a cup of coffee down on it at one point, and there was a ringed stain on the top left side of it.

By this time, the newspaper industry had decreed that photoshopping was a firing offense. I knew a guy formerly from the *Herald,* a very talented photographer, who was fired from his new job for tinkering with some clouds—clouds!—in the background of a spot-news picture he'd taken.

On *Whitey Watch,* I felt no compunction to observe such silly journalistic shibboleths. I instructed my technician to clean up the stain, while retaining a copy of the original. Then we ran the corrected mug shot and returned the original to the feds.

I mention this only because after Whitey's capture in 2011, my mug shot, the cleaned-up version, appeared at the top of the front page of the *New York Times*. I wrote the "ombudsman" that I wanted to report a violation of the newspaper's sacrosanct policies. I didn't mind the paper stealing my picture with no attribution, I said, but damn it, the photo represented the violation of the inviolable no-photoshopping rule.

I received no reply, let alone an apology.

The FBI also gave me all the handwritten letters and tracts Whitey had written during his sleepless night before he fled. They'd recovered them from his Quincy condo, the one with steel-reinforced back doors that he'd replaced the floor-to-ceiling glass with when he moved in.

I had more than enough material to cobble together about both brothers and the world they'd lived in and eventually dominated. I labored over the book weeknights after the show, and then on Sundays with the freelance editor that I'd hired.

The editor in New York who'd commissioned the book was fired, and my project was handed over to a guy who didn't like me or the book very much. I had to cut it down from 140,000 words to 100,000, which did make it better.

When I finally went down to New York just before the book was scheduled to be published, the editor grudgingly took me out to dinner. First he told me that no organized crime books ever sold unless they were about New York. I knew that wasn't true—think Al Capone. But I kept my mouth shut.

Then he told me it bothered him that everyone in the book seemed to have one of about four or five first names—"one of which is Howie," he added. I pointed out to him that there's a wedding scene in *Goodfellas* where everybody had the same two or three first names, and it's just something Henry Hill jokes about.

Finally, the editor told me that the best writing in the book was a jailhouse poem I'd included by a Mafia guy from Providence who'd been locked up with the Boston guys in Plymouth in the late 1990s. It was entitled "Who's Minding the Puppies?"—a reference to Whitey leaving his girlfriend's two miniature French poodles behind when he went on the lam in 1994.

Obviously, the editor didn't think *The Brothers Bulger* was going to do very well. But I got lucky, and as I always say, I'd rather be lucky than good.

Kevin Weeks was a younger guy from Southie who'd gone to work for Whitey at an early age. His two brothers were both Harvard graduates, but Kevin was a fat thug who'd been put on the MBTA before he went into the rackets full-time. The hours were better than at the T. So were the women, and the money.

Like most guys, Whitey had a "type" that he liked to go after. All the males Whitey was close to, however you want to define "close," had the same physical look—black hair, thick, combed straight back.

Down through the years they always looked the same—the Choctaw Kid, his Native American boyfriend in Alcatraz. Then Sal Mineo, the fifties heartthrob later murdered by gay hustlers whom Whitey met when Mineo was performing in South Boston at Blinstrub's. Then John "Zip" Connolly. And finally, Kevin Weeks.

Weeks had remained behind in Boston when Whitey became a fugitive, and he'd held out until 1999, when it was revealed beyond a shadow of a doubt that Bulger was an informant, a rat. When Weeks was arrested, it took about two weeks for the cops to flip him.

When he made his first court appearance, he turned around and looked at me and said, "Be kind, Howie." (The *Globe* edited the quote to, "Be kind." No free publicity for the competition, I suppose.)

In Southie, he'd long been derisively referred to as "Kevin Squeaks." I gave him a new moniker—"Two Weeks," for how long he'd stood up before going full-blown rat.

Once again, Gaga Murray had the perfect description of Weeks during his days running the Rotary Variety, next door to the South Boston Liquor Mart.

"He's wearing all pink. Pink hat. Pink shirt. Pink pants. V-neck shirt. Tight ass pants . . . Weeks talks about knocking out guys. TWO HUNDRED GUYS HE KNOCKED OUT. He knocked nobody out. Not even a wino. In his whole life, Weeks knocked nobody out."

Before he was arrested in 1999, the *Herald* had been searching for Weeks. One of our photographers had found him in Framingham at a spa or something, and Weeks had chatted with the guy. He told our photographer that he and Whitey had known where I lived—in Acton, across the street from an old cemetery that dated back to Colonial times, where some of the Minutemen killed at Lexington and Concord in 1775 were interred.

It's a nice old graveyard, and I used to walk through it on warm weekend afternoons, reading the rhyming Federalist-era inscriptions and the quaint old Yankee names.

Given how much Whitey detested me, and what often happened to anyone who crossed Whitey, Weeks apparently found it amusing that I lived across the street from a graveyard.

Later, he made it out like he and Whitey had made it their mission to find out where I lived, as if they were hunting me. But they'd had no need to go out of their way to track me down. One of his Harvard-educated brothers lived in Acton, had been elected selectman in fact, and lived behind my house.

I figure one day the two brothers were driving around, and Kevin's brother pointed out my house, across the street from the graveyard, and . . . well, you know how stories can get embellished and take on a life of their own.

When someone is arrested by the feds, a determination is made by the courts as to whether to grant bail. The cops must determine, among other things, flight risk and dangerousness. If they want to keep somebody *in durance vile*, the better to squeeze him, they'll include in the official filings whatever they can to make him look like a menace to the community.

So in their affidavit, the state police working with the feds included the story about me and the graveyard and Weeks's dark threats. (They also included the threats they made against me earlier at the South Boston Liquor Mart.)

After the affidavit was filed, I didn't write anything. I figured it was just more Southie fake-tough-guy bullshit. I could have made a big deal about it then—it was out there, on the public record, not some Brian Williams–Mike Barnicle–Kevin Cullen made-up nonsense. But I still gave it a pass, for the obvious reason.

Fake tough guy is a very bad look.

In my introduction to *The Brothers Bulger*, I mentioned the usual stuff, such as my hamming it up at the Billy Bulger congressional hearing, and the fact that in Somerville I'd been a neighbor of Howie Winter's. And I mentioned in passing the federal affidavit about how Whitey and his obese grave digger had known where I lived.

By 2006, as my book was about to be published, Weeks had finished his five-year stint in prison. He'd ratted out everything and everybody he could. He'd even pointed out where to find the skeletal remains of seven of Whitey's missing victims, including the two twentysomething female girlfriends of Stevie Flemmi. They'd all been dug up from shallow graves on public lands in and around Boston.

When Weeks got out, he got a book deal from Judith Regan, the dodgy New York literary agent who was working for Rupert Murdoch's publishing house, HarperCollins. She would soon be fired for her O. J. Simpson book, *If I Did It*.

Regan had endless connections in the New York media, and she quickly scored a major coup—a *60 Minutes* story about Weeks's book, *Brutal*, which was

UNITED STATES DISTRICT COURT
DISTRICT OF MASSACHUSETTS

UNITED STATES OF AMERICA)
)
v.)   Crim. No. 99-10371-EFH
)
KEVIN J. WEEKS and)
KEVIN P. YO'NEIL,)
)
Defendants.)

REDACTED AFFIDAVIT OF THOMAS B. DUFFY IN SUPPORT OF PRETRIAL
DETENTION OF THE DEFENDANTS KEVIN J. WEEKS AND KEVIN P. O'NEIL

Sep-21-2005 03:53pm   From-US ATTORNEYS OFFICE   6177483954   T-451 P.003   F-492

81.   WEEKS also has threatened, in a veiled fashion, a
member of the local news media in an apparent effort to chill
that reporter, who has regularly described WEEKS in print as a
member of Bulger's and Flemmi's criminal organization, from
writing about WEEKS. In approximately February of 1996 or 1997,
a photographer from the Boston Herald went to a local tanning
salon to photograph persons tanning themselves during the winter
months. WEEKS and his girlfriend were at the tanning salon. The
photographer attempted to photograph WEEKS' girlfriend. WEEKS
rebuked him and then engaged him in a discussion regarding Herald
columnist Howie Carr, the reporter referred to above. WEEKS told
the photographer, in substance, "We used to know where Howie
lived; it's across from a graveyard." The photographer relayed
this statement to Carr, who lived at one time across from a
cemetery. In addition, in approximately 1987 or 1988, a
colleague of Carr's entered the liquor store at 295 Old Colony
Avenue in South Boston. The clerk behind the counter engaged
this person in a discussion about Carr in which the clerk stated,
in substance, "How come Howie never comes in? Tell him if he
ever comes in, we've got a brand new dumpster for him, another
Robin Benedict." Benedict was the victim in a widely publicized
murder case. Portions of her remains were found in a dumpster.

3.   Risk of Flight

82.   There is evidence showing that WEEKS likely has been in
contact with Bulger while Bulger has been a fugitive. As noted

60

Feds' detention affidavit for Kevin Weeks 1999: First official mention of
Mob threats against me.

coming out the same week as mine. Sales prospects for *Brothers Bulger* appeared grim, but I had one big thing working in my favor.

Weeks had gone way overboard on the story about me and the graveyard—to get press attention for a book, you always offer them something new and juicy. The publishers want to put "untold story" in the title, and on the cover. So just before both our books were coming out, I got an unexpected call from *60 Minutes* asking me if I was willing to sit down at the Four Seasons Hotel on Boylston Street for an interview with Ed Bradley.

Hell yes I was willing! When you've got a book coming out, any publicity is good publicity. So I went downtown, before my radio show, and Bradley seemed a decent enough guy. He was asking me the usual questions, and then he hits me with what he and the producers thought was the big one—the "gotcha!"

Did you know that Kevin Weeks had you staked out in the graveyard, and that he was going to shoot you, only when you walked out the front door that morning holding your young daughter's hand, to drive her to school, he couldn't bring himself to blow you away?

Well, yes, I said, as a matter of fact I had known that. And I'd even mentioned his threats in my own new book, which I just happened to have a copy of in my lap. I held it up for the camera. I could see from their expressions that this fact greatly surprised the crew from what I've always called See-BS. Weeks must have told them that he had never ever shared this allegedly blood-curdling story before, even though it had been on the public record since 1999.

Bradley and the producers quickly exchanged glances, but they needed me for their "untold story," and I suddenly realized that I was an important part of *60 Minutes'* latest Fake News story. So Bradley adroitly asked me a slightly amended question, had I ever been concerned, really concerned?

I said, yeah, I'd heard Whitey wanted to kill me. Then I paused for emphasis before adding, "But I never figured Kevin had the stones to do it."

That was the money cut right there! Bradley and the producers glanced at each other again, and they all nodded. Now they were happy. They had what they needed—a *60 Minutes* soundbite. Now they could go back to Kevin and play him the cut, and, as they knew from interviewing him, he would bluster and issue hollow threats and puff out his chin(s).

As I said earlier, *60 Minutes* isn't journalism, it's melodrama, schtick. You're not so much interviewed as cast, in a role. With Jane Swift, I was the villain. For Kevin Weeks, my original role had been to play the victim.

But then I stole the show, as they used to say in Hollywood. I elevated myself to . . . Crusading Journalist.

I left the *60 Minutes* crew to go back to Brighton to do the usual prep work for my own show. The CBS crew would be coming over later, to get some B-roll. I had gotten a big banner of my book's cover that I would be using at the book signings, so I unfurled it and hung it up behind me in the studio.

I'd also had some magnets made—they served two purposes, promoting the book and also reminding listeners who got ratings diaries to remember me. I spread those magnets out on the console. Then I covered the desk and all around the microphone with just-printed copies of *Brothers Bulger*.

It didn't do any good. The camera crew shot super-tight shots of my face. The only wide shots were from the rear of the studio, so they wouldn't have to show the banner of my book's cover. I asked them what was going on, and they explained that they'd been told that *60 Minutes* had a deal with Judith Regan— no one else's book was to be mentioned.

It was only to be expected. After all, *60 Minutes* had tried to fix the 2004 presidential election with the infamous "fake-but-accurate" Texas Air National Guard story about President George W. Bush. That was the Democrat hoax that cost See-BS anchor Dan Rather his job.

A decade earlier they'd done a puff piece on Billy Bulger—as was their usual M.O., they'd cribbed it from an earlier print story, this one in *The New Yorker.* They'd mixed up facts, let him give Whitey a big wet kiss on camera, and finally recorded his St. Patrick's Day breakfast.

Locally, *60 Minutes* had earlier promoted another hoax involving a junkie murderer from Charlestown named Joseph Yandle. His life sentence had been commuted after a series of fawning columns in the *Globe* by, you guessed it, Mike Barnicle and Kevin Cullen. They had described the druggie killer as a "decorated hero" with a "fistful of medals."

Neither the *Globe* pipe artists nor See-BS news bothered to check with the Pentagon on the accuracy of that statement. Birds of a feather flock together.

So it was no surprise that *60 Minutes* was in the satchel for a serial killer, or for a serial killer's 300-pound gravedigger. But no matter how See-BS cut it, they were still going to have to use my "He doesn't have the stones" sound cut, and I was going to come across to a national audience as the crusading, courageous reporter.

Also, my book was going to beat Kevin's into the stores—and onto Amazon—by a week. I tipped off the *Herald* to the upcoming *60 Minutes* story.

On the Friday before it was to air, I was the splash story on the front page: "Howie Carr to his would-be assassin: 'You Didn't Have the Guts.'"

I guess "stones" was too much for the *Herald*'s delicate sensibilities.

When I went down to New York, I was told that my book was already at number 30 on the *Times*' bestseller list, even before its release. That number didn't appear in the print edition, but everybody in the book business got the rankings.

In New York, I did some radio interviews, then was driven over to Fort Lee, New Jersey, for a shot on MSNBC. The big one, though, was *The O'Reilly Factor* on Fox. In those days, what Oprah Winfrey was to female, daytime TV, O'Reilly was to the working-class audience that a decade later would be described as "Deplorables."

After authors appeared on the *Factor*, O'Reilly would often tell them, matter of factly, that their books were going to make the bestseller list. He wasn't bragging. It was fact.

As significant as the O'Reilly appearance was to my book sales, *60 Minutes* was an even greater boost. It was the kind of coverage I could never have created for myself—it would have seemed like self-aggrandizement.

Weeks would admit at Whitey Bulger's trial in 2013 that he'd been lying his whole life. But that was years after he claimed that he and his boss had been planning to murder me. And when his original story about me was picked up and embellished by a corrupt TV show that millions of gullible Americans still believed was on the level, it was my ticket to a big payday.

I'd have been a fool not to take the ball and run with it. For once, state-run media was doing me a favor, however inadvertently.

As dim as he was, Kevin Weeks realized what he'd done. He'd created a monster. I started doing two or three book signings every Saturday and Sunday. The only problem was, the publisher had believed my stupid editor and hadn't printed nearly enough copies. My state senator, the future U.S. Sen. Scott Brown, couldn't find a copy for his in-laws and had to stop by my house in Wellesley to pick up a few.

On the first weekend, I pulled into the parking lot of an independent bookstore in Orleans, down on the Cape, and the owners ran out to meet me and ask me if I had any extra books in the car.

I had a couple of cases I hadn't bothered to unload, and the owners immediately grabbed them and brought them into their store. The fans were already lined up outside, waiting to buy a book and get it autographed. We sold every book in my trunk that day, and still didn't have enough.

That Sunday night *60 Minutes* ran the story about the murder contract that had been out on me. The next morning, my wife had to appear in Palm Beach before the board of the lakefront building where we were buying a condo. It was in an old hotel, the Biltmore, where my father and uncle had worked briefly after World War II, before returning to The Breakers.

Later I saw some of the old brochures my mother had saved from the old hotel. It had had more than 500 rooms, which had been converted into about 130 condos. It had the biggest pool in Palm Beach, clay tennis courts, and a beachfront club with luncheon service.

I wanted that place bad, but I was worried that some of the old-timers on the Biltmore board might have seen *60 Minutes* the previous evening and might object to having someone in the building who had been on the Hit Parade. Thankfully, even by 2006, *60 Minutes'* ratings had collapsed. No one mentioned it to my wife, and we were in.

Meanwhile, I fell off the bestseller list for one week because there were no copies anywhere. But by reading the *New York Post* I learned that I'd be back on the list the next week, as soon as another print run was completed. In that story, I was identified as a reporter for the *Boston Globe*—much to the amusement of my radio audience.

By this time, Judith Regan had also realized her mistake, and her minions began trying to plant stories ripping my book, and extolling Kevin Weeks's, well, fabulousness. This I also learned from the *New York Post's* Page Six gossip column, which busted Regan's disinformation campaign. It wasn't a major item for Page Six, but to me it was a big deal, just to get it on the record.

It was only to be expected that one publisher would try to put the knock on another publisher. But most of the anonymous whispering about me was coming from Boston, where everyone in the protected classes was now lining up to take a shot at me. I'd expected some blowback, of course. At this late date, I understood that I wasn't going to win any Mr. Congeniality awards. Going up against the orthodoxy is never good for one's social standing. Journalism is no different than any other racket.

But lately, I hadn't been nearly as in-your-face as in the days of *Poisoned Politics*. Many of the *Globe* hacks who despised me had been RIFed themselves—the *Times'* profit margin was already plummeting as their classified-advertising market evaporated.

Paper Boy

Marooned by myself on a pitiful AM station with no signal and no budget, I had my hands full battling my new FM talk-station competition to a standoff.

But once I was back on one of "their" state-run outlets—*60 Minutes*—it was suddenly 1989 all over again. The Beautiful People started coming at me. Naturally, those most outraged by my sudden good fortune were people I'd done favors for.

In the *Globe*, my book was excoriated by a reporter who used to work for the *Herald*. We'd shared a desk in the newsroom. When she was trying to get hired by the *Globe*, she wanted to do a long-form piece to show off her writing chops. *Boston* magazine gave her an assignment, but she had writer's block.

One day at the federal courthouse, I told her to go out to lunch, and while she was out, I sat down at her terminal and, with the help of one of our Mob attorney friends, we knocked out the top third of her magazine piece just to get her started. It appeared in the next issue pretty much as we'd written it, and she was hired soon after by the *Globe*—the velvet coffin, as it was called.

And now she said that my book was nothing more than a cut-and-paste rewrite.

The *Phoenix* had once been known as an alternative, or underground, weekly newspaper. Now the only section of the *Phoenix* that mattered was the "personals," where all the hookers, I mean escorts, advertised. But in the front parts of the paper that all the perverts buying it threw out, they still espoused a tired left-wing agenda.

So they ripped me up too, saying that *The Brothers Bulger* was a clip job, with nothing new in it. The writer worked for one of the local TV stations, and had recently asked me if he could use the video of Zip Connolly's FBI retirement dinner, which I'd been posting on *Whitey Watch*. I was the only one who had the video he needed. I gave it to him, no strings attached.

But now he said I'd written a book with nothing new in it.

Dapper O'Neil once told me a story about how sometimes James Michael Curley would get the word that someone he knew well was bad-mouthing him, behind his back. He would always feign surprise at such betrayals.

"He's speaking against me?" Curley would say. "That can't be so. I haven't done anything for the man."

In other words, no good deed goes unpunished.

One of Curley's great foes in Boston politics was Dan Coakley, a legendarily corrupt figure whose career is recounted well in the late Francis Russell's book, *The Knave of Boston*.

Coakley was an up-by-the-bootstraps guy, who'd started out working in bar-rooms and later graduated to the *Boston Herald* (as a sportswriter). He and I had had the same career trajectory, in other words. When I started getting slammed again after I made the bestseller list, I found my dog-eared copy of *The Knave of Boston* and reread this statement Coakley once made in a newspaper ad he'd bought for himself during the heat of a political campaign:

"As a bartender, as a reporter, I seem to have escaped these cultured antagonisms which of late have beset me. Perhaps it was a mistake to have moved onward from these humble but honorable occupations. In the canons of my antagonists it is in such callings that I and such as I belong. . . . My career occasioned no alarm to anyone, until I got my head far enough above water to look horizontally at some of those on whom Fortune had pinned the blue ribbon. . . ."

Not all the reviews were bad, and the negative ones had absolutely no effect on sales. One week, both Kevin Weeks and I appeared on the *Times* bestseller list.

Neither of our books was ever mentioned, let alone reviewed, in the *Times*, except on the bestseller list. That was not unexpected, of course. They were books about America, by Americans. Not exactly the sort of subject—or authors—that the *Times* cared anything about, even then.

Oh well, I was crying all the way to the bank, as Liberace used to say. Eventually another thought occurred to me. The high-hats and the swells hadn't been able to lay a glove on me, and I could feel state-run media's power ebbing from week to week.

I figured if I ever wrote another book, they would be even less able to take me down a notch or two. If I waited long enough, they might not even exist—knock on wood! The Internet was crushing them—the *Phoenix* would only linger on a few more years, as the city's hookers migrated online, just like all the *Globe*'s classified real-estate and employment ads.

The Brothers Bulger ended up spending 11 weeks on the *Times*' bestseller list—seven weeks hardcover and four weeks for the paperback edition. 2006 was a very good year for me.

Meanwhile, Mitt Romney decided not to run for reelection as governor in 2006. I was going to miss him, not because he was a particularly effective leader, because he wasn't. Realizing the futility of the task of reinvigorating the GOP in Massachusetts, he threw in the towel and decided to run for president.

We all know how that turned out—twice.

Paper Boy

But he did do me a couple of favors on the way out the door. One night he was in my tiny, filthy WRKO studio in Brighton, and I asked him to contribute to my daughters' Catholic elementary school in Wellesley. He told me, I'll give whatever you gave. I thought that was a great answer. He matched the $2,500 I'd contributed.

My longtime producer Virgin Boy (as we nicknamed him because of his nonexistent social life) got a job at the local Fox TV affiliate. So we asked Mitt for a resolution honoring VB's years of service to me. It was a small thing, and I had to write the citation myself, but it's the little things that you remember.

What I recall most of all is that while Mitt was governor, I got to run the annual license plate lottery out of my radio studio. If you don't come from Massachusetts, or some other state like Rhode Island where low-digit license plates are considered political currency, you may not understand the bragging rights that come with having a low-number plate. In fact, you may think it's insane and I'm willing to concede that you may well be correct. What can I say?

Trafficking in low-digit license plates was a small-time grift in the hackerama. It was a staple of my *Herald* columns. After many scandals involving the trafficking in the low-digit plates during Dukakis's governorship, a lottery was established to select the year's recipients of the returned low-digit plates. The system worked well. The winners were picked out at random—in my studio. Naturally I always entered both cars in my household.

In Mitt's final year as governor, we went through the drawing of a few dozen plates during the last hour of my show—which I reserved for "local" issues, if needed. My old producer, Virgin Boy, was there with his Channel 25 camera crew. For some reason, in the last segment, with only a few plates left to pick, Mitt got nervous and bolted out of the studio, along with his entourage of state police and assorted coat holders.

I just shrugged and went on picking the winners out of the bowl. Finally, I was down to the last license plate. I reached in and drew out the slip of . . . Howard Carr of Wellesley.

It was a nationwide search! I had scored 9823, and wonder of wonders, it had previously belonged to a guy from Greenfield who just happened to also be a graduate of Deerfield Academy.

Ever since then, I've been accused of fixing the license plate lottery. I offered to let anyone see the video shot by VB's camera crew. But just as when I was

Mitt Romney sent me this photo when we were still on speaking terms.

charged with assaulting a member of the Republican state committee and the video exonerated me, my detractors accused me of "deceptive editing."

After the Democrats regained the governorship in 2006, the new Registrar of Motor Vehicles (a former legislator) announced that henceforward she would be running the annual plate lottery—"so that we don't have the same questions about the honesty of the process that we've had in the past."

How dare she!

When I officially moved to Florida a few years back, I handed the plate over to my daughter Carolyn. When she got engaged, her future in-laws were very, very impressed with her four-digit license plate.

As for me, all I can say is that I won 9823 fair and square. As the late Vinnie Piro once said of one of his deals at the State House, "It was so fucking legit it was ridiculous."

That's my story and I'm sticking to it.

15
JAILBREAK

Nature abhors a vacuum and Boston talk radio had a big vacuum—the only station offering the format was an AM station with a weak signal and a weaker lineup: my station, WRKO.

It was only a matter of time until another talker was started in Boston. Sure enough, in 1999, Greater Media flipped an also-ran FM music signal into a talk station with the call letters WTKK.

Fortunately, as I've told you, the initial lineup was lackluster. Still, the handwriting was on the wall. If they ever got their act together, WRKO was doomed. I was doomed.

Meanwhile, at the age of 80, Jerry Williams was dying.

The *Globe's* Sunday magazine did a story about his decline into irrelevance—mostly, I think, as an excuse to print a photograph of him in which Jerry looked more than half-dead, not unlike what Elvis Presley looked like in his casket in that *National Enquirer* photo printed after his death in 1977.

The *Globe* called me up for a comment to the accusation that I'd destroyed Jerry's career. I told the reporter, "My name is Howie Carr, not Father Time." I was quoted accurately.

At the time, I was briefly doing a weekend radio show out of WRKO studios for KFI in Los Angeles. One Saturday I walked into the studio and was shocked to see shuffling slowly down the hall toward me what appeared to be the ghost of Jerry Williams. He had been allowed to come in for a final show on WRKO, basically to say goodbye.

He was doddering along, staring down at the floor. I briefly considered speaking to him, then thought better of it. I ducked into the little backup studio I was using and did my fill-in KFI weekend show.

A couple of weeks later, Jerry Williams was dead.

I wrote a farewell column about his passing, but the *Herald* didn't seem to care. He was already a forgotten man, not by me certainly, but in Boston and in the business. It's like the Eagles' song, *New Kid in Town*, the story of all human life, including my own someday in the not-too-distant future.

They will never forget you 'til somebody new comes along.

The last line of my column was addressed directly to Jerry:

"Jerry invented me, at least my talk-show persona. When Jerry started reading my columns on the air, I lived in Somerville, and now I live in Wellesley. What can I say to Jerry except, thanks pal!"

The *Herald* editors threw the column into the back of the paper. Nobody saw it, except for maybe Jerry's old producer, who was now the program director at WTKK. I was told she showed it around to the people at her new FM station, presumably to impress upon them what an ungrateful bastard I was.

Marooned on the hopeless AM band, sometimes WRKO had good ratings books and sometimes not so good. After 9/11, the numbers spiked. Bad news is always good for talk radio.

And 2004 was a good year for me—Sen. John Kerry ran for president. I was soon writing columns about Kerry for the *New York Post*. National reporters were calling to ask me how I knew so much about his mother's family, the Forbeses. I told them the truth—I'd read Cleveland Amory's classic Boston book, *The Proper Bostonians,* which was full of Forbes family lore.

I didn't share with them my favorite story from the book, about a 19th-century Brahmin named T. Jefferson Coolidge who visited Montserrat in the West Indies. He wrote back to Boston that "We were tormented on landing by the Negroes. They were coarse and seem to have an Irish accent."

The Yankees still felt that way, at least the ones at the *Globe* did—about me anyway.

In 2004, not only was a Massachusetts politician the Democrat nominee for president, but the party's national convention was in Boston. It was made to order for me—actually, John Kerry's entire career was made to order for tabloids and talk radio, i.e., me.

There is an old French expression, *nostalgie de la boue*, which refers to an affection for the lower sorts of things. Slumming you might say. As the world's most successful gigolo, Kerry should have been immune to such sentiments. But he did have a variant of *nostalgie de la boue*. He tried to pass himself off as . . . one of the guys.

His second wife, Teresa, was the widow of the late Sen. John Heinz of Pennsylvania. She was an immigrant from Angola. That made her an African-American, I guess, like Elon Musk.

You might have called her a gold digger, and I know I did. And then she married a gigolo. It was so very Palm Beach. One day during the 2004 New Hampshire primary I was in a diner in Manchester. A couple of booths over, Gen. Wesley Clark, a short-lived candidate for president himself, was chatting with some voters.

Teresa walked in, test-marketing her own version of *nostalgie de la boue*, going table to table to commune with the hoi polloi. When she reached Gen. Clark's table, she had no idea who he was.

Kerry was promoting higher taxes, for other people, because that's what Democrats do. But he and Mama T, as we called her, had stashed hundreds of millions of her inheritance from her first husband in tax-free municipal bonds. Kerry denounced American corporations taking their manufacturing offshore, as H. J. Heinz moved factory after factory to Mexico. No one was supposed to say anything because . . . Democrats.

John Kerry was the beneficiary of Teresa's half-billion-dollar inheritance. He had six mansions owned, as I always put it, by his second wife's first husband's trust fund. Each mansion included an SUV. Even then he was a climate-change alarmist, so I asked his spokesman how Kerry justified owning six gas-guzzlers.

"He doesn't own them," Kerry's flak said. "His family does."

It was hilarious. We'd been observing him firsthand in Massachusetts for more than 30 years, and now he was finally exposed before a national audience. His absolute cluelessness was in full display when he tried to go Joe Sixpack and talk about sports.

Naturally the Democratic sporting magazines—which was all of them—wanted to do slobbering profiles on the likely next president. He told a motorcycle monthly about his bike—not a made-in-Wisconsin Harley-Davidson, but an imported Ducati. To a fish-and-game monthly, he recalled being on Cape Cod, tracking down (but finally not shooting, because of, you know, Vietnam) a 24-point buck. Not very likely, my listeners all agreed.

He bragged to a running magazine that he had once run the Boston Marathon—but unlike every single other runner who's ever trudged up Heartbreak Hill, he couldn't recall the year.

Somebody got videotape of him off Nantucket, windsurfing. Asked about his enjoyment of that quintessential leisure-class pastime, he sniffed and said he often went out with "tradesmen."

Then there was baseball. He was asked who his favorite baseball player was in his youth. For someone born in 1943, with New England roots, it should have been a no-brainer—Ted Williams. Or at least some other Red Sox, or maybe even, given his age, one of the old Boston Braves. Warren Spahn. Eddie Mathews.

But no, Kerry said his favorite ballplayer was Roy Sievers, who spent most of his career with the old Washington Senators. It was just another reminder that Kerry, despite his Forbes lineage, was not a local boy (his father had worked for the State Department).

That summer, on the campaign trail, as the Red Sox headed for their first World Series victory since 1918, Kerry took to reading the evening's scores, backward, as if he were calling a tennis match:

"Detroit 3, Red Sox 5!"

Finally, the weekend before the election, Kerry jetted to rural southern Ohio, in his stiff, pressed, brand-new hunting jacket. He strolled into a general store and asked a question that is still on my radio loop even now:

"Can I get me a hunting license here?"

Still, the mainstream media were doing their best to keep Kerry afloat. In October, *60 Minutes* ran that totally fabricated hit piece about George W. Bush's service in the Texas Air National Guard—"fake but accurate," as it was later described.

Kerry was leading in the polls, and if he won, his Senate seat would be vacant. The interim appointment, before a special election, would be made by Romney. During an appearance on my show in October 2004, I asked Romney whom he would appoint. He said he'd appoint me. I immediately asked him to put that in writing, and he did. I kept that piece of scratch paper for years, although it seems to have disappeared somewhere along the way.

Paper Boy

For a few days after Mitt promised me the appointment, callers would ask me if I planned to give up my talk show when I became a senator. No way, I said. I'll make every roll call, even in the afternoon during the show. The only change might be that there would be more floating breaks, because occasionally I'd have to hustle down to the floor to cast my vote.

But I could still do the show, I told everybody, because to vote all I needed to do was look up at the tote board and see how my "colleague" Ted Kennedy had voted. If the light next to his name was green, it was going to be red next to mine, and vice versa.

Election night 2004 was another nail-biter, just like 1988. It's disturbing, to say the least, when you have firsthand knowledge of the utter inadequacy of someone who might be on the verge of becoming the next president of the United States.

On election-day afternoon, after seeing the exit polls, one of Kerry's syco-phants asked him, "May I be the first to call you 'Mr. President'?"

Before the polls even closed, U.S. Rep. Steve Lynch of South Boston publicly announced that he would be holding a news conference the next day to announce his candidacy to succeed President-elect Kerry in the Senate.

Thank God, the nation was spared. I was briefly worried that Kerry would dispute the results, much like the hanging chads in Florida in 2000. Bush had won the popular vote by several million, which the Democrats always claim is the only fair way to determine the winner of any race. But in this case, I figured, they might claim a couple of states had been "stolen" because . . . Democrats.

I've heard since then that Kerry still privately believes that he was robbed in Ohio, but at least he didn't litigate the loss. Like most people, I had hated that whole 40 days of recounts in Florida in 2000, and I dreaded going through another of those catastrophes.

The 2004 election should have been great for ratings, but it wasn't. When the numbers came out in January, for the first and only time ever, I was edged by WTKK in the 25–54 demographic, by one-tenth of a point.

WTKK's afternoon host, Jay Severin, who claimed to have a Pulitzer Prize for Internet commentary (there is no such award), immediately declared my professional demise.

I wasn't happy, but somehow I didn't think this was the end of the line. For one thing, Severin knew nothing about Boston or Massachusetts politics. When it comes to local politics on Boston radio, it's always been my way or the highway.

More significantly, I was on a station on a dying band that fewer than 20 percent of the audience ever listened to. And 40 percent of that dwindling listenership couldn't even pick up WRKO after nightfall. By contrast, WTKK was a 50,000-watt Class A FM signal, and the best they could do was edge me by one-tenth of a point, in the prime advertising demographic, although my overall audience still dwarfed theirs.

All things considered, I thought I was hanging in quite well. But I had to do something, soon. The AM-FM trend line was not promising.

WTKK did not appear to be an option, as long as Jerry's old producer was the program director there. To her, I was *persona non grata*. Fortunately for me she couldn't figure out how to take out even an AM clunker like Entercom-owned WRKO. She was fired from WTKK, and a new general manager and program director were brought in. By 2007, as my contract with Entercom was expiring, I began talking with Greater Media, WTKK's owner.

Negotiations didn't take long. I desperately wanted out of Entercom. The jock sniffers at WEEI were still driving me crazy, with their endless ass kissing of all the local professional teams.

After the briefest of negotiations, I signed a five-year deal to switch to morning drive on WTKK. It was a no-brainer.

Don Imus, their syndicated morning host, had just been fired for his most recent racist diatribe, after which I had taken to calling the station WTKKK. They needed a replacement in morning drive. Under the deal, I would take my two producers with me. I would make less guaranteed money, but on FM the bonuses were likely, which they no longer were at WRKO. And the FM band wasn't going anywhere anytime soon. As for AM—who knew?

In the summer of 2007 I informed Entercom I was leaving when my contract expired. I took off to my new condo in Palm Beach. I figured it was a done deal—after all, Entercom hated the very format of talk radio. Too edgy. My salary was a huge drain financially, and my departure would mean they'd have more money for WEEI to use for sucking up to jocks, going on junkets and buying up rights to games that nobody listened to on the radio anymore.

Under my contract, Entercom had a right to "match" my offer, but no one in my camp took it seriously, because what could they "match?" I was going to a Class A FM signal. All Entercom had was a shitty AM stick.

To match the Greater Media offer, Entercom would have had to flip one of their FM music stations. Like all Entercom stations everywhere, their FM were dismally run also-rans. One, an alt-rock, or AAA (adult album alternative) station, was particularly dreadful.

Paper Boy

WAAF was licensed to Worcester, with weak coverage in the city. I called it the Beavis and Butt-Head station. Some of the "talent," now deceased, would snort cocaine in the men's room. It was about as professional an operation as your average community-access cable TV show.

But the arrogant rich boy who'd inherited the company was so enamored of the Beavis and Butt-Head format that he spent $27 million for a second FM stick, with an even weaker signal. That enabled Entercom to deliver a format shunned by most white people to the blacker parts of the metropolitan area—Mattapan, south through Randolph to Brockton.

Any rational, well-managed company would have realized that my new FM deal had given them the perfect excuse to throw in the towel on a format that required some programming know-how to run properly, something Entercom never managed to accomplish anywhere.

Instead, though, Entercom decided to fight. They "matched" the offer from Greater Media. My mistake, which I never should have made, was that I believed that I would prevail because there could be no "match." I was right about that, of course, but what I hadn't figured into the equation was that it was now payback time for the state's appallingly corrupt judiciary.

For decades, judges had been a regular part of my cast of cartoon characters in the hackerama. Most judges were, and are, failed lawyers. If you're worth a damn as a lawyer, why would you want to be a judge when you can make so much more in private practice? The fact is, the only lawyers who want to be judgeships are those who are starving to death.

Under state law, all judicial nominees had to publicly disclose their contributions to political candidates. In Massachusetts, as in many other states, judgeships are basically cash 'n' carry.

George Washington Plunkitt of Tammany Hall once explained that there's honest graft and dishonest graft. Bust-out lawyers funneling cash to politicians who can hand them no-heavy-lifting early retirement falls into the "honest graft" category, meaning it's legal, if not ethical.

It was Michael Kinsley who once said that in Washington, it's not what's illegal that's a scandal, it's what is legal. Same thing in Boston, and everywhere else for that matter.

You'd look at the lawyers' contributions, and you could see how hungry they were. Sometimes, they've been giving money to every candidate for governor (who appoints them) going back three or four administrations. Some starving lawyers would somehow max out, and have their parents max out as well.

Sometimes their secretaries too, although nowadays a lot of the real bust-out future jurists don't even have a secretary. They just rent a room—I mean, an office—in some random commercial building.

I always say that I'm not claiming all Massachusetts judges are corrupt, it's just the 98 percent of them who give such a bad name to the other 2 percent.

I also dusted off Lenny Bruce's famous quip about the root cause of all his legal problems:

"In the halls of justice, the only justice is in the halls."

Every few months, there would be another scandal involving one of these failed lawyers. Looting trusts, or clients' accounts. Drunk driving—all the time, they were drunk driving. They're as bad as state legislators. Plus, getting into barroom brawls, using the n-word in their chambers, being lugged for hit-and-runs or for lifting other people's watches at Logan Airport security gates, etc.

One of the unintended consequences of the War on Poverty is the collapse of the defense bar. Because nowadays almost every client, especially members of protected classes, claim to be "indigent." All those big-time criminal defense attorneys—in Boston they included such colorful types as F. Lee Bailey and Tom Troy—were once well-known public figures. They provided much of the blended Canadian whiskey that was delivered to the *Herald American* city room every Christmas.

Even gangsters now claim to be indigent. Whitey Bulger ran up a tab of millions of dollars when he was on trial in 2013. It went to "public defenders." They do all right, but their hourly rates are capped, unlike those of private attorneys. As criminal defendants followed the rest of society onto welfare, defense lawyers who had been making good livings saw their revenue streams dry up. Suddenly judgeships were even more lucrative.

I remember getting a call from one of my defense-bar friends, calling on behalf of one of his colleagues who was up for a judgeship around 2006. This guy had been the lawyer for Stevie Flemmi at some of the Mob hearings, and I still remembered what he would do whenever the prosecutors would ask Stevie about a murder.

The lawyer, Kenny Fishman, would hold up his open right hand—five fingers, meaning Steve should take the Fifth Amendment. Now he was up for a judgeship.

Please, my friend said, just lay off Kenny when he comes up for confirmation. No column, please. He needs the job, bad.

I gave him a pass. He's now retired. I just looked up Fishman's pension—$118,836 a year, state tax free. And, of course, the free health care.

Usually, though, I didn't pull my punches. I just slammed the judicial nominees as they came up for confirmation before the Governor's Council. Many of the nominees were former assistant district attorneys, who were already in the regular state pension state. Once they became judges, they went into a different, even sweeter pension system. So when the judges had to take mandatory retirement at age 70, many were collecting not one, but two, kisses in the mail.

And on top of that they could get "recalled" as part-time judges, collecting per diem pay. Triple-dippers, as Dapper O'Neil would say.

Pretty sweet, considering most of them had been starving to death in their little one-room solo practices, waiting to get some work on Aunt Gertrude's will, in between the occasional real-estate closings.

The *Globe*, of course, gave all this a good leaving alone. As I've told you, their motto is "Afflict the afflicted and comfort the comfortable," and few in Massachusetts are as comfortable as the state's judges.

So I went to court needing a simple ruling that Entercom had not matched the offer, which they obviously hadn't. But it was payback time. I had inadequate legal representation. The lawyer told me he knew the judge. Apparently, the judge had never told my attorney how much he hated me.

That judge was another failed lawyer, and he was already over the retirement age of 70. He was about to retire, and he decided to screw me on the way out the door.

I was taken off the air until a decision could be reached, and it wasn't long in coming. The judge ruled that Entercom had "matched" the Greater Media offer, and thus I had to remain on a crippled, underfunded AM stick rather than jump to a full-power FM station where I could actually compete, and win.

I appealed, but I was off the air. I described myself as an "indentured servant." So Entercom had George Regan, Kevin White's hack, leak my salary to the Globe—$790,000 in 2006. I know that sounds like a huge payday, and it is, but all I can say is you have no idea how horrible a company Entercom was, and still is, under its new name of Audacy. If you're stuck in a place you hate, working for assholes, and you can't leave, you are in fact an indentured servant.

It may sound tone-deaf to say such a thing, but I'll stand by my statement.

In their pleadings, Entercom also made public the contract I'd signed with Greater Media. They said it could be worth as much as $1.4 million a year—"could" being the key word—if I hit number one in the 25-to-54 demographic every quarter, which would of course be impossible.

We moved for an expedited hearing, because there was no way Entercom could win if I were granted an honest hearing on the facts. Unfortunately, I was in Massachusetts. My worthless counsel and I sat down with the Entercom attorney—another real sleazeball, but who else would you expect to be working for such a company? Entercom wanted me to agree to work for them for another year. There was no point whatsoever to that demand except to force Greater Media to find someone else for morning drive and prevent me from salvaging my career.

I told the Entercom lawyer that he knew as well as I did that this wasn't a matching offer and that we could prove it very quickly. The guy laughed at me.

"And you think you're going to get a fair hearing?" he said with a laugh. "You? After what you've done to the judges in this state?"

Off the air, I was just hanging around the house, still writing my column for the *Herald* but generally going crazy. My agent did some research to show the actual comparison between AM and FM audiences. By 2007, the AM share in Boston had slipped to 12 percent, and Boston was one of the better markets for AM.

The appeals court finally scheduled my hearing—for January. It was still October. Entercom had no replacement for me. Their ratings were utterly in the toilet, just like the last time I'd been riding the pine in 1993. But they didn't care. They just wanted to fuck me over. I could work again; I just couldn't work in Boston, unless I was toiling for them *in durance vile.*

I had to throw in the towel. They insisted on five years—five years, plus a one-year option! By then, the 12 percent who still listened to AM radio would be down to maybe 5 percent. Okay, I said, I'm screwed. I told my agent, take it but insist on a two-year option, because by 2012, there will be no audience left on AM and there's no way they'll want to pay me another $1.5 million for an additional two years just for spite.

Entercom immediately agreed to the two-year option. Seven years!

I had gotten a seven-year sentence in a maximum-security radio prison for the crime of not wanting to work for assholes. Incompetent assholes at that.

It was a terrible place to be, in every way. The only silver lining in a very dark cloud was the stock market crash in late 2008. Entercom's stock price plummeted to under a dollar a share. Every day, after the market closed at 4 p.m., I'd read the closing price and then we'd play a sound effect of Ted Knight's cackling from the *Mary Tyler Moore Show*, followed by the pop of a cork from a champagne bottle.

After about a week of that, my board op was fired—excuse me, laid off. I made a call and he got a job at Greater Media, which owned WTKK—best break he ever got, he's told me since. Everybody who's ever been let go by Entercom says the same thing.

The fall book in 2008 was the last time the Boston ratings were computed using so-called diaries, a notoriously inaccurate way of computing audiences, although I shouldn't complain, because I finished first again. Then the ratings company switched to PPMs—Portable People Meters, a little remote-control-like device that picks up encoded signals to indicate what you're listening to.

It's all bullshit, whether it's diaries or PPMs. There was a host in the revolving door at WRKO who later landed in Providence. His house somehow ended up with multiple books, and suddenly he was dominant in the Providence "book."

But then somebody from one of the competing clusters went down to Beltsville, Maryland, where the ratings company had its headquarters. They checked out the addresses of the people listening to the new ratings champ and saw that they were all living in a house that the host just happened to own. And that was that.

You used to be able to work hustles like that. Maybe you still can in the smaller markets where diaries continue to be used instead of PPMs. Not that ratings mean as much now, with all the different ways there are to listen or watch. But the lesson of that Rhode Island guy was that you can't get too greedy. It's the old story: pigs get fat, hogs get slaughtered. Just grab one, or at the most two, books at a time.

I knew a guy at the State House whose aunt had worked at the *Herald American*. He was a Dukakis hack but we always got along. When he came up for a promotion, he called me. This was when I was doing a lot of the Sunday notes column, "Pols and Politics."

I could dump pretty much whatever I wanted into that column. A column is—or was, before newspapers died—a marvelous way to win friends and influence people.

So one day this guy called and asked me if could I drop his salary somewhere into next Sunday's column. I said sure. Then he paused a moment and said he needed one other small favor. He wanted me to add a few hundred bucks to his weekly total, so he could get some extra dough at his new job.

You couldn't do this today. Everything's online. But back then, whatever number I used was accepted as gospel, because everybody knew I went over to the comptroller's office in the McCormack Building once a month or so to check out salaries.

I don't like to make shit up, even minor things. It's a bad habit to get into—look at the *Globe*. But this guy was a friend; I knew his family. He needed a favor and, ultimately, what was the harm? So I did it, threw him into some forgettable item in the Sunday paper, inflating his weekly salary by a few hundred bucks. He got the new job, at the higher rate of pay. (I checked later.)

He didn't call to thank me, nor did I expect him to. Some kinds of things you don't brag about. In fact, you want plausible deniability. As we used to say at the State House, "I didn't see you, you didn't see me."

A few years later, though, after I got the full-time afternoon shift at WRKO, the same guy called me. He'd gotten a ratings diary and he wanted to know how I wanted him to handle it. (This was before I was trying desperately to get fired by Entercom so that I could move to a real radio station.)

I told him, I need you to mark down that you listen to me four hours a day, every weekday. Whatever else you do is up to you. Beyond my own four hours a day, I just have one request: even if you do listen to WEEI, give 'em nothing. Now that I think about it, I'm sure I also asked him to give no mentions to anyone else at WRKO.

Number one, I didn't care much for any other "talent" at WRKO. After all, they worked for Entercom. Ergo, they had to be assholes. Number two, the more everyone else failed, the more indispensable I became. When you've been fired as often as I have, you're always sizing up the competition for a head shot, even if they're in house.

Especially if they're in house.

Until now, I never told anybody what I did with that ratings book. I've pulled similar stunts a few times over the years—all well outside the statute of limitations if you know what I mean. As I say, radio ratings are another thing that's pretty much gone by the wayside in recent years, at least as far as my business model is concerned.

Grace Curley started working for my network just out of Providence College in 2014. That Christmas I took her with me to a book signing on the North Shore as my assistant, passing out magnets, glad-handing the fans and so forth.

On the store's public-address system, they were playing whatever FM station was doing Christmas music that year. I explained to Grace that anyone who walked into the store with a PPM would be recorded as listening to whatever

Yuletide crap was coming through the loudspeakers. That's a big reason the Christmas programming always wins the so-called holiday book every year—passive listening, or more precisely, passive non-listening.

I don't think Grace comprehended exactly what I was telling her until a guy walked into the store to buy one of my books. Then he pointed to his belt—he had a PPM. He told me he listened to me every afternoon. I thanked him, and after he left, I asked Grace if she understood now how the system worked, or more precisely, didn't.

It didn't matter if that guy was my talk-show listener or not. For that quarter-hour or so that he was in the store, telling me how much he enjoyed my show on a different station (it was during my 15 minutes on WMEX), at that moment, he was being recorded as a Christmas-music listener.

I always tried to make up for WRKO's inherent handicaps with various stunts. Writing for the *Herald*, I'd use a tagline at the end of my column reminding readers to listen to the show. I had those magnets, which people would put on their refrigerators. If they filled out their diaries at their kitchen tables at the end of the week, as radio people suspected most did, they might notice my smiling face on the magnet and give me a mention—or five.

To survive my stretch, I had to learn every trick in the book, all the while looking for a way to break out of radio prison.

16
HITMAN

After my *60 Minutes* interview in 2006, Ed Bradley asked me if I knew Johnny Martorano, the local hitman who had pleaded guilty to 20 murders.

I didn't know Johnny, but I was friendly with his younger brother Jimmy, who'd been out of prison for several years. Johnny had been arrested in Boca Raton in 1995 after being on the lam for more than 16 years. He'd been tight with Whitey and Stevie—his youngest son was named Stephen James—but when he realized they were rats, he'd flipped, but only against them and Zip Connolly, the crooked FBI agent. He cut a deal that required him to testify against no one else.

In return for his cooperation, which had blown the lid off the FBI-Bulger conspiracy, Martorano got a 12-year sentence. He would be getting out in a few months, and I told Ed Bradley I was hoping to get an interview with him.

"You'll have to wait until I get mine," he said with a smile. "He promised me the first one."

It turned out that Ed Bradley had briefly gone to prep school with Johnny in Rhode Island. Johnny had only lasted at the school long enough to get a nickname from his teammates on the football team. They called him "the Milkman," because as the star fullback he had always delivered.

As it turned out, Bradley was dead by the time Johnny was released. But Johnny kept his promise to *60 Minutes*—slimy Steve Kroft got the exclusive first interview. But soon afterward I was sitting down with Martorano at Daisy Buchanan's in the Back Bay.

We agreed to do a book together, and began shopping it. The editor of *The Brothers Bulger* apparently hadn't been kidding when they told me the publishing house hadn't liked the book, no matter how well it had sold. My first publisher wasn't interested, even though Graham King, the producer of *The Departed,* had already brought the film rights to Johnny's story for hundreds of thousands of dollars. (The movie has yet to be made.)

But we did eventually sell the book to a subsidiary of Macmillan, and I began interviewing Johnny every weekend, usually on Sunday mornings in the *Herald* newsroom, which was still in the South End. Johnny, I discovered, had a near-photographic memory, and having pleaded guilty to 20 slayings, he was one of the few wiseguys anywhere who could speak candidly about anything in his past.

Recounting some of the murders, I couldn't name the shooters who were still alive—Howie Winter, for example, became "the guy from Somerville." But mostly I had *carte blanche* to make the story as accurate—and as compelling—as I could.

I'd been thinking for a long time about how I wanted to write a first-person, "as-told-to," true-crime account. I had some techniques I was itching to try. For instance, when Mike Royko wrote *Boss* about the late Chicago mayor Richard J. Daley, he had led off every chapter with a short transcript of sworn courtroom testimony from the mayor. All these years later, I still remembered how well that had worked as a literary device. So I asked Johnny to get me a transcript of his testimony in the Zip Connolly murder trial in Miami.

It was perfect. I had so many dramatic courtroom passages to choose from that I used them inside the chapters as well.

I also wanted to break up the text with photos, rather than have 8 or 16 pages of glossy pictures in the middle of the book. Macmillan was fine with that.

Another thing I wanted to do was get as many police reports as I could on the murders. It took a while, but the Boston Police Department finally turned over a lot of documents, which I worked into the account of as many of Martorano's murders as possible.

This irritated Johnny. He was telling me what happened, he pointed out, so why did I need anyone else's accounts, especially those of cops who (a) weren't there and (b) lied a lot.

I shrugged. I got some great status details from the Boston police reports. How one of Johnny's victims (a female black teenager shot in what amounted to a tragic mistake) was found in a car in Roxbury during a snowstorm with a cigarette still burning in her hand.

How the widow of one of his victims complained that when her husband's body was found in the trunk of a hot car in Charlestown, it was missing the pinkie ring he'd been most proud of.

It was good stuff, and Johnny eventually understood why I was using the police reports. He still didn't like me relying on them, but he finally figured out the advantage to quoting police reports.

"You use them because they're public record, don't you?" he said to me. "That way you don't have to worry about ever being called out on anything in a police report, because you can always blame it on the cops, right?"

He was right.

In the spring of 2011, just before *Hitman* was to be published, we had torrential rains in Wellesley. My basement, where I'd been storing all my notes and records, was flooded with half a foot of water. Much of my research for the book was destroyed. I called Johnny to tell him the bad news.

"That's great!" he said. Now, if he—or I—got called to testify in a new organized-crime case, we could truthfully say there was no documentation. I had been "memorializing" everything in the notes, "contemporaneously" as they say, but now everything was gone, washed away in a flood.

Hitman was published and immediately landed on the *Times'* bestseller list. I went back out on the road. I'd always meet a lot of interesting people, and sometimes they provided me with new material for my next book, or column.

My first weekend out on the road selling *Hitman*, on the South Shore an older woman waited patiently in line. When she reached my table, she handed me an old photo of a bunch of kids dressed as if they were at a casting call for an old Bowery Boys movie.

The woman asked me if I recognized the blond boy. It was Whitey. I told her I just had to have the picture. I didn't even wait to see if she'd offer it to me for free. The line of buyers behind her was too long. I just asked her, how much?

She smiled and requested a free autographed copy of *Hitman*. What a deal!

A few days later I wrote a column for the *Herald* that of course included the photo. The *Globe* had bloggers at that point. One of them wrote a snide little piece about how all the people who had had any sort of association with Whitey, including those at the *Globe*, venerated each new little bit of historical evidence about him as if it were a splinter from the True Cross. He cited my Whitey-as-a-youth photo as the latest example.

Hitman sold well, but only briefly, and after two weeks it fell off the bestseller list. Whitey had been gone now for more than 16 years, and he seemed to be fading into the past tense like other once-famous vanished celebs of yore, another Judge Crater or Amelia Earhart, or maybe D. B. Cooper would be a more apt comparison, given the criminal angle.

About a week later, early one morning I was asleep in Wellesley when the phone rang. It was a reporter from Channel 4, a guy who'd been an intern at Channel 56 when I worked there. He told me Whitey had finally been arrested, in Santa Monica, California.

The guy wanted to know if he could interview me. Is the Pope Catholic? We did it across the street from my house outside the little private elementary school, in the dark, under a streetlight.

He told me he figured he wouldn't be bothering me by waking me up, and he was right. By dawn, I was sitting on the set for the local morning news on Channel 5. A couple of more TV crews showed up for the start of my radio show.

That afternoon, I got a call from ABC News. They wanted permission to use my photo of young Whitey, which the *Globe* blogger had been giving me the needle for just days earlier.

Hitman jumped right back on the Times bestseller list. I don't know how often that happens, a book coming back on after dropping off the list, but I was very grateful.

The Whitey cottage industry was back in business.

I enjoyed being on the road every weekend. I was still wasting away at WRKO, doing time in indentured servitude. I was coming up on my fifth year, and while I was desperately hoping that Entercom wouldn't pick up my option, I wasn't optimistic.

I had three years left in the hole. For years now, I'd slowly been adding stations, setting up my own little radio "network" around New England. Entercom couldn't complain, given the station's wretched signal. My most important affiliate was in Worcester, because it covered most of the 40 percent of the market that AM 680 didn't after the sun went down.

I picked up stations in areas where I had a background—among them, Portland and Springfield. My wife despised Entercom as much as I did, and she began fantasizing about how maybe we could just shear off from Entercom and take our own network with us. It had only rarely been done, but so what?

So to promote my potential new independent radio network during my short time remaining in radio jail, I went out on the road more and more. On the weekends, I'd hit bookstores. I passed out thousands of magnets (except for Boston and Hartford, all of my affiliates were still in diary, as opposed to PPM, markets).

One day at the Barnes & Noble bookstore in Peabody, a guy came in wearing a jacket he'd worn back in the 1970s when he was a bouncer at Triple O's, Whitey's bar in the Lower End. With my cell phone, I took pictures of the jacket and then turned out white sweatshirts with the Triple O's shamrock logo.

Another Saturday at the Paper Store in Billerica, a Lowell police detective dropped off hundreds of pages of files on the Winter Hill Gang's takeover of the betting rackets in Lowell around 1974. In one of the reports, a Lowell cop tells Jackie McDermott, an old buddy of mine who was murdered by one of Fat

We always made a magnet from the cover of the latest book.

Tony Ciulla's old enforcers in 1988, that the guy he knows as "Nick" is actually Johnny Martorano.

Jackie tells the cop that he knows that. The cop then asks him, so why aren't you carrying a gun when you meet with him? And McDermott replies something to the effect that, with guys like that, it doesn't matter if you carry a gun or not, they'll still clip you.

Which, in Jackie's case, they eventually did. But even more interesting to me was that Jackie gave almost the same reply that the hitman Dillon gave to his cop handler in George V. Higgins' novel, *The Friends of Eddie Coyle*. The fictional character Dillon tells his cop handler how if you drive a car, they'll get you with a car, and if you ride on a bus, they'll find a way to get you on the bus.

At another signing, I met a woman who gave me the Catholic girls' high school yearbook of the black teenaged woman Johnny Martorano murdered by mistake during that blizzard in Roxbury in 1968. A relative of Stevie Flemmi gave me a bunch of photos of Stevie's older brother, Jimmy the Bear, taken in prison back before he died of a drug overdose at MCI-Norfolk in 1979.

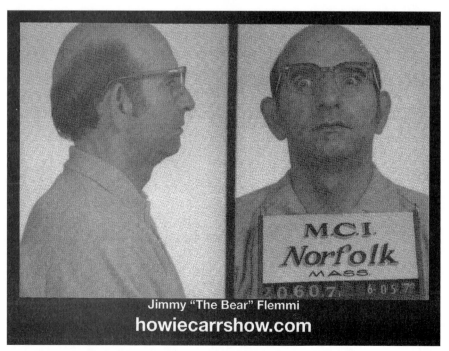

Jimmy the Bear Flemmi: one of my favorite mugshots ever.

One day at the Book Ends bookstore in Winchester, the older wife of a retired criminal lawyer walked in with a box of files and state police reports from the 1960s, including all the files on the murdered hoods in the Irish gang war and on the Plymouth mail truck robbery in 1962.

When I looked over the MSP files on the 30 or so dead gangsters, I realized I'd just been handed a chapter in a book, a book that would require practically no effort on my part to produce.

By now, I had put together a traveling road show—*Night of Crime.* My wife was instrumental in setting it up. We were both looking ahead to the day when I'd be free of Entercom.

To make any radio network succeed, I would need loyal affiliate stations. And what better way to bond with my stations than to make personal appearances like *Night of Crime.* In most cases, they would get me the venue, usually as trade. In return, I'd give them some free tickets for their VIPs, and then we'd sell the rest to listeners. At the events, we'd peddle books, and T-shirts, as well as give away magnets and other free stuff. I gladly posed for what must have been thousands of photos and selfies with whoever wanted one.

Having a New York publisher was prestigious, to be sure, but by now I'd learned how much prestige was worth. I'd been an instructor at Harvard, I was a member of the Radio Hall of Fame, a *New York Times* best-selling author, and it didn't mean shit to a tree, to quote Jefferson Airplane. When it came to the elite, I was still an outlaw in their eyes, to quote an old Steely Dan song. I was never going to be accepted in polite society, but so what?

Living well is the best revenge.

Not only did I want to get out from under the corporate thumb—Entercom in particular—but more generally I was all done with bosses, period.

So my wife and I decided that we would self-publish my next book. When we ran the numbers, it was clear what a better deal it would be. No advances, of course, but the fact was, on the New York–published hardcovers, I made about four bucks per book. On *Hitman,* I had to split both the advance and the royalties with Martorano—cut up the pot, to use his phrase, in addition to the agent's percentage.

On the other hand, if I were to print my own books, they would cost me maybe $1.50 per copy to produce. I could charge $19.99 or $24.99, whatever. With that kind of markup, and the middlemen removed, I could make four times as much money per unit than I could writing for Hachette or Macmillan.

Most authors need an organization behind them, to get the book into the stores, generate publicity, and so forth. That's what a publisher used to do. But like everything else in all media, old-line publishing has fallen on hard times. By 2012, I realized that, for better or for worse, I would soon be my own organization. I had a radio show—and a newspaper column—to promote my books.

Another thing: an ever-larger percentage of books were being sold online. I could sell through Amazon, and then fulfill the orders myself. Even more profitably, I could set up a website and sell directly to my listeners—even eliminating the Amazon middleman.

One more plus: once I got out on my own, I could start selling remote broadcasts. And to draw crowds into the restaurants or car dealerships or wherever, I could give away some of my books. I'd autograph them, personalize them. At a buck-fifty per copy, I could afford to give away a few hundred if I was being paid, say, $5,000 for each appearance.

The more remotes I did, the more selfies I took with my listeners, the more they bonded with me. That meant my ratings would go up, and more listeners would show up at the next remote with more great material that I could put into my next book, and the one after that.

Pretty soon I owned what had to be the biggest collection of old police mugshots anywhere in New England. And all of them were public record, meaning I didn't have to pay anybody to reprint them.

Our new business model developed slowly. Like every other small start-up business, the Howie Carr Radio Network learned by hit and miss. How much equipment do you need to have? How many employees? Do you need to pay for PR, or to buy ratings?

The biggest roll of the dice is on employees—a bad hire is about the worst mistake any small businessman can ever make. If you survive, you start asking other questions later. For instance, if we set up 401(k)s for everybody, will it save the corporation money on taxes?

Even while I remained on the Entercom payroll, I was already a short-timer. I was getting ready to bolt.

The first book we did on our own was *Rifleman*. It wasn't at all like the first two. It was basically a police report with photographs. It didn't make the *Times'* bestseller list. But it made a lot more money than either of the first two, because I owned it 100 percent. As I'd hoped to do, I had cut out the middleman. This was perhaps the most valuable early lesson for the Howie Carr Radio Network.

The genesis of *Rifleman* came from Stevie Flemmi's guilty plea when he became a rat for the feds. Part of his plea agreement was to provide the feds with a complete account of his entire criminal career. He sat down, not with the FBI, because along with Whitey he'd been paying the G-men off, but with agents of the Drug Enforcement Administration (DEA).

The document they produced on Stevie was called a DEA-6. A lawyer for one of the survivors told me about Stevie's DEA-6. He said it was "very dark," and that was an understatement. It was a fascinating document, and there were no copyrights on it. After I took possession of the DEA-6, I went through my now voluminous collections of mug shots and found dozens of grainy photographs to illustrate the dry, bureaucratic Joe Friday prose.

I paid an illustrator at the *Herald* to produce a map of Greater Boston to show where the gangs had been operating in the 1960s. One of my daughters' classmates at Wellesley High was a talented graphic artist, which I knew because he'd done a portrait of my two pugs. I commissioned him to do the *Rifleman* cover—in black and red, of course, because I'd learned from my first two books that those two colors somehow attract the attention of male readers, who make up most of the buyers for true-crime works.

On the back of the dust jacket I used the first-ever court photo of Stevie, from 1957, which I'd found while rummaging through the *Herald* morgue one Sunday morning.

I pulled photos out of ancient high-school yearbooks—I had both H. Paul Rico's and Larry Baione's. As it turned out, Larry's nickname at Franklin High School back in 1938 was "Zip"—it's amazing the tidbits and ironies and, yes, those little status details that you can come up with if you just keep digging and asking questions.

Whitey's murder and racketeering trial was starting in June 2013 in federal court in Boston. Two competing biographies of Whitey were coming out from current or former *Globe* reporters. My photo of young Whitey was in one of them—the authors, who had never ripped me publicly, probably because I'd never done them any favors, had asked for my permission to use the photo. I was glad to give it to them. It had already served its purpose for me, in the books and in the *Herald*.

There was enough on the market already about Whitey. I figured with Stevie, maybe I could cash in on a related topic, even if it wasn't exactly a "major" work. We found a publisher in Ohio who printed mostly vanity books. *Rifleman* was privately printed, but it was for profit, not vanity.

Paper Boy

The more books I did, the more I came to appreciate photographs. One of the most exasperating experiences with *Hitman* was the New York publisher's refusal to print a photo of one of the men framed by the FBI for the murder of gangster Teddy Deegan in 1965.

The lawyer for the family had given me the photo—it was his military photo from World War II. He was smiling and wearing an overseas cap. The publisher's lawyers asked me who had taken the photo. I told them it was an Army picture, the subject was dead, the photographer was dead, the family wanted the picture in the book, etc. But nothing could convince them to include the photo. They were afraid of getting sued.

I came to understand their fear later, when my website was sued by a predatory lawyer (since disbarred) who made a good living just going after careless people who hadn't bothered to check copyrights before reposting photographs.

But in the case of that World War II photo that didn't make *Hitman*, I knew I wasn't going to be sued. They were hassling me over nothing. The older I got, the less I liked any interference from . . . clerks, as I was starting to call them, the corporate bean counters and pencil sharpeners I'd grown sick of answering to.

After all my years in stir at Entercom, I'd lost whatever tolerance I may have once had for clerks. Years earlier, in Winston-Salem, after I was named assistant city editor, one of the old-time reporters, a good guy, came up to me and said, "I never figured you for middle management, Howie."

He had said it amiably enough, but it was a needle nonetheless. And he was right—and as much as I hadn't been cut out for middle management, as I got older I was even less inclined to suffer those same paper-shuffling yes-men gladly.

Advertisers, I could listen to them. They paid the bills. The customer is always right—that is a cliché to live by. But timid corporate bureaucrats and timeservers are another thing altogether.

It wasn't just an aversion to taking orders. I didn't like other people making bad decisions that affected my own finished product, and maybe the bottom line as well. For instance, in *Hitman* the publishers had agreed with me about putting the photos alongside the copy, rather than in a center section. But they had used what seemed to me to be an inferior grade of paper—not terrible, but not ideal for reproduction of photographs, especially the superior black-and-white photographs, including mug shots, that I delivered to them.

So for *Rifleman*, we decided to use glossy, slick paper. The photos looked fantastic, but then I had another question to ponder. Was it worth the extra cost?

Ditto, the hardcover. Who cared anymore whether a book is hardcover or not, especially if it meant the book was priced at $24.99 rather than, say, $15.99?

These are the types of issues you deal with if you're a publisher, and that's what my wife and I were now—publishers.

Another conundrum—how the hell were we going to get the books out to the local booksellers? We wanted to use them for book signings, obviously, but how would we handle distribution? Returns? Past-due bills from struggling local bookstores being driven to the wall by Amazon?

Slowly, we began adjusting our marketing model. We still did some bookstore signings, but more and more we moved to venues where we could sell the books ourselves and not have to worry about collecting money later. Eventually we would stop taking cash—too many sticky fingers, another elementary business lesson you can only learn the hard way.

Fewer and fewer people were going to bookstores anyway. On one level, it was sad, the passing of another venerable tradition. On the other hand, with Amazon, you just posted your book and it was sold online. You fulfilled the order, cut Amazon in, and that was it.

Of course Amazon was evil—how evil we didn't know just yet—but partnering with them was easier than making your own deliveries and chasing people endlessly for money. And anyway, who was to say that we would always have to rely on Amazon? Maybe someday not so far down the road we could set up our own store, and sell everything through it. We'd already used the Amazon middleman to eliminate the other middlemen.

Now if we could just eliminate the Amazon middleman . . .

17
THE TRIAL
OF WHITEY
BULGER

Whitey Bulger's murder and racketeering trial in the summer of 2013 was going to be big. I was asked by my *Hitman* publisher if I wanted to do a book on it, with a female co-author who was a lawyer.

I thought about it. I considered the profit margin for *Rifleman* and the headaches of dealing with New York publishers, not to mention splitting the money with a co-author and potential clashes of ego.

I also factored in the lead time. With a major publisher, the book would take at least a year to get out. In an age of rapidly diminishing attention spans, that was far too long. So my wife and I decided we would do our own book on the Whitey trial. It was starting in June and would run into August. We needed to get it out by Christmas—another thing I'd learned was that close to half of all book sales are made during the holidays.

We had a good relationship with our *Rifleman* publisher in Ohio. The photos wouldn't be a problem—everything that the prosecutors put into evidence became public record, and anyone could use anything. Now I would have unlimited access to some of the classic old *Globe* photos, like the ones of Eddie Connors, murdered in a phone booth in Dorchester in 1975 just up Morrissey Boulevard from the *Globe*.

One of the police surveillance photos of Whitey and Stevie made public at the 2013 trial that we turned into a popular magnet.

I didn't think any other reporters in the Bulger trial pool knew enough about the mechanics of the publishing industry to even be considering any of these possibilities.

Dr. Johnson said that when a man is being hanged in a fortnight, it concentrates his mind wonderfully. So does being in business for yourself, I've discovered.

The trial was starting on a Monday. That Friday night, I was having dinner in Wellesley when I got a phone call from the U.S. attorney's office. Whitey had included me on his potential defense witness list. Thus, I would not be allowed to come into the courtroom (therefore theoretically preventing me from learning what other "witnesses" were saying, and then tailoring my own testimony accordingly).

It was total nonsense, of course. There were five reporters among the 50 or so people on his "witness list"—the four *Globe* reporters who had new biographies out about him, and me. It was just a typical fuck-you by Whitey to all his "foes," as his brother Billy always called his own political adversaries.

UNITED STATES DISTRICT COURT
DISTRICT OF MASSACHUSETTS

UNITED STATES OF AMERICA)
)
V.   )   NO. 99-CR-10371-DJC
)
JAMES J. BULGER   )
)

DEFENDANT'S AMENDED WITNESS LIST

The defendant, James J. Bulger, submits this witness list pursuant to the Court's Order dated March 26, 2013. ECF Dkt. No. 851. The defendant reserves the right to supplement, modify or withdraw witnesses from this list.

1.   Michael Albano
     Medford, MA

2.   Earl Anderson
     Roseau, MN

3.   Jeannette Benedetti
     Walpole, MA

4.   Richard Bergeron
     Quincy, MA

5.   Sam Berkowitz
     Royal Palm Beach FL 33411

6.   Brian Burke

7.   Howard Carr
     Brighton, MA 02135

8.   Jerry Campbell
     Boston, MA

9.   Neal Cherkas
     Chelsea, MA

1

2013: My name on Whitey Bulger's list of defense witnesses.

The *Herald* was already feeling the financial pinch, and I knew they wouldn't pay for a lawyer to go into court and ask Judge Denise Casper to let me in. But the *Globe*, which was also reeling, was willing to spend a few bucks (they had four people to protect, after all), so for once I would just ride in on the *Globe*'s coattails.

First thing Monday morning, even before the opening statements, Judge Casper lifted the ban preventing the five newspaper "witnesses" from attending the trial. Not one of us was ever called to the stand by Whitey's taxpayer-funded lawyers.

It was a small courtroom. With so many survivors and other assorted victims who wanted to attend, there wasn't nearly enough room for the reporters. So the feds set up a spillover room downstairs, with large-screen TVs. I came to prefer being there—you could drink coffee, browse through newspapers or your emails during dull stretches, put your feet up, and even occasionally grab a few winks if things got slow, as they occasionally do in every trial, except the ones in made-for-TV movies.

It was a motley crew downstairs in the spillover room. Some days Maureen Dowd from the *Times* was there. She was a lot easier to take in person than in her columns. T. J. English, who's written some excellent organized-crime books, moved into the North End to cover the trial.

I got along fine with T. J., told him how much I'd admired his earlier work. But when his own book about the Whitey case finally came out, more than a year later, he made clear that he thought that Kevin Cullen and I had not always treated the trial with the seriousness it deserved.

As necessary as that trial was for so many reasons, I believe that the young Winston Churchill was onto something when he said after surviving combat in the Boer War:

"Nothing in life is so exhilarating as to be shot at without result."

Okay, so they hadn't shot at Cullen or me. But they had certainly threatened both of us. That much was not in dispute. That was not Brian Williams bluster. It was all on the record.

Now the serial killer who'd wanted me dead would never see the light of day again. And what turned out to be his empty threats had only increased my stature and made me a lot of money. Exhilarated—yeah, I'll admit to being a little exhilarated.

When Weeks took the witness stand, Whitey's defense attorney baited him with the nickname I'd bestowed on him—Two Weeks. Then he brought up his alleged attempts to murder me. I was watching downstairs, and some of the other reporters were glancing over at me, as Weeks was asked about their alleged murder plot against me when I lived in Acton.

To drive home his point—I guess that he was a homicidal maniac who'd do anything Whitey ordered him to—Weeks blurted out, "We knew his address—99 Concord Road!"

Then he said it again, almost spat out the address—99 Concord Road. I started giggling. I guess it must have seemed an inappropriate response, because some of the other reporters immediately tweeted out my baffling reaction.

The reason I was amused was because my actual address in Acton hadn't been 99 Concord Road. I had lived at 91 Concord Road. I explained this to all the reporters during the sidebar conference that had immediately been called.

When I got the trial transcript the next day—which included those sidebar discussions between the judges and the lawyers that the jury and spectators hadn't been privy to—I discovered that they had been debating whether to strike "99 Concord Road" from the official record, to protect me or something.

Judge Casper, God bless her, instructed the court reporter not to include my supposed address. She was only trying to do the right thing. I still appreciate her concern for my safety.

Somehow a lot of casual trial observers seemed to believe that Whitey still controlled some underworld organization in Southie that would seek vengeance on his foes, his persecutors.

One of the spectators who was coming to court every day was Stippo Rakes, the Southie hustler who'd had the South Boston Liquor Mart stolen from him by the gang. I'd written about that crime at some length in *The Brothers Bulger*, and had gotten to know him well. I'd even written a letter on his behalf to his sentencing federal judge when he was convicted of lying to a grand jury about his dealings with Whitey.

Stippo was an interesting character. For a guy who claimed to be a victim, he seemed to know a lot about the rackets in Southie. In fact, one of his sisters was allegedly an upper-level distributor in Whitey's cocaine crew. Her name and mug shot were featured on one of the gang's organizational charts during the trial.

When Whitey muscled in and stole the Liquor Mart from Stippo, he'd paid Rakes some nominal sum. But unlike so many of the others in Southie, including Weeks, Stippo hadn't been handed a job at the MBTA—Mr. Bulger's Transportation Authority. He'd had to take $3,000 from the pittance Whitey gave him to launder his theft of the package store. He used Whitey's cocaine cash to buy a shitty T job from the bagman of a South Boston politician whose last name was not Bulger.

By now, Stippo was retired, living on his monthly kiss in the mail from the MBTA. But he was still outraged by what Whitey had done to him all those years ago. Who could blame him? He showed up at the courthouse every morning. He was on the feds' original witness list, but they'd decided not to call him. Given his past, Stippo would have been vulnerable on cross-examination.

The prosecutors figured why take a chance with a slam-dunk case? Don't let the jury get even the slightest shred of a reasonable, or even not so reasonable, doubt.

But Rakes still liked to sit in the front row of the courtroom every day and stare at Whitey, trying to get his attention. He was always ready to give an interview to reporters. But then one morning he didn't show up at the courthouse. Stippo had vanished.

A few hours later, a body was found in the woods off Route 128. It was Stippo's. He'd been poisoned. For a few hours, on a slow summer afternoon, it was a huge story nationally. Whitey witness—Whitey victim—found dead in the woods in Lincoln. No car, no wallet, no visible signs of trauma. It was an unsolved mystery.

Now, knowing Stippo's sketchy background, and knowing how defunct Whitey's criminal organization was, I was not at all concerned about my own safety. There was no Murder Inc. roaming through Southie, exacting vengeance on behalf of the imprisoned gang bosses.

But Stippo's murder was such a made-for-tabloids story that I was deluged with messages. Some friends just texted me not to take any chances. A few radio talk shows wanted me as a guest. I agreed of course.

The conjecture was ever so much more fascinating than the reality. Once again, like in the old John Ford movie, when the truth became the legend, print the legend.

The truth came out a day or so later. An autopsy showed Stippo had been poisoned with potassium cyanide. He had loaned a lot of money to Bill Camuti, a businessman so shady that he had his own weekend finance show on WRKO. He'd met Stippo at a McDonald's on 128, poisoned his iced coffee, and then dumped his body on some conservation land in Mike Barnicle's affluent suburb.

It was a disappointment to fans of true-crime TV that Whitey hadn't had a hand in murdering Stippo. For me, it was yet another reminder how terrible a place Entercom was to work. As I mentioned earlier, it was the second poisoning involving WRKO in a decade—in 2004, one of the younger part-time staffers had been convicted of poisoning his wife.

Whitey's trial was like yet another old home week for me. One of Whitey's real defense witnesses was a former Boston FBI agent named Bob Fitzpatrick. Right before Brian Halloran was murdered by Whitey Bulger in 1982 (on Northern Avenue, just down the street from the new courthouse in which the trial was now taking place), Fitzpatrick happened to mention in passing, publicly, that he wouldn't want to be standing next to Halloran.

Fitzpatrick parlayed that prescient statement into his own personal 15 minutes of fame, and then a book, by the same publisher as I had for *Hitman*. So on a Saturday afternoon in 2011, I found myself doing a series of dual book signings with former agent Fitzpatrick. He was an amiable enough companion, and we had lunch together.

Two years later, I was somewhat surprised when I saw Fitzpatrick's name on Whitey's witness list—the real witness list.

His direct testimony was anodyne, forgettable. But Brian Kelly, the assistant U.S. attorney, was loaded for bear on cross-examination. He picked up a well-thumbed copy of Fitzpatrick's "nonfiction" tome, and began asking him, was it a fact that he himself had found the rifle that was used to kill Dr. Martin Luther King Jr. in 1968? Had he slapped the handcuffs on Mafia boss Jerry Angiulo in 1982? Did he in fact know what Whitey Bulger had said to John McIntyre before he shot him in the head in 1984?

Remember, Fitzpatrick was under oath. But he still claimed he'd in fact done everything he'd claimed in the book (except for the story about McIntyre's final moments before Whitey murdered him—he blamed that one on his ghost-writer's "research").

That afternoon, after being savaged on cross-examination for more than an hour, Fitzpatrick reeled out of the courthouse and headed straight for the nearest barroom—the Barking Crab.

The next morning, Kelly resumed his grueling cross-examination. He went over Fitzpatrick's testimony from the prior day.

KELLY: "You don't remember yesterday's testimony?"

FITZPATRICK: "No, I don't."

KELLY: "You don't recall your testimony from yesterday?"

FITZPATRICK: "You're asking me to recall something that I may not recall."

KELLY: "I'm asking you, first of all, to recall something you said yesterday and you don't recall."

FITZPATRICK: "Fine. I just don't recall."

KELLY: "Are you on medication or something?"

FITZPATRICK: "I am on medication, yes."

KELLY: "Does it affect your memory?"

FITZPATRICK: "I don't believe so, but I'm on medication."

KELLY: "Do you have any medical issue with your memory?"

FITZPATRICK: "Not that I recall."

I put that entire exchange in *Ratman*. I included every important, or amusing, bit of testimony—verbatim. Because of my other obligations, especially the four-hour radio show, I couldn't make it to the courthouse every day. But I needed to have an accurate record, especially if I was going to get the copy to Ohio in time to be set in print for Christmas.

Fortunately, through a source at the courthouse, I got the daily trial transcripts as soon as they were generated. Whether I was in the courtroom or not, I could keep knocking out the book day by day as the trial continued, as long as I didn't tell anybody what resources I had access to that they didn't.

My chapter on Fitzpatrick was shipped off to Ohio a week or so after he committed all those felonies in the courtroom. It was great for me, not nearly so great for the "decorated" FBI agent.

More than two years later, the forked-tongue G-man pleaded guilty to six counts each of perjury and obstruction of justice. At age 76 he got a suspended sentence, and more importantly he got to keep his pension until his death in 2021. Of course so did Zip Connolly and his boss, John "Vino" Morris, both of whom took thousands of dollars in bribes from Whitey. They're still collecting, well into their eighties. So why not good old garrulous Fitzie?

Once a week, we even did the entire radio show from The Barking Crab, with guests from the trial. It was fun, almost like the old days in radio, before Entercom ruined everything.

In August, Whitey's case went to the jury. Before it did, though, the defendant was given one final opportunity to testify in his own defense.

"This trial is a sham," Whitey yelled at the judge. "Do with me what youse will!"

Youse? That use of faux vernacular disappointed me—Whitey wasn't Italian. *Youse* as the plural of *you*—that was an Italian thing, not Irish. That was the mark of a guy trying to . . . I don't know what exactly. Who the hell did Whitey still need to impress at this point? Youse indeed.

The verdict was a foregone conclusion, and the afternoon it came in, I went down to Channel 25 in Dedham to do a live shot. I'd been wearing long pants to court all summer, so I stopped off at home in Wellesley and changed into shorts and sandals, forgetting that all of Channel 25's live interviews were conducted on tall stools, using wide shots.

In other words, even though I was wearing a sport coat, formal shirt and tie, the viewers would see me in shorts and sandals. The audience was greatly amused, and the screenshots still live on the Internet. I even made a magnet using the photo.

I finished writing *Ratman* within 10 days of the verdict, and three weeks later I was editing the galleys. It was the final hardcover printed by my publishing arm—Frandel, named after my late parents, Fran and Del Carr, just like Harvey Weinstein named his company Miramax after his mother and father, Mira and Max.

With *Ratman* in production in October, I went back to court for the two days of sentencings. I got another chapter of unbelievable stories out of the victim-impact statements, including Whitey calling up the 11-year-old son of one of his victims one Christmas and identifying himself as Santa Claus.

The sentencing was too late for that first Christmas edition, but we quickly had the new chapter set in type and added to the text. We ordered the printing of another edition of 5,000 updated copies, this time soft cover, cheaper, and more up to date. Naturally, we sold even more of the paperbacks, and had to keep ordering more printings.

My only regret about the sentencing was that the prosecutors were unable to work yet another reference to Whitey's hatred of me into their final statement to the judge. The feds had access to all his jailhouse recordings with his relatives at the Plymouth County Correctional Facility.

On at least one of their visits, Whitey had gone off on a long rant about how much he wanted to kill me. That was a harangue he would repeat, I later found out, not only to assorted local jailbirds in Plymouth, but also to his fellow federal BOP inmates later in Tucson. According to one later podcast, in Arizona Whitey supposedly expressed his desire to "eat my fingers."

If the feds had played that tape from Plymouth at sentencing—to show how much Whitey still wanted me dead—then I'd have had another round of the kind of publicity money just can't buy. Everyone in the press would have used it, because they could have interviewed me outside the courthouse about my indomitable, aw-shucks, stoic courage in the face of the threats of this unspeakable serial-killing fiend.

It was not to be, however. Whitey's latest rant about me was left on the cutting-room floor. That's showbiz, I guess. You can't win 'em all.

Ratman was out for Christmas 2013, and sold quite well. It actually made the *Globe's* local bestseller list. The other trial books, put out by the more reputable New York publishers, came out years later, and quickly died. The Whitey story might not have been quite over, but it had peaked. Still, ultimately, Whitey had been good to me, a real résumé enhancer as Rush Limbaugh used to say.

18
2,555 DAYS
IN THE HOLE

Jailbirds say that you can do good time or you can do bad time. Meaning, you can try to relax and just get the sentence over with as painlessly as possible. Or you can rant or rave—that way madness lies, as King Lear put it. But sometimes you can't help yourself. King Lear tried to do good time. Speaking of the madness, he said, Let me shun that, no more of that.

Easy for King Lear to say. Despite everything, he was still the King. I wasn't. I was pissed—beyond pissed.

When I was in radio prison, I did bad time. But the good news about doing time is that, sooner or later, it's always over, one way or another.

But in the meantime, I acted out. To again quote Dr. Johnson, "He who makes a beast of himself gets rid of the pain of being a man."

I made a beast of myself.

I made the front door of my office a bulletin board for anti-Entercom stories—bad ratings, lawsuits, delisting threats from the New York Stock Exchange, etc. The stooge for whoever the local cluster manager was that month would take photographs of my door. I'd come out of my office and ask him if he wanted me to pose beside the door.

The jock sniffers were getting free cases of Smartwater, which I liked. Every Sunday morning I'd come in to their deserted offices and steal however many cases they'd gotten that week.

On weekdays, I would steal toilet paper from the men's room, and try to make sure that I was observed while pilfering multiple rolls.

The WEEI hosts got free review copies of books. I took to stealing many of their expensive coffee-table sports volumes, selling them to a used bookstore on Newbury Street until it finally went out of business, like most of the other independent bookstores I'd always frequented and done book signings in.

The less valuable books I shipped down to a struggling bookstore on the Cape whose owners I liked. I sent them out from the station mailroom—at Entercom's expense. I ordered the mail-room clerk to send everything first class, no matter how heavy. Anything to cut Entercom's profit margin.

The other hosts would sometimes inquire about their missing books, which they'd ordered from the publishers. Eventually even the dimmest of the dim WEEI hosts realized what was going on.

Just in case they were particularly slow, when I ripped open the book packages, I'd toss the mangled, torn-up packing envelopes, which included the names of the hosts who'd ordered the books, onto the floor of the mailroom. That way they could confirm that their deliveries had been stolen.

If I'd just put everything in the trash, they might not have figured out what I was doing.

I was trying everything I could think of but they still wouldn't fire me. If I got fired, I'd just go over to WTKK, and WRKO would collapse, and my ratings might take a bite out of WEEI as well. So it was a standoff. I had always liked Humble Pie's song, "Thirty Days in the Hole." Now I was doing seven years in the hole.

The first crack in the Entercom armor came in 2009. Years earlier I'd taken to working out at Babson College every morning, walking for miles on a treadmill while reading the papers. (I hadn't yet made the switch to the Internet.) After a few years, my right hip was totally shot. I was forced to get a hip replacement. In the summer of 2009, I was laid up at Mass General post-op, comfortably numb with a morphine drip. That's when I got the text.

WEEI was about to get a competitor. On FM. That meant WEEI was finished.

It was the news I had always assumed would come someday. I just hadn't known which competing radio conglomerate would pull the trigger.

It was CBS that had decided to flip one of its also-ran music stations to an FM sports-talk format. It was what I'd always been hoping for, a competitor to WEEI, because I knew that anything on FM could beat anything on AM, especially a product as wretched as Shillville's. You didn't have to be in radio management to understand this. You only needed to drive around the city for 20 or 30 minutes a day with your radio on.

The only ones who didn't instantly know that WEEI was doomed were the jock sniffers who worked there. From my hospital bed at Mass General, I emailed the CBS GM, who used to work at the old American Radio, and told him that the news had made me so ecstatic that I'd turned off my morphine drip. (That was a slight exaggeration.)

The only thing listenable on Shillville was the morning show, with Gerry Callahan and John Dennis, my former colleagues. Later they were joined by Kirk Minihane. They were running a real talk show, not just a slobber-fest for Tom Brady, Bill Belichick, and whichever other local teams were on a historic, unprecedented two-game winning streak.

Somehow, even the dimmest Shillville sycophants believed they were immune to a challenge. Even if they'd been competent broadcasters, they were still stranded on the AM band. It was difficult enough for me to survive the twin catastrophes of being on AM and having Entercom management. I had to work hard to keep my head above water, even as I tried to get fired. Obviously, the jock sniffers had never studied the history of AM versus FM. Neither had the below-average clowns who ran Entercom.

Within six months, WEEI's ratings had been demolished. Over the years Entercom had tried to keep WRKO on life support by moving one pro team or another's play-by-play over to AM 680. As usual, management was oblivious, in this case to the fact that nobody under the age of 80 was listening to play-by-play on the radio anymore.

For a while WRKO had the Celtics. Their pregame show, which had even lower numbers than the games themselves, was costing me a half hour at the end of my show twice a week. My bonuses were based on the entire four hours of my show, 3 to 7.

I didn't get an asterisk for nights I was preempted by the pregame shows. As I knew it would, it ended up hurting my ratings—and my bonuses. It was the same later with the Red Sox. As with the Celtics, the end of my show was preempted, cratering my numbers. I always announced the preemption by saying that we were now going to the "very exciting" Red Sox pregame show.

As soon as the dimensions of WEEI's ratings collapse became clear, the Red Sox were likewise shifted back to Shillville. Then they decided, finally, to blow up one of their wretched also-ran rock music stations—not WAAF or its $27 million translator—and move Shillville over there.

Too late!

As the self-inflicted disaster unfolded day by day, it became almost fun to go to work again. They were shuffling the deck chairs on the *Titanic*—on both WEEI and WRKO.

Until I started writing this book, I'd forgotten what a revolving door WRKO had become. An ex-Congressman who'd lost his job for going on a topless booze cruise during working hours was briefly the morning host. His partner was a morbidly obese former part-time undercover narc on the Cape who'd busted Robert F. Kennedy Jr. and one of his cousins in the early 1970s for selling him a couple of joints while he was driving a cab.

That guy died of a heart attack in his sleep, and the ex-Congressman was fired. He was replaced by that former House speaker I told you about who was a convicted felon. Another short-time, ratings-challenged yakker was fired for calling a candidate a "fat lesbian."

Another was canned for calling for Palestinians to be, well, nobody was ever clear about what he had said, because nobody listened to his show, including management. That guy had been brought over on waivers from WAAF, the Beavis and Butt-Head station. He called himself "Ozone."

The program directors likewise came and went. One of them had an assistant who looked like Fatty Arbuckle. Another had a goatee. That one had had a French surname that he'd changed, so we called him "Frenchy." Then, to save money, they turned the programming on WRKO over to the 63-inch-high program director of WEEI, who was named Jason Wolfe. He was a career yes-man that I nicknamed "Coffee Boy." Predictably, Coffee Boy knew even less about news talk than he did about sports talk, about which he knew nothing.

The WRKO sports reporter, the traffic guy, and then everybody in the "news" department were already gone. Nobody noticed.

They fired the hag female GM who hadn't even realized that WEEI had been gut shot by CBS's FM competition. They brought in a new manager for the cluster, a very appropriate word for Entercom's Boston clusterfuck.

Do you see how I could get frustrated?

I continued doing everything I could to keep the "fuck" front and center in the Entercom clusterfuck. At one point WRKO hired yet another new morning host, a black guy named Reese Hopkins.

He didn't last long, and a couple of days after his firing, Hopkins was arrested and charged with sexual abuse of a child. (He was eventually acquitted.) This happened two nights after he had appeared on CNN as a guest political analyst. He was lugged in Malden one night after the *Herald*'s deadline. So first thing the next morning I tipped off the *Herald*, and a reporter called up Jason Wolfe.

Coffee Boy hadn't known anything about the arrest. He phoned and asked me why I hadn't told him. I told Coffee Boy he hadn't asked me. Then I laughed.

The next day the *Herald* splashed with the headline, "Reese's Gone to Pieces/ Fired WRKO Host Faces Child Rape Charges."

There was a female midday host who likewise didn't last long. (I was the only one who couldn't catch a break and get fired.) Soon after her termination, she was arrested for drunk driving. I obtained her mug shot—she had a couple of black eyes and cuts all over her face—and asked the *Herald* to be sure to identify her as a "former WRKO host."

Who said there's no such thing as bad publicity?

Yet another new morning host, who'd blown in from parts unknown, began disparaging Dunkin' Donuts, claiming they employed only illegal aliens behind the counter. That seemed a rather harsh criticism, especially considering that Dunkin' was one of his dismal show's few remaining advertisers.

I got tape of his asinine comments and had them posted anonymously on social media, making sure Dunkin' was alerted to them. End of sponsorship. I began to understand how valuable social media could become in my Entercom destabilization campaign.

With revenues plummeting, they hated paying me my still-sizable bonuses more than ever. Twice, after bonus money didn't show up in my first paycheck after the ratings, I phoned the attorney general's office. I filed formal unfair labor practice grievances against the corporation, then leaked the news to the papers.

Coffee Boy came into my office and asked me why I hadn't just asked him about the bonuses. Again, I just laughed at him.

Entercom kept trying to fuck me over, of course. My contract—my prison sentence—had been written before the advent of PPMs, and the bonuses were based on the ratings from the four traditional "books" of three months each— 48 weeks, with no numbers recorded for four weeks during the Christmas holidays.

With PPM, a 13th ratings period was added—holiday, it was called. Being Christmas, it was a black hole for talk radio, so suddenly they had a way to drag down my fall numbers. One year they refused to pay me a fall bonus. It was a clear violation of my contract terms—sort of like what they'd pulled in 2007, come to think of it.

The Boston Marathon is run every year on Patriots' Day, a state holiday in Massachusetts and Maine commemorating the battles of Concord and Lexington—"the 18th of April in '75/ hardly a man is now alive . . ." as my man Henry Wadsworth Longfellow once wrote.

In 2013, a pair of Muslim Chechen "asylees" living in Cambridge on welfare decided to blow up the Boston Marathon. The pressure-cooker bombs went off at the finish line on Boylston Street just as my show began at 3 p.m. By 4:30, the latest GM had preempted programming on all the other Entercom stations in Boston for my show. He really had no choice, not because my show was so good, but because everything else on the Entercom stations in Boston was so dreadfully amateurish and fourth-rate.

That afternoon, the new GM brought in pizzas for me and my crew, since we were the only crew left broadcasting in the entire cluster. He'd been in Boston for maybe six months, and until that moment he had not bothered to introduce himself to me. It was the first time I ever spoke to him, and also the last.

For days afterward, WRKO was on all three stations—in fact four, considering that WAAF was still simulcast on a second FM signal.

For a few days, anyway, Shillville had to shelve all their usual fascinating talk about whether the hosts wanted to have Tom Brady's baby, or his twins, or his triplets.

Next, the Celtics fled the sinking ship of S.S. *Shillville*. Their contract was up and they kept calling that new GM, but he never bothered to call them back. So they signed with the new sports station.

Entercom brought in still another new GM, to replace the pizza delivery guy. This latest guy hired one of his old buddies, another goodradioman, as his consultant. Every day it felt more and more like *Hogan's Heroes*, and I was in the custody of Col. Klink and Sgt. Schultz. They knew nothing—literally.

One day in 2013, these two goodradiomen took me out to lunch. I brought my wife with me, since we were getting down to the end of the contract. The "consultant" was still putting out a printed newsletter with his insights into the biz, because he'd once been a weekend guy at WPRO back in the day when it was the "station that reaches the beaches," or something like that.

That weekend shift at WPRO seemed to be the highlight of his career, the way he prattled on about it. He started sharing some of his insights as to what wet-behind-the-ear hosts could do to get their ratings up. He said he'd discovered that few modern-day hosts did "time checks," nor did they give out the station call letters the way they did back in the Golden Age of radio, when he was doing weekends at AM 630 in Providence.

When you give out the call letters, he informed me, the listeners are more likely to remember your station when they're filling out their diaries.

I had been listening placidly—as a short-timer, I was now trying to do good time. But nonetheless, I felt compelled to point out to him that the Boston market hadn't had any diaries since 2008—five years earlier.

Then the two goodradiomen asked me if there was anything I wanted. Other than the obvious, that is, which was a pink slip. I told them I only had one thing on my wish list. They thought I was serious. They leaned forward to hear my proposal.

What do you want? they asked.

I want, I said, one of those shitty second-rate FM sticks that WAAF had. I pointed out that WAAF was on two FM frequencies—two!—and they didn't have half the numbers I had on an AM signal that didn't reach 40 percent of the market half the year.

I told them that their beloved WAAF couldn't get any lower ratings than it already had, so what did they possibly have to lose?

WAAF has no listeners with two sticks, I said.

So WAAF can just as easily have no listeners with just one stick, I told them.

I informed them that I wasn't asking for WAAF's primary signal. I knew that was a nonstarter. Give me the shittier of the two WAAF FM signals, I said, the one that covers the black districts, because Kurt Cobain is still so popular on Blue Hill Avenue.

After that modest suggestion, I didn't get any more advice from the erstwhile weekend guy at WPRO.

The next shoe to drop was the firing of Jason "Coffee Boy" Wolfe, the ratings-challenged program director of both WRKO and Shillville. I began tweeting as soon as he was whacked.

"Those are going to be some mighty small shoes to fill."

"Heard he's going to work at another station: Sunoco."

"No, Jason, I would not like my fries supersized."

"As Gore Vidal once said, 'No talent is not enough.'"

"There isn't a wet eye in the house."

The *Herald* called and asked me for a column. I told them, just run the tweets. My contract had been written pre-Twitter, so they couldn't claim I was violating it by dumping on this month's scapegoat.

At this point, in 2013, I was fairly certain I was walking out the door. There was no noncompete in my sentence, er, contract. But I wanted to keep grabbing as much money as I could for as long as I could.

I kept tweeting throughout the day.

"Whitey Bulger's going to have a bigger going-away party than Jason Wolfe."

"Coffee Boy says 'What a ride!' Has he checked the ratings lately? It's a ride all right—like Thelma and Louise's."

"Jason's 'ride' is over. . . . NTSB investigators are being called to the scene of the wreckage."

Just before I went on the air that afternoon, I remembered the words of Whitey Bulger just before his case went to the jury, and I attributed them to Coffee Boy:

"His final words before he left the building: 'This trial is a sham. Do with me what youse will.'"

19
BACK IN THE
SADDLE AGAIN

WMEX had been the first big Top 40 station in Boston. Arnie "Woo Woo" Ginsberg was their superstar, and Jerry Williams wasn't far behind.

But that was the 1950s, and AM 1510's glory days before long were in the past. Ironically, Jerry Williams had had to sue 'MEX when he wanted to flee to WBZ for the clear-channel signal and the big money in the late 1960s.

Like most weak AM signals, WMEX had suffered through all sorts of in-carnations and ownerships. I got my radio start of sorts there as a fill-in host around 1980. The *Daily News* in New York had a "Bulldog Edition" on WOR with reporters talking about their stories in the next day's paper. I was the fill-in when *Herald* political columnist Peter Lucas couldn't do the Boston version of the Bulldog Edition.

In early 2014 the station was taken over by a guy from New Jersey who owned an ambulance service or some such thing. His ambition, his dream, was to become a mass-media mogul. He didn't know much about radio, but he knew how weak WRKO programming was—he was a listener, in other words—and he instinctively understood that they could be taken out.

I realized WMEX was under new management when I saw their ads on top of cabs and the backs of buses—something WRKO hadn't done in decades. I let my wife handle the negotiations for a new deal. We first talked with WRKO, that wasn't happening, obviously. WTKK had expired—without me, they had no marque talent, and they finally threw in the towel and shifted formats.

So I quickly cut the deal with WMEX, and all of my more than 20 affiliates agreed to go with me. Next I needed a place to broadcast from. Barry Armstrong, who had a paid two-hour weekday-morning financial show on WRKO, agreed to let us use his studio in Needham, a much shorter commute from my home in Wellesley.

When WRKO announced I was leaving, the news was treated as if I were being fired. The local press show on Channel 2 devoted a segment to my career obituary. Only one of the "experts" had even the slightest idea what was going on.

When I had worked summers in Kennebunkport, I had a '59 Chevy Impala. It was the early 1970s, so naturally I only listened to Top 40 on AM. There were no FM receivers in cars of that vintage. On the left side of my dial was WRKO, on the right side was WMEX.

I knew the 2014 WMEX signal would be a problem in the western suburbs—what else was new?—but I figured I'd be okay running up the coast, just like 40 years earlier. But now somehow the coverage was different, weaker. On the modern WMEX, I could no longer be heard on the New Hampshire seacoast.

Suddenly we had to hustle for new affiliates—in Lowell, to cover the Merrimack Valley, and in Portsmouth, New Hampshire, for the seacoast. Another problem was that coming out of the gate, our payroll was too big, not productive enough. But we got leaner and meaner fast. And since the WMEX guy was paying us enough money to cover our payroll, and we had no rent, we never went into the red.

This went on for a few months, but then the guy in New Jersey realized that his start-up was not doing nearly as well as ours. He stopped paying us. Now we would have to get nimble really fast.

Fortunately, we had an ace in the hole. As I've said, Entercom had never developed a successful program, let alone format, on its own. Its luck didn't change with my successor. His ratings were lower than that proverbial whale shit I keep mentioning.

My wife went to WRKO and asked if they wanted me back—not as an employee but as a vendor, an affiliate. I would be making less money. That was the bad news. The good news was that all the rights fees from my affiliates were going straight to me, not to the world's worst radio company.

More importantly, my wife was selling the advertising, and she was a lot more committed to the bottom line than the "sales associates" at Entercom.

They were mere hired hands, just doing time, like I had been, behind the walls at MCI-Entercom.

Entercom, though, was justifiably wary of how I might behave if I were back on their airwaves, especially after my months-long furlough at WMEX. So they offered me a sweetener—for every quarter in which I could keep my mouth shut and not insult Entercom, I would receive a bonus of $50,000.

Obviously, they never thought I'd be able to keep my end of the bargain. Just as obviously, they still didn't know me very well, or understand that I despised them so much that I wanted to relieve them of as much money as I possibly could in revenge for those seven lost years.

Maybe they thought that they could pull some sort of bait and switch like they had with the "matching" clause, or with the "holiday" book. That's the kind of connivers they were. But from then on, never was heard a discouraging word from me. Because they made it worth my while.

I think that in those three years as a syndicated host on an Entercom station, before WRKO was spun off to iHeart in December 2017, I only returned to the Big House once, when our signal failed in Needham. After that, I made sure we had a fail-safe system so I would never have to venture behind the walls again.

There was no blueprint, no how-to book, for setting up a regional radio network. Like most start-ups, it was all trial and error. Fortunately, I'd been saving my money during all those wasted years. Plus, I still had a paycheck coming in from the *Herald*.

We tried to keep our affiliates happy. If they wanted me to, I did weekly call-ins on their morning shows. I recorded spots for them. We even produced individualized magnets for every affiliate to hand out. Anything that helped them, helped me.

And my wife soon developed new ways of monetizing, to use the popular buzzword, the Howie Carr Radio Network.

We sold the daily poll question, and the Chump Line. We only had four spots per hour on the network, so we learned to "embed" live reads into the show. A few of our stations complained, but our programming was inexpensive, it was local, and, yes, it was better than any of the alternatives (admittedly, that's not saying much in modern radio).

We started charging for remote broadcasts. We set up an online store—that was a real winner. In the online store, we sold "Cheap Bastard Deals." The way

Every station got its own set of magnets to promote the show.

those worked was, we would go to a potential advertiser—say, a restaurant, or a chain of restaurants—and offer them what used to be called a trade or a barter deal. We would trade spots on the show in return for product, which we would sell, at a discount.

Thus, on the website we would sell $50 gift certificates to a restaurant for $25. If we got 200, we'd make $5,000 in cash (plus shipping and handling fees). In addition to the free segment promoting the deal, the business would then get $5,000 worth of advertising on the network, or on the live streaming, social media, and the podcasts that we eventually incorporated into the network.

Why no one had ever thought of this concept before, or at least used it on a regular basis, we had no idea. I'm glad the way it's worked out, though, because it's a great way to make money and we have it all to ourselves.

Radio's got a lot of problems these days, but I'm still doing okay, so I can't complain.

20
MAKING
AMERICA
GREAT AGAIN

The first time I ever tried to get Donald Trump on the show, he was making a speech to a big Chamber of Commerce breakfast in New Hampshire. This was in 2007, and there were rumors even then that he was running for president.

I booked him for that afternoon, but he cancelled at the last minute. At that point, I figured he was just messing around, trying to jack up the ratings for his network TV show, *The Apprentice*. So in 2015, I didn't pay much attention to all the early buzz about his candidacy.

I knew him more from the New York tabloids than from *The Apprentice*. People forget that when he bought Mar-a-Lago for $8 million in 1985 from the Town of Palm Beach, he was a controversial, polarizing figure on the island—because he was admitting Jews and blacks as members of his new club.

Diagonally across South Ocean Boulevard from Mar-a-Lago was the ultra WASPy Bath & Tennis Club, where I'd taken those ballroom dance lessons as a little boy.

As always, so near, and yet so far.

The B&T (as we called it) hated parvenu Trump. At the time, the *New York Post* gossip column, Page Six, ran an item about how the rapper then known as P. Diddy and his then girlfriend Jennifer Lopez were staying at Mar-a-Lago.

They wandered down in front of the B&T's dining-room window overlooking the beach and engaged in, well . . . you know.

Then Trump was sued over the huge American flag he put up in front of the mansion, easily visible from South Ocean Boulevard. It was of a size you seldom see except outside the showroom of a truck dealership in DFW.

Trump was basically a pariah in Palm Beach—still is, to some degree. Certainly in the pages of the *Palm Beach Daily News*—the local newspaper formerly known as "the Shiny Sheet."

On the day he announced in 2015 on TV, I watched him come down the escalator at Trump Tower and then listened to him speak. The more he talked, the more I liked the guy—just like millions of other voters. When he started talking about the need to build a wall on the southern border, and how "they" weren't "sending us their best," I was hooked.

I told my producers to try to get Trump on the show, and they did. He was great. But shortly after he announced, he went off on a rant on a Saturday afternoon in Iowa about Sen. John McCain. Trump sneered that he preferred people who hadn't been captured by the enemy.

I was crushed. I thought it was all over. Sean Hannity called him and begged him to apologize. The next morning, I was in Waltham doing my weekend shopping at Market Basket, and I saw the headline in the *Post*, above a cartoon of Trump:

"Don Voyage," it said.

But it wasn't. He didn't even apologize to McCain. Veterans called up my show and said they agreed with Trump. They too had had it up to here with virtue-signaling McCain. That week, I got a call from Ernie Boch Jr., the billionaire car dealer from Norwood. He was one of our network's first advertisers. I'd worked for his late father when he had owned our Cape Cod FM affiliate, WXTK.

Ernie has a huge estate on Route 1 in Norwood—the Automile, as it's called. As the largest property taxpayer in Norwood, he even got a zoning variance to build a mausoleum, which he now uses in this life for, among other things, the dessert tables when he brings in a band like Aerosmith for a private performance.

Ernie wanted to know if I knew somebody in the Trump campaign, because he wanted to sponsor an event for him.

A few weeks later, on a Friday afternoon, Trump flew up to Norwood on Ernie's private plane, because Trump Force One was too big to land at Norwood

Airport. Ernie's estate was swamped with people. A big tent was set up, and all the cable networks were broadcasting live. I was also broadcasting live. I felt like Murray the K, or Ed Sullivan when The Beatles first arrived in New York in 1964. When Trump got out of his limo, he was chased into the tent by his adoring fans, male and female alike.

I was stuck doing my show, but as Trump reached the stage, I could hear him yelling, "Where's Howie? Where's Howie?" For years, we had it on one of the loops we play on our audio streaming.

By the time I finished my show, I couldn't get close to Trump, so many people and camera crews had surrounded him around the stage. As he was leaving, he called my cell phone and left a message that he'd see me soon. I played it on the show Monday, to prove that I was on the team, even if I didn't have a selfie from Ernie Boch Jr.'s.

I loved having him as a regular on the show. So did the listeners. He would rip the mainstream media, saying exactly what all of us had been thinking for years.

The *Daily News* in New York was teetering yet again on the edge of bankruptcy, and they'd rashly decided that the way to fend off oblivion this time was to attack Trump. Didn't seem like a wise business decision to me. After all, the *Daily News* was Archie Bunker's newspaper, and Archie Bunker would have loved Trump, at least this latest version of him. I was certain of that.

One of the people sniffing around to buy the *Daily News* was a guy who'd been three years ahead of me at Deerfield—Jimmy Finkelstein. One afternoon, after Trump talked about how much the *Daily News* sucked, I mentioned that Finkelstein was looking to buy it.

"Tell Jimmy not to do it," Trump said. "He'll lose his shirt."

I'd started doing a little work for the new Newsmax cable news network, which was owned by Chris Ruddy, an old *New York Post* hand. He'd hired Ken Chandler, another Murdoch minion who'd run the *Herald* for a while. Chandler was managing the print/Internet arm of the operation.

On the TV side, Ruddy had developed what seemed like it might be a workable business model. He said, publicly, that if the Fox News Channel was making $1 billion a year, if he could grab just 5 percent of their audience, he should be able to make $50 million a year. Sounded like a plan to me.

Ruddy was building new headquarters in Boca Raton, and in the meantime operating Newsmax out of an old PBS station in Boynton Beach. I wasn't doing much with them, but when I was down in Palm Beach, sometimes I would get together with Ruddy.

One day, at the end of 2015, I was in Palm Beach and Ruddy asked me and my wife if we wanted to join him at Mar-a-Lago. That sounded great. Even though I'd had Trump on the air several times now, I'd never met with him face to face, since I'd missed him in the throng at Ernie Boch Jr.'s that Friday night in Norwood.

It was a few days after Christmas, and we'd had lunch and we were sitting outside Mar-a-Lago, facing Lake Worth and basking in the South Florida sunshine. Suddenly Trump and his wife Melania were coming toward us. Ruddy introduced us and we chatted. Finally Trump said to me, "You like it here, Howie?"

"Oh hell yes," I said, or words to that effect. Trump nodded and turned one of the club guys who was trailing behind him.

"Put Howie down on the list," he told the guy. Then he turned to me and Kathy.

"You guys are members now," he said. Just like that.

Then he said he had to get going because he was flying up to Nashua, New Hampshire, for a rally.

2015: Hanging out at Mar-a-Lago.

"Anybody want to fly up there with me?" he said.

It was maybe 75 degrees. We were all wearing polo shirts. In Nashua, it wouldn't have been much more than 15 degrees. We said we had . . . dinner plans, or something, so we begged off. But now we were members of Mar-a-Lago.

We still had to pay for all the services of course, but the big thing was the membership. Once he became president, it was an even greater perk. I'd always known how businessmen used their memberships in certain prestigious clubs as a way to impress their clients. But until I became a member at Mar-a-Lago, I'd never seen the actual value of being able to take somebody somewhere special, a place that he or she will remember for a long time, where they might actually get to meet the president of the United States. Talk about winning friends and influencing people.

I used to fret that someday I'd be asked how I'd become a member. If I told the truth, perhaps it could be made to look like I was being paid off. And if I lied and said I'd had to pay—I think the initiation fee was then about $200,000— then I'd look like a Beautiful Person.

It wasn't something I obsessed over, but I wondered how I'd handle it if I was ever asked. Fortunately, the *Globe* solved my problem one day when they ran some snarky list of members, and my name was on it. At the end of the item or whatever it was, the *Globe* ran a sentence saying that membership costs $200,000.

The *Globe* was trying to give me a shot, but they'd done just the opposite. Now, if anybody ever asked me how much it had cost me to get into Mar-a-Lago, I could just refer them to that piece in the *Globe*. And if they wanted to know more, I could just tell them that it's all right there in the *Globe*, and we all know the *Globe* never makes shit up, right?

What the left has never understood about Trump supporters is that it's not so much their blind loyalty for Trump himself, but for what he represents—his willingness to fight for Americans who work for a living.

And almost as importantly, his determination not to take any crap from anybody.

During the primary campaign, "traditional" Republicans often couldn't believe how some of Trump's base—especially evangelical Christians—could so enthusiastically support a guy who'd been married three times, who'd hung out at Studio 54, who wasn't born again, who didn't even pretend to be.

Tucker Carlson, I thought, got it exactly right in a magazine piece he wrote during the 2016 campaign, a year or so before he took Bill O'Reilly's prime-time slot on Fox.

Tucker said that evangelicals weren't looking for a spiritual leader, they were looking for a bodyguard. Precisely! They were tired of being pushed around and being sneered at by people who had absolutely no reason to be looking down on anybody who worked with their hands, or who went to church on Sunday, or because they hadn't gone to an Ivy League school, or because they lived in Flyover Country or . . . whatever.

One of the Democrats who ran against George W. Bush in Texas said he was born on third base and thought he hit a triple. There was an element of truth to that, but by the time Trump came along, practically all the well-born, trust-funded snobs in politics were Democrats. The Democrats were now the ones who'd been born on third base and thought they'd hit a triple.

They'd been for busing in Boston—because they lived in the suburbs. They didn't mind affirmative action being used against working-class whites and Asians because their kids were legacies. They wanted higher taxes—on income, but not so much on capital gains, or inheritance, because they were living on trust funds while "working" for nonprofits.

The more I saw of these people—and they are thick on the ground across New England—the more I detested them and their suffocating sanctimony, haughtiness, and hypocrisy. But even though I had a radio talk show, and got four hours of feedback from the listeners every weekday, I always asked myself, is this just me, or are other people getting the same vibe—that we're being asked to make all these sacrifices—for illegal aliens, for the "climate," for transgenders or whatever this week's latest woke insanity is—while our sanctimonious betters are just getting richer and richer and richer and pricing the rest of us out of all the nice stuff, whether it's beachfront property or a good college education?

Obviously, there are millions who feel the same way as I do. Obama called us "bitter clingers."

A once-famous quote is applicable here. I seldom cite it, given its provenance, but in 1861, Jefferson Davis, the former Democratic senator from Mississippi who became the president of the Confederate States of America, said:

"All we ask is to be let alone."

And that is all that Trump supporters—of whatever race, color, or creed—asked. Get off our lawn! He was just telling all these Democratic grandees who'd been born on third base and thought they'd hit a triple that they weren't any better or smarter than us, and that if in fact they thought they were, well, maybe the next time they had a flat tire, they should change it themselves. Or try to.

Early in the campaign, he went to some Christian college and, reading from a prepared text, quoted from, not Second Corinthians, but "Two Corinthians."

For state-run media (and some of Trump's opponents in the GOP presidential primaries) it was another gotcha moment—Trump claims to be a Christian but he doesn't know the Bible, or go to church and so on.

But hardly anyone cared. What everybody understood was that Trump was willing to let them alone. And that's all they wanted. To be let alone.

What was happening was unlike anything that had ever happened before in American politics. His campaign manager was Corey Lewandowski, originally from Lowell. Corey scheduled an event for January 2016 in Lowell, at the Tsongas Arena. Do you know how cold it can get in Lowell in January—as cold as Nashua in December. Still, there were lines winding around and around the building.

We did a remote broadcast that winter from another New Hampshire event, in a huge heated tent. Again, it was wicked cold. But outside, in the parking lot, before they opened the doors, everyone had their grills fired up and were drinking beer in the subfreezing temperatures. They were tailgating, like it was an Indian summer Saturday afternoon in October during football season.

Earlier, in November 2015, Trump had done an event at the DCU Center in Worcester—another full house with 10,500 in attendance in addition to cable TV coverage. As he was denouncing welfare fraud—specifically, food stamps—an obese, unkempt hippie jumped up and began screaming at Trump.

Trump stopped speaking midsentence and watched, along with everyone else, as the cops dragged the shabbily-dressed fat man away. Then Trump shook his head and leaned in close to the microphone and spoke softly:

"You know it's amazing. I mention food stamps and that guy who's seriously overweight went crazy. He went crazy! That's an amazing sight."

The crowd exploded into raucous laughter and applause. All 10,500 people had been thinking the same thing. But Trump was the only politician who would dare voice his—and their—thoughts aloud.

My daughter Charlotte was a junior at Southern Methodist University in Dallas. At Mar-a-Lago one night in the winter of 2016, she asked the candidate if she could be a summer intern with the Trump Organization in Manhattan. He said sure.

I was spending more and more of the winter in Palm Beach. We started getting a few invitations to GOP-type fundraisers. One was for the *National Review*. It was to be held at Mar-a-Lago—Trump was doing the magazine a favor.

So my wife and I drove down there. We had ulterior motives of course—doesn't everyone? My first *Kennedy Babylon* book was coming out, and I was hoping for a good notice in *National Review*—it seems now like this all must have happened a century ago, caring about a book review anywhere, but especially one in a magazine.

So we went down to Mar-a-Lago and it was a very nice spread. Top-shelf booze, a fine spread of hors d'oeuvres, just what you would expect. Rich Lowry, the editor, spoke. Mark Foley, the gay ex-Congressman from Lake Worth (and originally from Massachusetts of course), was there. It was a well-heeled crowd. We wrote a small check and I introduced myself to Lowry. By the way, *Kennedy Babylon* never got a review from the magazine—silly me.

The reason I mention this is because about a month or so later, *National Review* devoted an entire issue to denouncing its host that evening. The hysterical attacks took up the entire news section, or certainly seemed to. Even Glenn Beck checked in with an unhinged screed—which he followed up by dipping his face into a bowl of crushed Cheetos—orange, get it? Orange Man Bad.

It was another example of that adage: No good deed goes unpunished. Then there was Joe Scarborough, the former GOP congressman from Pensacola with the dyed hair and the high Deliverance-esque inbred white-trash cracker forehead.

I remember seeing him one night at the bar in Mar-a-Lago, standing by himself, scanning the crowd. Three words came to mind: On the arm. Maybe I'm wrong, but "Mourning" Joe didn't look like he was running a tab.

Imagine my surprise (not!) when he and his third wife Mika turned on his former patron. This time, Trump at first said he would have a lot to say about the MSNBC lovebirds at some point in the future. And he did. He released an old, slobbering voicemail message from Mourning Joe.

Pre-Congress, Scarborough was a jackleg lawyer up in the Panhandle, so I guess he loves those millions he annually makes carrying the water for the Roberts family's low-rated morning show. One of his sidekicks, besides his "flotation-device third wife," as talk show host Chris Plante calls Mika, is Mike Barnicle.

Need I say any more about Scarborough's commitment to journalistic ethics, among other sorts of ethics?

In June 2016, Trump held a late-morning fundraiser at a downtown hotel in Boston. Afterward he would fly to Bangor, Maine, on his private jet for an afternoon rally. Trump's campaign was supposedly disorganized, but they knew how to count electoral votes—Maine is the only state other than Nebraska that apportions its electoral votes to whichever candidate wins the most popular votes in each congressional district.

Trump knew he was competitive in Maine's 2nd Congressional District—Down East. And he ended up winning it.

The campaign asked me to introduce him, because of my connections to the state, not the least of which were my radio affiliates across Maine.

My wife and I first went to the Boston fundraiser. Afterward we were hustled into SUVs and driven in a convoy to Logan Airport. We had to run a gauntlet of people lining the sidewalks, some cheering, others screaming and giving us the finger.

It was a new experience for me. I'd never been in a convoy before.

There were only a few people on the plane—Trump, one of his flaks, and maybe a couple of others. The aide delivered Trump a sheaf full of printouts and he glanced at them briefly before setting them aside and turning on the television.

He flipped back and forth among the cable channels. He seemed to know the names of even the most obscure reporters. His aides handed him bags full of McDonald's, and he walked down the aisle, offering the fast food to everyone on the plane.

We arrived in Bangor and another convoy rushed us to the Cross Insurance Center, where a packed house of almost 6,000 Trump supporters was waiting for the candidate. While Trump was meeting with local dignitaries—including a lot of cops in uniform—I warmed up the crowd, most of whom were listeners of my show. Some of the cable networks were there, broadcasting live.

The Maine crowd knew my bits well, among them, the "fake Indian" meme about Sen. Elizabeth Warren, who had decided in middle age to falsely declare herself an American Indian, to jumpstart her piss-poor career as a law school instructor. I'd been calling her out since day one. I don't know what it was about her that aroused my suspicions—maybe her blonde hair and blue eyes.

More importantly, she didn't have a card from the Bureau of Indian Affairs—the *sine qua non* if you wish to claim Native American heritage. Her only credentials were the fact that she alleged that a grandparent had told her she had "high cheekbones like the Indians do," and the fact that she'd contributed to a supposed Indian cookbook called *Pow Wow Chow*.

Her recipes, however, had been lifted from melanin-impaired sources, as I had proven in about 30 seconds of Google research during her 2012 campaign for the U.S. Senate. Her favorite: cold crab omelet, apparently a tasty treat on the Trail of Tears. It turned out to have been taken, verbatim, from a recipe in the *New York Times* by Pierre Franey, "the 60-Minute Gourmet."

At his restaurant, Le Pavilion, cold crab omelet was a favorite of such noted sachems as Noel Coward and the Duke and Duchess of Windsor.

During the 2012 campaign, as she was campaigning in Kelley Square in Worcester, one of my guys got her to autograph a copy of *Pow Wow Chow*. She took off the cap of the pen with her teeth, and we sent off the cap to a DNA testing service, hoping to find out her exact genealogical background. Alas, there wasn't enough saliva on the pen, but that was $200 I didn't mind parting with, to try to bust her once and for all. (That wouldn't happen until 2020, when she conducted her own private DNA test, after which the *Globe* lied about the results to assist her faltering campaign.)

Once the fake Indian had started checking the box, her career blossomed, and she was soon handed a tenured professorship first at the UPenn law school, and then at Harvard Law.

On this weekday afternoon, in the summer of 2016, I was there in Bangor, in front of what was for me a huge crowd. I knew how these arena appearances worked—you played them your greatest hits, like an over-the-hill rock band.

I was just the warm-up act, and the natives were getting restless, so I decided to give them something familiar, one of my Greatest Hits. I asked the crowd if they were familiar with Sen. Elizabeth Warren, the fake Indian from Massachusetts.

Then I let out a fake war whoop, straight out of an old Republic Pictures B-movie western.

That got their attention, by God. They started cheering and hooting. It wasn't long before I got the signal, and I introduced Gov. Paul LePage or Trump, I can't remember who. What I do recall is that as I was leaving the stage, one of Trump's advance men handed me his cell phone with a headline about me on one of the state-run websites.

"They're already coming after you!" he said.

Apparently, it was racist what I had done, making sport of a racial fraud perpetrated by a woman who was whiter than me. The blue checkmarks on Twitter were in an uproar. They were shocked, shocked! Did they not know she was a flat-out grifter who'd been busted, repeatedly, for scamming the affirmative-action racket? Or were they just manufacturing fake outrage for their low-info viewers and followers?

Whatever, it didn't concern me very much. I listened to Trump's speech, and then we jumped back into the convoy to head back to the Bangor airport. We were flying to LaGuardia, where my wife and I would be met by a car we'd hired to drive us back to Boston.

Once we were in the air, I told Trump what had happened. As I expected, he didn't give a shit. He'd been calling Warren "Pocahontas" himself.

"Whatever you do, don't apologize," he said. "Jimmy the Greek was doing fine until he apologized, and then he was gone. Remember that?"

I sure did. I also recalled the old saying, which in Boston was always attributed to James Michael Curley:

"Never complain, never explain."

Or as P. J. Wodehouse put it somewhat more formally:

"It is a good rule in life never to apologize. The right sort of people do not want the apologies and the wrong sort take a mean advantage of them."

What did I have to apologize about anyway? She's the one who lied and stole a job from a real Native American, not me. My war whoop was all over the media for a few hours—the *Daily Mail*, Rachel Maddow, all the usual suspects—and then it was over.

My wife loved Trump, and she'd run to become one of his Massachusetts delegates to the Republican convention in Cleveland. She won—the only competition in our congressional district came from the Ted Cruz campaign.

Trump of course had suggested that the Texas senator's father might have been one of the JFK shooters in Dallas in 1963. He also brought up some of the problems Cruz's wife had had over the years. It's less remembered now, but Cruz was tough on Trump as well—on my show he mentioned Trump's "New York values," for instance, which was in its own way a dog whistle.

We had a good time in Cleveland, hanging out on radio row, seeing the likes of George Will wandering around, unrecognized, forgotten but not gone.

From radio row to Desolation Row—that was George Will's career trajectory.

You always meet such unlikely people at national conventions. In 2004, in Boston, I had Jesse Jackson on my show as a guest, not to mention Mitch McConnell. Both of those interviews were my one-and-onlys with them.

In Cleveland, my interviews included Diamond and Silk—the Trump people sent them over—and the gay Brit Milo Yiannopoulos, before he went totally crazy. Diamond and Silk were a lot better as guests.

As the fall campaign began, I wasn't optimistic. The media were so in the satchel. Remember when Hillary collapsed on 9/11? CNN was accusing Fox of making up the story right up until the moment Fox ran the cell phone video of her tumble on air, after which CNN immediately shifted into high dudgeon about how-dare-anyone-raise-health-issues-about-any-candidates?

The Democrats and the media (but I repeat myself) had no shame. But I wanted to do as much as I could for Trump because I was worried about my own career prospects as an independent broadcaster. We had just moved into our own studios, in Needham, on the other side of 128 from our old offices. I had signed a five-year lease, and I was concerned about the future of talk radio.

The Democrats were veering further and further hard left. Hillary was not a big believer in the Bill of Rights. She was campaigning promising to appoint new Supreme Court justices who would repeal *Citizens United*, i.e., freedom of speech protections under the First Amendment.

I figured if she'd say that publicly while she was running, what would she do once she controlled every lever of federal power? She didn't like the Second Amendment either—she was also vowing to do something about *Heller* v. *D.C.*

One Friday night in Manhattan, she described Trump supporters as "deplorables." I was surprised, but not shocked. After all, she knew she was going to win, so what did she care about what she said about us?

The next day, I was emceeing the official opening of the Massachusetts Trump campaign state headquarters, in Hudson. It was a sunny Saturday afternoon. As soon as I got there I noticed first the size of the crowd, hundreds of people, of every age and race, and second, how many of them were wearing pieces or strips of paper pinned to their chests with safety pins or paper clips.

On each piece of paper was scrawled, "Deplorable."

Wow. My wife and I looked at each other. We are always trying to find something new to sell in our online store. After the ribbon-cutting, I posed for photos with any Trump supporters who wanted one. A lot of them were older, and they were as inept with their cell phone cameras as I am with mine. It was going very slowly until a 10-year-old girl with her mother stepped up and said, "Mr. Carr, do you want me to take the pictures?"

She knew how to use every one of those cameras, even the flip phones. Suddenly the line was moving along quickly. Once my wife and I got back in our car, we immediately decided that we needed to start marketing our own T-shirts.

"Proud to Be a Deplorable."

I think we were among the very first in the country to offer them on our website. Within days we were shipping out scores of them every day. We couldn't get them in-house fast enough from our supplier in Maine to keep up with the orders.

In late October, I got a call from the Trump campaign. The last debate was coming up in St. Louis that Sunday night. It was a "town hall" format, meaning questions from the audience. Corey Lewandowski was on the CNN payroll at the time, but he was still involved in the Trump campaign, off the record and off the payroll.

He told me Trump wanted to do a practice town hall, with a raucous crowd (a specialty of mine), and would I be the moderator? Absolutely! It was held on a Thursday night at the town hall in Sandown, New Hampshire. I did the radio show at my affiliate in Manchester and then drove over to the Sandown Town Hall.

The place was already packed, and the crowd had submitted questions. Corey and I went through them to pick appropriate ones—it was going to be covered live, of course, by all the cable networks.

Trump arrived with Chris Christie, the ex-governor of New Jersey. He hadn't had much of a presidential run, but he had taken out Sen. Marco Rubio in one of the free-for-all debates in New Hampshire before the primary. So he was there to critique the candidate's performance.

It was fun being there, running the show. Trump was in fine form, and afterward, I drove back home, where I appeared on CNN with Don Lemon at the Videolink studio in West Newton. There were floods or weather problems somewhere, so I was kept around longer than usual, as filler between the rain live shots. I didn't mind. It was the first time I'd been on CNN in ages, maybe since Larry King got kicked down the stairs. And I haven't been back since.

The reason I remember that evening so well is because of what happened the next day, Friday. The *Access Hollywood* audiotape was released by the *Washington*

Post, which had been spoon-fed the sound by NBC. Couple of Harvard guys apparently, conspiring, doing their rich-kid sneaky stuff. The tape was about 12 years old, and Trump was just goofing around with one of the Bush family's distant relatives, Billy Bush.

Trump, who was then the network's number-one prime-time star on *The Apprentice*, mentioned how stars could get away with . . . but you remember.

It was another one of those "No good deed goes unpunished" moments. After all the millions he'd made for the Roberts family, their little stooge Noah Oppenheim took time out from sucking up to serial rapist Harvey Weinstein and trying to sell some crappy screenplays to leak the ancient tape to his fellow trust-funded legacy Beautiful People at the *Washington Post*.

The story broke during my show, and of course it was going to be the end of the Trump campaign, just like everything else. Some spineless Republicans began calling on him to drop out of the race. Sen. Kelly Ayotte of New Hampshire told a press conference early the next morning that she was cutting all ties with his campaign, and she was doing it for her teenage daughter.

Ten days later, she would be defeated for reelection by 1,017 votes, but on the plus side, she'd be put on the board of News Corp., where she would be joined a couple of years later by House Speaker Paul Ryan, the RINO who had urged his GOP incumbents to cut Trump loose about the same time Ayotte was holding her press conference.

But Trump wasn't done. The town hall debate was in St. Louis that Sunday night. Trump had a press conference scheduled that afternoon, before the debate. He was the only politician ever who would schedule a combative press conference before the biggest debate of his life, while reeling from a state-run-media-concocted "scandal." But he did.

And when Trump walked out in front of the cameras, he was accompanied by four women—three of whom had accused Hillary's husband of either raping or sexually assaulting them. The fourth had been the victim of a violent sexual assault by a thug whom Hillary as a young lawyer in Arkansas had gotten off.

It was an amazing press conference. I had once interviewed the rape victim, Juanita Broaddrick. Bill Clinton had allegedly assaulted her when he was attorney general of Arkansas. To keep Juanita under control while he was raping her, he'd bitten her lower lip and drawn blood. Afterward he had brusquely told her, "You'd better put some ice on that."

Paper Boy

Juanita had written a book, and I'd had her in studio. She was an old-fashioned kind of Southern lady, quite intelligent, but I wondered how she'd do under this kind of pressure. She was perfect, all four of them were. They spoke in usable sound bites of under two minutes. They were concise. Nobody rambled or stumbled or teared up.

The Democratic operatives with press passes were shocked. Once again, they'd thought that they'd finally driven a stake through the heart of Orange Man Bad. And yet again he was rising, Freddy Krueger–like, from his political grave.

That night, the four women sat in the front row at the debate, staring at Hillary. There's a memorable photo of Bill Clinton, sitting next to Chelsea Clinton, his jaw dropping as his victims walked into the hall.

As the debate began, Trump took advantage of the ambulatory format. He lurked behind Hillary as she spouted out her usual woke nonsense. At one point, she said it was good that "someone with the temperament of Donald Trump is not in charge of the law in this country."

He replied, "Because you'd be in jail."

That was Sunday night. Despite his stellar performance, it was still a depressing time. The election seemed over, but we had commitments. The show must go on, to coin a phrase.

The next Friday, I was doing a remote broadcast from the Kowloon, the big Chinese restaurant on Route 1 in Saugus. It was owned by the Wong family, good Republicans. Every Tuesday for years, they'd delivered us a huge free spread. Before I broke out of Entercom, the jock sniffers loved our chicken wings and crab Rangoon. They were like seagulls, hovering above an old-style, open-air dump near the seashore.

Ann Coulter was my guest at the Kowloon, and we were selling or giving away her newest book, I can't remember which, because about 10 minutes before the show, FBI director James Comey announced that he was reopening the case into Hillary Clinton's laptop and the "missing" 30,000 emails that she had destroyed after they were subpoenaed by Congress.

You know the story—by the time the show ended, Hillary was squealing like a stuck pig. As I drove back to Wellesley, I was thinking maybe, just maybe . . .

But I didn't want to get too excited. I never do. Four years earlier, when Mitt Romney was supposedly running neck and neck with Obama, I'd nixed doing a remote from Willard's campaign-night party in the Seaport, because . . . I just knew.

On Monday, I was back in Manchester for my radio show, after which my wife and I went to Trump's election-eve rally at the SNHU Arena downtown. Trump and Pence were flying around the country for final events in various swing states. Most of the statewide New Hampshire candidates were there, or at least represented—except for Sen. Kelly Ayotte. The crowd chanted, "Where's Kelly?"

Preparing her concession speech, apparently.

By the time we got there, after the show, the place was packed, and the only seats we could find were way up in the back. Right in front of us was a family with two young sons. The mother appeared to be Hispanic.

The kids were playing, and enjoying themselves, and in my glum mood I was thinking to myself, these boys aren't going to have nearly the opportunities that my generation had. It was supposed to be an upbeat night, but I couldn't shake my gloom, my dread of what was about to happen.

Trump arrived and he was on fire, as always. About midway through, he pulled a letter out of his coat pocket and read what amounted to an endorsement from Bill Belichick, the coach of the Super Bowl–bound New England Patriots.

At the end, Trump announced that he and Pence were flying out to Grand Rapids for a final, post-midnight rally. I was impressed by their never-say-die attitude, but I also understood that you never want to leave anything on the table. It's devastating enough to lose, at anything, but you never want to be wondering, what if I had worked just a little bit harder?

On Tuesday, I dutifully voted, but my bleak premonitions continued. One of my producers I knew to be a closet Hillary supporter, not because he loved her—how could anyone?—but because on Wednesday, he wanted to be able to tell everyone in the office that he'd told us so. We knew this because one day he'd left his computer open and one of the other guys had seen his emails to one of his friends.

My wife had told the local Trump campaign that I would emcee the "victory party" that night at the (now defunct) F1 Boston "race track" in Braintree. It was about 6:30 and I was already wondering how long I'd have to stick around that wake when my producer informed me that "the big guy" was on the phone.

The big guy? This was four years before Hunter Biden's laptop. Surely this big guy couldn't be . . . but it was. Trump surely was taking it to the bitter end.

Massachusetts wasn't in play, but New Hampshire and the 2nd District of Maine were. He only had a few minutes left before the Granite State polls closed at 7. I think I may have been the last interview before whatever happened, happened.

Driving down after the show to Braintree, I was listening to Fox News Channel on satellite radio. They were touting exit polls from Florida that Clinton was going to win easily. The state was changing blah-blah-blah. It was probably Chris Wallace, but it could have been almost any of them except for Sean Hannity. Even then, most of Fox News was trending RINO.

I got down to Braintree and sure enough, the crowd was outnumbered by the waiters. I knocked out an early-edition *Herald* column with no interruptions from the crowd because there wasn't any . . . crowd, that is.

I finished my first-edition column and chatted with the staff. There were no more than two or three Trump supporters there. I paid little attention to the results, but slowly it started to get interesting.

A few stalwarts were arriving, and I addressed the "crowd" and said the usual things that you're supposed to say at such a moment—namely, that it might be a long night and don't believe exit polls and so forth. I didn't believe any of it, but I said it anyway. By 8:30, there were finally more partygoers than waiters and bartenders.

By 9 it was clear Trump was doing a lot better than had been predicted. Forecasts of a Democratic takeover of the House seemed greatly exaggerated. Republican Mayor Bob Hedlund of neighboring Weymouth showed up. I'd known him since his first campaign for the state Senate in 1990, when he owned a garage in Quincy.

We talked and then I knocked out a second-edition column. The states began falling, and they were mostly going Trump's way. We decided to set up a live Facebook feed. Hedlund was glad to be my cohost. A *Globe* photographer came by and snapped a photo of us. A few minutes later the photo showed up on their website. My face was blurred out—the *Globe* must be at least a little bit concerned, I figured.

By 11 o'clock, people were streaming into the ballroom. It actually began to look like a victory party. At Shillville, I'd seen more than my share of bandwagons, cheerleaders, front-runners, bum kissers, and groupies. But this was perhaps the most egregious case of open and gross rump swabbery that I had ever witnessed.

The Republican state committee was controlled at that time by Gov. Charlie Baker. At least half of them had hack jobs on his payroll. And he had just haughtily announced that morning at his precinct in Swampscott that he had not voted for either Trump or Hillary.

By 11:30, all of Baker's payroll Charlies were swarming into the F1. Hedlund was more familiar with them than I was—he'd served in the legislature for more than 20 years—and he pointed the hacks out as they came giddily skipping into what was by now a full-blown celebration.

As we were doing our little Facebook show, the mayor would identify the committee members, and I'd shout out their names. I don't know how many people were watching us, but it was fun. By 12:30, we had a quorum of the Republican state committee.

We set up another computer and checked out the odds on the *New York Times* calculator. Trump's needle kept moving higher and higher. Wolf Blitzer on CNN wondered if "we" could still pull the election out if North Carolina went "our" way. Some other Democrat reminded him that North Carolina had been called for Trump a half hour earlier.

On ABC, my old local-TV running mate, Martha Bradlee, now known as Martha Raddatz, was openly weeping on the set (although she later denied it). Barack Obama had been at her post–Ben Bradlee wedding, to a Harvard Law School pampered puke from whom she was now divorced as well.

Hedlund joked about his desire to become ambassador to Finland, and I pointed out to him that he'd been with Sen. Rand Paul in the primaries. But I said I'd put in a good word for him with the president-elect. It was all in good fun. I'm sure we weren't the only ones joking that night about our prospects in this New World Order, as the *Times'* needle indicating Trump's chances of victory climbed up over 99 percent.

If it hadn't been for the Town of Braintree's closing hours, F1 Boston could have stayed open all night, and made a mint. But they had to finally close the bar, and I drove home. Sitting in my living room in Wellesley, I watched the candidate declare victory at Trump Tower. I was amazed to see Chris Christie up on stage with him—I'd read that Christie had run away from him after the *Access Hollywood* tempest in a teapot over the weekend, when only Rudy Giuliani had still been willing to endure the slings and arrows of outrageous fortune for Trump on cable television.

I knew I had to get a few hours' sleep, but I was up again by 6. Talk about must-see TV. But my wife told me she had something to tell me. Despite the euphoria we both felt, she seemed very serious, so I looked up from my laptop.

She told me she just wanted me to know that she'd given the Trump campaign some money.

I shrugged. What did it matter now? We were all set for a while. The First Amendment wouldn't be on the table again for at least four years. But she was still staring at me, so I just asked, okay, so how much did you give?

"Twenty-five thousand bucks," she said. She had the money, I knew that. At the time, we owned a five-unit apartment building in Framingham—North Framingham, as the area was always described in the real-estate listings, meaning near the Wayland line, far away from the illegal aliens on the other side of Route 9. I'd cashed out my *Herald* 401(k) as soon as I'd reached the magic age—59½—and we'd paid off the mortgage.

Being a landlord was a pain in the ass, especially after Obamacare, because our younger tenants would get dropped down to part-time by their employers, who could no longer afford to pay their health insurance. And then our tenants had to move back in with their parents. Oddly, the so-called mainstream media showed no interest in discussing this rather widespread national phenomenon.

Despite the headaches with our tenants, my wife still had more than $50,000 in her landlord account, and she hadn't wanted me to know.

"Are you mad?" she asked me.

"No," I said. "He won!"

"But if he hadn't?"

I shrugged. One thing I've learned from covering politics all these years. Never answer a hypothetical.

I was concerned when Hillary et al. started demanding "recounts." Long before 2020, I knew what kind of "recounts" they were talking about. I remembered what the Democrats had tried in Florida in 2000. I knew they were capable of anything.

When the recounts faded out—the ballot boxes in Democratic precincts in Wayne County, Michigan, were found to contain significantly fewer actual ballots than the official vote totals indicated had been cast, a sort of dress rehearsal for 2020—they tried to get "faithless" GOP electors to change their votes. That was a nonstarter as well.

On New Year's Eve in Palm Beach, we usually went to The Breakers for their big party. But in 2016, there was only one place to be—Mar-a-Lago. It was black tie, of course, and it's one New Year's Eve I'll never forget. The bars and appetizer stations were laid out around the adult pool, on the lake side of the mansion.

After everything horrible he'd been saying about Trump on MSDNC, Mourning Joe Scarborough and his flotation-device third wife showed up. Scarborough didn't even bother to put on a tuxedo. It was like he was trying to . . . stand out, maybe. I'm sure he hadn't paid to get in—that's just not Mourning Joe's M.O.

Later, some liberal reporter tweeted out that he was there, and he claimed he'd only stopped by as a "journalist," to ask the president-elect for an interview. What a tool!

As midnight neared, after dining with some rich Arabs, Trump sauntered onto the stage to address the crowd of about 1,000 people.

"Tonight I just want to thank all the members," he said, more in his traditional role of maître d' than soon-to-be Leader of the Free World. "The rest of you—I don't give a shit about you!"

It was hilarious! At our table, I glanced over at one of my tuxedoed neighbors at the Biltmore, another club member. His jaw dropped as he heard the president-elect utter what a Nixon-era judge once called a barnyard epithet. Half the audience had been recording his remarks with their cell phones, and I'm sure many immediately posted his barnyard epithet on social media. I know I did.

Which made it even more humorous 12 hours later, on New Year's Day, when CNN posted their "scoop"—that Trump had been swearing in front of his well-heeled crowd at Mar-a-Lago.

CNN—what a bunch of assholes.

Just a few days later, CNN hysterically ran with the bogus Steele dossier, bought and paid for by Hillary Clinton, through a string of cutouts. As so often seems to happen, the story broke in the middle of my show. CNN had convened the usual Democratic operatives—among others, Jake Tapper, formerly employed by Chelsea Clinton's mother-in-law, who was married to another congressional grifter who'd gone to prison for bank fraud (Bureau of Prisons #55040-066). Also pretending to be shocked was Carl Bernstein, famous long ago, who'd just written a slobbering hagiography of Hillary Clinton.

Among the more preposterous charges in Hillary's dossier was that an obscure Trump volunteer named Carter Page had been offered an $11 billion bribe to introduce some Russians to the candidate. Even more absurd was the accusation that in Moscow, Trump had rented the hotel suite that the Obamas had once stayed in, and then hired prostitutes to piss on the bed they'd slept in.

It made absolutely no sense for anyone to have done such a thing, but especially Trump, who had a phobia about physical contact with others. Still, the Clinton operatives on CNN couldn't get enough of it—recounts and faithless electors hadn't worked, so now it would be Russia, Russia, Russia.

My wife and I traveled to Washington for the inauguration. I hadn't seen street riots like that since busing days in Boston. There were even burning limousines in the street. We went to the big inaugural ball and ran into Juanita Broaddrick and Paula Jones, whose lawsuit against Bill Clinton had led to his impeachment and disbarment after he lied under oath about Monica Lewinsky. (Paula also got an $850,000 settlement from him.)

I'd never expected to be friendly with a president of the United States. It just hadn't seemed to be in the cards. But now there was a guy in the Oval Office who was not only from Palm Beach, but who was also in the same industry—resort hotels—that I had started out in, following in the footsteps of my father and uncle.

And the new vice president, Mike Pence, had been, among other things in his adult life, a regional radio talk-show host.

I could never have imagined having people with backgrounds even remotely similar to mine being in control of the federal government, although of course as it turned out they weren't really in control.

They were hamstrung from the very beginning by Hillary's Russian collusion hoax. And to this day, only a handful of corrupt cops, Democratic fluffers, and other assorted coat holders have been punished or even reprimanded in the slightest for what they did. And so-called journalists played an outsized role in this, the largest political scandal in American history.

I continued doing my radio show, of course. But for the first time ever, I was being called by powerful people who were seeking big federal jobs for themselves or, more often, for some friends of theirs. Others were just seeking to prevent their own foes from getting said jobs. I didn't have any real clout, but the people seeking me out didn't seem to understand how low I was on the Trump totem pole.

The local federal patronage job I cared most about was U.S. attorney in Boston. Rod Rosenstein was the swamp creature who had become de facto attorney general after Jeff Sessions was railroaded into recusing himself from the Russia investigation, or should I say inquisition? Word was that Rosenstein was going to hand off the big job in Boston to one of his Harvard Law classmates, a big liberal Democrat from Newton.

I got this Beautiful Person's campaign contributions—to both Obama and Hillary Clinton—wrote a *Herald* column, and made sure Sessions saw it. Rosenstein's pal didn't become U.S. attorney. I was used to writing columns pointing the finger at this reprobate or that scandal, but usually the bad guys got away with it. It was, after all, Massachusetts. I wasn't accustomed to winning much of anything except the accolades of my fellow losers in local politics.

For years, I'd been irritated by the fact that the Justice Department wouldn't identify criminals as illegal aliens. The arrest of any kind of Third World thug would invariably be headlined as something like "Lawrence Man Arrested," when in fact he would be an illegal alien from the Dominican Republic or some other Third World shithole, as Trump would say.

You often had to delve deep into the press release to discern the truth—that the immigration agencies were listed as cooperating in the investigation, or the welfare-fraud cops. Sometimes, I'd have to request the actual detention affidavits, in which the cops would point out that so-and-so was not lawfully present, as they say, in the United States.

Sessions had been politically neutered by the Deep State so that they could pursue their Russian collusion hoax with no pushback. Still, he was permitted to do occasional interviews with friendlies—and I'd gotten to know him slightly during the Trump campaign. When he came on my show, I implored him to implement a Truth-in-Press-Releases policy at the DOJ. Without fanfare, he did so.

A small win, but I was grateful.

I spent Christmas 2017 in Palm Beach, as always. Mar-a-Lago was different now that Trump was president. Billionaires teemed in the dining area every night, hoping to get a moment to bend POTUS' ear. I wrote about one such night in *What Really Happened,* my book about the 2016 campaign.

That Christmas, I got a call from a reporter at the *Washington Post.* She introduced herself as the former assistant of Maureen Dowd, who as I've told you I met during the Whitey Bulger trial. She wanted to know if I was planning to go to Mar-a-Lago anytime soon. I thought she might be angling for an invitation, which was not in the cards. But all she wanted was for me to ask the president how he'd rank his first year as president in historical terms.

I considered her request for a few moments, then told her I'd be willing to ask him that, but only if I could tell the president that I was working that evening as a legman for the *Washington Post.* She said that would be fine.

So that night, I walked in and saw him. I went up and identified myself as a one-night legman for the *Post* and asked him to assess his initial year as POTUS. He answered instantly.

"I have had the best first year of any president—ever!" he said.

'The best ever?" I asked.

Like everybody, I know how much Trump likes to paint in broad strokes, shall we say. But I thought maybe he might want to put it in slightly more nuanced terms, like perhaps he'd had the best first presidential year in a generation, or our lifetime, or some such modification.

I wasn't taking notes because it was only a single quote I needed. So I recited it back to him and asked him if that's what he wanted in the paper.

"Absolutely," he said.

I spent dinner thinking perhaps I should give him one final opportunity to fine-tune, shall we say, his comment. As I was leaving, I walked past the roped-off presidential table and caught his eye. He waved me over—the Secret Service would stop anybody he didn't want to talk to. I asked him if he was sure he wanted me to give his quote to the *Post* about how he'd had the best first year of any president ever.

"Of course," he said. "I told you already."

So I gave it to the reporter and she put it in the paper. Nobody was shocked, or even surprised. In retrospect, I don't know why I'd been concerned about it. But that wasn't the end of my career as a legman for state-run media.

Two years later, in early January 2020, I was having dinner on a weeknight with my wife and a client of our show at Mar-a-Lago. There seemed to be somewhat more activity than normal for what was the end of the Christmas break, with lots of Secret Service and assorted other suits lurking around the stairs that led up to the president's personal quarters.

Finally, around 8 o'clock, a little later than usual, Trump strode into the dining room. With him was Rep. Kevin McCarthy, the House minority leader from California. He got the usual standing ovation from the weeknight crowd. On the way out, I waved to him and he called me over and introduced me to McCarthy. It was just another night in sunny South Florida.

Then he asked me, "Howie, who do you think would be the better opponent for me, Bernie or Biden?"

"Bernie," I answered automatically.

Trump nodded and gestured toward McCarthy. "That's what Kevin thinks too. Everybody says so."

Everybody was right. I asked McCarthy if he'd come on my show—you always have to make the pitch when you get a chance. He said sure and I said good night to him and the president and drove home. When I turned on the TV, cable news was in an uproar.

Gen. Qasem Soleimani, the Iranian terror boss, had just been blown up on the tarmac of the airport in Tehran by a U.S. drone strike. Trump had ordered it from Mar-a-Lago a couple of hours earlier, just before he'd come down into the dining room for dinner.

He had said nothing about it to me. This was a huge story, and Trump had handled it nonchalantly, like he was signing off on a new nominee to the board of the Tennessee Valley Authority.

I tweeted out something, about how calm and collected he'd been. I guess I'd been the only press there that night, so the next morning, I started getting calls from the national media. They wanted me to elaborate on how he'd been behaving, and I told them.

Then, one of them hit me with the tough question, "When you were at his table, did you notice what he was having for dinner?"

Damn, that was one of those status details that I always like to include in my own stories. But I hadn't paid any attention. I had had no idea it was an evening for the history books. I thought I was just shooting the breeze, and trying to line up an interview with the House minority leader. (It turned out that the president was having Mrs. Trump's meat loaf, which is also one of my favorites, along with the filet and the Dover sole.)

After the 2016 election, I'd decided to do a book about Trump's victory. Hillary had put out another book, which I doubt she even read, called *What Happened.* So I decided to call mine *What Really Happened.*

It turned out okay. It had a great photo on the cover, taken by a *Herald* photographer, of Trump waving at a rally. He was wearing one of his trademark red ties with the usual blue suit.

We weren't expecting to make a huge amount of money with it. But as I've told you, the markup on your own product makes it worthwhile—selling 2,500 copies printed by Frandel is as profitable to me as maybe 15,000 sales of a book put out by a New York publisher.

We got the books and they were selling well enough. We had them for sale on Amazon too, of course. Nothing spectacular, but the market for 2016 campaign books was already saturated. One night my wife and I were going down to Mar-a-Lago for dinner with some Boston people, which is usually our M.O. That's where visitors always want to go, even now when he's not president.

We knew Trump was there—his presence was always reported in the local papers, mainly because the air traffic patterns at PBIA were changed, which meant more to most of the town's residents than Trump's actual presence.

We decided to take a copy of *What Really Happened* with us to dinner. And when the president waved us over, I handed him the book. He was immediately taken with the cover.

"That's a really nice picture," he said. "Where's that from?"

I told him and then we moved on to our table. I didn't want to ask him for a blurb, because that would make me too much of a supplicant. When you're the president, everyone is a supplicant, in one way or another. And you never want to wear out your welcome, with anyone, but especially not with the president of the United States.

My wife and I looked at each other and shrugged. We'd done our best, and what more can you do? We went home after dinner and got a good night's sleep. When authors have a new book out, many (including me) fall into the habit of checking to see how it's doing on Amazon at least a few times a day. It doesn't make a lot of sense—it's like the watched pot that never boils that my Aunt Mabel always used to tell me about. But it's human nature.

The next morning, I got up and immediately checked Amazon to see how the new book was doing. The previous night, the last time I'd checked, I think it was probably somewhere around number 50,000 in sales. It had fewer than a dozen reviews, with an average rating of four or four and a half stars.

But now, this morning, I was amazed that *What Really Happened* was up to around number 250 in sales. Even more jarring, suddenly the book had several hundred reviews—and the average number of stars on the ratings had plummeted from four-plus to under two. Many of the "reviews" were nothing more than a few obscenities, with no stars. And they did not have that official Amazon seal of approval—"verified purchase."

What had happened? There was only one possible answer. The president had tweeted about the book. He'd given it a rave review, of course. Which was the absolute best possible way to sell books while simultaneously generating the worst possible reviews from the Democratic troll community.

We quickly sold hundreds of books through Amazon and through our own website (which we of course preferred, because it cut out the middleman). I sent an email to Amazon about the reviews, explaining the circumstances but expecting that nothing would be done.

I was pleasantly surprised when most of the one- and no-star reviews by Trump-hating trolls who hadn't bought the book vanished. In the next few days, we even got a few bulk orders, one from a Trump campaign committee.

As the months went by, we got two more positive tweets from the president. Each time, we sold a few hundred more books. During the 2020 campaign, Donald Trump Jr. stopped by the studio before a fundraiser at Ernie Boch Jr.'s estate in Norwood. We were talking about his book, and I mentioned that his father had given me three rave tweets.

"That's two more than he gave me," Donald Trump Jr. said.

2023: At Mar-a-Lago with Karoline Leavitt, former NH congressional candidate.

21
CHARLIE BAKER'S DISAPPOINTING DISAPPOINTMENTS

The Massachusetts Republican Party has been a mess forever—I wrote a column on the local GOP's dysfunction for *Boston* magazine back around 1986 headlined "Shootout in the Lifeboat."

Very little has changed. There was a brief resurgence in 1990, when William F. Weld was elected governor over John Silber, the president of Boston University whose candidacy had been largely created by Billy Bulger, the Senate president.

Silber was probably more conservative than Weld, but because of the Bulger connection, I had to be with Weld. In his first term, Weld did a good job of getting the state budget back under control, but he had a short attention span. In public, he was soon slurring his words. At a St. Patrick's Day breakfast, he admitted to Billy Bulger that he sometimes drank in the morning—"just a wee small taste." As the years went on, he began pulling the occasional bizarre stunt, like diving into the Charles River, in front of TV cameras, fully clothed.

Weld finally resigned in 1997 in a quixotic attempt to become ambassador to Mexico. Out of office and divorced, he kept drifting further and further left, into general incoherence and crapulence. These days, at his rare public appearances, he looks more dissipated and disheveled than Tip O'Neill or Ted Kennedy ever did.

During the organized-crime hearings in federal court in 1998, he was called as a witness for the government about the FBI's Top Echelon informant program that had enabled the serial-killing spree of Whitey Bulger and Stevie Flemmi.

Nobody in politics had seen much of him since he left office, so outside the courtroom during a recess, several of us asked Weld what he'd been doing. He told us he'd been writing novels, one of which was about the Quabbin Reservoir, the construction of which required the flooding of four small communities in central Massachusetts. It was an odd book. Set in the 1930s, Weld had the affected residents of the towns riding around in buckboards.

"It's slow going," he said of his writing. "It's not like when I was governor, and I had nothing to do all day long."

Then Weld began giggling. It was sad. He seemed like he wasn't all there.

As the years went by, he just kept going downhill. In 2016, like the RINO that he'd become, Weld denounced candidate Trump as little more than a modern Nazi, saying that his proposals about ending illegal immigration reminded him of Hitler's Kristallnacht against the Jews.

Trump responded with a statement:

"I don't talk about his alcoholism, so why would he talk about my foolishly perceived fascism."

Asked to respond to that, Weld refused to comment. What was he going to say?

Then there was Paul Cellucci, Weld's lieutenant governor, my state senator when I lived in Acton after fleeing Somerville. He was alright, was elected on his own in 1998. Like Weld, though, he became bored with the Corner Office. He was tight with the Bushes—he'd been a driver for Bush 41 during the New Hampshire primary in 1980. He resigned as governor in 2001 to become Bush 43's ambassador to Canada.

Cellucci's lieutenant governor was Jane Swift, a former state senator (first elected in the Weld landslide of 1990). As I've told you, she was such a disaster that *60 Minutes* did a piece about her, with me as the designated comic-book villain required in every *60 Minutes* melodrama.

She was forced out by Mitt Romney, who won the 2002 race. But he quickly lost interest in the job, like Weld and Cellucci before him. In 2004, he even invested a lot of effort in trying to elect more Republicans to the legislature.

He spent his last two years of his single four-year term preparing to run for president—the only judges he appointed were prosecutors, because he didn't want any rogue jurists coming back to haunt him, the way Mike Dukakis's weekend furloughs (Willie Horton, Jimmy the Bear Flemmi, etc.) were used against him by Bush 41 in 1988.

Willard—for that is indeed his first name—liked the state police detail, but that was about all he liked about Beacon Hill. He didn't enjoy horse-trading with the ward heelers in the legislature. It was all just so tawdry and low-rent.

The state agencies were hopelessly infested with small-time hacks and grifters who were as corrupt as they were shiftless. Romney had long dreamed of becoming president, fulfilling the dream his father could never quite realize—President Romney! And he quickly realized that ultimately nobody cared what you had gotten done as governor, only what scandals had occurred on your watch.

By 2004, Mitt figured that if he had an entire year or two to plot his presidential campaign, maybe he could win in 2008. So he announced he wouldn't be running again—perhaps I should have entitled this chapter "Republican Lame Ducks I Have Known." That opened a pathway to the GOP nomination for his lieutenant governor, Kerry Murphy Healey.

Kerry Murphy was from Daytona Beach, Florida—a social climber *par excellence*. She went to Harvard and hooked up with a future investment banker, Sean Healey. In 2002, Mitt was looking for a running mate, and he needed a Catholic, which he naturally assumed Mrs. Sean Healey was.

But no, she was a convert—she had become an Episcopalian. Now, let me state for the record that I have nothing against Episcopalians. I am not a "devout Catholic" (unlike Joe Biden and Nancy Pelosi). But my father always told me that any Catholic who converted to Episcopalian was nothing more than a social climber. And in his estimation, that was even more ridiculous than a "left-footed Irishman," one who was born Protestant.

My father's belief, which I have come to agree with, was that it shouldn't matter what your religion is, and that most likely the people you're trying to impress by "converting" will not be fooled in the slightest, which I have also found to be pretty much true.

When I found out that Healey was a Protestant, I was as surprised as Mitt. So I began calling her "Muffy," the most demeaning WASP nickname I (or actually one of my sources) could come up with. It caught on, much to her chagrin.

Muffy was crushed in 2006 by Deval Patrick, an affirmative-action blow-in drifter from Chicago who despite his Milton Academy/Harvard/Harvard Law pedigree needed two tries to pass the bar exam. He was a disaster, of course, or so it seemed until he decided not to run for a third term in 2014 and was replaced by another Republican, Charlie Baker.

Baker had been a State House aide during the Weld/Cellucci administrations, eventually running the state budget. He was a Harvard legacy. His father had been in the Nixon administration.

Back in the sixties, when Ronald Reagan was first being promoted as a candidate for governor of California, one of the old-time movie moguls shook his head and rendered his verdict on the potential Reagan campaign.

"No, no," he said. "Robert Taylor for governor. Ronald Reagan for best friend."

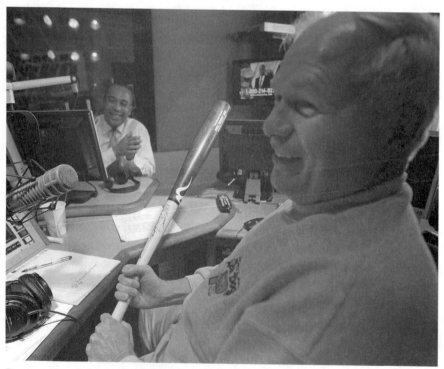

Batting around the issues on WRKO with then-Gov. Deval Patrick.
Source: Photo by Stuart Cahill/MediaNews Group/Boston Herald via Getty Images.

When Charlie first ran in 2010, I asked one of the veteran Democrats at the State House about Baker as a candidate for governor. Like the mogul, this guy shook his head.

"No, no, not Charlie for governor," he said. "Charlie for governor's chief of staff. His proper role is as the guy who briefs the reporters off the record before the governor comes out for the press conference."

Which was probably why he lost his first time out in 2010, to the protected-class incumbent Deval Patrick. But as Mitt Romney had already learned, the Republican farm system in Massachusetts was failing. So he was nominated again by the GOP in 2014 after a fractious state convention.

But in 2014 Baker had a couple of things going for him. The legislature had just passed a law instituting an automatic annual gas tax increase. Which meant that the legislators could not be held accountable by the voters for ever-increasing gas prices.

It was just the kind of outrage you see in a one-party state, but it was an overreach, even by Beacon Hill standards. Working-class people, led by then state Rep. Geoff Diehl of Whitman, gathered signatures to repeal the automatic gas tax increases by referendum.

In my last days at Entercom, I got heavily involved in the campaign, promoting signature drives to put the question on the ballot. On weekends, I made appearances at the malls where the petitions were being circulated.

We got the question onto the statewide ballot, but our prospects did not look bright. All the usual Deep State suspects—I dubbed them Big Asphalt—were behind the automatic gas-tax increase, because it meant billions of dollars every year to keep their assorted pork projects for the protected classes going.

I concentrated my fire on the MBTA pension funds, especially all of Whitey Bulger's relatives and in-laws who'd done their 23 years and retired in their 40s with full pensions. Not to mention assorted ex-pols, gangsters, and relatives of mobsters who'd been run as straw candidates to split the anti-Bulger vote in assorted legislative primaries, and who were now enjoying their monthly kisses in the mail at their beachfront retirement condos in Florida.

Big Asphalt had more money than they knew what to do with. I remember watching *Monday Night Football* one evening in October 2014. During a single break, I saw two ads about how the automatic "modest" increases in the gas tax would go to, you guessed it, the crumbling infrastructure.

But an odd thing happened. The more money the hacks spent, the more working people realized what a grift the whole thing was.

In his second campaign for governor, Charlie Baker was running against Martha Coakley, the attorney general. He was the underdog until he decided to become a crusader against Beacon Hill overreach. He attended the anti–gas tax rallies. He was photographed by his state police driver pumping his own gas.

On Election Day, the automatic gas tax increase was repealed by 110,000 votes, a margin of 53–47 percent. Given that we were outspent 30–1, it was quite an impressive win, if I do say so myself.

Charlie Baker, meanwhile, defeated the woman Patches Kennedy had once dubbed "Marsha" Coakley by a mere 40,000 votes.

In his own mind, of course, Charlie became "Landslide" Baker. It was like *Boston* magazine's old Best and Worst awards—if you won, it had to be God's will.

Christmas 2015: At Downtown Crossing with Gov. Charlie Baker before he became the Pope of Panic Porn.

As with so many other pols, it could be said of Charlie Baker that if you ever named a street after him, it would have to be one-way. As time went on, Charlie came to regard himself as a one-man electoral wrecking crew.

That was tolerable for a while. He wasn't great, but he seemed marginally better than Deval Patrick. At least at first. But as time went on, it became clearer and clearer that he wasn't. Soon we were calling him "Tall Deval." (He's 6'6".)

Then Donald Trump arrived on the scene. He offended Charlie's RINO and Harvard sensibilities. On election day 2016, as I've mentioned, at his precinct in Swampscott, Baker pompously announced that he couldn't vote for either of the two candidates because they were . . . well, unworthy, I guess.

Who the hell ever blanked a presidential race? Especially someone in politics.

At Trump's inauguration in January 2017, the Mass GOP, like all the state committees, hosted its own parties in Washington. My wife and I went to one of them just to show the flag, so to speak. Guess who walked in—Tall Deval. And here I had thought that his minions at the F1 in Braintree on Election Night had been front-runners!

I just shrugged it off as one of those things. But once Trump was in office, Baker started criticizing him on absolutely everything. He always used a variation on the same word—disappointing. The governor would just be so disappointed in Trump's disappointing disappointments.

Finally, about six months after the inauguration, I just googled the words *Trump, Baker,* and *disappoint.* I came up with more than 15 instances of his . . . disappointment.

I wrote a column and even the *Globe* picked up on it and did a follow-up. But that didn't stop Baker from continuing to be disappointed, although sometimes he threw a changeup and expressed his frustration or irritation or something else, although disappointment was always the first option.

Throughout his eight years in office, Baker supposedly polled as one of the "most popular" governors in the nation. I never detected any such groundswell. He was supposed to be a micromanager—he had after all run the state budgets under Weld and Cellucci. Yet so many state agencies were riddled with scandal and corruption—the state police, the Registry of Motor Vehicles, the Department of Children and Families.

His sanctimonious hectoring and virtue-signaling became so intolerable that in 2018, I blanked the governor's race, the fight at the top of the ticket. That was only two years after I'd thought Baker had been lying about not voting for either Trump or Hillary. There is a first time for everything, I guess.

Bottom line: Baker was terrible even before the COVID-19 Panic was ginned up in early 2020 and he totally lost his mind. He was worse than any other Republican governor (except possibly Larry Hogan of Maryland). He overreacted more than most of his Democrat counterparts.

He believed the bullshit Fauci et al. were spewing out, unlike some politicians who were just swept up in this latest outbreak of extraordinary popular delusions and the madness of crowds.

The (silent) skeptics couldn't do anything else in the midst of such a mass panic. Locally, I would put Boston Mayor Marty Walsh and New Hampshire Gov. Chris Sununu in that category. They didn't cover themselves in glory, far from it, but at least they balked at some of the insanity, or at any rate didn't lead the masked mobs.

But Charlie Baker? He swallowed the Democrat agitprop hook, line, and sinker. I think he realized early on that the real goal was not so much public health, whatever the hell that means, as the destruction of the president who had so disappointed him, Donald J. Trump.

Even before the Wuhan flu, I hadn't been overly optimistic about Trump's chances for reelection in 2020. I'd laid out my fears in *What Really Happened*—that he might end up as a kind of modern-day equivalent of the latter-day Roman emperor Julian the Apostate.

Julian's reign had been a reaction to the proselytizing Christians who were settling old scores all over the empire with the pagans, also known as "Romans." The Deplorables of their day, you might say. Julian had promised to Make Rome Great Again, but he died on a military campaign in Persia. Then it was back to business for the Christians, converting temples to churches, evicting the Delphic Oracle and the Vestal Virgins from their shrines, etc.

It's a depressing story, even for Christians. The Dark Ages lasted for a long, long time.

At the beginning of 2020, the U.S. economy was roaring. Gas prices were low. The nation was energy independent and the world was at peace. Crime, inflation, and the border were under control. It's hard to beat any incumbent running on peace and prosperity.

But then came the Chinese virus. Like most sane people, I wasn't much concerned about COVID-19 killing me. But it gave the Deep State an excuse—many excuses, in fact—to shut down everything, and then blame Trump. Which of course they did.

Paper Boy

Never let a crisis go to waste, as Rahm Emanuel famously said. You couldn't expect anything less from the Democrats, even if the only real crisis was their hysterical overreaction, which they quickly understood was their only way to defeat Trump.

Fake news called it a pandemic. I began describing it as the Panic. You can't turn a panic into a pandemic without "dem."

It is a truism that if you believe in nothing, you'll fall for anything. That was Charlie Baker, not that he was any different than almost all the nation's political class, Republican as well as Democrat.

As human beings, we are hard-wired to believe in something, even if it's a cult, which is what the Deep State had been promulgating in various, ever more demented iterations—global warming, transgenderism, critical race theory, etc.

Overnight, if only temporarily, the Cult of the Mask supplanted "climate change" as the prevailing faith of the people without the Word—those who had forsaken religion for secular humanism and, God help them, the Democrat party.

As a kid, I was always taught in CCD that saints had to be dead before they could be beatified. Again, though, the old rules went out the window—suddenly we had St. Anthony Fauci, who'd had his snout buried in the public trough since LBJ, when he was dodging the Vietnam draft. It didn't matter that Fauci's pronouncements changed from live shot to live shot—no mask, one mask, two masks . . . the true believers didn't care.

They never do. Predict the end of the world and then it doesn't happen—to the committed snake-chuckers listening to gospel radio down south, a missed date (or two) for the Rapture or the Second Coming is nothing more than a speed bump on the dusty trail to the Mount of Olives. The reverend clergy just proclaim a new date—and pass the collection plate one more time.

That was one lesson I'd learned driving around Winston-Salem listening to the daytime-only gospel station all those years ago whenever I grew weary of the Top 40 fare on AM radio.

In early 2020, Charlie Baker instantly appointed himself the Commonwealth's Cassandra of COVID-19, the Pope of Panic Porn. He was intoxicated by his absolute power. The legislature was more than willing to stay at home and cash their paychecks. All those endless pay raises for his hack judges meant that they would rubber-stamp his extra-constitutional overreaches and executive orders.

All the old sayings applied. Power is the ultimate aphrodisiac. Power corrupts; absolute power corrupts absolutely.

In Massachusetts, when you register to vote, the best bet is to remain "unenrolled." That way, you can take a ballot in either primary. Why would anyone ever become a member of either, or any, party? More than 60 percent of the Massachusetts electorate has come to the same conclusion—they're unenrolled.

In Massachusetts, I usually, but not always, voted Republican, at least in the general election. The way I looked at it, if I took a Democratic ballot in the primary, I had two chances to vote against the worst candidates. Not that I succeeded in defeating them very often. Still, I was basically a Republican, just not officially—like most conservative voters in the state.

During COVID, most of us semi-Republicans became totally pissed off by Charlie Baker's imperious, obnoxious behavior. And his stewardship of the state was a complete disaster. His veterans' agency ran the Holyoke Soldiers Home, and the superintendent was a hack from a multi-generational Democratic family of payroll patriots from Springfield. The guy had given Baker $950 and the lieutenant governor $1,000.

Baker's payroll patriots at the Holyoke Soldiers home botched the outbreak of the virus, and 76 veterans died. The lawsuits were massive. He fired the Hispanic boss of the agency, and then rehired him for a six-figure salary at an obscure quasi-public agency. Better to have him inside the tent pissing out than outside the tent pissing in . . .

The death toll in the private, state-regulated nursing homes rivaled those in New York and New Jersey (whose Democratic governor Phil Murphy was a classmate of Baker's at Needham High and, of course, Harvard College).

In charge of monitoring the nursing homes was the Department of Public Health, which had earlier been responsible for the falsification of tens of thousands of criminal drug tests, resulting in the wrongful imprisonment of hundreds of drug dealers, many of them people of color.

But since Charlie was perpetually "disappointed" in Orange Man Bad on COVID, he got a complete pass on everything from the lapdog Boston media, what little remained of them.

I went over Baker's contributions reports—he had taken $52,000 from the nursing homes, Lt. Gov. Karyn Polito another $35,000, and the speaker of the House, an unindicted co-conspirator in the probation department scandal, about $45,000.

None of the hacks on Beacon Hill ever gave back a dime. They didn't care. All the state office buildings were shut down. The hackerama began what amounted to an almost endless vacation—early retirement, with full pay.

When local businesses and churches began suing the state, the judges always ruled in favor of the state. Sometimes the judges, in their pajamas on the Zoom-call hearings, would talk about how wonderfully the governor was handling the "crisis," by closing the courthouses while they continued to collect full pay for doing nothing.

Was I the only person who noticed that most of the extinguished jurists seemed to be putting on a few pounds in their unending indolence? Or was it just that all those Zoom hearings packed on an extra 10 pounds, as TV news live shots supposedly did?

Meanwhile, people who had real jobs were paying the price of the public sector's endless vacations. A great new bakery that had just opened in Wellesley—it was suddenly out of business! The coffee shop within walking distance of my house that was like a breakfast club in downtown Wellesley for a whole bunch of us—gone!

The Eastern Standard in Kenmore Square, where I used to do live broadcasts before Red Sox home games—shuttered.

It became a staple of my show, bemoaning the closures of our favorite restaurants, bars, and mom-and-pop stores. Two weeks to flatten the curve my ass.

I wrote about it—the rest of the media didn't care. They were all in on the Panic. Charlie Baker was in charge of fear-mongering, and the Democrat operatives with press passes were his amen chorus.

As for the real churches, the ones that didn't venerate Fauci, they were shuttered. So much for the First Amendment.

Every month, the death rates would come out for all the states. With an almost complete police-state lockdown, Massachusetts still had the third-highest mortality rate, behind only New York and New Jersey. Then there was unemployment—for several months in 2020, Massachusetts was tops among the 50 states.

Every week the state posted charts showing the age of the dead. Most weeks the age of the average victim was over 80. The vast majority of the COVID-19 dead were over 75, and most had multiple comorbidities. The handful of younger victims were usually already very ill or very fat—or both.

But hardly anyone in the media had the slightest interest in showing that the emperor—Tall Deval—had no clothes.

Printing Panic Porn 24/7 was so much easier than having to go out and, you know, report real news. The press, so-called, could just take those daily numbers from the ever-so-reputable Department of Public Health and run their dire headlines.

The reporters went to work about as often as state judges. Newspaper circulation plunged, TV ratings less so, but day by day fewer and fewer people bought into the grift. But the media never shed their credulity. The press had the same attitude as the judges—they were still getting paid, so promoting the Panic beat working.

Every day, Baker would hold a live press conference in his squeaky beta-male voice. Nobody ever challenged his bullshit. When I wrote the story about his $52,000 in blood money from the nursing homes where they were stacking up dead bodies like cordwood, I thought a logical follow-up question might be:

"Governor, will you give back the $52,000?"

The *Herald* reporter was too frightened of the governor to ask the question. She wanted to stay on Team Panic. The next day Baker was down in Bristol County. I got my producer, who's from New Bedford, to hire a guy to ask the governor if he'd return the blood money. Of course, Baker just walked away, not providing me with any sound, knowing that no Boston "reporter" would follow up.

That's how pathetic state-run media have become.

In 2020, with the senseless lockdowns destroying the state, his lieutenant governor threw a kegger at her lakefront mansion in Shrewsbury. The Boston papers were well aware of it, but wouldn't touch it—too damaging to Team Panic's narrative. The scoop had to be reported by a local blogger, Turtleboy.

Turtleboy broke other big stories, often about scandals in law enforcement. Once the newspapers would have been competing among themselves to break such stories, exposing corruption, generating front-page headlines, winning prizes, etc.

Now digging into such scandals was almost unthinkable. Too complicated, too much work. And it would have required the one thing newspapers no longer have—real reporters.

When the Panic began, Baker's administration ordered the firing of state employees who refused to get the "vaccine." The corrupt state police began firing cops, hero cops some of them, not in the fake-news headline sense, but troopers who'd in fact put their lives on the line.

In the K-9 unit, troopers keep the dogs with them 24/7. If the cops have children, the dogs become family pets. So they would wait until the troopers were off-duty before they went to their homes to grab the dogs. The kids would naturally start screaming and yelling as their pets were dragged away to a kennel in Acton that cost $50 a day to board them at.

I got to know some of these troopers because, let's face it, who else could they turn to for relief? One trooper whose wiseguy uncle I'd written about called me "Winston" in his texts, from the hero of *1984*.

That I did take as a compliment.

There was a young trooper, a combat veteran, an actual Sunday school teacher if you can believe it, who didn't believe in the Panic or the vaccine. The brass waited until he went to a day of training at the academy in New Braintree. He was pulled out of class in front of his peers, stripped him of his badge, his gun, his uniform, and his cruiser.

He was left stranded in the middle of nowhere.

A trooper told me about the record of the superior officer who'd done this. He had an uncle even higher up in the MSP hierarchy, and this jackbooted thug cop been charged in western Massachusetts with pushing his wife's head into a toilet bowl he hadn't bothered to flush.

I knew this was a story the *Herald* wouldn't touch in a million years. But it had to get out there. So I pulled the court documents and handed them off to Turtleboy. He knew what to do with the story.

When the story ran, the state police brass began trying to track down the source of the information. They narrowed it down to my source and we had to halt communications. Internal Affairs grabbed his cell phone. I had to change my voicemail, although I'm afraid it didn't do much good.

This entire jihad by the state police was orchestrated by a colonel from the Cape. His son got popped in Hyannis, hanging halfway out of his truck at 2 in the morning in February. He'd been drinking for hours at one of the local downtown bars. Inside his truck the local Barnstable cops found an unregistered gun. No charges were filed.

I worked on that story with the Turtleboy of the Cape, an ex-cop named Robert Bastille who runs the Hyannis News website. He sells spot-news police video to the Boston TV stations.

The Boston media had neither the skills or the stones to handle such stories anymore. I stopped even calling in tips. What was the point?

What a mess—a government consumed by scandal and dysfunction, yet the press was utterly uninterested in reporting the news. Baker was anti-Trump, and that was his get-out-of-jail card. As always in the media, the sin of omission—not reporting something—was worse than the sin of commission—making shit up, like the Russian collusion hoax.

The people of Massachusetts, though, or at least the handful of Republican voters who remained, were slowly coming to a realization of what Charlie Baker was doing to the state.

In my experience, most voters are willing to forgive, or at least overlook, a lot from politicians they've supported in the past. Increasing a fee, turning a street one way, restricting hours on a beach—those issues can be infuriating, but not necessarily a deal-breaker.

Abject betrayal is another thing altogether.

Charlie Baker lost me and a lot of the rest of his base when he came out for something called the Transportation Climate Initiative (TCI). It was nothing more than a massive increase in the gasoline tax. The gasoline tax!

After he'd first gotten elected on a platform fighting that very thing, he was now pushing a tax that according to one study could have jacked up the state tax per gallon from 24 cents a gallon to 62 cents a gallon.

And Baker claimed he could do it without approval either by the legislature or the people (whom he didn't want to allow to vote on the question). The TCI was concocted by the Church of Climate Change as a region-wide scam, for every state to raise their taxes together, as far south as Virginia.

The gag was, it would save the planet. What a crock. The United States represents 5 percent of the world's population, and Massachusetts is 3 percent of that 5 percent. But by giving billions in additional taxes to the same arrogant fools who were already wrecking the state with their incompetence, somehow polar bears would survive. And penguins too, I suppose, at the South Pole.

But a funny thing happened on the way to the Green New Deal. The Democrat-run states began pulling out of the "compact," because even they realized it was insane. But Baker refused to throw in the towel. Even more so than on COVID, on gas taxes he was a bigger fool than any Democrat in the Northeast.

It was the last straw for the Massachusetts Republicans who'd dragged him across the finish line with the anti–gas tax referendum in 2014. There's an old saying in politics, you go home with the one that brung you to the dance. Charlie had obviously forgotten that old saw.

By this time, Biden was president. He loved Charlie Baker, but of course he couldn't get his name right. Biden called him "Charlie Parker." You know, like

Bird, probably the greatest jazz saxophonist of all time. Clint Eastwood made a movie about him.

We began calling Baker "Charlie Parker." An elderly black listener called to complain, asking why we were disrespecting Bird by comparing him to Charlie Baker? The caller had a point, but it was too good a moniker not to use. Then Sen. Ed Markey called Baker "Gov. Bacon."

For a few days, we tried calling Baker Charlie Bacon, but it didn't catch on. That's the way it is with nicknames. Like any other new product, you never know how they'll sell until you test-market them.

Parker—as we now called him—just kept tightening the screws. At Thanksgiving 2020, he bragged of sending "folks" out to supermarkets to make sure that no one was buying turkeys of more than 12 pounds. He thundered against Super Bowl parties—don't share chips, and keep the windows open, in early February.

It was great sport for Charlie, screwing over his own base and reveling in the accolades of the people who'd never voted for him. The problem for Charlie Parker was that in 2022 he would still have to be re-nominated in the Republican primary, and his base now despised him.

Soon calls were being made to Mar-a-Lago, not by me, but by Jim Lyons, the GOP state party chairman, and by ex-Rep. Geoff Diehl, the unsuccessful 2018 U.S. Senate candidate against the fake Indian.

One thing Trump can't stand is backstabbers, and that's what Charlie Parker was, and is.

Finally, in November 2021, Trump issued a press release endorsing Geoff Diehl for governor. Polls of likely GOP primary voters quickly showed that the incumbent—still touted by the supine Boston media as "the most popular governor in America"—was running more than 20 points behind Diehl.

A few weeks later—after a final flurry of $1,000 fundraisers—Parker and Polito announced their "retirements" from politics.

They retired, as I always say, due to ill health—the voters got sick of them.

A few days later, their monthly campaign finance reports came out, and I ran the names of all the marks, I mean donors, who had given to Baker and Polito in their final cons. I demanded that the Boston Police Department's bunco squad open an investigation.

But Charlie Parker didn't care. He had checked out. Like Bill Weld before him, he put out a book.

It was called *Results,* as if he'd had any, beyond his son beating the rap. When it was issued, to tepid reviews even in the lapdog Boston media, someone posted a scathing comment on Amazon:

"Odd, the book doesn't mention the dozens of state police convicted of felonies on Gov. Baker's watch. Nor does it mention the 25% of small businesses that closed and fled Massachusetts due to his failed policies . . . Where's the chapter on his son being escorted off a plane at Logan Airport for allegedly groping a stranger? He doesn't mention his Lt Governor having a graduation party for a member of her family at the height of the pandemic while everyone else is locked down."

The review was signed by Pierre Delicto Jr., a variation on Mitt Romney's *nom de plume* on Twitter until he was outed. I was immediately blamed for the notice, and I deny it.

That's my story and I'm sticking to it.

22
THE END OF
NEWSPAPERS

It used to be said that in a recession, if the *Globe* caught a cold, the *Herald* would come down with pneumonia. In other words, if any company bought ads in two dailies, the first one they'd pull was the *Herald*'s.

But it wasn't just department store display ads that were carrying the *Globe*, it was the auto dealerships and even more importantly, the classifieds of all sorts. Because the Internet was such an economical and effective way to advertise, the real estate companies and the car dealers were fleeing the *Globe* faster than the common nightwalkers had deserted the *Phoenix*.

By 2008, as the *Herald* was having financial heart murmurs, the *Globe* was keeling over with a massive coronary thrombosis in its business model. I could see it with my own eyes in Wellesley. Early Sunday mornings, I would drive in to the *Herald* plant in the South End to pick up my mail and the weekend editions.

Sometimes I'd get behind a *Globe* deliveryman. He'd be going down my narrow suburban lane way over the speed limit, tossing fat Sunday editions out of his car onto every driveway. But around 2003, I'd say, things started changing. Fewer people were buying the dead-tree edition.

Now I didn't have to worry about getting run off the road by the *Globe* deliveryman. Now I had to worry about being stuck behind him, as he crawled along, constantly braking as he consulted his notes or smartphone to see who'd cancelled their subscriptions this week.

Ernest Hemingway wrote a famous line in *The Sun Also Rises* about going bankrupt—"first gradually, then suddenly."

That's what happened at the *Globe*. Overnight, seemingly, the classified ads vanished. In 2009, the *Times* abruptly threatened to shut down the suddenly bust-out newspaper if the pampered unions didn't approve tens of millions of dollars in concessions.

The news broke on a Friday night. The next evening, I walked into an up-scale seafood restaurant on Boylston Street with a friend of mine named Harold Brown. Patrons began standing up and shaking my hand, congratulating me. I accepted their congratulations and compliments, even though I was, like them, just an onlooker. A very happy onlooker.

The next day CBS News called me. At my house in Wellesley, I did a taped interview for the evening newscast about the *Globe*'s impending bankruptcy. For the establishing shot, they taped me walking my pugs on the sidewalk across the street from my house.

In my interview, I acknowledged that the *Herald* too was on the ropes. But I added, "I don't care what happens. As long as we stay in business an hour longer than the *Globe*, we win."

Nobody complained about my lack of empathy, or was shocked by my attitude. In fact, most people just shrugged. They'd already moved on. Newspapers were all done. It was just a question now of who was going to get to write the obituaries.

In 2013, the *Times* sold the *Globe* and the *Telegram* to John Henry, the woke owner of the Boston Red Sox, for $70 million. It was all about the real estate at 135 Morrissey Boulevard. The actual newspaper itself was worth nothing. As for the *Worcester Telegram*, it was apparently worth less than nothing—in the next couple of years, it would change hands three or four times.

The *Herald* likewise was on its last legs. Like the *Globe*, its physical plant was worth more—much more—than the newspaper itself. First Pat Purcell sold off his suburban papers, near the top of the market, just before the collapse of local print journalism. Then he got rid of the plant in the South End, settling with the back-shop unions and the Teamsters and then farming out the printing to the *Globe*.

The *Herald* had once had a somewhat robust reporting tradition, at least after Murdoch bought it. But at the end of Purcell's ownership, a couple of lawsuits decimated the paper's finances. One involved a member of the band Boston.

It was a ridiculous complaint, not even worth explaining, but defending against a deep-pocketed musician cost Purcell millions in legal fees.

The other suit involved a state judge named Easy Ernie Murphy. He had purportedly made inappropriate remarks to a young rape victim, and the *Herald* reported the story. I mention this only because if anyone relies on Wikipedia for their information, they may read that I was somehow to blame for this lawsuit. What happened was that I wrote a column, carefully, not including any of the material that was later in dispute.

That morning, on the message board under my column, one of the anonymous commenters said that because of what Murphy had said, his own daughters deserved to be raped. Whoever said it was way out of line, obviously, but I wasn't the one who said it.

However, at trial, the judge was asked for his reaction when he read the comment in what was described as a "chat room," not by me, but by some anonymous online troll.

"I wanted to kill Howie Carr," he said. The *Globe* loved that quote and played it very high in the next day's story. Now on the Internet I've somehow become the defendant, the guy who cost the *Herald* all that money, however much it was.

You ask, why don't I just edit the Wikipedia entry? Because it'll just be changed back.

If you're a Democrat, any embarrassing facts anywhere on the Internet tend to be expunged permanently, even if they're true. *Especially* if they're true. If you go against any woke orthodoxy, the record is often manipulated, twisted, falsified. If you try to correct the bogus information, some beta male who's probably sporting a man bun and a squirrelly goatee and sipping a Bud Light immediately gets online and just changes it back.

They have a lot more time on their hands than I do. I still have to work for a living.

After Pat Purcell sold the Harrison Avenue plant to developers, the *Herald* moved to the Seaport District, formerly known as South Boston. But within a few years, it became clear that even our much smaller offices were way too much for the incredible shrinking formerly feisty tabloid. The *Herald* had two floors on Fargo Street, but after another series of layoffs even one floor would have provided us with more than enough space.

By 2015, the *Herald* moved again, this time out of the city, to rented digs in suburban Braintree.

Pat Purcell filed for bankruptcy in 2017. Several companies bid for what little remained of the paper, and the winner prevailed with an $11 million bid. There were more layoffs. The library—the morgue—disappeared. The photo editors were laid off—this on a newspaper that had won four Pulitzer Prizes for photography, back when a Pulitzer meant something. The gossip column was first turned into just another collection of PR releases, and then the plug was pulled altogether.

The paper shrank in size and the price rose. I never once stopped into the Braintree offices before they too were shut down in the wake of COVID. The *Herald* is now printed in Rhode Island, at the plant of the *Providence Journal*. They too have plenty of excess printing capacity, considering that their afternoon paper, the *Evening Bulletin,* is long gone.

When I started out in newspapers, there was a farm system of sorts in journalism. Of course some people didn't have to work their way up—Chris Wallace comes to mind immediately. He started out at the *Boston Globe*, appropriately enough, given that paper's record of open and gross nepotism.

But most of us Jimmy Olsen types still had to work our way up. When I hired at the *Winston-Salem Journal,* the old-timers still talked about Tom Wicker, the political columnist of the *New York Times*. He'd started out at the *Journal*. They chuckled over how he'd written potboilers, those paperback novels that were so popular back in the 1950s.

Wicker was by then a "serious" journalist, a paralyzing snore-monger as Tom Wolfe would have described him. He wrote some dreadful 500-page novel fraught with weighty issues, *Facing the Lions,* it was called. It didn't even rise to the level of paralyzing snore-mongering.

Just recently, I came across some ancient copies of Wicker's youthful "potboilers." You know what? They were good reads. He wasn't always a paralyzing snore-monger. I think maybe the unfortunate metamorphosis began when he got that Neiman Fellowship to Harvard. Nine months in Cambridge is almost impossible to recover from. As they say, you can always tell a Harvard man, but you can't tell him much.

But I digress. The point is, until the 1970s, almost everybody in the newspaper business came up like Wicker . . . or me. Newspapers or television, it was the same process. You started out in a small market and worked your way up. If you weren't having any luck moving up the ladder, you eventually threw in the towel. You either ended up on the copy desk, or went to work in public relations for a bank or a college or something like that.

Paper Boy

The only reason I broke into television news in a major market was because I'd already worked my way up in newspapers.

Now, though, the old farm system is defunct. Consider what Hunter S. Thompson sardonically used to call the "cream" of the national press—the D.C. political reporters. The apprenticeships now involve working as rabid partisan hack aides for Democratic politicians—George Stephanopoulos, Jake Tapper, Chuck Todd, etc., etc.

Or they're the coat holders' offspring—Chelsea Clinton, Valerie Jarrett's daughter, etc. Or one of the Bush kin—RINOs can get on the media gravy train as well.

Tim Russert was the first of the erstwhile Capitol Hill payroll Charlies to become a—drum roll please—journalist. But Russert was on the level, even if he did allow Mike Barnicle to brownnose him endlessly. Russert had worked for a decent senator—Daniel Patrick Moynihan—not the kind of Democrat grifters that the new breed gravitates to. Even Chris Matthews, crazy as he was, at least seemed somewhat authentic—a working-class sort of guy from Philadelphia.

No young people come to me for avuncular advice, thank goodness, because I have no desire to be anyone's mentor. But if anyone did approach me, I'd tell them to stay the hell away from "the business." On the rare occasions when some parent has approached me on behalf of his or her child, I've replied, as diplomatically as possible of course, "What the hell are you thinking of?"

In fact, I'd advise anyone against going into the corporate world these days, especially if they are white, more so if they're male, even more so if they're straight, or is it cisgender now?

Most of the media companies I've worked for either no longer exist, or soon won't. That's just a fact. Capitalism, as I've mentioned, is sometimes described as "creative destruction." These days, in newspapers, it's just destruction, period.

The daily *Herald* now never runs more than 40 pages—tabloid pages, which means 20 broadsheets. When the *Herald American* was about to go out of business in 1982, the Saturday paper was never that small. Now, 40 pages is standard.

When my producer and now fellow talk show host Grace Curley got married on the Cape, one of her guests approached me at the wedding. He'd moved out of state (who hasn't?) and earlier that Saturday, had visited an old friend who was recuperating from an operation in a local hospital.

He'd decided to bring his friend a few presents, one of which was a Saturday *Herald*.

317

"Howie," the guy told me, in shocked tones. "It cost $4.50. And it was thinner than a supermarket flier!"

And probably had less news in it. At least Market Basket's weekly will tell you what's on sale. What could I say? He won't be making that same mistake again. Very few people do anymore.

I still write three columns a week for the *Herald*. Sometimes I wonder if anyone is reading them. People I've known for decades often have no idea anymore what I've just written. It's not just the *Herald* either. Nobody reads the *Globe,* either, as far as I can tell.

When I turn up something newsworthy now, I seldom bother to call the *Herald*. That would be like beating my head against a wall. For years—decades—I'd been trying to get the dirt on ex-Rep. Gerry Studds's predatory sexual behavior with young men when he was a teacher at St. Paul's School in Concord, New Hampshire.

Maybe I was trying to make up for that puff piece I wrote on him for *Boston* magazine that helped me win that National Magazine Award. Finally, St. Paul's did a report, using numbers rather than names for the pervert "masters."

I finally figured out the code. Then two of the students sued, and used Studds's name, among others. I wrote a lengthy report—for Breitbart, not the *Herald*. The great thing about outlets like Breitbart is that you don't have to worry about length.

It wasn't just Studds that I could write about forever. Sen. Ed Markey—the man that time forgot. What a fool he was, even back in his days as a state rep on Beacon Hill. Again, I just unloaded for Breitbart.

As time went on, I decided to cut out editors—middlemen—altogether. It was just so much easier to do a Twitter thread. Instant posting, instant feedback. No bullshit, except of course the death threats from the Democrat trolls.

I also keep dabbling in new media, to try to keep my name out there. I did a podcast on the Bulgers. We called it *Dirty Rats*. It turned out well, I thought, but we couldn't make any money off it. I still have 90 minutes of interviews I taped with Howie Winter, the boss of the Winter Hill Gang, before he died in November 2020.

I used some of the Howie Winter interviews in a four-hour documentary about organized crime, *Bloody Boston*. Like *Dirty Rats,* it was fun to be involved in something like that (it runs on the Reelz channel) but it didn't make me a lot of money. I think I was credited as a "contributing producer."

I sat down and recorded a long interview with ex–Winter Hill boss Howie Winter shortly before his death in 2020.

I continue nosing around for such kinds of showbiz projects. You know, like everybody else in the world.

After the 2022 elections, which were disastrous for the GOP in Massachusetts, some of us decided we had to oust the party chairman, Jim Lyons, whom I'd initially backed when he was trying to take down Charlie Baker. The enemy of my enemy is my friend . . .

But once Baker was taken off the board, Lyons turned out to be a complete disaster. He lost every race and eventually gave up even trying to defeat Democrats. Instead, he squandered the local GOP's ever-dwindling resources on private detectives to snoop on and stalk members of his own committee, as well as tracking the lesbian Democrat candidate for governor and her girlfriend, a state appellate court judge.

I began calling him Jim "Jones" Lyons. I described his followers as the "Kool-Aid Kult."

The stuff our group turned up on Lyons and his cult was beyond the scope of the modern *Herald,* so I just tweeted it all out, complete with embarrassing photos of the Kult members culled from social media.

Everything I tweeted out was solid, and the *Globe* would sometimes pick up my threads a few hours later. I would always retweet the *Globe* stories with a notation of how many hours I'd beaten them by.

Lyons was ousted by the state committee in January 2023. I still had some clout, at least in minor political races. But very little of it seems to come from my column in the *Herald.*

Sic transit gloria mundi. . . .

EPILOGUE

"TOTAL COVERAGE,
FINAL WISDOM,
FREE LUNCH"

Tucker Carlson was fired last week.

I finished writing *Paper Boy* on a Sunday night in late April. The next morning, news broke that Carlson was out at Fox News. To me, it seemed like a coda, an exclamation point for what I'd been writing about.

I had déjà vu watching the firing unfold. Tucker was whacked when he was at the top of both his game and the ratings, for murky reasons that may well remain unknown for years, if not decades. He's still getting paid, but Fox insists he can't work anywhere else.

Welcome to my old club, Tucker.

I'm not putting myself in Tucker Carlson's class. For one thing, I can't remember exactly what my pay was when I was fired from WRKO in 1993, but it couldn't have been much more than $100,000 a year. Didn't seem bad at the time, especially when I was going through a divorce, but Tucker was—is— earning $1.9 million a month.

I doubt Tucker is sweating his long-term prospects. He's already on Twitter. He's not going to be silenced.

Another thing about Tucker: he's been fired almost as many times as I have. The first time is tough. After that, you start getting used to it. Like baseball managers, people like us are hired to be fired.

As you write a book like this, you keep getting new information.

When the Twitter files started coming out, I reached out to Matt Taibbi, the son of my old colleague Mike Taibbi, and asked him if he wanted to come on the show. He didn't get back to me for a few weeks, but then I got a DM from him:

"Howie, hi from fellow Bostonian Matt Taibbi. Sorry I didn't answer you before. I'm going through Twitter Files stuff still and came across your name—did you know you'd been flagged by the ADL for writing: 'Very Odd: Michigan Found Over 100,000 Ballots and Every Single One Has Joe Biden's Name on It.'"

It was just a retweet of a *Red State* article. No one disputed the facts. The problem was that it made Democrats look bad. But what the hell did that have to do with the ADL—the Anti-Defamation League?

Big Brother is getting pretty far down the list of co-conspirators if they're flagging my retweets of stories that happen to be true.

The winter 2023 Boston radio ratings came out and it was the worst book ever for WEEI, Shillville. In the target demo, men 25–54, Sports Hub crushed Shillville 19.4–4.0.

I'm still stuck on AM, although that's not nearly as much of a handicap as it used to be before all the new technologies. I still did very well—number three in my prime demo, adults 35+.

To me the most pleasurable part of the winter book were my numbers in that sports radio demo, men 25–54.

Despite my AM handicap, I was number three, with a 7.9 rating. WEEI finished 15th, with a 3.6 share, on the FM band.

When the numbers were released, some random guy on Twitter posed the question:

"I wonder if Carr's numbers would change much on FM."

You know, I've been asking myself that same question for more than 20 years.

Entercom, now known as Audacy, was just delisted by the New York Stock Exchange. The entire corporation, with more than 230 radio stations, not so long ago had a market capitalization of $2.4 billion.

Now Entercom is worth about $6 million. They just did a reverse stock split—30 shares for one. That got the price up from about seven cents a share to a little over two bucks.

Paper Boy

When they made the catastrophic decision to buy CBS Radio in 2017, Entercom had to spin off some of their Boston stations. WRKO went to iHeart—a blessing to me, finally being able to work once again for programmers who aren't totally clueless, and even more importantly aren't assholes.

Entercom was forced to divest some other stations in Boston, either their own or CBS's. It was left to Entercom to determine which ones to get rid of, and which to retain.

Some choices seemed like no-brainers. They had to choose between keeping Sports Hub, CBS's now-dominant sports station, or Shillville, even then a shell of its former self. As usual Entercom made the wrong decision—they kept WEEI.

Entercom likewise had to choose between a top-billing classic rock station, WZLX, and WAAF—the Beavis and Butt-Head station that sounded like piss-poor college radio. Guess which one they picked. (And a year later, Entercom had to unload WAAF to a Christian broadcaster for $10 million—that's how destitute they'd become.)

Whenever I consider Entercom's demise, it always brings a smile to my face. I recall the words of Oscar Wilde:

"It would take a heart of stone not to laugh."

As I've been writing *Paper Boy*, I've occasionally asked myself whether I was being too hard on somebody or something. Was I perhaps misremembering, as George W. Bush would say, long-ago events that had become foggy in my mind?

For instance, the class distinctions at Deerfield Academy. Don't get me wrong, I remain eternally grateful to Mr. Boyden and everyone else in my life who has given me the opportunity at one time or another to get . . . so near, and yet so far.

A while back, some of the other "Deerfield boys" from the Class of '69 set up a kind of chat room to while away their golden years. One of the other alums posted a *Herald* column I did about a drunk-driving state rep. It had everything—dialogue from the police reports, his drunken confusion, the Harvard connection, the two middle names, etc.

It was probably the best drunk-driving state rep column I'd done in years. The alum who posted it observed, "Howie Carr in fine form."

A different classmate typed back that I was "still spewing forth the Fox News–type partisan hackery he's been spewing forth at the *Boston Herald*."

Then he added this:

"I always felt Howie's Deerfield years were the source of his lifelong professional bitterness and rage—his father worked in the mailroom of a school whose students he saw as elitist and entitled liberals (really?) who looked down upon, or worse didn't notice, people like his father."

My critic took some heat from our classmates, but I was somewhat grateful to him for reminding me where I stood, at least among some of the old crowd.

By the way, the title of this final chapter is lifted from Hunter S. Thompson's tongue-in-cheek description of his own and in fact all journalists' careers.

I just didn't want to get called out by some book reviewer for stealing somebody else's material, although my guess is that *Paper Boy* will be getting one of those good leavings-alone that we often talk about on the show. (More full disclosure: I stole the good-leaving-alone line from *The Friends of Eddie Coyle*. Consider it a homage.)

In May, I returned to Massachusetts from Florida, and one weekend came down with a stomach bug that was going around. I figured I could handle two hours of the Monday show—those live reads are good money, after all—and I had a substitute coming in at 5.

As it turned out, I couldn't even make it through the first hour. Just before 4, I started sweating profusely. My speech slowed and then I fainted, right on camera, in front of the microphone. Down in Florida, at Newsmax headquarters, they thought I might be dead. Grace Curley was afraid I'd had a stroke.

It wasn't all that different than what happened to Jerry Williams back in 1991 during the Kennedy rape trial in Palm Beach. Like Richard II, I wasted time and now time doth waste me.

Turns out it was just dehydration from the stomach bug. I was taken by ambulance to a small local clinic and was released by 9, when they got my blood pressure back up to a tolerable level. But my collapse made all the local newscasts.

The *Globe* caught up with me the next day. I should have known it was one of them calling me by the fact that the cell phone was from California. Another blow-in drifter. But I gave them a comment and the story ran. I was surprised that after all these years, almost 200 *Globe* readers cared enough to comment about me. The first four or five comments were blocked. I wonder why.

My favorite comment was from someone with the handle Reask who described me thusly: "Ah, the Tucker Carlson of the T."

Obviously Reask hasn't ridden the T recently.

One woman said she "was hoping this was his obituary." Another said, "A health scare involving Howie Carr would be that he survives."

Paper Boy

Karl from beyond Forest Lawn: "Howie created an audience, knows what they wanted, bleats it out hour after hour; the last ghoul on the sinking-slow ship named *Local Talk Radio*."

As on the Deerfield message board, I did have my defenders. Somebody said, "The *Globe* commenters did not disappoint today! They haven't been this happy since Rush Limbaugh got cancer."

Numeral wrote, "I wonder how many people spewing negative comments about Carr have signs and bumper stickers saying 'Hate Has No Home Here.'"

Another one said I should have stuck to what I was best at—exposing Boston criminals like Whitey Bulger. To which someone responded:

"The problem is there isn't much left to document. The Irish and Italian mobsters he used to write about so often have largely gone the way of the dinosaurs."

Robert F. Kennedy Jr. announced his candidacy for president as a Democrat in Boston. I've been trying to get him to come on the show but so far no luck. Do you suppose he's read *Kennedy Babylon, Vol. 2*? Would it help or hurt if I mentioned that my flagship station used to employ the fat guy who busted him for a couple of joints down on the Cape back in 1971?

A poll just came out, showing that if Charlie Parker ran for the U.S. Senate in 2024, he would have a 15-point lead over the Fake Indian. You can get a poll to say anything you want, as long as you pay for it.

Two days after the supposed poll came out, his son Gropey was busted again, not for allegedly assaulting a woman on an airline flight as in 2018, but this time for driving drunk on 128 in Lynnfield. He stupidly took the breathalyzer and blew a .0152—almost double the legal limit. In Somerville, we used to call that "Double Bubble Trouble."

The news got out on Sunday afternoon and my phone lit up. It was Mother's Day, but all my old trooper sources found a moment to text me, even the guy who called me "Winston."

I hadn't spoken to him in 18 months, since Internal Affairs had grabbed his cell phone. He's still trying to get back on the job. So far he's out $200,000 in legal fees. And Charlie Baker still wonders why people hate him.

I'm still always looking for different, nonpolitical topics for the show. We used to have a guy on every Monday night to talk about network TV. Boy, is that over.

We also used to do a segment on standing—recurring—headlines in newspapers. Of course the problem there is one we've already discussed. Nobody reads newspapers anymore.

Recently, I was considering a segment or two on magazines the audience misses, or still subscribes to. Magazines—another industry I used to work in that's pretty much vanished. I printed out a few stories to introduce the segment.

One headline was "The Woke Mob Ruined *Bon Appetit*, and I'm Still Salty About It." Another was "*Scientific American* Compares DeSantis to Mussolini." And finally, "*Vogue Magazine* Features Stormy Daniels—But Ignored Elegant First Lady Melania Trump for 4 Years."

I decided there was no point in talking about any magazines anymore, even for nostalgic purposes. I threw the stories in the trash.

People I used to know, and write about, are dying with ever-increasing frequency. Not a surprise, of course, when you get to be a certain age, which I certainly am now.

George Frazier used to say that every death of someone he'd covered just made his job as a columnist that much easier, because it didn't take as much work to knock out a few hundred words about somebody you knew well.

There is that, I suppose, but on the other hand. . . .

Bob Popeo, my old lawyer when I first got audited, just died at the age of 85. When I ran into him at Bob Crane's wake a few years back, Popeo mentioned the obit I'd just written for Crane.

He asked me, "Are you going to write something nice like that about me after I'm gone, Howie?"

These are the kinds of conversations I never used to have.

A week earlier it had been David Bartley, the old House speaker from Holyoke. He was 88. As a kid, Bartley caddied at Holyoke Country Club, and he used to say that the Yankee golfers were always the cheapest tippers. Bartley and I were never best buddies—I always mentioned his $158,316-a-year state pension—but I always liked him for putting the knock on the same kind of people who put the knock on me.

Somebody sent me an obit from New Orleans. It concerned the death of one of the revolving-door cast of morning-show hosts when WRKO was owned by Entercom. This guy was fired in Boston by Entercom, then moved to New Orleans, where he got a new radio job with Entercom, only to be fired by the company a second time.

I opened the story, looked at the name in the headline, and didn't recognize it. Then I read down and saw that the host, whom I had known as "Ozone," had been known in his final days as "Rebecca Pratt." He was transitioning, the story said.

Entercom affected different people in different ways, I guess. But never for the better.

So this is it for *Paper Boy*. I plan to keep my show going for as long as I can. My father made it to 103, my mother to 90. Chances are I have a few years left. At least I hope so.

I don't want to retire. Bobby Bowden, the former football coach of Florida State, summed it up rather well, I think:

"After you retire, there's only one big event left . . . and I ain't ready for that."

Me neither.

HOWIE CARR BIBLIOGRAPHY

The Brothers Bulger, 2006

Hitman, 2011

Hard Knocks (a novel), 2012

Rifleman, 2013

Ratman, 2013

Plug Uglies, 2014

Killers (a novel), 2015

Kennedy Babylon, Vol. 1, 2017

What Really Happened, 2018

Kennedy Babylon, Vol. 2, 2018

Paper Boy, 2023